CITIES OF EUROPE

Check for CD @ i

Studies in Urban and Social Change

Published by Blackwell in association with the *International Journal of Urban and Regional Research*. Series editors: Harvey Molotch, Linda McDowell, Margit Mayer, Chris Pickvance

The Blackwell Studies in Urban and Social Change aim to advance debates and empirical analyses stimulated by changes in the fortunes of cities and regions across the world. Topics range from monographs on single places to large-scale comparisons across East and West, North and South. The series is explicitly inter-disciplinary; the editors judge books by their contribution to intellectual solutions rather than according to disciplinary origin.

Published

Forthcoming

CITIES OF EUROPE

CHANGING CONTEXTS, LOCAL ARRANGEMENTS, AND THE CHALLENGE TO URBAN COHESION

Edited by

Yuri Kazepov

Cities of Europe © 2005 by Blackwell Publishing Ltd
except for the CD-Rom *Visual Paths Through Urban Europe* © 2004 by Yuri Kazepov

BLACKWELL PUBLISHING
350 Main Street, Malden, MA 02148-5020, USA
108 Cowley Road, Oxford OX4 1JF, UK
550 Swanston Street, Carlton, Victoria 3053, Australia

The right of Yuri Kazepov to be identified as the Author of the Editorial Material in this
Work has been asserted in accordance with the UK Copyright, Designs, and Patents Act 1988.

First published 2005 by Blackwell Publishing Ltd

Library of Congress Cataloging-in-Publication Data
Cities of Europe : changing contexts, local arrangements, and the challenge to urban cohesion
/ edited by Yuri Kazepov.
    p. cm. — (Studies in urban and social change)
    Includes bibliographical references and index.
    ISBN 1-4051-2133-5 (alk. paper) — ISBN 1-4051-2132-7 (alk. paper) 1. Cities and towns—
Europe, Western. 2. Sociology, Urban–Europe, Western. I. Kazepov, Yuri. II. Series.

    HT131.C56 2004
    307.76′094—dc22

                                                                                2004008399

A catalogue record for this title is available from the British Library.

Set in 10.5/12pt Baskerville
by Graphicraft Limited, Hong Kong
Printed and bound in the United Kingdom
by MPG Books Ltd, Bodmin, Cornwall

The publisher's policy is to use permanent paper from mills that operate a sustainable forestry
policy, and which has been manufactured from pulp processed using acid-free and elementary
chlorine-free practices. Furthermore, the publisher ensures that the text paper and cover board
used have met acceptable environmental accreditation standards.

For further information on
Blackwell Publishing, visit our website:
www.blackwellpublishing.com

Contents

Table of Contents of the CD

III: Social Exclusion, Governance, and Social Cohesion in European Cities

Ethnic Villages
Manuel B. Aalbers (University of Amsterdam)

Local Community
Manuel B. Aalbers (University of Amsterdam)

Urban Poverty
Nico Giersig (Humboldt University, Berlin) and *Manuel B. Aalbers* (University of Amsterdam)

Additional text

The Transformation of Inner and Outer Space. Reflections on Space after 9/11
Robin Harper (New York University)

Interviews

Susan Fainstein (Columbia University, NY)
Hartmut Häussermann (Humboldt University, Berlin)
Chris Hamnett (Kings College, London)
Paul Kantor (Fordham University, NY)
Chris Kesteloot (Catholic University of Leuven)
Patrick Le Galès (Sciences Po, Paris)
Peter Marcuse (Columbia University, NY)
Guido Martinotti (University of Milan-Bicocca)
Enzo Mingione (University of Milan-Bicocca)
John Mollenkopf (City University of New York)
Harvey Molotch (New York University)
Saskia Sassen (University of Chicago)
Richard Sennett (London School of Economics)

The CD-Rom includes also about 2000 pictures, 14 city data sheets and more than 120 thematic maps. The credits of the CD mentions all those who participated.

Notes on Contributors

Marisol García is Professor of Sociology at the University of Barcelona (ES). She was the President of the International Sociological Association (ISA) RC21 on Urban and Regional Research, 1998–2002. She has been Fellow of the Citizenship Forum at the European University Institute in Florence (I) and has been involved for many years in European comparative research (ESOPO, INPART, SEDEC, EUREX, EUROPUB). She is a member of the editorial board of the *International Journal of Urban and Regional Research*. Her publications range from urban sociology to the question of social justice and citizenship.

Anne Haila is Professor of Urban Studies at the Department of Social Policy at the University of Helsinki (FIN). From 1994 to 1998 she was Vice-President of the ISA Research Committee on Urban and Regional Development and its Scientific Secretary from 1998 to 2002. Since 1999 she has been a member of the editorial board of *Planning Theory and Practice*. She has a strong international record of publications and research on globalization, East European cities and science parks.

Hartmut Häussermann is Professor of Urban and Regional Sociology at the Institute of Social Sciences of Humboldt University, Berlin (D) and President of RC21, the Research Committee on Urban and Regional Development of the ISA. He is involved in a range of comparative research concerned with social and spatial inequalities, urban renewal, urban development policies such as URBEX and EUREX. He is a partner in the Urban Europe RTN project. He has published extensively on these issues.

Yuri Kazepov is Professor of Urban Sociology and Compared Welfare Systems at the University of Urbino (I). He has been Jean Monet Fellow at the European University Institute (Fiesole, I) and Visiting Professor at the University of Bremen (Germany). Since the early 1990s he has been involved as national partner or as coordinator in several EU funded research projects on urban poverty and segregation, local social policy, welfare reforms and activation policy. For the period 2002–2006 he is the secretary of RC21 Research Committee on Urban and Regional development of the ISA and a founding member of ESPAnet (European Social Policies Analysis).

Christian Kesteloot is Professor of Social and Economic Geography at the Catholic University of Leuven (B), and also teaches at the Free University of Brussels, Belgium. He is a former Research Director of the Fund for Scientific Research, Flanders and member of URBEX and EUREX. He specializes in socio-spatial structures and urban restructuring in West European cities and participates in several European networks on these topics, including ethnic minorities, the socially excluded, and young people. He has published extensively on these issues.

Patrick Le Galès is Directeur de Recherche au CNRS at CEVIPOF and Professor of Politics and Sociology at Sciences Po Paris (F). Previously, he was at CRAPE (IEP Rennes, 1992–97). He has been also a Visiting Fellow at the Robert Schuman Center (IUE Florence, 1996–97) and a Visiting Professor and Fellow at UCLA (1999) and at the University of Oxford (2002–03). He is Editor of the *International Journal of Urban and Regional Research* and is involved in European comparative research on local societies, urban and regional governance, economic development, urban policies, and state restructuring.

Guido Martinotti is Professor of Urban Sociology at the University of Milan-Bicocca (I). Since 1986 he has been Visiting Professor at the Department of Sociology of the University of California at Santa Barbara (UCSB). In the spring semester of 1998 he was Fellow of the E.M. Remarque Institute, New York University. Between 1992 and 1996 he was Chairman of the Standing Committee for the Social Sciences of the European Science Foundation (ESF). Since 1999 he has been a member of the External Advisory Group of DG Research on Improving the Human Potential and enlarging the socio-economic knowledge base of the European Union.

Enzo Mingione is Professor of Economic Sociology at the University of Milan-Bicocca (I). He has been Visiting Professor at the University College of London (UK, 1974–75) and of the University of California,

Los Angeles (UCLA, 1992–93), LSE (2003) and Sciences Po Paris (2004). He has been a member of the editorial board of the *International Journal of Urban and Regional Research* of which he is now a corresponding editor. He has been Italian Coordinator of ESOPO and of the National Research Council project on Governance and Economic Development. He is President of the Bignaschi Foundation and responsible for the Observatory of Urban Poverty at the University of Milan-Bicocca (together with F. Zajczyk and Y. Kazepov).

Enrica Morlicchio is Professor of Sociology of Development at the University of Naples Federico II (I) where she carries out research on segregation, ghettoization and poverty, with special reference to Southern Europe and in particular Italy. She has published extensively on the issue, both nationally and internationally. She was a member of the URBEX and EUREX projects and is a member of the UGIS project.

Alan Murie is Professor of Urban and Regional Studies and Head of the School of Public Policy at the University of Birmingham (UK). He has published extensively, nationally and internationally, with a focus on social and spatial changes related to housing and residence and the policy issues associated with these. He was a member of the URBEX and EUREX projects and is a member of the RESTATE project.

Sako Musterd is Professor of Social Geography at the University of Amsterdam (NL). He specializes in segregation and integration and in urban development issues. Among the books he has edited are *Urban Segregation and the Welfare State* and *Amsterdam Human Capital*. He is on the management board of *Housing Studies* and is a corresponding editor of the *International Journal of Urban and Regional Research*. He has been the International Coordinator of the URBEX research project and participates in the RESTATE (5th framework) program and in the EUREX online seminar.

Wim Ostendorf is Associate Professor at the Department of Geography and Planning of the University of Amsterdam (NL), where he teaches research methodology, urban geography and geography of the Netherlands. His main research interests concentrate on urbanization processes in metropolitan regions and on issues of population, segregation, and housing. On these topic he has published extensively, both nationally and internationally. He is engaged in comparative European research projects such as Cost Civitas, URBEX and RESTATE.

Saskia Sassen is the Ralph Lewis Professor of Sociology at the University of Chicago, and Centennial Visiting Professor at the London School of Economics. She is currently completing her forthcoming book *Denationalization: Territory, Authority and Rights in a Global Digital Age* (Under contract with Princeton University Press 2004). She has also just completed for UNESCO a five-year project on sustainable human settlement for which she set up a network of researchers and activists in over 50 countries. Her most recent books are, the edited *Global Networks, Linked Cities* (Routledge 2002), and the co-edited *Socio-Digital Formations: New Architectures for Global Order* (Princeton University Press 2004), and *The Global City* (fully updated edition in 2001).

Richard Sennett is Professor of Sociology and Chair of the Cities Programme at the London School of Economics (UK), an interdisciplinary teaching and research program joining urban visual design to the social sciences. In the Sociology Department he teaches courses on narrative theory and its application to practical ethnography, and the sociology of the arts. He is internationally well known through his publications: *Flesh and Stone: The Body and the City in Western Civilisation* (W.W. Norton, 1994) and *The Corrosion of Character: The Personal Consequences of Work in the New Capitalism* (W.W. Norton, 1998) and, more recently, *Respect: The Welfare State, Inequality, and the City* (Penguin, 2003).

Patrick Simon is a senior researcher at Institut National d'Etudes Demographiques (INED) (F) where he studies, as socio-demographer, social and ethnic segregation in French cities, discrimination in social housing and the labor market, and the integration of ethnic minorities in European countries. He was a member of the URBEX and EUREX projects, is the coordinator of a European project on the measurement of discriminations, and represents INED in the Network of Excellence, International Migration and Social Cohesion in Europe (IMISCOE) in the 6th framework program.

Ronald van Kempen is Professor of Urban Geography at the University of Utrecht (NL). His research activities are focused on housing low-income groups and immigrants, neighborhood developments, segregation and the links between policy and theory in these fields. Many of his projects are internationally comparative projects. He has published in numerous international journals and has edited several books. He is currently managing an extensive project on large estates funded by the European Union (RESTATE).

Jan Vranken is a Professor at the University of Antwerpen (B). He teaches courses on social inequality and stratification, poverty and social exclusion, and social problems, and coordinates the Research Unit on Poverty, Social Exclusion and the City (OASeS) (www.ua.ac.be/oases). Since the late 1970s he has participated in several European poverty programs and initiatives. From 2000 to 2003 he coordinated a large project on Governance in European cities (UGIS) within FP6. Recently he became a member of the Management Committee of COST-A26 on European City-Regions.

Acknowledgments

The complexity of the editorial project which brought about the publication of this book and the enclosed CD, would have never been managed without the help of many people and the financial and infrastructural support of several institutions. Let me first thank the University of Urbino, in particular the Institute of Sociology and Guido Maggioni, who was heading it at the time the manuscript has been prepared. The freedom I had in developing new ideas and to embark into such an ambitious project are rare to be found in any institution.

The European Commission should also be gratefully mentioned as it allowed this project to become real by providing generous funding within the stream of *accompanying measures* targeted to *dissemination* of the *Improving Human Potential* programme of the DG Research, contract (Nr. HPHA-CT2000-00057). The EU official in charge of the project, Fadila Boughanemi supported me with all its capacity and competence helping the project through all bureaucratic complexities.

The link to the European Commission and its research policies is even stronger. In fact, most of the chapters make an explicit or implicit reference to empirical results from EU funded research in which most of the authors were involved in the recent past. The following projects and their coordinators should be gratefully mentioned:

1) ESOPO: Evaluating SOcial POlicy. A project on local policies against poverty, coordinated by Chiara Saraceno (University of Turin, Italy).

2) URBEX: URban poverty, EXclusion and segregation. A project on the spatial impact of socio-economic transformations, coordinated by Sako Musterd (University of Amsterdam, the Netherlands).
3) UGIS: Urban Governance. A project on governance issues tackling mainly regeneration projects at the local level, coordinated by Jan Vranken (University of Antwerp, Belgium).
4) EUREX: Online seminar on Poverty, Exclusion and Governance in European Cities, coordinated by myself within the Minerva programme of DG Culture.

To the authors of the chapters go many thanks for supporting the ambitious project of a young colleague with comments and constructive criticism aimed at improving the accessibility and readability of the book. Warmest gratitude goes also to Patrick Le Galès and Harvey Molotch for their support throughout the whole project. Being a non-native speaker I benefited from the help of Terry McBride, who also prepared the first version of the manuscript according to the publishers guidelines.

My introductory chapter benefited from comments by Alberta Andreotti, David Benassi, Domenico Carbone, Angela Genova, Patrick Le Galès, Harvey Molotch, Enzo Mingione, and Matteo Villa to whom I express my gratitude for their help. The usual disclaimers apply.

Very special thanks go also to all those involved in the realization of the CD-Rom on *visual paths through urban Europe*. The CD is the result of a really very complex collaborative work, which involved more than 80 people from 11 countries and different scientific backgrounds and institutions. To all of them – named in the credits section of the CD-Rom – goes my deepest gratitude for their commitment and support throughout the whole project. In particular I would like to thank Daniele Barbieri professor at ISIA (Istituto Superiore Industrie Artistiche, Urbino), who codirected with me the realization of the CD-Rom, for his immense patience toward my never-ending requests. Valter Toni, also a professor at ISIA, provided essential technical support during the final rush. Daniela de Bartolo and Daniela Gravina, who were students of ISIA at the time in which the CD has been finalized, provided the concept and the nice graphic design of the CD, implementing most of its functions and surfing options. Franco Mariani, director of ISIA made the framework for this fruitful collaboration possible and should be gratefully mentioned for that.

Among the many other people who helped me, I would like to mention Eduardo Barberis and Giovanni Torrisi, who not only helped me with excellent technical and editorial support for both the book and the CD, but were always available when needed with their problem-solving oriented minds, a rare quality.

Henning Moser, Anja Nothelfer and Erica Barbiani provided not only pictures, but also extensive visual advice and support.

The editorial team for the CD included Manuel Aalbers, Eduardo Barberis, Nico Giersig, Maarten Loopmans, and Justin Beaumont, who enthusiastically provided texts, pictures, and comments. They helped me also revizing the whole written and visual material in the CD. Maarten Loopmans played also a substantial role in linking the images with the chapters.

Finally, there are no words which can express my deep gratitude to Simona, my wife, and Alexander, my son. They gave me the energy to bridge the difficult moments simply existing. This book owes much to them and to them it is dedicated.

Series Editors' Preface

The Blackwell *Studies in Urban and Social Change* series aims to advance theoretical debates and empirical analyses stimulated by changes in the fortunes of cities and regions across the world. Among topics taken up in past volumes and welcomed for future submissions are:

- Connections between economic restructuring and urban change
- Urban divisions, difference and diversity
- Convergence and divergence among regions of east and west, north and south
- Urban and environmental movements
- International migration and capital flows
- Trends in urban political economy
- Patterns of urban-based consumption

The series is explicitly interdisciplinary; the editors judge books by their contribution to intellectual solutions rather than according to disciplinary origin.

Proposals may be submitted to members of the series Editorial Committee:

Harvey Molotch
Linda McDowell
Margit Mayer
Chris Pickvance

Foreword

The city has long been a site for the exploration of major subjects confronting society and the social sciences. In the mid-1900s it lost that heuristic capability. This had partly to do with the actual urban condition; the city of the mid-1900s is no longer the entity that captures the foundational dislocations of an epoch as it had been at the turn of the century and into the early 1900s. The massive effort to regulate the urban social and spatial order had succeeded to a certain extent. Further, and in my view crucial, the strategic dynamics shaping society found their critical loci in the government (the Fordist contract, the Keynesian state project) and in mass manufacturing, including the mass production of suburbs.

Today the city is once again emerging as a strategic lens for producing critical knowledge, not only about the urban condition but also about major social, economic, and cultural refigurings in our societies. Large complex cities have once again become a strategic site for a whole range of new types of operations – political, economic, cultural, subjective – both urban and non-urban. They are also in part the spaces for post-colonial history-in-the-making. One question, then, is whether studying cities can today, as in past periods, help us produce critical knowledge and analytic tools for understanding the broader social transformation underway. The old categories, however, are not enough. Some of the major conditions in cities today challenge many, though not all, of the well-established forms of theorization and empirical analysis.

One set of challenges arises out of the intersection of major macro-social trends and their particular spatial patterns. The city and the metropolitan region emerge as one of the key sites where these macro-social trends instantiate and hence can be constituted as objects of study. In this regard then, the complex city or city-region becomes a heuristic zone: it actually can produce knowledge about, and make legible, some of the major transformations and dynamics shaping society. This is the city not as a bounded unit, but as a complex structure that can articulate a variety of macro-social processes and reconstitute them as a partly urbanized condition.

This volume is an important contribution to this larger effort. Its particular contribution lies in the specification of a European city type. In a conceptual and historical tour de force, Häussermann and Haila locate this European city type for us and set the stage for the volume. The effort of this volume is not to find homogeneity. Rather, together the chapters document the fact of enormous heterogeneity among European cities, but within a framework that does not deborder the European city type.

In a strong, detailed and illuminating introduction, Kazepov shows us the complexity of the notion of a European city. Kazepov notes that what binds these chapters into a European type is their emphasis, whether explicit or not, on the regulatory heritage and current policy apparatus within which these cities function. A critical variable for all authors is the set of changes that came about in the 1980s and the pressures they produced on welfare states throughout Europe. In sharp contrast with cities in the USA subject to similar pressures, in Europe the welfare states and the role of the state remain strong and consequential. It is at this juncture that the model of a European city finds one of its key moorings.

Within this broader framing, each author focuses in great detail on one particular feature. This makes reading these chapters truly rewarding as they go, as I like to say, digging into their issue. It raises the level of complexity in the specification of a type of European city.

At the most general level, one consequence of the changes emerging in the 1970s and 1980s in Europe has been the development of new forms of governance through which different actors have become increasingly involved in policy design and delivery. In an earlier phase, the notion of urban policies, Le Galès emphasizes, was related to national efforts to address the threats of urban violence, delinquency, and the fear of the working class. Urban policy is the development of welfare state policies; often they are simply public state policies.

Le Galès examines the increasingly constructivist frame within which urban policies are produced today. The complex processes of stucturation include a wider range of actors coming from different sectors of society, with different interests and acting at different levels. This brings about a

field of experimentation by local actors, who are no longer simply implementing decisions taken at other levels of government, but are active
participants in redesigning policy. Cities become a key site for aggregation and representation of interests. For Le Galès, organizing a mode of
governance is critical, and it is here that European cities reveal themselves
as different from US cities. The ongoing importance of the welfare state
in Europe also means that urban elites are less dependent on business
interests.

Introducing complexities, Martinotti shows us how specific populations
with specific interests today cut across older class differences and so make
regulation more difficult. Most of the social problems in today's metropolitan societies are related to the way in which potential conflicts among
inhabitants, commuters, city users, and businesspeople are played out and
are structured. Despite some measure of convergence with US cities, the
fact remains that the less market-oriented local governance arrangements
and the more binding regulation systems and urban planning constraints
give European cities more control over the tensions different interests can
produce. The effect is to temper the consequences of economic globalization
and neoliberal adjustment, the spread of flexibility and of vulnerability.

However, Vranken, on his part, finds limits in the governance
approach to cities and their problems. He shows how urban policies have
not captured the complexity and the key dynamics of cities in seeking to
address the breakdowns of cohesion: the mix of organic and mechanical
forms of solidarity present in a city, the particular dynamics through
which cohesion can be achieved (e.g., by allowing a community to establish its identity), the need to recognize that edges and borders can be
fruitful zones contributing to cohesion rather than strengthening divisions.

Kesteloot emphasizes that even as state action makes the critical difference in Europe compared with the USA, state action varies across
Europe. The social issues confronting European cities may be the same but
the socio-spatial arrangements of cities vary and have different effects on
how the social issues are handled. The socio-spatial structure of the city
results from historical processes: older spatializations of economic, social
and political processes; the material and social modes for collective
organization and consumption of older periods; the organization of the
economy and the conditions for class struggle. These differences can shape
different futures for these cities, especially their social relations.

The weight of these differences in social relations comes sharply to life
in the disturbing findings by Mingione and Morlicchio, respectively. Each
notes the differences between Northern and Southern Europe. In the latter,
the importance of clientelism, segmented labor markets, locally fragmented
social assistance schemes, and unsupported family responsibilities, produce specific burdens and major responsibilities on families rather than

the state as in Northern Europe. The redistribution of resources is confined to the family, thereby trumping the European welfare state. This reproduces already high inequality. But the vicious cycle goes deeper. Mingione shows how the instability arising out of changes in the market and the family spilled over into the welfare state, affecting its capabilities and leading to breakdown in its fiscal and crisis management capacities.

Murie adds to this type of analysis by emphasizing the importance of going beyond income when we measure and explain poverty. His findings also point to a particular kind of trumping of the welfare state. He is concerned with the resources households can draw on, resources that can determine their life chances. Murie emphasizes the importance of a wider definition of poverty, one that specifies the terms of access to resources other than income and employment. Important in this context are decommodified services (not provided through markets) and how poor families can access them. Different neighborhoods are positioned differently as a result of a variety of conditions such as stereotyping, racism, mobility, and transiency. We cannot assume that such decommodified services will be evenly distributed and that they go to all those who need them. This can in turn generate inequalities. Poverty is then a far more dynamic and embedded condition than indicated by income and by the features of the welfare state.

García addresses the challenge to social citizenship, crucial to the European city, contained in the fact of the persistence of poverty. She emphasizes the importance of a broader form of social inclusion, not only income, in order to secure social citizenship. Given increasing inequality in the terms of inclusion into the social, political, and economic spheres, García wants to make more explicit the implicit notions of social justice emerging in the policy context for addressing poverty in the European Union (EU). To some extent, social citizenship has been realized in the EU (welfare regimes, Social Europe), but the context has changed from strong welfare to one where more private/market mechanisms enter the picture. Hence new understandings of social justice need to be developed in today's Europe. It comes down to a specification of what we mean by social inclusion: an increasing focus on the multidimensional causes of poverty beyond narrow economic definition, highlighting the importance of participation in society.

In yet another twist on the limits of welfare states, Ronald van Kempen shows us how the housing conditions of migrants in Europe are still worse than those of nationals. He finds that segregation persists in all the cities examined and that it has failed to decline over time; for some groups it has increased. He also finds, interestingly, sharp differences for the same group across countries and, within a given city, sharp differences for different groups and among cities in a country. Different dynamics in each city, country or group may be part of the explanation. Van Kempen finds that spatial segregation exists in different combinations with inequality.

Musterd and Ostendorf focus on ongoing segregation and social exclusion and their potential reinforcement through the spatial clustering of socially excluded people. They find a mix of dynamics: that the extent of social welfare development has a significant effect on the reduction of polarization, that higher unemployment can result from structural or spatial mismatch, and that globalization has reduced the role of the state in welfare and increased that of the market. In their detailed analysis they find that welfare states and urban histories make a difference, and explain much of the difference in social segregation and exclusion between US and European cities. Further, the types of welfare policies also make a difference. Thus, in Dutch segregated neighborhoods the authors find that those who were in a stronger position (e.g., had a job) in a weak neighborhood, fared worse after losing the job than those who start out unemployed in a weak neighborhood. Current Dutch welfare policies can neutralize the negative effects in the second case but not in the first. The major policy implication is that government policy should not target areas but do more individual targeting.

The question of politics as distinct from governance is addressed in oblique ways in the last two chapters I discuss here. In his study of a gentrifying neighborhood, Simon shows us the diversity of possible patterns. While he recognizes that this is perhaps the less common situation, he emphasizes that we need to recognize it is one trajectory. The gentrifiers are particular types. However, at the same time within this self-selected group there are differences, one group wanting to preserve the diversity which includes the long-term poorer residents, and the other group acting according to the familiar image in the gentrification literature, i.e. trying to drive the long-term residents out. The latter group fails, in good part because of the efforts of the former gentrifiers who seek to ensure that even if old-time residents are forced to leave their housing because of price rises, that they relocate in the same neighborhood. Thereby these gentrifiers are not only protecting the old-time residents but also their own interest in having a diverse neighborhood, and one where they can be certain to be able to stay too. Simon retheorizes class relations by showing the possibility of political projects that join different classes.

Sennett reminds us that the peculiar value of urban life, even in decaying cities, is that cities are places where learning to live with strangers and with those who are not like ourselves, can happen directly. Cosmopolitanism arises from this. Urban life can teach people how to live with multiplicity inside themselves: it is not just about registering differences – of identity, language, etc. – out there. As we interact with others who are different, there also is a shift in who we are. How our identity is constructed will vary in different types of interactions. Urban life then, gives us the concrete materials for developing that consciousness. Crucial for Sennett is that this is a possibility, not an inevitability. There are cities whose features actively exclude that possibility. In this sense, European cities are far more amenable than US cities to this possibility.

Saskia Sassen
University of Chicago and London School of Economics

Introducing European Cities

1

Cities of Europe: Changing Contexts, Local Arrangements, and the Challenge to Social Cohesion

Yuri Kazepov

Introduction

European cities are back on the agenda of researchers in social sciences as a distinct topic. In the last few years scientific production has markedly increased, highlighting their distinctiveness in comparative terms.[1] This increased interest towards *difference* is the outcome of the scientific debate and empirical research emerged from the need to understand the transformation trends set in motion at the end of the 1970s, their impacts and the resulting growing diversity at different territorial levels.

The deep process of spatial reorganization which began in the aftermath of the crisis of Fordism brought about two apparently contradictory directions of change, running partly parallel and bringing about this distictiveness. From the economic point of view, the extensive globalization of production strategies and consumption behaviors, with multinational firms and financial markets playing a decisive part, has been paralleled by an increased localization of production into regional economies and industrial districts with varying impacts at the local level. From the political point of view, the rise of supranational institutions and political configurations (e.g., the European Union, the International Monetary Fund, the World Trade Organization (WTO)) gaining strategic guidance in fostering the mobility of capital, goods, services and labor, has been paralleled by a transfer of regulatory authority downwards to subnational territories, namely regions and cities.

These processes bring about a growing complexity which needs to be disentangled and this book is one of the few available contributions in that direction from the perspective of European cities. In fact, the way in which *converging trends* characterized by the spread of market regulation mechanisms in a framework of increased and global economic competition have been played out is characterized by *diverging impacts* bringing about an increased heterogeneity at different territorial levels. This points to some distinctive elements that European cities have retained in this process, a distinctiveness that derives, according to an emerging body of literature with which I tie in, from the regulatory framework that structures the processes of social cohesion and integration taking place at the urban level. As will become evident, these opposing directions of change do not occur in an institutional vacuum, but take full advantage of the regulatory heritage within which they are embedded.

Even though not all chapters explicitly address the distinctiveness of European cities as their main focus, their difference from other contexts – in particular the USA – emerges as a recurrent trait. The varied and partly mitigated impact of resurging inequality and poverty linked to the spread of market relations, the new forms of governance linked to the emergence of new local actors and innovative policies are just a few examples of how change might produce new contexts for cities. Investigating these changes in Western European urban societies, understanding the tensions they might give rise to, their multiple dimensions, the potential patterns of social vulnerability that might emerge, the impacts on the built environment, and the solutions provided are the aims of this book.

The authors address these issues, providing the reader with a rich and diversified set of analytical tools and empirical evidence from comparative research to understand these processes. The book is complemented by a highly innovative CD-Rom on *visual paths through urban Europe* to which all authors of the book refer to for any visual accounts given in the individual chapters (see the specific section on the CD-Rom).

The chapters have been grouped into three main sections. The first section addresses the changing contexts and the link with the local dimension this process might have. The second section concentrates on the impact of these transformations on the built environment in European cities, in particular investigating potential neighborhood effects, segregation and gentrification. The third section deals with the governance and social cohesion issues arising, and in particular the local policies against social exclusion and poverty.

The three sections are complemented by two opening chapters focusing on European cities at a more abstract and theoretical level. In particular, in order to understand and frame the distinctiveness of European cities, I divided this introductory chapter into three parts. In the first part I propose a specific explanatory path, starting from a relatively abstract level of analysis of how regulation frames work and the need to understand their institutional context. This implies bringing in also not specifically urban issues that are relevant to understand how the distinctive elements of European cities become structured. The second part briefly presents the institutional mixes characterizing the European context. This discussion intersects with the ongoing debates on urban change and is not separate from the structure of the book, being fuelled with the arguments put forward by the different authors. These are briefly presented in the third part where I connect them with my explanatory path. I will not sum up here the theories and the empirical evidence presented in the current literature and in the different chapters of this book. The literature on the topic has been extensively reported by Le Galès (2002) and Chapter 2 reviews the conceptual framework and normative project within which 'the European city' as an analytical category is in general embedded. Moreover, the different chapters provide – in most cases – an introduction and discussion of the main contributions in the literature of the topic they are dealing with, so I would have run the risk of being repetitive. Therefore, my strategy is aimed rather at understanding what cuts across most chapters and what I consider crucial in understanding the characteristics of European cities.

The Importance of Considering the Context

Let me start with an obvious and rather theoretical statement: context matters. Scholars from most disciplines of the social sciences increasingly underline its importance: it is not possible to understand social phenomena without embedding them in their context, but what does this really mean for the analysis of European cities? Is it enough to say that the context of European cities is different from other contexts and therefore European cities are different? Such a tautological answer only shifts the question to another – more abstract – level. We have therefore to define first what a context is, what are its dimensions, which are relevant and how they intermix. The next step is to consider the implications of different mixes. It is those *specific mixes that contribute to define differences*.

Most theoretical approaches in social sciences refer – implicitly or explicitly – to the concept of "context" as a quite powerful tool at the very basis of their investigations. This is true for sociological thought since its foundation as a discipline: the classical dichotomy of *Gemeinschaft* (community) and *Gesellschaft* (society) is clearly a contrast of contexts, in which different dimensions interact in a relatively coherent way, providing two different sets of constraints and opportunities to actors. The concept of *embeddedness*, which characterizes most of the debates on the working of the economy and its social foundations (from Polanyi 1944 onwards), has at its very analytical basis the crucial role of contexts. The same is true for the analysis of cities and urban governance. The concept of *nested cities* (Swyngedouw 2000; Hill and Fujita 2003; Hill 2004), besides highlighting the interconnectedness among cities and different territorial levels of regulation, makes explicit the need to consider cities as open systems, *nested* (or embedded) in a wider context of social, institutional, and economic relations (see also DiGaetano and Strom 2003). But what is a context? Generally, it can be defined as a set of alternatives made of constraints and enablements, within which individual (or collective) actors *can* or *have* to choose. In this sense, a context implies a classification exercise that allows actors to define events as constraining or enabling, to posit meanings and to act strategically. This quite abstract and loose definition is scalable in different directions: different levels of abstraction can be contexts to one another; the same is true for different territorial levels and timescales. The nation-state and regions are contexts for the city, just as the past is a context for the present.

The concept was used for the first time by Bateson (1972), who was interested in understanding how learning processes take place and work at different levels of abstraction. Actors learn, but they also learn to learn: they acquire frames through which they interpret the world, consolidating routines and structuring *Weltanschauungen* (world views). From this perspective actors acquire – interacting with the context – both the cognitive frameworks to refer to and the routines that point to a shared understanding of reality.

Sociologists usually investigate these processes in order to understand how the social bond is produced and reproduced in the tension between *agency* and *structure*. From their disciplinary point of view, contexts are usually considered the structural dimension of social life. This identification, however, is not so clear-cut, because contexts entail founding relational characteristics in which *agency* and *structure* are contexts for one another. For this reason, after the 1970s, sociologists increasingly focused on the process of *structuration* (Giddens 1984; Archer 1995, 2003). This entailed the recognition that social (cultural, economic, political, etc.) constraints have the power to impede or to facilitate different kinds of projects expressed by agents and, at the same time, that agency – through human reflexive abilities in interacting strategically with constraints – influences structural settings and mitigates their impact in a dialectical process that puts the two in relation with one another.[2] As we will see, these two dimensions acquire specific features in Europe.

At the intersection of macro-social constraining logics and the micro-social foundations of agency we find institutions, which have a crucial and mediating role. On the one hand they provide specific contexts, and on the other they reflect the results of the institutionalization process of actors' action. They incorporate structural features reaffirmed through recursive praxis (Giddens 1984) but, at the same time, they express a genuine structural constraint, external to the individual (or collective) actor, defining the space for free action (Archer 1995, 2003).

Institutions as contexts

The crucial and mediating role of institutions has been underlined in most of the chapters included in this book as a strategic starting point for understanding cities and their emergent role. It is at this level that we should begin asking about the distinctiveness of different urban settings, including the question of why European cities are different from other cities. The answer is again banal: European cities are different because they are embedded in different institutional arrangements, providing specific contexts to actors, characterized by a specific mix of constraints and enablements, and structuring specific *Weltanschauungen*. But how, and which institutions are structuring specific contextual mixes? In what ways do they differ in Europe? These are difficult questions, which need some preliminary definition of what an institution is.[3]

In the sociological tradition some founding differences can be traced back to Durkheim and Weber. In his classical work *De la division du travail social*, Durkheim used the legal system as a proxy for the existing forms of solidarity, assuming that it institutionalizes the social bond holding society together (1893: 24–5). In doing so, he addressed the underlying collective normative framework institutionalized in the legal system, highlighting its constraints on human action. This concern also characterized Weber's analysis, even though he was more interested in understanding the ways in which cultural rules define social structures and govern social behavior, influencing the meaning actors give to their actions. His more actor-centered perspective aimed at developing an interpretative understanding of social action in order to arrive at a causal explanation of its course and effects (1922/1972: 1). Here, he pioneered a context-bound rationality approach, maintaining that rationality and choice must be understood within the context of the institutional framework of a given society and historical epoch (Nee 1998: 6).

The divide between the two classics[4] is reflected in the shifting focus of new institutionalism.[5] Despite the fact that there is no consensus on all characteristics of new institutionalism, it is possible to synthesize the difference between the old and the new in the higher degree of autonomy credited to the individual actor and to the role of culture. Actors are supposed not only to interiorize social norms during their primary social-ization process, but they are also considered more proactive in the con-struction of their cognitive framework of reference and their institutions.

Considering the different existing theoretical positions, Scott provided an *omnibus* definition of institutions as "cognitive, normative and regulat-ive structures and activities that provide stability and meaning to social behavior" (1995: 33). The implications of these characteristics – which are strictly interwoven with one another and are separated only analytically – are that institutions provide a *structured context for action*. On the one hand, their constraints (normative, cognitive, and regulative) limit and modify the free play of interactions; on the other, they provide resources for actions to take place. In other words, they define through complex social inter-actions borders, i.e. *in–out* relations. From the normative, cognitive, and regulative points of view, defining borders implies defining identities and differences, as well as the related processes of social inclusion and exclu-sion, i.e. processes of *social closure* (Weber 1972). In this sense, institutions are the result of power relations that became institutionalized, i.e. they reflect the outcome of conflicts and struggles resulting from agency taking place within a framework of specific power asymmetries. These are trans-lated into regulations and define the roles of actors, who is *in* and who is *out* and – more particularly – who gets what, when and for how long in the redistributive process (Korpi 2001).

The path-dependent character of institutions

The above-outlined characteristics last over time because institutions are considered by most scholars to be *path-dependent*, i.e. they constrain choice to a limited range of possible alternatives, reducing the probability of path changes and presenting an evolutionary tendency, given the acquired routines. Agency takes place within a given context and path dependency is one of the most likely (but not the only) results of the interaction between the two, which brings about relative stability. There are many reasons why this is the case. For example, the reproduction of the institu-tional context occurs through recursive reflexive action. This implies, from the cognitive point of view, inevitable learning effects. Routines, taken-for-granted, and practices tend to consolidate the existing institutional settings. Moreover, the regulative nature of institutions, by establishing more formal rules (through the state) or fewer (through communitarian arrangements), contributes to the formation of mutual expectations – "a system of nested rules, which are increasingly costly to change" (Goodin 1996: 23) – and produces a self-reinforcing effect over time. Both examples show that the stabilization process works through the crucial mechanism of "increasing returns," i.e. positive feedbacks, which encourage actors to focus on a single alternative and to continue on a particular path once initial steps are taken (Pierson 2000a). At the very basis of all this lies the law of parsimony, which consists precisely in not re-examining the premises of habits, routines and rules every time they are used (Bateson 1972: 276). This tendency should not bring us to conceive of institutions as uniquely targeted to maintain stability. The other side of the coin is that institutions are not only constraining but also enabling contexts. Being at the intersection between path-dependent structural inertia (North 1990) and path-shaping activities, institutions provide a theoretical and empirical bridge between macro-social trends and micro-social foundations. As Jessop and Nielsen put it: "institutions always need to be re-interpreted and re-negotiated, they can never fully determine action; but nor do they permit any action whatsoever so that life is no more than the product of purely wilful contingency" (2003: 4; see also Berger and Luckmann 1967: 87). This implies that the path-dependent character of institutions has to do with the interplay of agency and structure, their different temporal frame of reference and the evident *long dureé* of the latter. This interpretation implies that paths might be changed, but connects this possibility to the given contextual opportunities.

Institutional mixes and regulation

All the chapters in this book implicitly or explicitly underline the importance of contexts and institutions: living in a European city is quite different from living in a North American city, just considering the Western industrialized world. Even within Europe, living in a Scandinavian city is different from living in a South European city (see Chapter 14). Where do the differences lie? Most chapters here agree that they lie in the peculiar mix of institutions regulating social interaction in the different European states and cities (e.g., see Chapters 3 and 6) and in the differences between them and the other industrialized countries. But how does the issue of difference become concrete and empirically investigable? A favorite starting point has been the analysis of the regulative framework that institutions provide (Regini and Lange 1989: 13). In particular, the fact that they are:

- coordinating the relationship between different actors;
- regulating the allocation of resources; and
- structuring conflicts.

These intrinsic structural qualities of institutions in mediating agency and structures have influenced the building typologies exercise, which most social scientists use for reducing social complexities and explaining differences in comparative work. The advantage of this perspective is to consider laws as a crucial starting point, but to go beyond the formal settings and to include also the practices different actors put forward, and the struggles implicit in the political process.

At least since Polanyi (1968, 1977), it has become quite popular in scientific debate to identify the *family* (*community*), the *state* and the *market* as the relevant institutions to be considered in analyzing the different types and mixes. The literature on the issue is constantly growing in a quite articulated way. Some scholars added *associations* or organized social interests (Streeck and Schmitter 1985) as a further relevant institution working through specific mechanisms of regulation. Others stick to the dualism between *Gemeinschaft* and *Gesellschaft* outlined by classical thinkers such as Weber and Durkheim (e.g., Mingione 1991). We briefly discuss some of the typologies and the *classification exercise* later on. Here it is enough to say that these institutions regulate social interaction through their specific cognitive frameworks, the norms they put forward and the rules and resources they mobilize. In short, these institutions define – through their own specific principles of reference – specific modes of coordination and regulation, addressing what Polanyi defined as *mechanisms of socio-economic integration*. The *integrative effect* emerges – according to Polanyi's holistic view of society – out of the economic process which consolidates, through specific movements of goods, the interdependence of individuals within institutionalized social relations. Within this framework, economic relations are considered to be both a means of fostering and consolidating social integration and the expression of wider social relations (Polanyi 1977). This implies not only defining specific contexts of constraints and enablements, but also the patterns through which social order is produced, and the crucial mediating role institutions have in putting agencies and structures in relation to one another.

Family, state, and market and the underlying principles of regulation have been widely used to construct typologies aimed at simplifying the complexity of society and explaining differences, at least descriptively. The prominence of one regulating institution produces an ideal typical configuration that – according to the different disciplines and models – helps to investigate analytically specific social systems of production (e.g., Hollingsworth and Boyer 1997; Crouch et al. 2001), particular welfare regimes (e.g., Esping-Andersen 1990, 1999; Mingione 1991; Gallie and Paugam 2000) and certain modes of governance (e.g., Jessop 2002; Le Galès 2002; DiGaetano and Strom 2003). Unfortunately, the complementarities between these approaches have been rarely investigated (for some exceptions see Ebbinghaus and Manow 2001; Huber and Stephens 2001; Hall and Soskice 2001). What all approaches share is the relevance of the systematic interconnectedness and complementarity among the different institutions and their organizational characteristics, which mutually adjusted over long periods of time. Referring to Gramsci's (1949/ 1971) concept of *hegemony*[6] and to the Regulation School (Aglietta 1979; Boyer 1986), the terms "regime" and "system" have often been used to underline precisely this aspect.[7] How the interconnectedness is achieved and the way it gave rise to varieties of capitalism is, nevertheless, a matter of how agency and context structured one another over time, i.e. how the different dimensions interacted – through conflicts and struggle – bringing about specific historical paths of change.

The Prominence of the Political and the European Context

Within the picture outlined above, the state has a particular position. The command over resources and the capacity to enforce its regulation framework puts the state at a different level of abstraction compared with the other institutions. The state is not just one of the sources of regulation, but *the* regulative institution, which defines the role of the other institutions through its ability to impose decisions that concern the whole society or parts of it. As Hollingsworth and Boyer maintain: "it is the state that sanctions and regulates the various non-state coordinating mechanisms, that defines and enforces property rights, and that manipulates fiscal and monetary policy" (1997: 13). In so doing, the state establishes the prominence of the political by linking the different institutions through its policies, which explicitly (through rights and duties, resources redistribution, and so on) or implicitly (e.g., without intervening in or regulating specific issues) define the social responsibilities of the other institutions, their obligations and constraints on one side and the rewards and opportunities on the other. From this point of view, political power has an intrinsic *paramountcy* (Poggi 1991). This does not mean that the other institutions are irrelevant; on the contrary, but their "jurisdiction" has to be defined in relation to that of the state which regulates their functioning.

This was not always the case. The state emerged as a regulatory institution in Europe in the sixteenth century (Tilly 1975; Rokkan 1999), but its effectiveness increased only after the French and the industrial revolutions, when it extended its supremacy in regulatory terms over most other institutions through *the rule of law*. This increased role of the legal dimension of political processes defined rights and duties as the outcome of the institutionalization of political choices and struggle (Poggi 1991). Underlying this crucial historic shift was the fact that the state became *the* means through which political rights were defined and the participation of the population regulated (Tilly 1975). This situation was further consolidated after the two World Wars, when the development of national compulsory insurance schemes and the removal of rigid guild systems and corporatist protections, most often organized at the local level, established new spaces for social membership (Marshall 1950; Alber 1982). Economic growth fuelled the nation-state with resources to be redistributed through welfare provisions and services.

Underlining the importance of the state and the *political* already defines the framework I will mainly refer to for understanding the context of European cities. However, the political is not separated from social reality. Despite important intra-European differences, to which we will return, we can identify, along with Kaelble (1987), Therborn (1995) and Crouch (1999), some broader commonalities characterizing (West) European countries on the eve of the nineteenth century. Here I will just mention some that distinguish them from other industrializing countries at that time, most prominently the USA.

1   European countries had a relatively low degree of religious diversity with just one (Catholic) or two dominant institutionalized Christian churches (Catholic and Protestant). Other religious diversities were limited to small and marginal groups (Crouch 1999). The religious cleavages have been linked for a long time with parties influencing the policy-making process in specific directions (Alber 1982; Rokkan 1999; Huber and Stephens 2001). These cleavages were not given in the USA, where the existing complexities, also in terms of ethnicity, brought about a bipartitism that was completely detached from religious values.
2   In European countries, some family structures, such as single young adults and nuclear families, were over-represented and, comparatively, later marriages characterized their reproductive strategies. These characteristics were present elsewhere, but not altogether and at the same time. According to Kaelble (1987: 14–23), this had three major implications. First, the development of social policies, which were needed to back up the nuclear families' weak sheltering capacities in the industrialization phase. Only South European countries followed a different path; stronger primary social networks have been accompanied on the whole by weaker states and other redistributive means. Second, late marriages contributed to the availability of a considerable and potentially mobile workforce. Third, the presence of single young adults might have had political consequences in the participation in mass political movements during the extension of voting rights. Even though it is not possible to speak about a unique European family model for the time being, it is nonetheless possible to differentiate it from the USA where the transformation processes have not been accompanied by the development of social policies.

3   European societies were characterized by widespread industrialization and a significant share of industrial employment, which favored class consciousness, cleavage and conflict. Nowhere else did industrial employment become as large a part of the economically active population as in Europe (Therborn 1995). This brought about a high level of class stratification with relatively low inter-class social mobility but, at the same time, also created greater political mobilization opportunities for the lower socio-economic classes, which brought about a more equal redistribution of resources and the development of the welfare state.

4   European societies since the Middle Ages developed a dense network of medium-sized cities (Hohenberg and Lees 1996), which had some important common traits, summarized by Bagnasco and Le Galès (2000) and Le Galès (2002). First, their morphology and history. European cities developed in most cases between the tenth and the fourteenth century, predominantly around a central place where political power and citizenry had, and still have, their symbols. This picture contrasts quite sharply with the grid structure of North American cities, their central business districts and the tendency towards suburbanization. Second, European cities have political and social structures that are embedded in relatively generous and still structuring nation-states. This implies, given the higher public expenditures, a relatively high share of employees in the public sector, who make the city's economy – in contrast to US cities – less dependent on market forces. Also, the low geographic mobility helps to stabilize urban contexts, favoring the development of collective actors. Third, European cities present public services and infrastructures that are strongly related to the regulative capacity and planning traditions of the respective nation-states. There are, of course, important differences among countries and cities (and this book reports some of them); nevertheless, they mitigate tendencies to segregation and poverty, which are quite widespread in the USA.

These characteristics are historically interconnected. European cities, for instance, had an important role in the development of the nation-state itself (Tilly 1975; Rokkan 1999; Le Galès 2002). Cities were political and cultural laboratories of participation and government. The specific administrative tools and techniques developed at the urban level – from town planning to differentiated functional roles and tax collection – were crucial to the rising nation-states, which extended their remit to the whole of society, promoting new mechanisms for regulating associative life.

In his analysis of power carried out within *Wirtschaft und Gesellschaft*, Weber devoted one chapter to the city (1922/1972: 727–814), underlining precisely the importance of this aspect. He considered the way in which the political deliberative processes were organized to be a crucial analytical dimension for understanding differences. Comparatively, he highlighted the peculiarity of the medieval European city, where the *Bürger's* membership was based on his individual involvement in the regulation of social matters as a citizen and bearer of rights and duties, subject to common legislation (see Chapter 2). This was considered by Weber to be quite revolutionary for that time, because it contributed in the long run to free the individual from communitarian and ascribed bonds, and to set in motion a deep process of change, giving rise to the building of the nation-state on the one hand and to the development of capitalism on the other. Once these processes were completed – in Europe it was with the unification of Italy (1860) and Germany (1871) – state domination became the strongest organizing principle of the European urban system. Cities lost their autonomy and became agents of the state as local and regional bases for putting national policies into practice and for legitimizing the forms of territorial management defined by the State (Le Galès 2002: 76).

Institutional configurations and welfare regimes as structuring contexts

All the distinctive elements briefly outlined above are related to the specific role institutional configurations have in addressing and structuring social life. How do scholars deal with these differences? We mentioned previously the use of typologies as a heuristic device. A first distinction is provided by *comparative political economy* approaches which, addressing social systems of production, consider European countries – with the partial exception now of the UK and Ireland – as *coordinated* market economies and contrast them with uncoordinated ones, such as the USA. This approach provides a systemic view of how institutions and economic systems interact and considers institutions not only as a constraint on actor's (firms) behavior, but also as an opportunity to increase competitive advantages through the provision of collective public goods (Fligstein 1996; Hall and Soskice 2001: 31; Le Galès and Voelzkow 2001). This implies, for instance, that educational policies are important to attain a skilled labor force, and that social policies are important in managing social risks. They stabilize consumption and deter social tensions from degenerating. But where do the differences lie? They do *not* lie in the economic performance of the two models, as neoliberal rhetoric would suggest. In fact, as Hall and Soskice (2001) maintained, both liberal and coordinated market economies were able to provide satisfactory levels of economic performance and competitiveness. The World Economic Forum (2004), by ranking Finland, Denmark and Sweden among the top five most competitive countries in the world, contradicts neoliberal assumptions about the negative role of the state on competitiveness. These countries are, in fact, also the highest welfare spenders. Differences lie more in the explicit and important role of institutional arrangements in shaping – through their complementarities – the two social systems of production. These arrangements bring about relatively coherent outcomes (e.g., in terms of social protection, labor market structure, financial markets) and reinforce the differences between the two kinds of political economy. However, despite the revitalization of the convergence hypothesis (for the debate see Berger and Dore 1996; Crouch and Streeck 1997), coordinated market economies show that a considerable diversity in national responses to exogenous (e.g., global competitiveness and trade liberalization) and endogenous (e.g., demographic structure, institutional inertia) pressures still prevails. The debate on welfare regimes provides insightful elements to understand these differences. The term *coordinated market societies* is, in fact, too vague. What becomes crucial is *how* they are coordinated, besides the institutions targeted directly at regulating market forces.

The important work by Esping-Andersen (1990, 1999) takes us a step further. Esping-Andersen uses the prominence of one regulative dimension as the main criteria to identify specific welfare regimes. The market, the family, and the state intermix in a peculiar way, giving rise to the *three worlds of welfare capitalism*: the *liberal*, the *conservative* and the *social-democratic* regime. The three regimes are characterized by different relations of dependence/independence from the market[8] in relation to meeting one's own needs, and by specific outcomes in terms of social stratification and inequality. In the liberal regime, market-dependency is the greatest and inequality the highest (Förster 2000). In the conservative regime, we have an intermediate level of market-dependency, related to position in the labor market, with a tendency to maintain the status quo. Finally, in the social-democratic regime market-dependency is the lowest and redistribution the highest.

Esping-Andersen's model is well known and much debated,[9] so we do not need to go deeper into it here. Its advantages lie in the plausible simplification it operates, which can be considered a good starting point to systematically address the intra-European differences among coordinated market economies. In order to give an adequate picture of these differences, however, several scholars criticized Esping-Andersen's typology and made a plea for grouping the specificities of South European countries into a specific regime (e.g., Mingione 1991; Leibfried 1992; Ferrera 1996, 1998; Gallie and Paugam 2000). The importance of clientelism, segmented labor markets, locally fragmented social assistance schemes, and unsupported family responsibilities underline the important differences between these countries and those of the conservative regime. For more details see Chapters 2 and 12, which address the specificities, opportunities, and threats of this particular regime, under particular stress as a result of the ongoing changes.

Table 1.1 provides a series of important indicators to understand the main characteristics of the four welfare regimes of *social Europe* resulting

Table 1.1 Socio-economic and social expenditure indicators for selected EU countries (1990–2000)

Welfare regime	Liberal		Social-democratic		Conservative		Familistic		EU-15	
	UK		Denmark		Germany		Italy			
	1990	2000	1990	2000	1990	2000	1990	2000	1990	2000
Population										
Old age index[1]	24.0	23.9	23.2	22.2	21.6	23.9	21.5	26.6	21.6	24.3
Child in single parent family[2]	11.9	19.8	n.a.	n.a.	6.7	10.3	3.3	4.1	6.0	9.7
Fertility rate[3]	1.83	1.64	1.67	1.34	1.45	1.34	1.33	1.25	1.57	1.53
Births out of wedlock[4]	27.9	39.5	46.4	44.9	15.3	23.1	6.4	9.2	19.5	27.2
Divorce[5]	3.0	2.6	2.5	2.7	1.7	2.4	0.5	0.7	n.a.	1.9
Non-EU immigrants[3]	0.6	2.7	2.8	3.9	6.3	6.7	0.9	1.9	n.a.	n.a.
Employment rates[6]										
Male (15–64)	80.5	77.9	80.1	80.7	78.7	72.7	72.0	67.6	n.a.	72.4
Female (15–64)	61.7	65.1	70.7	72.1	54.0	57.9	36.4	41.1	n.a.	53.8
Youth (15–24)	64.3	55.9	65.0	67.1	57.9	46.1	33.3	26.1	n.a.	39.9
% of fixed term contracts	n.a.	6.7	n.a.	10.2	n.a.	12.7	n.a.	10.1	n.a.	n.a.
Unemployment rates										
Male (55–64)[7]	8.4	5.5	5.1	3.9	7.0	12.6	1.6	4.4	6.1	8.0
Female[8]	6.6	4.9	8.4	5.3	9.6	8.3	13.7	14.4	n.a.	9.7
Youth (15–24)[8]	10.8	12.7	11.4	7.35	8.0	9.1	27.2	30.7	n.a.	16.2
Long-term (15–64)[9]	33.5	28.0	28.8	20.0	45.9	51.5	69.0	61.3	n.a.	45.2
Expenditure on social protection										
Per capita in PPS[10]	3410.1	6180.7	4543.5	7671.5	4316.5	7267.9	3749.5	5891.4	3823.9	6404.9
As % of GDP[11]	25.7	26.8	29.7	28.8	26.1	29.5	25.2	25.2	26.4	27.3
On family/children[12]	9.0	6.9	11.9	13.1	7.6	10.5	4.4	3.8	7.9	8.1
On old age and survivors[12]	46.2	48.7	36.8	38.0	45.8	42.5	54.7	58.5	45.4	46.6
On labor policies[13]	n.a.	0.5	n.a.	3.9	n.a.	2.9	n.a.	1.2	n.a.	2.0
On active labor policies[13]	n.a.	0.07	n.a.	1.6	n.a.	0.9	n.a.	0.5	n.a.	0.7
Unemployed covered[14]	24.1	26.2	79.4	63.8	62.4	72.3	4.4	4.4	n.a.	n.a.
GMI for 1 parent + 1 child PPP[15]	n.a.	575.79	n.a.	800.11	n.a.	534.62	n.a.	219.57	n.a.	n.a.

Poverty									
60% median pre-transfers[16]	32	29	29	23	22	20	23	21	26	23
60% median post-transfers[16]	20	19	10	11	15	10	20	18	17	15
Gini index[17]	n.a	33	n.a.	23	n.a.	28	n.a.	33	n.a.	31
Competitiveness[18]										
Growth 2003 ranking	n.a.	15	n.a.	4	n.a.	13	n.a.	41	n.a.	n.a.
Business 2003 ranking	n.a.	6	n.a.	4	n.a.	5	n.a.	24	n.a.	n.a.

[1] Old age index: people over 65 years as a percentage of the working age population (15–64 years). *Source:* Eurostat (2003a)

[2] Children (0–14 years) living in families with only one adult as a percentage of all children living in families with two adults. *Source:* Eurostat (2003b)

[3] Data for non EU-immigrants first year 1994. *Source:* Eurostat (2003b)

[4] As a percentage of all live births. For Italy, Denmark and EU-15, last year 1999. *Source:* Eurostat (2003a)

[5] Per 1000 persons. *Source:* Eurostat (2003b)

[6] Employed persons as a share of the total population aged 15–64. Last year 2001. *Source:* Eurostat (2003b)

[7] *Source:* OECD (2002)

[8] For Germany, first year 1993. *Source:* Eurostat (2003b)

[9] Long-term unemployed (12 months or more) as percentage of all unemployed. *Source:* Eurostat (2003b)

[10] In PPS (purchasing power standards). *Source:* Eurostat (2003b)

[11] First year 1991, last year 1999. *Source:* Eurostat (2003a)

[12] As a percentage of social benefits. *Source:* Eurostat (2003b)

[13] As a percentage of GDP, last year 2001. *Source:* Eurostat (2003b)

[14] Unemployed covered by unemployment benefits. *Source:* ECHP version 2001, first year 1994 (wave 1), last year 1998 (wave 5). Calculations by Carbone (2003)

[15] Guaranteed minimum income (social assistance and existing relevant benefits/allowances) for one parent plus one child aged 2 years 11 months. PPP = purchasing power parities (Euro = 1). Situation July 31, 2001. *Source:* Bradshaw and Finch (2002)

[16] Eurostat (2003a). First year 1995, last year 2000

[17] EU-13. *Source:* Marlier and Cohen-Solal (2000)

[18] *Source:* World Economic Forum (2004). The CGI (competitiveness growth index) and the the BCI (business competitiveness index) aim at ranking countries according to the factors that favor the growth and business of an economy. It considers at its very basis a mix of qualitative and quantitative set of indicators and a survey conducted on 7707 senior business leaders in 101 countries. The report and full methodological details are available online at: www.weforum.org. Retrieved: September 15, 2003

from this typologic readjustment. We clearly see that data confirm to a large extent the clustering of the four models, their relative internal coherence and the different part played by the peculiar mixes of institutional arrangements.[10] Just a few examples will make this more concrete.

Within the conservative regime the family is considered to have a major role (Esping-Andersen 1999). This role is socially recognized and supported by the state through *active subsidiarity* (García and Kazepov 2002), which implies family allowances and services only slightly less generous than in the social-democratic regime. Women balance caring activities with an European Union (EU) average activity rate and there are slightly fewer children born out of wedlock than in the EU average. In general, reciprocity relations are backed up by state intervention, and even though market dependence is higher than in the social-democratic regime, it is definitely lower than in the liberal and the familistic regimes. If a person becomes unemployed, there is an unemployment benefit that replaces wages by approximately 60 percent for a minimum of 6 months up to 2.5 years, according to age and length of paid contributions. After this period of time people can claim unemployment assistance or, most probably, social assistance as long as the condition of need persists. Replacement income rates are lower, but benefits allow individuals and families to be just above the poverty line (Kazepov and Sabatinelli 2001). Labor activation policies (training, requalification, job insertion) accompany passive policies.

All these indicators point to an institutional context in which the state and the family provide, through a specific mix of redistributive and reciprocity relations, a set of resources aimed at protecting families from social risks. Poverty is kept at relatively low levels and the relation to the market is mediated through the provision of public goods that bring about relatively competitive coordinated market economies.

South European countries of the familistic regime, despite some commonalities with the conservative regime, present quite a different picture. *Passive subsidiarity* characterizes the way in which the state supports the family. Family allowances are very low, in-kind services rare and locally fragmented. Women's activity rates are much lower than the EU average (Schmid and Gazier 2002), as are divorce rates and children born out of wedlock. Protection is (was, if we consider the recent reform trends) provided more than anywhere else through the male breadwinner. Relatively low unemployment rates for male adults, but high ones for youth and women point in this direction. The same is true for the high share of public expenditure absorbed by pensions vis-à-vis other social protection policies, which are left aside. Unemployment benefits are much lower than in other regimes (40 percent of the last net income for 6 to a maximum of 9 months) and other income-maintenance schemes aimed at the unemployed provide a fragmented landscape of access criteria and benefits which protect only selected categories. Social assistance schemes are in most cases local and intervene only residually. As we will see in Chapters 3 and 13, within this framework families become overloaded with social and caring responsibilities and are not able to redistribute resources except within the family itself. This brings about an unequal distribution of income (i.e. a relatively high value of the Gini index) and also a drop in fertility rates. Having children becomes extremely costly (De Sandre et al. 1999). There are, of course, exceptions, which are located in economically and institutionally more dynamic regions of Southern Europe (e.g., the Basque country in Spain, some North-Eastern regions in Italy), but they confirm the overall problematic situation.

The typology briefly outlined in this section considers the nation-state as the main organizing territorial unit in the type-building exercise of welfare regimes. The same is also true of the coordinated market economies, which operate mainly through institutional settings defined at the national level. This prominent position of the nation-state has been widely challenged in the last 30 years, bringing about processes of rescaling and redesign. Does this mean that we are looking through the wrong lenses, if we focus on nation-states to understand European cities? In the following sections I try to show how the national frame of reference is still important and that the growing importance of cities (and regions) has to be considered through this perspective. In particular, I proceed on two parallel tracks. On one side I pursue my main argument about the distinctiveness of European cities rooted in the political dimension and the role of the welfare state; on the other side I present some of the main arguments put forward by the authors of the chapters collected in the three sections of this book as examples of this line of thought.

Changing Contexts

Undoubtedly, nation-states are changing. The issue is much debated in the literature on welfare capitalism and globalization[11] as well as among urban scholars.[12] Changes are emerging out of specific endogenous and exogenous pressures that the nation-state has to face. These pressures have had various sources since the virtuous synergies of the post-war welfare capitalist economies, which fed the expansion of public expenditure, were interrupted in the 1970s. Economic restructuring, technical innovation, and shifts between sectors brought about deep changes in employment and working conditions: relatively stable jobs in the manufacturing sector declined and flexible forms of employment in the service sector increased together with an increase in women's activity rates. Demographic changes, like the aging of the population or the weakening of families' sheltering capacities, brought about increasing welfare demands for pensions and care services (Gullenstad and Segalen 1997). As Mingione notes in Chapter 3, the instability emerging from these changes in the market and the family spilled over into the protection capacities of the welfare state, giving rise to its fiscal crisis and that of its *crisis management mechanisms* (Offe 1984). This brought about a deep process of institutional redesign and rescaling, which Mingione sketches in relation to its diversified spatial impact on the different welfare regimes. In particular, he focuses on the consequences for the familistic regime, providing a picture within which the emerging patterns are, together with the liberal regime, the most fragmented and diversified. On the one hand, local institutions and family networks foster flexible and innovative competitiveness in self-employment or in small and medium-sized enterprises, like in the *Third Italy* or Catalonia (Bagnasco 1977; Piore and Sabel 1984). On the other hand, cities and regions with chronically high rates of unemployment and poverty remain locked in their situation, like in the Italian Mezzogiorno. The reasons for these differences are complex and both historically and institutionally rooted. The problems lie in the fact that the changing socio-economic and demographic contexts seem to exacerbate pre-existing differences. Cities and regions tend to polarize according to their ability to lessen the burden of caring responsibilities and to make strategic use of local social capital in addressing flexible and economically innovative arrangements. Within this picture, the nation-state has an important role. It provides only selectively the local economies with competitive public goods and it has difficulty keeping the divergent trends under control, because it is no longer able to guarantee its redistributive functions. Institutionally, the reliance on the family bears the risk of reproducing inequalities if the family's role is not backed up by state intervention. Resources are pooled just within the smaller *Gemeinschaft*. In other welfare regimes – including the liberal one, even though at a lower level – these protective functions, despite the increasing diversity, are still provided by the nation-state. There, the tensions generated by the changing contexts are kept under control through new forms of governance based on innovative mixes between passive national and active local policies.

It is within this framework that we should view the scenario presented and the trends highlighted by Martinotti, Sennett and Kesteloot in Chapters 4, 5 and 6 of the first section of the book on changing contexts. The existing regulative settings also influence the way in which the changing morphology of cities and the resulting urbanization patterns are filtered into concrete socio-spatial configurations.

The outlined changes make cities more complex, and to understand this complexity we have to refine our analytical tools. Martinotti proposes to focus on how different populations, with different interests, cut across traditional class cleavages and make regulation much more complicated. Most of the social problems contemporary metropolitan societies experience are related to the way in which potential conflicts among inhabitants, commuters, city users, and metropolitan businesspeople are played out and are structured historically. Despite certain degrees of convergence with US cities, however, less market-oriented local governance arrangements, embedded in more binding regulation systems and urban planning, provide European cities with a higher degree of control over the tensions these different interests might bring about. These tensions are related to the ways in which the consequences of economic globalization and neoliberal adjustment are dealt with and, in particular, with the underlying spread of flexibility and vulnerability (Castel 2000). Sennett, in Chapter 5, addresses the implications of this trend on the social virtues of urban life: sociability and subjectivity. In particular, he maintains that just as flexible production brings about more short-term relations at work, it creates a regime of superficial and disengaged relations in the city, weakening the social bond. This is true, in general, but it should not be forgotten that it is also crucial how flexibility is dealt with in institutional terms. Sennett does not develop on that, but he warns us of the intrinsic risks institutions have to face. Flexibility undermines citizenship practices, which have to recompose increasingly fragmented interests. In this sense, we can surely affirm that the way in which flexibilization impacts on individuals' interaction patterns and feelings of insecurity depends also on the ways in which it has been institutionalized in different welfare regimes. Being a protected *flexiworker* in a system that bridges conditions of work instability through extensive and generous coverage, rather than a precarious worker left alone within unstable market relations, makes an important difference (see Table 1.1 for some relevant data supporting this argument).

Kesteloot, in Chapter 6, takes up Sennett's warning and deploys it in relation to the socio-spatial configurations of European cities. Using a geologic metaphor combined with an adapted regulationist approach, he shows how different types of residential environments are associated with the organization of the economy, the conditions of class struggle, the types of housing and the material and institutional modes of organization for collective consumption existing at the time they were built. These spatial patterns overlay and combine with the patterns produced in previous periods in a complex and historically rooted mosaic, which varies across cities, regions and countries. This results – according to Kesteloot – from the specific balance of power between employers and workers existing in the different accumulation regimes. As we have seen, however, this relation is strongly mediated by state policies, which influence levels, security, and replacement rates in case of market failure. Consequently, production, consumption, and housing patterns are molded according to the ways in which taxation and social security contributions are redistributed through services and provisions. Our claim is that this produces different socio-spatial configurations in different welfare regimes. The neoliberal turn and the emergence of a flexible accumulation regime after the 1970s challenges the forms of mediation and negotiation that were institutionalized in the post-war period, and tends to polarize the possible directions of change (see also Jessop 2002). Kesteloot suggests two options. The first points towards a *repressive city*, where fear and insecurity develop into spatial displacement and concentrations of less privileged social groups. The second points towards a *negotiated city*, in which new forms of governance institutionalize the legitimacy of different populations to participate in the co-definition of socially relevant goals and how to attain them.

Rescaling and redesigning welfare

One of the consequences of the above-mentioned changes is that the local dimension is becoming more important in regulatory terms. This can occur in different ways. On the one hand, the state can decentralize some of its functions to lower levels of government, reforming the existing system. On the other hand, there might be an *implicit* decentralization resulting from a shift in the relevance of different policies, operating one at the national and the other at the local level. The two ways usually co-evolve and feed reciprocally. Let me give an example that shows how the two relate to one another. I will mainly refer to social assistance schemes and how they have changed in the last 15–20 years.[13]

The causal sequence of events is well known: the rise in unemployment in the late 1970s, triggered by deindustrialization and economic restructuring, brought about the spread of long-term unemployment by the mid-1980s. Unemployment benefits are based on contributions and regulated at the national level in most European countries. They aim at providing benefits up to a certain period of time. After that period, unemployed people who are unable to re-enter the labor market shift to unemployment assistance or, most probably, to social assistance schemes. The latter are regulated mainly at the local level (e.g., in terms of funding and accompanying measures) and operate on the basis of the means test (see Figure 1.1 on the CD-Rom). The increased number of unemployed claiming social assistance exerted growing financial pressure on cities, which stirred the debate on welfare *dependency* and how to hinder it, highlighting mainly the potential poverty and unemployment traps (Dean and Taylor-Gooby 1992) that passive social assistance measures bear.

This paved the way for deep reforms of most of the social assistance schemes in Europe. *Not being passive anymore* become the new slogan from Scandinavian cities to the Southern European ones, heading towards what Jessop called the "Schumpeterian Workfare Postnational Regime" (2002). Activation has become the magic word for finding a solution to dependency and attaining, at the same time, two goals:

1 *Getting people off the payrolls*, thereby cutting public expenditure on social assistance and unemployment measures and reducing the social costs of poverty and unemployment.
2 *Empowering the people* out of work by improving their life conditions and increasing their opportunities through wide social support provided by ad hoc designed accompanying measures.

Despite the fact that the tools developed for the attainment of these goals are relatively similar (e.g., providing subsidized jobs, training, requalification), European welfare regimes differ in relation to conditionality, compulsion, generosity, and to the local fragmentation these policies give rise to.[14] The emerging differences cluster relatively coherently around the four welfare regimes that characterize Europe's social model. The stronger accent on compulsory activation and conditionality is to be found in the *liberal regime*, even though all other regimes also introduced it. *The social-democratic regime* fosters more empowering policies, while the *conservative (corporative) regime* balances obligation and empowerment. The *familistic regime* is the most problematic one because, despite the path-breaking reforms of the second half of the 1990s introducing Revenue Minimum d'Insertion (RMI)-like schemes (e.g., in Spain, Portugal, and part of Italy), their implementation still reproduces in most cases past arrangements. The latter regime is also the one in which spatial differentiation is the highest in Europe (see also Mingione et al. 2002).

These trends are not just occurring within social assistance schemes. They reflect a more general shift towards local regulation, which took place in social policies throughout the 1990s (OECD 2003). In general, this regulatory shift addresses mainly in-kind services, public employment services, local partnerships, activation and accompanying measures rather than the definition of thresholds and the level of benefits. These are still defined at the national level. Even where they are defined at the local or regional level, as in Germany for instance, the variation is negligible. This holds true in all European welfare regimes, with some limitations in the familistic one where, on the contrary, the differences existing in access criteria and welfare provisions are not able to compensate existing differences in the other spheres of regulation, ending up institutionally reproducing and reinforcing the existing conditions of inclusion and exclusion.

The spatial impact of ongoing transformation processes

The implications of the increasing differentiation in local welfare state services and practices are highlighted by Alan Murie in Chapter 7. Their role in addressing the social consequences of the changes described above is becoming more and more important, because they are structuring the ways in which vulnerability and poverty are becoming concrete in cities and neighborhoods. The processes of social exclusion are, in fact, increasingly triggered by differential access to participation, redistribution, and rights, which are also shaped by local practices (see also Mingione 1996). Where you live makes a difference, and the rescaling process that welfare regimes are undergoing increasingly constrains and enables individual and families' agency according to the qualities of decommodified services they can have access to at the local level.

This implies, as all the chapters in the second part of this book highlight, that the patterns of social stratification emerging in European cities increasingly incorporate *space* as an important dimension in the structuring process of social exclusion and inclusion.

Musterd and Ostendorf (see Chapter 8), for instance, investigate the role of space in relation to segregation in cities. In particular, they address the possible neighborhood effects of spatial concentration of social disadvantage. The assumption in the literature is that the changing socio-economic and demographic contexts tend to increase inequality. Increasing socio-economic inequality is assumed to activate processes of spatial segregation, which negatively influence opportunities for social mobility, particularly in socially and economically weak neighborhoods (Wilson 1987; for a review, see also Burgers and Musterd 2002). Inhabitants of these neighborhoods become trapped in their condition of disadvantage. This question has been much debated in the North American literature. The evidence from comparative research shows that in European cities the impact of ongoing transformation processes does not automatically translate into high levels of segregation (Musterd and Ostendorf 1998). European cities have only moderate levels of segregation compared with US cities. Even in neighborhoods that concentrate social and economic conditions of disadvantage, people can easily "get in touch with the other" and experience socially mixed environments. The role of social policies in this process – in particular, welfare transfers coupled with targeted area-based projects – is considered to be particularly relevant in reducing segregation and neutralizing the neighborhood effect for the poor and socially excluded. Institutions (including the family and reciprocity networks) mediate the consequences of the changing contexts and mitigate their impact on people's living conditions. The authors report empirical evidence for Dutch cities. Similar outcomes characterize European cities in general, even though differences can be found in relation to the characteristics of the welfare regimes within which cities are embedded. These differences are also confirmed when we consider the housing conditions of immigrants, who are in general one of the most vulnerable parts of the population with higher levels of segregation than nationals. In order to understand these differences, van Kempen makes a plea for a comprehensive approach in which the state plays an important part and interacts in a specific way with other dimensions (income, demographic structure, choice, etc.). Concrete housing conditions result from the interrelation between all these dimensions. Van Kempen shows that, despite the migrants–nationals divide in segregation levels, social housing supply and local welfare practices provide European cities with resources to reduce the levels of segregation much more than is the case in US cities. Marcuse follows the same line of reasoning, maintaining that social divisions within cities depend upon state action which "can ameliorate the extremes of inequality in income, in the first instance, and it can directly control the spatial patterns produced by [economic changes], in the second. State action in fact makes the critical difference between European cities and cities in the United States today" (Marcuse and van Kempen 2002: 29). However, the situation is not homogeneous in Europe, and the ongoing rescaling processes can bring about an increased differentiation at the local level, with liberal and familistic regimes being the most diversified.

The different role of the state in regulating access to housing influences the way in which gentrification processes take place and social mix is encouraged. Simon (see Chapter 10) shows how the pace and intensity of gentrification depend upon the flexibility of the housing market. European cities are, from this point of view, particularly resilient compared with US cities. The prominent role of home ownership, of public investors, and relatively low residential mobility limit de facto the negative effects of gentrification processes and sharp divisions. Public intervention in the renovation process and public urban planning in general tend to minimize the effects of the rent gap and to promote social mixing. Another limitation comes from local communities. In order to understand the processes at stake, Simon analyzes the case of Belleville in Paris. In particular, he addresses the implications of gentrification for the structuring of social integration and social mixing as part of a wider process of urban renewal in which different actors with different interests participate. In this sense, he is interested in showing how the encounter of different populations within the neighborhood changes the patterns of social integration. From this point of view, gentrifiers are not a homogenous group and the resulting interactions with the local inhabitants point to complex forms of mediation and interclass collaboration. Among gentrifying groups,

new middle-class *multiculturals* – as Simon calls those who enjoy social and
ethnic mixes, look for an atmosphere and are willing a priori to respect the
neighborhood – might mediate between business and politics, bringing
about new forms of social cohesion from below, which are increasingly
gaining ground in European cities.

Local governments, new forms of governance, and social cohesion

Within the trends of decentralization and devolution emerging at the
end of the 1970s, cities gained autonomy and became actively involved in
the policy design exercise. The basic assumption underlying these trends
is that local policies should facilitate more targeted and flexible solutions
which are able to adapt to increasingly varying social needs in differentiated local contexts. The degrees of freedom localities have, however, vary
across countries and regions and depend very much on the institutional
frames of reference, which constrain and enable context-specific options
at the different territorial levels. The relationship these policies retain with
national regulatory contexts remains crucial in understanding the impact
devolution has in fragmenting and differentiating access to resources and
establishing and institutionalizing new territorial inequalities. The four
regimes characterizing the European social model present, from this point
of view, distinct even though partly converging *path-dependent patterns*. This
implies that similar policies embedded in different institutional contexts
produce different impacts.[15]

To understand the complexity of this process and the fragmenting
effect it might bear, we have to consider preliminarily that decentralization
is often accompanied by a broader process of privatization and diffusion
of neoliberal principles of regulation within public social services (Ascoli
and Ranci 2002). Besides introducing *new public management* criteria inspired by the rhetoric of efficiency and the adoption of cost–benefit relations and performance indicators within public services and administrative
bodies, this has brought about an increasing separation between funding
and delivering services. In this context, public bodies are funding and
regulating contracted-out services, which are supplied by third parties,
mainly non-profit actors.

According to Ascoli and Ranci (2002), these changes are transversal
to any welfare regime and should no longer be seen as a mere devolution
of management responsibilities from public to private actors driven *only* by
neoliberal ideology. Rather, they reflect increasingly *also* processes of systemic realignment of the spheres of regulation, implemented to meet the
new emerging needs. These processes of realignment do not necessarily
neglect the role of the state, but involve a reorganization of the institutional

forms through which services are being delivered, financed, and coordinated. Social expenditure did not decline radically as heralded and the state did not disappear. The territorial impact of these changes, however, depends on how they intersect with the existing institutional settings. As the chapters of the last part of the book clearly show, this situation is characterized by highly ambiguous synergies. On the one hand, they open up new opportunities for developing local partnerships and democratic participation in the co-definition of goals; on the other hand, they might have negative and unequal effects in terms of redistribution of both economic resources and opportunities (Geddes 2000; Geddes and Le Galès 2001).

One of the consequences of the above-mentioned changes from the mid-1980s onwards has been the development of new forms of governance through which different actors have become increasingly involved in policy design and delivery. Le Galès (see Chapter 11) addresses these issues, disentangling the elusive nature of urban policies and underlining the increasingly constructivist frame within which they are produced. Urban policies are, in fact, becoming more fluid as a result of a complex process of structuration, during which a widening range of actors, from different sectors of society, with different interests and acting at different levels, interact and produce policies. This brings about "an immense field of experimentation undertaken by local actors," who are no longer merely implementing decisions taken at other levels of government, but are taking an active part in the redesign of public policies through conflicts and negotiations. In this framework, urban government has not disappeared; on the contrary, cities become a privileged site of aggregation and representation of interests. The crucial issue is then, as Le Galès clearly underlines, "bringing them together to organize a mode of city governance." In this exercise, European cities present important differences compared with US cities. They still have strong capacities for initiatives and control, and – most importantly – they can rely on a welfare state with powerful mechanisms of redistribution. These provide relative stability, an *institutional milieu* that the new forms of governance can build upon: "a political domain in which the structural context of economic and state structuring and restructuring, political culture and the political actors intersect in the process of urban governance" (DiGaetano and Strom 2003: 363). The relevant role of the welfare state in European cities provides a specific political domain and makes European urban elites less dependent upon business interests. Not only do large groups within cities mobilize against radical cuts, but the vast majority of the population in Europe defends the welfare state (Gallie and Paugam 2002). It is true that state restructuring has partly weakened the protection from market forces and there is general agreement that competition is growing (Jensen-Butler et al. 1997). However, according to Le Galès, "the reality of competition translates into public policies presented in the language of competition" to make cities more attractive to investors, also through the production of local collective competition goods (see also Le Galès and Voelzkow 2001). This tendency is supported by new forms of European-wide urban coalitions, which emerged with the support of the European Commission and its funding policies, promoting the new forms of urban governance with the aim of balancing competitiveness and cohesion (Geddes 2000; Le Galès 2002).

A good example of how the new forms of governance work and what impact they might have at the local level is provided by urban development programs, which are the focus of Jan Vranken in Chapter 12. These programs, developed throughout the 1980s and the 1990s, target a wide range of issues, from poverty and social exclusion in specific neighborhoods to the promotion of social cohesion and economic dynamism at the city level. Vranken's analysis focuses on the implications of these programs for the changing patterns of solidarity and cohesion in the city. Do they impact on the life chances of the inhabitants? Are they just displacing a problem from the neighborhood in which they intervene to the neighborhood where they do not intervene? Does the intrinsic integrated approach foster solidarity and cohesion? Vranken's answer is yes to all three questions, but under certain conditions. We have to consider how the context of action is structured, who are the actors involved, who is excluded and whose interests are represented.

Vranken shows that the most recent urban development programs tend to be rather comprehensive, foreseeing also the participation of inhabitants (or claimants) in the planning and implementation processes. This *participatory turn* dramatically improves the life chances of the poor and the excluded, and effectively fosters solidarity and cohesion. However, targeting some neighborhoods or areas might bring about varying degrees of territorial displacement, increasing inequalities within the city by isolating neighborhoods from their wider urban context. Here Vranken ties in with Le Galès and underlines another important aspect: the complementary nature of these programs to social policies, which cannot be substituted, because it "would imply an important breach of basic principles of solidarity." This also has important implications in relation to fragmentation and to the ability of these programs to recompose the "pieces of the puzzle." Their success depends not only on their ability to pull together actors, interests and available resources, but also on the quality of the resources social policies can provide.

This latter aspect implies that the characteristics of social policies influence the types of urban development programs that can be promoted in different welfare regimes and their degrees of freedom. In short, they help to structure the emerging modes of governance, coordination, and regulation, without determining them.

In the last few years, several scholars have tried to systematize the debate, developing typologies to understand the different underlying principles making the different modes of governance work (e.g., Pierre 1999; Geddes and Le Galès 2001; Jessop 2002; DiGaetano and Strom 2003). The aim of these scholars has been to understand how the public–private resource mobilization takes place, how partnerships are built and how actors interact, with a major focus on economic activities. Despite some divergence in the construction of the typologies in terms of criteria adopted and resulting types, there seems to be wide consensus on the driving forces fuelling the spread of new governance arrangements (e.g., economic restructuring, devolution of state authority). There also appears to be consensus on the crucial importance of the nation-state and the institutional embeddedness of these new forms of governance. Institutions reflect values, norms, and practices, providing, at the same time, the context for actors' bounded rationality. What clearly emerges from the analysis that the different scholars provide is, again, the tendency to develop forms of governance that seem to be in keeping with the existing institutional settings. According to DiGaetano and Strom (2003), different *institutional milieus*, with their structural contexts and political cultures, seem to furnish environments that are more receptive to some modes of governance than others. This depends on the fact that urban governance is related to the role of local governments (Pierre 1999: 375), which implies different institutional settings – also defined at the national level – and underlying values, norms, beliefs, and practices. Geddes and Le Galès (2001) refer to the four welfare regimes prevalent in Europe, as does Jessop (2002) in an adapted form.

Taking up the example of increasingly localized activation and social assistance policies mentioned earlier, we can recognize – using Jessop's classification (2002: 247–75) – some degrees of coherence between welfare regimes and the emerging new forms of partnership and governance (Lehto 2000). The prefix *neo* underlines the path-dependent character of the four regimes.

In the *neoliberal welfare regime*, typical of Anglo-Saxon countries (e.g., the UK), we find broad multi-actor partnerships, with a strong presence of private actors. *Delivery through partnership* characterizes employer coalitions, which provide a wide array of training and job insertion opportunities in a privatized market context in which variety is high and the claimant cannot necessarily choose. Efficiency, accountability, competitiveness, and contractual forms of relations regulate claimants' activation in a trend towards increased use of compulsory work activity and conditionality in defining access to means-tested benefits (Trickey and Walker 2000; Evans 2001).

In the *neostatist welfare regime*, typical of North European countries (e.g., Denmark), we find partnerships in which the main partners are state agencies and, to a much lesser but increasing extent, the social partners. The former tend to foster collaboration between employment services and social assistance agencies. The latter operate under strict guidance of the local authority, which keeps the degrees of freedom for non-state actors quite low (Lødemel and Trickey 2000; Kautto et al. 2001). Compulsion exists, but is less relevant than in other regimes and accompanying measures aim at including a wide range of empowering services, which are often also designed to improve the participation of claimants in the definition and design of the policies' implementation.

In the *neocorporative welfare regime*, typical of continental European countries (e.g., Germany), we find partnerships in which the main actors are social partners, third-sector voluntary agencies, and state agencies. They all increasingly negotiate with the local authority on the design of the active policies to be consensually implemented. Most of them follow a *carrot and stick* strategy (compulsion and empowerment), providing chances to escape the conditions of need within a framework of diffuse conditionality and increasingly fragmented provision of accompanying measures, also at the territorial level.

In the *neofamilistic regime*, typical of South European countries, we find an extensive and highly heterogeneous presence of third-sector voluntary and non-profit agencies. Possible relations can range from particularistic and clientelistic forms of partnerships to highly advanced empowering and participatory arrangements. The reforms undertaken at the end of the 1990s in most South European countries tried to overcome the first aspect by supporting the latter. Their implementation, however, did not succeed in the majority of cases. Weak state initiative, the legacy of clientelism and reciprocity relations gave rise to a highly fragmented landscape in the context of an overall tightening of resources.

These modes of governance have to find ways of integrating structural constraints and opportunities for action for people in a condition of need. The final two chapters provide a glimpse of the influences that different modes of governance, embedded in different welfare regimes, have on individual agency. They reflect specific regulating and coordinating frames, and structure (but do not determine) specific coping strategies that individuals and families develop in the different contexts. Enrica Morlicchio describes in Chapter 13 some illustrative cases of how these processes take place in South European cities. The lack of either support from the state or local welfare arrangements, coupled with high unemployment, place a considerable amount of pressure for protection on the family. This does not imply automatically that the family is able to cope adequately with the problems it may have, but that poverty and social integration may coexist. Poor people in South European cities are not necessarily socially excluded, they are often just poor and integrated in a frame of precarious living conditions, which allow them to "merely maintain a level of daily subsistence" in a context of neo-communitarian governance arrangements.

Similar accounts are given by García in Chapter 14. In contrast to Morlicchio, however, she embeds her analysis in the wider debate on the conceptions of social justice underlying social policies in general and minimum income policies in particular. Her focus is on how the latter provide individuals and families with adequate or inadequate resources to cope with conditions of economic hardship. The empirical evidence presented ties in with the analyzes put forward here and in the other chapters of the book, providing a coherent picture of similarities and differences existing in the European social model(s). Regulation principles and conceptions of social justice are not merely abstract terms of an academic debate, but become concrete through policies that define how needs are met, which actors will or should be involved, what resources will be mobilized, their generosity and coverage. Garcia shows that these differences have to be understood in a framework of multilevel governance in which both the local level and the European Commission are gaining regulative capacities. In particular, within the framework of increased fragmentation in the social policy landscape, the European Commission is fostering coordination processes aimed at advancing common European objectives while respecting national diversities. To attain this goal, in 2000 the Lisbon Council adopted the *Open Method of Coordination*, i.e. a *soft* instrument working through recommendations, benchmarking, monitoring, exchange of good practices, and the joint elaboration of performance indicators (Ferrera et al. 2002).

The impact of this method has still to be assessed. However, steering capacities are low and the instruments used – such as the adoption of National Action Plans for labor market policies and for policies on social inclusion – have no real binding character. Awareness of these shortcomings prompted the Commission to foresee a substantive streamlining, making objectives more targeted. A road map has been already set up for reviewing the impact of this method in 2006, but it is still unclear how much flexibility the path-dependent character of the national institutional setting will allow.

Conclusions: Challenging European Cities

In this introductory chapter I have tried to show that in order to understand the specificities of European cities we have to understand their contexts and how they changed from the end of the 1970s onwards. In particular, I have highlighted the importance of considering institutions as relevant contexts, and how different regulatory frameworks produce different forms of social integration. I have also underlined the important role of the nation-state and the *rule of law* as a privileged perspective to frame the meaning of different institutional settings in filtering the impact that changing contexts have on cities. Economic restructuring and the relatively high levels of unemployment have, in the last 20 years, challenged the forms of social integration and cohesion that developed in Europe, particularly after World War II, within different national welfare states. These differences influenced the ways in which nation-states faced these challenges, and the way in which they redesigned and rescaled their policies.

In this framework, cities become increasingly important. The strong accent on devolution, decentralization, and active welfare policies has provided them with new regulatory autonomies which, in a framework of overall fragmentation, brought about the need for coordination of an increased number of different actors. New forms of governance emerged almost everywhere as an attempt to keep this complexity under control and to find ad hoc solutions to contextual and differentiated problems. The degrees of autonomy cities have and the resources at their disposal, however, still very much depend on the overall regulation at the national level. In fact, even though the processes of social exclusion and social fragmentation that the changing context produced at the local level have been increasingly counteracted by local policies, the latter retain a double territorial nature. They are both local and national (urban or regional). Passive policies (such as unemployment or social assistance benefits) are still defined mainly at the national level, while activation policies are defined more at the local level. It is for this very reason that the nation-state's influence on local policies is still pervasive, in particular in relation to redistribution, which still has an important role in Europe. In this sense, the new forms of governance may well be highly differentiated and fragmented, but as long as unemployment benefits, family allowances and minimum income support policies are regulated at the national level – and they are regulated at the national level in most European countries – the degrees of fragmentation and polarization are lower than in other countries, such as the USA. There, the low level of policy intervention exposes people in need to the increased speed of change of the market. The market changes faster than political redistributive institutions, which are more resilient. The conservativeness of resilience, however, should be seen in the light of cities being actors of institutional innovation. In fact, as we have seen, institutions define not only constraints but also enablements. This implies that changes are *metabolized* by the institutional system through claims, negotiations and conflicts among actors, and the outcome of the structuration process is a new institutional setting connected to past institutions but not entirely dependent upon them.

Being bold we could say that – as in the Middle Ages – cities are once again laboratories of how citizenship, in terms of membership, social inclusion and participation, is going to be constructed in the future; that is Weber's claim for Europe's specificity. The real challenge plays out in the definition of who is included and who is excluded. The increasing complexities cities have to face – new populations, migrants, more unstable labor markets, individualization of needs, segmented segregation – all point to rising struggles over citizenship. Less than ever can social rights be taken for granted. Fragmentation, flexibilization, and heterogeneity are indeed factors that foster social vulnerability and the spread of social risks, but these risks are not distributed evenly. European cities took up this challenge and provided diversified capacities of adaptation. They do that drawing on the full institutional heritage nation-states provide them with, a heritage that we have to consider in order to understand the paths undertaken in the different contexts, which the authors of this book describe in their chapters, highlighting the strengths, weaknesses, threats, and opportunities European cities have.

ACKNOWLEDGMENTS

I would like to thank Harvey Molotch, Patrick Le Galès, Enzo Mingione, Alberta Andreotti, and David Benassi for their valuable comments on the much longer draft version of this introduction.

NOTES

1   The distinctiveness of European cities has been investigated by important contributions by Bagnasco and Le Galès (2000) and Le Galès (2002). Also, other scholars highlighted important distinctive characteristics. Just to mention some of the most recent ones: Andersen and van Kempen (2001); Marcuse and van Kempen (2002); Moulaert et al. (2003).

2   There is no consensus among scholars on the topic. For an overview see Alexander et al. (1987), for the main contributions see Giddens (1984) and for recent developments see Archer (1995, 2003).

3   The concept of institution gave rise to a vast literature in the social sciences. Durkheim defined sociology as the *science of institutions*, but also other disciplines are closely associated with the study of institutions. For an overview of different disciplinary perspectives see, among anthropologists, Douglas (1986). Among economists, see Williamson (1975) and North (1990). For sociologists and their different positions, see Durkheim (1893), Berger and

Luckmann (1967), Goffman (1974), DiMaggio and Powell (1991), Nee (1998), and Jessop (2002). For political scientists, see Hall and Taylor (1996), Nielsen (2001) and Pierson (2000b).

4   For the sake of simplicity we will consider these categories as undisputed, even though we recognize that the identification "Durkheim/structure" and "Weber/agency" is too crude. In the last decade, Durkheim's work has been reconsidered in the light of agency-based theories, and *social facts* are no longer considered an external and coercive factor but concrete elements of social construction produced by the actors through their practices (Hilbert 1992; Rawls 1996; Poggi 2000; Garfinkel 2001).

5   For an overview of the diversified theoretical landscape of neo-institutionalism, see DiMaggio and Powell (1991), Hall and Taylor (1996), Nee (1998), Korpi (2001) and Nielsen (2001).

6   By *hegemony*, Gramsci meant the permeation *throughout* society of an entire system of values, attitudes, and beliefs that support the status quo in power relations. From this point of view, hegemony can be defined as an "organizing principle," like institutions in the sense given above; that is, diffused by the process of socialization into every area of daily life. To the extent that this prevailing consciousness is internalized by the population, it becomes part of the "common sense," so that the values of the ruling elite come to appear as the natural order of things.

7   Even though the term *regime* has been used in quite a different way in North American urban studies (e.g., Stone 1989), the relational focus played an important part in those debates as well. Urban regimes are considered as collaborative arrangements through which local governments and private actors assemble the capacity to govern. By privileging the government–business link, however, these models are inadequate to analyze the context of European cities (Harding 1997; Mossberger and Stoker 2001). The different policy environment of European cities – despite the increasing role of city entrepreneurialism (Harvey 1990; Mayer 1994) – makes these approaches biased towards the economic point of view. Partnership is not only business related; it also involves quite differentiated policy fields and actors, such as welfare provisions (Kazepov 2002). In addition, the national influence, also in terms of resources transfer, is still predominant and European cities do not have to rely heavily on business investments as US cities are forced to do. For these reasons we will use the term regime in a wider sense, including other actors besides business.

8   Esping-Andersen uses the terms commodification and de-commodification, referring to Marx and Polanyi. Social policies are seen as instruments to free individuals and families from market dependency and to protect them from the inherent risks this dependency might bear in case they are unable to work any more.

9   For an overview of the debate on Esping-Andersen's seminal contribution, see Art and Gelissen (2002).

10 Despite the fact that some scholars put the UK in the same welfare regime as the USA, it is evident that the UK also presents substantial differences.

In the UK, claimants have well-established rights to moderately generous benefits. The contributory, non-contributory, and means-tested forms of state assistance are integrated and highly centralized, providing an overall coverage of risks. We cannot ignore the fact that the British welfare state was founded on the universalistic principles of the Beveridge report and has, for instance, a National Health Service which has provided since 1948 a tax-financed universalistic service, and a significant proportion of publicly owned council housing which accommodated – at its peak in the 1970s – nearly one-third of the population. It is also true, however, that entitlements have been progressively eroded since the 1980s, poverty and income inequality has increased more than in other European countries, and a path change towards neoliberalism has taken place (Kleinman 2002: 52–7).

11 The literature is immense. For an overview of the relation between the national welfare state and globalization, see, for instance, Pierson (2001), Sykes et al. (2001), Jessop (2002) and Rieger and Leibfried (2003).

12 For the relationship between globalization and its impact on the urban and regional scale, see Mollenkopf and Castells (1991), Sassen (1991, 2001), Fainstein et al. (1992), Amin (1994), Amin and Thrift (1994), Peck and Tickell (1994), Swyngedouw (1997), Keil (1998), Brenner (2000), Sellers (2002), Jessop (2002) and Scott and Storper (2003).

13 The literature on this topic is expanding. For an overview, see Eardley et al. (1996), Guibentif and Bouget (1997), Voges and Kazepov (1998), Ditch (1999), Leisering and Leibfried (1999), Heikkilä and Keskitalo (2001) and Saraceno (2002).

14 The literature on activation policies is also growing. For an overview, see Lødemel and Trickey (2000), Hanesch et al. (2001), Barbier (2001) and van Berkel and Møller (2002).

15 This hypothesis is supported by the analysis of Tito Boeri (2002). Considering two periods (1980–90 and 1990–99), Boeri regressed the average yearly growth rate in social expenditure in four social policy fields (unemployment benefits, pensions, family and social assistance) as a percentage of GDP and against its initial level in all four welfare regimes. The resulting beta coefficient showed convergence rates that are barely significant from the statistical point of view. The existing low level of convergence, however, does not occur across regimes, but within them.

REFERENCES

Aglietta, M. (1979) *A Theory of Capitalist Regulation.* New Left Books, London.

Alber, J. (1982) *Vom Armenhaus zum Wohlfahrtsstaat: Analysen zur Entwicklung der Sozialversicherunge in Westeuropa.* Campus Verlag, Frankfurt–Main.

Alexander, J.C., Giesen, B., Münch, R., and Smelser, N.J. (eds.) *The Micro–Macro Link.* University of California Press, Berkeley.

Amin, A. (ed.) (1994) *Post-Fordism*. Blackwell, Oxford.

Amin, A. and Thrift, N. (eds.) (1994) *Globalization, Institutions and Regional Development in Europe*. Oxford University Press, Oxford.

Andersen, H.T. and van Kempen, R. (eds.) (2001) *Governing European Cities: Social Fragmentation, Social Exclusion and Urban Governance*. Ashgate, Aldershot.

Archer, M. (1995) *Realist Social Theory: The Morphogenetic Approach*. Cambridge University Press, Cambridge.

Archer, M. (2003) *Structure, Agency and the Internal Conversation*. Cambridge University Press, Cambridge.

Art, W. and Gelissen, J. (2002) Three worlds of welfare capitalism or more? A state-of-the-art report. *Journal of European Social Policy*, 12 (2): 137–158.

Ascoli, U. and Ranci, C. (eds.) (2002) *The Dilemmas of the Welfare Mix: The New Structure of Welfare in an Era of Privatization*. Kluwer Academic, New York.

Bagnasco, A. (1977) *Le tre Italie: La problematica territoriale dello sviluppo italiano*. Il Mulino, Bologna.

Bagnasco, A. and Le Galès, P. (eds.) (2000) *Cities in Contemporary Europe*. Cambridge University Press, Cambridge.

Barbier, J.C. (2001) *Welfare to Work Policies in Europe: The Current Challenges*. Document de Travail (see http://libserver.cedefop.eu.int/vetelib/nat/fra/ngo/2002_0001_en.pdf).

Bateson, G. (1972) *Steps to an Ecology of Mind*. Balantine, New York.

Berger, L.P. and Luckmann, T. (1967) *The Social Construction of Reality*. Doubleday, Garden City (NY).

Berger, S. and Dore, R. (eds.) (1996) *National Diversity and Global Capitalism*. Cornell University Press, Ithaca, NY.

Boeri, T. (2002) *Social Policy: One For All?* Centre d'Etudes Prospectives et d'Informations Internationales (CEPII), Paris. (see http://www.cepii.fr/anglaisgraph/communications/pdf/2002/29301102/boeri.pdf).

Boyer, R. (1986) *Théorie de la regulation*. La Découverte, Paris.

Bradshaw, J. and Finch, N. (2002) *A Comparison of Child Benefit Packages in 22 Countries*. Department for Work and Pensions, Leeds (see http://www.dwp.gov.uk/asd/asd5/rrep174.asp).

Brenner, N. (2000) The urban question as a scale question: reflections on Henri Lefebvre, urban theory and the politics of scale. *International Journal of Urban and Regional Research*, 24 (2): 361–378.

Burgers, J. and Musterd, S. (2002) Understanding urban inequality: a model based on existing theories and an empirical illustration. *International Journal of Urban and Regional Research*, 26 (2): 403–413.

Carbone, D. (2003) Percorsi incerti: analisi delle traiettorie di uscita dalla disoccupazione in Italia, Danimarca, Germania e Regno Unito. PhD Thesis, University of Milan-Bicocca, Italy.

Castel, R. (2000) The roads to disaffiliation: insecure work and vulnerable relationships. *International Journal of Urban and Regional Research*, 24 (3): 519–535.

Crouch, C. (1999) *Social Change in Western Europe*. Oxford University Press, Oxford.

Crouch, C. and Streeck, W. (1997) *Political Economy of Modern Capitalism: Mapping Convergence and Diversity*. Sage, London.

Crouch, C., Le Galès, P., Trigilia, C., and Voelzkow, H. (2001) *Local Production Systems in Europe: Rise or Demise?* Oxford University Press, Oxford.

Dean, H. and Taylor-Gooby, P. (1992) *Dependency Culture: The Explosion of a Myth.* Harvester–Wheatsheaf, Hemel Hempstead, Hertfordshire, UK.

De Sandre, P., Pinnelli, A., and Santini, A. (1999) *Nuzialità e fecondità in trasformazione: percorsi e fattori del cambiamento.* Il Mulino, Bologna.

DiGaetano, A. and Strom, E. (2003) Comparative urban governance: an integrated approach. *Urban affairs Review,* 38 (3): 356–395.

DiMaggio, P. and Powell, W. (eds.) (1991) *The New Institutionalism in Organisational Analysis.* University of Chicago Press, Chicago.

Ditch, J. (1999) The structure and dynamics of social assistence in the European Union. In: Heikkilä, M. (ed.) *Linking Welfare and Work.* European Foundation, Dublin.

Douglas, M. (1986) *How Institutions Think.* Syracuse University Press, Syracuse, NY.

Durkheim, E. (1893) *De la division du travail social.* F. Alcan, Paris.

Eardley, T., Bradshaw, J., Ditch, J., Gough, J., and Witheford, P. (1996) *Social Assistance in OECD Countries: Synthesis Report.* HMSO, London.

Ebbinghaus, B. and Manow, P. (eds.) (2001) *Comparing Welfare Capitalism: Social Policy and Political Economy in Europe, Japan and the USA.* Routledge, London.

Esping-Andersen, G. (1990) *The Three Worlds of Welfare Capitalism.* Polity Press, Cambridge.

Esping-Andersen, G. (1999) *Social Foundations of Postindustrial Economies.* Oxford University Press, Oxford.

Eurostat (2003a) *The Social Situation in the European Union 2003.* EUR-OP, Luxemburg.

Eurostat (2003b) *Year Book 2002.* EUR-OP, Luxemburg.

Evans, M. (2001) *Welfare to Work and the Organisation of Opportunity: Lessons from Abroad.* CASE Report 15, Centre for Analysis of Social Exclusion, LSE, London.

Fainstein, S., Gordon, I., and Harloe, M. (eds.) (1992) *Divided Cities: New York and London in the Contemporary World.* Blackwell, Oxford.

Ferrera, M. (1996) The Southern model of welfare in social Europe. *Journal of European Social Policy,* 6 (1): 17–37.

Ferrera, M. (1998) The four *social Europes*: between universalism and selectivity. In: Rhodes, M. and Meny, Y. (eds.) *The Future of the European Welfare State: A New Social Contract?* Macmillan, Basingstoke.

Ferrera, M., Matsaganis, M., and Sacchi, S. (2002) Open coordination against poverty: the new EU "social inclusion process." *Journal of European Social Policy,* 12 (3): 227–239.

Fligstein, N. (1996) Markets as politics: a political–cultural approach to market institutions. *American Sociological Review,* 61 (4): 656–673.

Förster, M. (2000) *Trends and Driving Factors in Income Distribution and Poverty in the OECD Area.* Labour Market and Social Policy Occasional Papers 42, OECD, Paris.

Gallie, D. and Paugam, S. (eds.) (2000) *Welfare Regimes and the Experience of Unemployment in Europe.* Oxford University Press, Oxford.

Gallie, D. and Paugam, S. (2002) *Social Precarity and Social Integration*. Report for the European Commission Based on Eurobarometer 56.1, European Commission, Brussels.

García, M. and Kazepov, Y. (2002) Why some people are more on benefits than others? Ways into social assistance. In: Saraceno, C. (ed.) *Social Assistance Dynamics in Europe: National and Local Poverty Regimes*, Polity Press, Bristol.

Garfinkel, H. (2001) *Ethnomethodology's Program: Working Out Durkheim's Aphorism*. Edited by Rawls, A. Rowman and Littlefield, Oxford.

Geddes, M. (2000) Tackling social exclusion in the European Union? The limits to the new orthodoxy of local partnership. *International Journal of Urban and Regional Research*, 24 (4): 782–800.

Geddes, M. and Le Galès, P. (2001) Local partnerships, welfare regimes and local governance: a process of regime restructuring? In: Geddes, M. and Benington, J. (eds.) *Local Parnerships and Social Exclusion in the EU*. Routledge, London.

Giddens, A. (1984) *The Constitution of Society*. Polity Press, Cambridge.

Goffman, I. (1974) *Frame Analysis: Essays on the Organisation of Experience*. Harper, New York.

Goodin, R. (1996) *The Theory of Institutional Design*. Cambridge University Press, Cambridge.

Gramsci, A. (1949) (1971 edn.) *Selections from the Prison Notebooks*. Lawrence and Wishart, London.

Guibentief, P. and Bouget, D. (1997) *Minimum Income Policies in the European Union*. União das Mutualidades Portuguesas, Lisboa.

Gullenstad, M. and Segalen, M. (eds.) (1997) *Family and Kinship in Europe*. Pinter, London.

Hall, P.A. and Taylor, R.C.R. (1996) Political science and the three new institutionalisms. *Political Studies*, 44: 936–957.

Hall, P.A. and Soskice, D. (eds.) (2001) *Varieties of Capitalism: The Institutional Foundation of Comparative Advantage*. Oxford University Press, Oxford.

Hanesch, W., Stelzer-Orthofer, C., and Balzer, N. (2001) Activation policies in minimum income schemes. In: Heikkilä, M. and Keskitalo, E. (eds.) *Social Assistance in Europe: A Comparative Study on Minimum Income in Seven European Countries*. Stakes, Helsinki.

Harding, A. (1997) Urban regimes in a Europe of the cities. *European Urban and Regional Studies*, 4 (4): 291–314.

Harvey, D. (1990) From managerialism to entrepreneurialism: the transformation of urban governance. *Geografiska Annaler*, 71: 3–17.

Heikkilä, M. and Keskitalo, E. (eds.) (2001) *Social Assistance in Europe: A Comparative Study on Minimum Income in Seven European Countries*. Stakes, Helsinki.

Hilbert, R.H. (1992) *The Classical Roots of Ethnomethodology: Durkheim, Weber and Garfinkel*. University of North Carolina Press, Chapell Hill, NC.

Hill, R.C. (2004) Cities and hierarchies. *International Social Sciences Journal*, forthcoming.

Hill, R.C. and Fujita, K. (2003) The nested city: introduction. *Urban Studies*, 40 (2): 207–217.

Hohenberg, P.M. and Lees, L.H. (1996) *The Making of Urban Europe*. Harvard University Press, Cambridge, MA.

Hollingsworth, J.R. and Boyer, R. (eds.) (1997) *Contemporary Capitalism: The Embeddedness of Institutions.* Cambridge University Press, Cambridge.

Huber, E. and Stephens, J.D. (2001) Welfare state and production regimes in the era of retrenchment. In: Pierson, P. (ed.) *The New Politics of the Welfare State.* Oxford University Press, Oxford.

Jensen-Butler, C., Shachar, A., and van Weesep, J. (eds.) (1997) *European Cities in Competition.* Avebury, Aldershot.

Jessop, B. (2002) *The Future of the Capitalist State.* Polity Press, Cambridge.

Jessop, B. and Nielsen, K. (2003) Institutions and rules. *Research Papers: Network Institutional Theory*, no. 11/03, Institut for Samfundsvidenskab og Erhvervsøkonomi, Roskilde, Denmark.

Kaelble, H. (1987) *Auf dem Weg zu einer europäischen Gesellschaft. Eine Sozialgeschichte Westeuropas 1880–1980.* Beck Verlag, München.

Kautto, M., Fritzell, J., Hvinden, B., Kvist, J., and Uusitalo, H. (eds.) (2001) *Nordic Welfare States in the European Context.* Routledge, London.

Kazepov, Y. (ed.) (2002) Le politiche di attivazione in Europa: frammentazione e coordinamento. *Assistenza Sociale*, 52 (2).

Kazepov, Y. and Sabatinelli, S. (2001) *How Generous Social Assistance Schemes Are: A Comparative Analysis of Benefit Levels.* Report 3. Stakes, Helsinki (see http:// www.stakes.fi/verkkojulk/pdf/socasstreport3.pdf).

Keil, R. (1998) Globalisation makes states: perspectives on local governance in the age of the world city. *Review of International Political Economy*, 5 (4): 616–646.

Kleinman, M. (2002) *A European Welfare State? European Union Social Policy in Context.* Palgrave, New York.

Korpi, W. (2001) Contentious institutions: an augmented ration-action analysis of the origins and path dependency of welfare state institutions in Western coun tries. *Rationality and Society*, 13 (2): 235–283.

Le Galès, P. (2002) *European Cities: Social Conflict and Governance.* Oxford University Press, Oxford.

Le Galès, P. and Voelzkow, H. (2001) Introduction: the governance of local economies. In: Crouch, C., Le Galès, P., Trigilia, C., and Voelzkow, H. (eds.) *Local Production Systems in Europe: Rise or Demise?* Oxford University Press, Oxford.

Lehto, J. (2000) Different cities in different welfare states. In: Bagnasco, A. and Le Galès, P. (eds.) *Cities in Contemporary Europe.* Cambridge University Press, Cambridge.

Leibfried, S. (1992) Towards a European welfare state? On integrating poverty regimes into the European Community. In: Ferge, Z. and Kolberg, J.E. (eds.) *Social Policy in a Changing Europe.* Westaview Press, Boulder.

Leisering, L. and Leibfried, S. (1999) *Time and Poverty in Western European Welfare States.* Cambridge University Press, Cambridge.

Lødemel, I. and Trickey, H. (2000) *An Offer You Can't Refuse: Workfare in International Perspective.* Policy Press, Bristol.

Marcuse, P. and van Kempen, R. (eds.) (2002) *Of States and Cities: The Partitioning of Urban Space.* Oxford University Press, Oxford.

Marlier, E. and Cohen-Solal, M. (2000) Social benefits and their redistributive effects in the EU. *Statistics in Focus*, theme 3-9/2000, EUR-OP, Luxembourg.

Marshall, T.H. (1950) *Citizenship and Social Class and Other Essays*. Cambridge University Press, Cambridge.

Mayer, M. (1994) Post-Fordist city politics. In: Amin, A. (ed.) *Post-Fordism: A Reader*. Blackwell, Oxford.

Mingione, E. (1991) *Fragmented Societies: A Sociology of Economic Life Beyond the Market Paradigm*. Blackwell, Oxford.

Mingione, E. (1996) (ed.) *Urban Poverty and the Underclass: A Reader*. Blackwell, Oxford.

Mingione, E., Oberti, M., and Pereirina, J. (2002) Cities as local systems. In: Saraceno, C. (ed.) *Social Assistance Dynamics in Europe: National and Local Poverty Regimes*. Policy Press, Bristol.

Mollenkopf, J. and Castells, M. (eds.) (1991) *Dual City: Restructuring New York*. Russell Sage Foundation, New York.

Mossberger, K. and Stoker, G. (2001) The evolution of urban regime theory: the challenge of conceptualisation. *Urban Affairs Review*, 36 (6): 810–835.

Moulaert, F., Rodriguez, A., and Swyngedouw, E. (eds.) (2003) *The Globalized City: Economic Restructuring and Social Polarization in European Cities*. Oxford University Press, Oxford.

Musterd, S. and Ostendorf, W. (eds.) (1998) *Urban Segregation and the Welfare State: Inequality and Exclusion in Western Cities*. Routledge, London.

Nee, V. (1998) Sources of the new institutionalism. In: Brinton, M.C. and Nee, V. (eds.) *The New Institutionalism in Sociology*, Russell Sage Foundation, New York, 1–16.

Nielsen, K. (2001) Review of institutionalist approaches in the social sciences: typology, dialogue and future prospects. *Research Papers: Network Institutional Theory*, no. 7/01, Institut for Samfundsvidenskab og Erhvervsøkonomi, Roskilde, Denmark.

North, D. (1990) *Institutions, Institutional Change and Economic Performance*. Cambridge University Press, Cambridge.

Offe, C. (1984) *Contradictions of the Welfare State*. Hutchinson, London.

OECD (2002) *Employment Outlook*. OECD, Paris.

OECD (2003) *Managing Decentralisation: A New Role for Labour Market Policies*. OECD, Paris.

Peck, J. and Tickell, A. (1994) Searching for a new institutional fix: the after-Fordist crisis and the global-local disorder. In: Amin, A. (ed.) *Post-Fordism: A Reader*. Blackwell, Oxford.

Pierre, J. (1999) Models of urban governance: the institutional dimension of urban politics. *Urban Affairs Review*, 34 (3): 372–396.

Pierson, P. (2000a) Increasing returns, path dependence, and the study of politics. *American Political Science Review*, 94 (2): 251–267.

Pierson, P. (2000b) The limits of design: explaining institutional origins and change. *Governance*, 13 (4): 475–499.

Pierson, P. (ed.) (2001) *The New Politics of the Welfare State*. Oxford University Press, Oxford.

Piore, M.J. and Sabel, C.F. (1984) *The Second Industrial Divide: Possibilities for Prosperities*. Basic Books, New York.

Poggi, G. (1991) *The State: Its Nature, Development and Prospects*. Polity Press, Cambridge.

Poggi, G. (2000) *Durkheim*. Oxford University Press, Oxford.

Polanyi, K. (1944) *The Great Transformation: The Political and Economic Origins of our Time*. Farrar and Rinehard, New York.

Polanyi, K. (1968) Primitive, archaic and modern economies. In: Dalton, G. (ed.) *Essays of Karl Polanyi*. Anchor Books, New York.

Polanyi, K. (1977) *The Livelihood of Man*, Pearson, H.W. (ed.) Academic Press, New York.

Rawls, A. (1996) Durkheim's epistemology: the neglected argument. *American Journal of Sociology*, 102 (2): 430–482.

Regini, M. and Lange, P. (1989) *State, Market and Social Regulation: New Perspectives on Italy*. Cambridge University Press, Cambridge.

Rieger, E. and Leibfried, S. (2003) *Limits to Globalisation: Welfare States and the World Economy*. Polity Press, Cambridge.

Rokkan, S. (1999) *State Formation, Nation-Building and Mass Politics in Europe: The Theory of Stein Rokkan*. In: Flora, P., Kuhnle, S., and Urwin, D. (eds.) Oxford University Press, Oxford.

Saraceno, C. (ed.) (2002) *Social Assistance Dynamics in Europe: National and Local Poverty Regimes*. Policy Press, Bristol.

Sassen, S. (1991) *The Global City: New York, London, Tokyo*. Princeton University Press, Princeton (second revised edition 2001).

Schmid, G. and Gazier, B. (eds.) (2002) *The Dynamics of Full Employment: Social Integration through Transitional Labour Markets*. Edward Elgar, Cheltenham.

Scott, W.R. (1995) *Institutions and Organisations*. Sage, London.

Scott, A.J. and Storper, M. (2003) Regions, globalisation, development. *Regional Studies*, 37 (6–7): 579–593.

Sellers, J.M. (2002) The nation-state and urban governance: toward multilevel analysis. *Urban Affairs Review*, 37 (5): 611–641.

Stone, C.N. (1989) *Regime Politics: Governing Atlanta, 1946–1988*. University of Kansas Press, Lawrence.

Streeck, W. and Schmitter, P. (1985) Community, market, state and associations? The prospective contribution of interest governance to social order. *European Sociological Review*, 1 (2): 119–138.

Swyngedouw, E. (1997) Neither global nor local: 'glocalisation' and the politics of scale. In: Cox, K. (ed.) *Spaces of Globalization: Reasserting the Power of the Local*. Longman, New York–London.

Swyngedouw, E. (2000) The local in the regional, in the national and in the global: the re-scaling of Europe and the process of "glocalisation". In: Bekemans, L. and Mira, E. (eds.) *Civitas Europa: Cities, Urban Systems and Cultural Regions between Diversity and Convergence*. Lang, Bruxelles.

Sykes, R., Palier, B., and Prior, P.M. (eds.) (2001) *Globalisation and European Welfare States: Challenges and Change*. Palgrave, New York.

Therborn, G. (1995) *European Modernity and Beyond: The Trajectory of European Societies 1945–2000*. Sage, London.

Tilly, C. (ed.) (1975) *The Formation of National States in Western Europe*. Princeton University Press, Princeton.

Trickey, H. and Walker, R. (2000) Steps to compulsion within British labour market policies. In: Lødemel, I. and Trickey, H. (eds.) *An Offer You Can't Refuse: Workfare in International Perspective*. Policy Press, Bristol.

van Berkel, R. and Møller, I.H. (eds.) *Active Social Policies in the EU*. Policy Press, Bristol.

Voges, W. and Kazepov, Y. (eds.) (1998) *Armut in Europa*. Chmielorz Verlag, Wiesbaden.

Weber, M. (1922) (1972 edition) *Wirtschaft und Gesellschaft*. Mohr Verlag, Tübingen.

Williamson, O. (1975) *Markets and Hierarchies: Analysis and Antitrust Implications*. Free Press, New York.

Wilson, W.J. (1987) *The Truly Disadvantaged, the Inner City, the Underclass and Public Policy*. University of Chicago Press, Chicago.

World Economic Forum (2004) *Global Competitiveness Report 2003–2004*. Oxford University Press, Oxford.

2

The European City: A Conceptual Framework and Normative Project

Hartmut Häussermann and Anne Haila

Introduction

Attempts to construct theories of cities not only face the problem that the city is not a "theoretical object" (Saunders 1981), but also run into the dilemma of generalization. Theoretical formulations cannot avoid making generalizations, but abstract urban models fail to describe the rich reality of cities. On the other hand, detailed and empirical descriptions of particular cities are far too accidental to be useful in comparing other cities. Such problems have always vexed urban scholars.

One early attempt to make generalizations and theorize the city was Max Weber's concept of the "Occidental city." Weber defined the concept of the European city by comparing European cities with cities in the Orient and by identifying several characteristics of cities in the West and in the East. Weber's object of study was the medieval city, and therefore it is no surprise that urban historians were challenged by his concept of the European city. In the community of urban scholars studying modern cities, however, Weber's ideas did not find followers. His concept of the European city was considered obsolete after the consolidation of worldwide capitalist relations and the emergence of the territorial states that demolished the autonomy of cities, because autonomy was of importance for Weber's concept of the European city. Instead of the Weberian approach, in the twentieth century urban scholars analyzed cities from an ecologic perspective or used the political economic framework. Both of these frameworks regarded cities as universal formations without paying attention to, for example, national differences.

In recent years, some European urban scholars have begun talking about European cities invoking Weber's notion of the "European city." The category of the European city is a tempting and challenging idea in different ways: in contrast to the overall pessimistic views of the declining significance of cities as actors in a globalizing world, the basic assumption of the reconsideration of a "European City" of this type could be – and to a certain extent is – a social and political actor with a higher degree of autonomy compared to the big metropolises in other parts of the world. In this chapter we will take up the challenge and discuss the usefulness of this category (see also Häussermann 2001). We also attempt to contribute to the debate on the question of making generalizations in urban studies.

We will begin by introducing some scholars and theoretical traditions in urban studies. These are Georg Simmel, the Chicago School, the Marxist-influenced political economy approach and the global city paradigm. Second, we will recall Weber's concept of the "Occidental city" and discuss a recent revival of Weber's ideas. After that we will explore the usefulness of the revived notion of the European city by analyzing some recent trends in cities in contemporary urban Europe.

Four Theoretical Traditions

Georg Simmel

It is fair to say that Georg Simmel was the first social scientist to deserve the title "urban sociologist." He provided a sociological definition of "the urban" and analyzed the interaction between spatial density, social behavior, and economic differentiation.

Simmel was born in 1858 and wrote his significant works *Die Großstädte und das Geistesleben* (The Metropolis and Mental Life) and *Philosophie des Geldes* at the turn of the twentieth century. He was interested in the question of what makes the urban culture of big cities distinctive. This distinctive character was found by contrasting big cities to small towns and rural villages. Big cities created the space of modernity, because they were dominated by the money economy and impersonal social relations (characteristic of the market economy). Impersonal relations constitute the mode of living and interacting in big cities. Unlike in the countryside, interactions between people are predominantly functional and segmented. This enables individuals to cope with the frequency of interactions and the heterogeneity of the people. The scarcity of close personal relations and emotional outbursts are, in Simmel's view, a precondition for living together in big cities. When people ignore each other they can live side by side without seeking to control each other or to repulse others because of their difference. City people, therefore, seem aloof and arrogant, but the distance they maintain makes it possible for them to preserve their personal freedom and develop as individuals; big cities liberate urbanites from social control and the traditional ties that restricted the life of peasants in the countryside and inhabitants of small towns.

Thus, Simmel presented a thesis that spatial density and social heterogeneity create a certain mode of behavior and "mentality." Because the density and heterogeneity were only to be found in big cities in Simmel's time, big cities (identified with the "money economy"), with their impersonal social relations, became the theoretical starting point for a sociologic definition of the urban. Based on this definition, Simmel also made important remarks on the cultural productivity of big cities: competition in dense and heterogeneous cities leads to economic specialization, cultural diversity and division of labor. This further increases the innovations and cultural productivity typical of cities.

The concepts of an urban mentality and the money economy refer ultimately to the heterogeneity of actors and the density of their interaction, not to the city as such. Simmel's object of study, therefore, was the effects of the intensified interaction between urban dwellers under the condition of the money economy, not exactly or exclusively (geographically defined) cities. The reason why Simmel connected individualized social relations and the money economy to big cities was that in his time modernity and developed economic relations were still limited to big cities. Indeed, at the beginning of the twentieth century a characteristic feature of Germany was the sharp contrast between rural and urban areas, both in social and cultural terms, and Berlin in particular – where Simmel had been living at that time – was at the cutting-edge of economic and cultural innovation. This context sheds light on Simmel's concept of the urban space as the space of modernity.

Simmel took one specific aspect of the modern city (aloof and arrogant urbanites), and regarded it as a straightforward and universal trend. Similar to Weber's method of identifying the ideal type, Simmel's general definition of the urban is based on one characteristic of the big city and ignores, for example, different types of cities and the neighborhoods that served as communitarian social spaces for the working classes, which also existed in Simmel's Berlin and which were vividly described, for instance, in Alfred Döblin's *Berlin Alexanderplatz* written in 1929. Simmel's addiction to one aspect of the city turned out to be fatal. The contrast Simmel made between big and small cities, which he equated with the distinction between *Gemeinschaft* (community) and *Gesellschaft* (society), soon lost its validity and in the modern world communication technologies spread urban culture around the human landscape. "The urban" was no longer bound to a specific geographic type of space – dense and heterogeneous.

The Chicago School

Simmel was born in Berlin and his "big city" was there. However, there was nothing specifically European in his thinking and his ideas found a receptive audience outside Europe and became popular in the USA. Simmel's ideas matched well with the intellectual tendencies at the University of Chicago. Robert Park, who had met Simmel in Berlin, americanized Simmel (Smith 1988: 121), and Louis Wirth reproduced Simmel's ideas in his famous essay on "Urbanism as a Way of Life" (1938).

The Chicago School, consisting of Robert Park, Ernest Burgess, Louis Wirth, and others, took Simmel's conception of the interrelation between the urban mentality and the density and heterogeneity as its starting point and gave a universal definition of "the city" as a heterogeneous, dense and large place. This definition was meant to be applicable to all cities irrespective of the differences in their cultures, economies, social relations and structures. Perhaps Berlin, known as *Chicago at the Spree* (Smith 1988: 44–5), was too similar to Chicago to make urban scholars question whether cities around the world have some universal qualities or whether there are merely individual and unique cities; different kinds of cities in different nations.

Chicago was divided into Polish, Italian, and Irish neighborhoods. Reflecting this, the Chicago School conceptualized the city as a "mosaic of small worlds", as a patchwork of communities in which the urban lives of individuals were embedded and restricted. In this the Chicago School differs from Simmel. The Chicago School saw individualization as endangering social integration, not as a form of emancipation as Simmel had perceived it.

The Chicago School added Darwin's theory of evolution to Simmel's thought. Competition and struggle were seen as the basic forces of urban development. Ethnic, national, racial and social groups competed for limited urban space and the segregation that was the result of this competition was conceived as "natural" and typical of cities. As Neil Smith says (1997: 123), "The Chicago School of urban research explained how social differences, squeezed through a sieve of economic and geographic competition, were the hallmark of a distinctly holistic, American urbanism (and this model was quite successfully exported)."

The approach of the Chicago School became the dominant paradigm for urban research in the 1940s and 1950s. This paradigm implied the idea of a trend towards similar structures of cities; competition between ethnic groups for urban space will produce a segregated city. The ecologic approach explained the urban structure by referring to natural forces. These natural forces were viewed as the same everywhere; hence there was no difference between cities in the East and West, between cities in America and Europe, between cities in the "First" and "Third Worlds." In this universalistic strain, the Chicago model naturally seemed to contradict empirical studies on cities (see, for example, Berry 1973; Castells 1977). This contradiction further urged urban scholars to carry out empirical studies on the diversity between cities in different cultural contexts. What soon became clear after the accumulation of empirical studies on real cities was that in addition to the neglect of cultures, another reason limiting the applicability of the Chicago model was its ignorance of politics. To amend this shortage, a new line of thinking, the political economy of cities, was developed. Political economists offered an alternative approach to understanding "the city".

The political economy perspective on the city

The ideas of the Chicago School were challenged by the "New Urban Sociology" in the late 1960s. The revival of Marxist theories and concepts simultaneously in European countries and in the USA produced a novel way of seeing cities. The ecologic approach was a target for criticism, particularly because of the lack of any political analysis of urban development. Critics such as Manuel Castells (1977) and David Harvey (1973) argued that cities are part of societies, and instead of analyzing cities as heterogeneous, dense, and large formations, they defined cities as units of collective consumption and analyzed them in the framework of investment flows and class struggle. The struggle for amenities in cities (as places of collective consumption) was seen as part of the class struggle that had its basis in the sphere of production. The "new urban sociologists" regarded the capitalist economy as a crucial force affecting the development of cities; hence the term "political economists".

Compared to the Chicago School, political economists paid more attention to politics. This could have opened up the possibility of treating cities with different political traditions and contexts differently. However, like Simmel and the Chicago School, they tended to analyze the structures and development of cities as universal rather than different and unique. The laws of capital were regarded as similar around the world. Although most political economists thought that "the logic of capital" had different manifestations in different localities (see, for example, the empirical case study by Harvey [1985] on the Basilica of the Sacred Heart in Paris), the critics (e.g., Gottdiener 1985), occasionally taking an exaggerating and simplifying tone, blamed political economists for ignoring urban

politics and analyzing cities as too straightforwardly determined by economic forces. They argued that political economists postulated a universal
model of urban development based primarily on economic forces – and
not always without justification – while occasionally a certain economic
determinism and functionalism can be discerned in some neo-Marxist
studies on urban affairs.

Marxist theory was only considered applicable to capitalist cities. Cities
in non-capitalist social formations did not have a role in the "new urban
sociology." It was widely agreed that socialist cities could not be analyzed
using Marxist concepts. Therefore, little attention was given to cities in
socialist countries.

The Regulationist School, which further developed the historical materi-
alist approach, gave more space to politics than some earlier versions of
the political economy approach. The concept of Fordism was introduced
to emphasize that relationships between capital, labor and the state vary
in different historical periods. This concept – implying an idea of different
types of contracts between capital, labor and the state in different historical periods and locations – paved the way to recognizing differences between cities, such as national differences. The concept of Fordism, referring
to power relations in various phases of capitalist development and various
national paths of welfare regimes, could easily have led to abandoning the
idea of a universal model of "the capitalist city." However, the paradigm
of the universal capitalist city stood firm and in most regulationist writings
a focus on similarities replaced the search for differences (for a different
perspective see Chapter 6).

Compared with the Chicago School, political economists took a step
towards more realistic theories and recognized the cultural and political
differences between cities. Unlike the Chicago School, political economists did not analyze cities as determined by ahistorical and natural forces.
They postulated a specific historical phase of economic development –
capitalism – which affects the pattern and inequalities of cities. Nevertheless, political economists preferred to regard cities in the capitalist world
as similar, influenced by the same economic forces: the capitalistic logic.
In the next phase of the history of urban studies, economic forces, celebrated by political economists, were taken as an object of study by global
city theoreticians who postulated the emergence of a new type of city –
the global city – thus differentiating various types of capitalist cities.

The global city

In the early 1990s, global cities became a hot topic in the community of
urban scholars. The category of "global city" refers to the specific economic

functions of the global economy. Some specific economic functions that are necessary for the global economy are concentrated in a few cities that have become strategic places for the control of this new economic system. Global cities have more producer services, headquarters of transnational corporations and financial institutions than other cities. As in the political economy approach, economic factors are seen as determining the social structure of cities, their income distribution and the accommodation of immigrants.

When Saskia Sassen originally formulated the global city hypothesis (1991), she used three cities, New York, London, and Tokyo, to exemplify the effects of global trends in cities. Characteristics of global cities, in Sassen's model, were spatial and social fragmentation, segmentation, and polarization. She saw global cities as dual cities: on the one hand there is a small world of high-salary elite workers active in transnational transactions, and on the other hand there are growing numbers of poor and relatively low-paid workers who produce services for the new transnational elite.

Saskia Sassen's global city hypothesis was a great success. Urban scholars around the world started to analyze their home towns to see whether they satisfied the criteria of global city. In this frenzied hunt for new global cities, the critical attitude that should have been a quality of academic urban scholars was forgotten and the structures Sassen postulated for a specific city type were understood as general and universal effects of globalization. The reason for this unwarranted generalization is that Sassen did not differentiate the economic trends forming "global cities" from general trends of post-industrial and transnational economies, and did not pay enough attention to national and local variations and to cultural and political differences, which are crucial in different labor markets. Here again, as in the cases of the Chicago School and the political economists, we find an inclination to identify cities around the world as similar and to neglect their differences.

Saskia Sassen's work has been harshly criticized from various perspectives. Some European scholars have refuted the idea that global cities are dual cities. Edmond Préteceille (2000) and Chris Hamnett (2003) have analyzed Paris and London, and have shown that the polarization of income – the central assumption of the dual-city thesis – does not hold for these cities. Instead of dualization, they found rapid increases in the salaries for highly qualified professional service jobs but also growth in the earnings for lower paid jobs. In these two "global cities" all income groups are earning more. The poor and the low-income groups seem to be better protected from the effects of globalization than the global city thesis would suggest. Increased polarization might be true for New York, and also for some other cities, but not necessarily for all "global" cities, and certainly not for all cities in general. The cities that perform as nodes in the global economy are not a new type in the sense that there exists only one type of income or residential pattern. Rather, it seems to be the case that there are different types of "global cities" and the differences depend on the national contexts and on local politics and traditions. The criticism by Preteceille and Hamnett and other European scholars made urban scholars more sensitive to national and continental differences.

As a result of several empirical studies on the effects of globalization in urban areas, urban scholars now widely accept the idea that there are no direct and simple links between economic globalization and local outcomes. There are remarkable differences between cities with different welfare regimes and different political-institutional and cultural contexts, despite the fact that most cities are now embedded in the capitalist system and influenced by the laws of capitalist development (Lehto 2000; Burgers and Musterd 2002).

The attempts to develop theories about cities we have discussed so far characteristically analyzed cities as universal formations. Simmel saw dense and heterogeneous cities producing aloof and arrogant behavior. The Chicago School constructed the model of the segregated city. The political economy approach postulated the model of the capitalist city, and regarded cities in capitalism as more or less similar, determined by economic forces. The global city paradigm, although originally focusing on a few particular cities, continued the tradition of regarding cities as similar and universal. In this tradition of searching for a universal definition of the city, does it make sense to recall Max Weber's old concept of the "Occidental City" as some contemporary European urban scholars are doing? Before answering this question we have to briefly discuss Weber's concept and the present-day invocation of Weber's ideas.

Max Weber

The Occidental city

In *Die Stadt* (2000), Max Weber defined the concept of the European city and contrasted it to the Oriental city. Weber was puzzled by the fact that European cities had become the birthplace of a new mode of economic development – capitalism – whereas the cities in the Orient did not have this incubating role. European cities, in contrast to Oriental cities, had the following characteristics in Weber's writings: the European city had fortifications (walls), a locally controlled market and a court of its own; European cities were associations, politically autonomous and had administrations of their own. The medieval cities, on which Weber focused, were city-states with their own politically representative bodies and self-governing. The concept of the "burgher" was most important in Weber's thinking. Burghers had a privileged status and an important role in European cities. The role of city dwellers also differentiated European cities from cities in Asia. Whereas in Europe citizens participated in the local administration, in China urban dwellers belonged to their families and native villages, while in India urban dwellers were members of different castes.

Landownership was closely connected to the status of being a burgher. European burghers owned land in cities and as urban landowners they established formal associations, or fraternities (*schwurgemeinschaftliche Verbrüderung*). Fraternities had the task of protecting the property of their members. They represented the interests of the city bourgeoisie. The concept of the burghers and their political participation explain Weber's concept of the city. The city, for Max Weber, was not a physical structure but a political association, a corporation. Weber was not interested in cities in the spatial sense, but the question that concerned him was that of the consequences of a distinct social and political institution. At the core of this social and political institution, the city as a corporation was the self-administering urban *Bürgertum*. The *Bürgertum* formed the city as a political and economic actor. Because the burghers were not completely suppressed and exploited by superior powers, together with their local associations they could develop unchained energies that were used for the benefit of European cities. Thus, the cities developed as a revolutionary power for dispelling the supervising and controlling power of clerical landlords and the aristocracy.

For Max Weber, cities were special kinds of societies. In Europe, the contrast between the city and the countryside was clearly defined. Up to the beginning of modernity, the border between the urban and the rural was demarcated by walls. The walls also separated different types of societies. Cities distinguished themselves sharply from the surrounding feudal countryside. Inside the city walls, economic and political life flourished and cities became the breeding ground for the new mode of production – capitalism – and Occidental modernity. In the city, people were free from the peonage that restricted the life of the rural population. Belonging to the urban community meant upward social mobility, compared with those left in the countryside. Cities were also sites of social and cultural innovation. This gave European cities the honor of symbolizing modernization and civilization.

Over the years and after several struggles, in the age of Absolutism the autonomous cities of medieval Europe were incorporated into the territorial states and lost their special legal status. Cities became part of nation-states and national economies. They were no longer special societies. This development made Weber's concept outdated for urban scholars studying contemporary cities. Textbooks on urban sociology, such as Peter Saunders'

(1981) *Social Theory and the Urban Question* and Savage et al.'s (1993) *Urban Sociology, Capitalism and Modernity*, bypassed Weber with a brief reference, as a scholar who was not interested in cities as such.

A new evaluation of Max Weber

Recently, two European scholars, Arnaldo Bagnasco and Patrick Le Galès (2000; see also Le Galès 2002) introduced a notion of the European city reviving Weber's old ideas. They begin by stating that "Europe is inconceivable without its cities" (Bagnasco and Le Galès 2000: 1) and provide a collection of studies in which "European cities are analyzed both as political and social actors and as local societies: not as metropolises, but as cities" (ibid.: 3). They appeal to Max Weber and characterize European cities by the participation of burghers in local government, rules applying to landed property, the legal status of citizens, and citizens' associations with relative freedom. Their basic argument is that the diminishing significance of nation-states (as a consequence of globalization) in Europe (and promoted by the European Union) has created a "power vacuum" that has provided new opportunities for local and regional action. Cities have quickly grasped this opportunity and have become political and economic actors and increasingly created identities of their own (Bagnasco and Le Galès 2000: 5–6; for more empirical information see Le Galès 2002).

Max Weber contrasted European cities to cities in the East, whereas Bagnasco and Le Galès contrast European cities to North American cities. Typically, European cities consist of a built-up area around a focal point (which can be administrative and public buildings, churches, squares and open spaces). They are relatively old and stable; their built-up form is old and has developed gradually. Europe is characterized by a large number of small- and medium-sized cities in relatively close proximity to each other; population mobility is relatively low. Public services are important in European cities. State intervention and town planning have regulated land use; public landownership and public infrastructure have a part to play; public investments are important in European cities. There are numerous civic associations and citizens are involved in local affairs. The urban has an important role in the European imagination.

How is this revival of Max Weber's notion of the European city to be understood? Is it a description of European cities? Or is it a new research paradigm to replace the Chicago School model, the political economy framework and the global city paradigm? In the following we examine the usefulness of this neo-Weberian perspective by analyzing some recent trends in European cities. We discuss landownership, burghers, metropolitanization, public services, the relationship between the state and cities, and "Americanization" in contemporary European cities. We will begin by a brief look at the history of so-called European "moderate modernism," because it forms an important historical heritage for European cities.

Moderate Modernism and Recent Trends

Modernism in America and Europe

The American city, in the models of the Chicago School and urban economics (Alonso 1964 and his followers), was the place of a radical modernity. Its spatial and social development has been subject to the power of the market. The use of land follows the profit-seeking of private investors, and the value of a place is determined by market forces. Minimal regulation leads to a sharp segregation of different groups in terms of income, status, and ethnic identity. The survival of neighborhoods is dependent on economic cycles. Local traditions, social concerns or urban cultures do not have a role in such urban models. The city center is not a place of identification, but is a *central business district* (CBD), in which culture and housing do not survive. In the American city, the tenement houses are owned by landlords who live outside the city, who are not interested in *the city* from a social point of view, but in the gains they can make out of their properties.

Unlike in such US cities, where market forces dictate the pace of urban development, in Europe, beginning in the second half of the nineteenth century, an opposition emerged to fight against market-led urban development. This opposition consisted of left-wing radicals and reformers, but also included members of the enlightened bourgeoisie. These philanthropists saw market-led urban development as responsible for the social contradictions and inhuman living conditions of the lower income classes in cities. Friedrich Engels' report on Manchester (1845) is one example of this concern about the antisocial effects of radical market development on the urban fabric.

European cities developed an urban regime that found a compromise between particular economic interests and social responsibilities and tried to take into account the interests of the city as a whole; examples are healthcare and anti-poverty initiatives, but also interventions into the provision of housing for the poor. This European urban regime felt responsible for "the city" and can be characterized by what Kaelble (2000) has called the model of "moderate modernity." Essential to it is the strong influence of the public administration on urban development and it has the following five characteristics:

1   Public landownership in European cities enabled the cities to play an important part in the decisions on land use and gave cities the opportunity to plan the urban structure from a long-term perspective (2291, 2864).

2   After some negative experiences with private provision and management of infrastructure, such as water, energy, and the transport system, these were organized as public services (6391, 5324, 3544). This so-called "municipal socialism" turned out to be an effective method of organizing such services and brought in revenue for the public purse.

3   The growing influence of economic interests in urban development was balanced with the development of legal instruments for town planning, legitimizing public intervention. Since the last third of the nineteenth century, local governments have increased their influence in the formation of cities. The laws regulating land use and development schemes were developed and implemented at the local level. The regulations became even more extensive and efficient in the twentieth century when the national states took over and unified legal regulations for urban development.

4   A typical feature of European countries was the development of welfare states, which began fighting against poverty and social exclusion and which succeeded in preventing homelessness from becoming an urban problem on a mass scale. After the take-off of industrialization and urbanization, and the concentration of proletarian masses in rapidly growing cities, programs of "social housing" (4427, 2779, 1983) were developed in order to break the connection between the quality of housing and the economic power of the tenant (Harloe 1995). To this day, European states and cities are significant providers of social housing (2231, 6504, 2864). Because of the social housing programs, European cities lack the type of slums and ghettos found in American cities. Also, the European states, through their urban renewal programs, attempted to improve the quality of high-density quarters constructed during early capitalist urbanization (5934, 2290, 4235). Although some of the urban renewal programs had unwanted consequences in relocating the working class and the "underclasses," it was never doubted that "the city" as a whole should feel responsible for the living conditions in the inner-city areas and for the poor, and that the city center or dilapidated neighborhoods should not be reconstructed solely by capitalist logic (5255, 5081, 3438, 0809).

5   Thanks to the tradition of the burghers' influence in urban development, there developed in Europe, during the first decades of the twentieth century, visions or ideal models of the good city. The most famous was the garden city (0697, 2947, 4428). Encouraged by the antipathy towards the capitalist city of the nineteenth century, urban reformers

and social revolutionaries envisioned a "modern city" that would overcome class contradictions and social inequality. They proposed the nationalization of land, the provision of public services and the building of sound infrastructure.

These features – city landownership, municipal socialism, the tradition of town planning, the welfare state and visions of urban development – moderated the effects of modernism in Europe and still make European cities different from those in the USA, which are predominantly organized through market processes. However, in recent years these features have been challenged. Cities have begun selling their properties, what used to be public services are increasingly provided by private entrepreneurs, public–private partnerships have replaced the tradition of regulatory town planning, the welfare state is in crisis, and the plans drawn up by town planners are contested by citizens. European cities seem to be modernizing along the lines of American cities. In the following we will discuss these challenges in more detail.

Regulation and public landownership

Rules applied to landed property, public landownership, the tradition of town planning, and public intervention were among the characteristics of European cities identified by Bagnasco and Le Galès, as well as by Kaelble. The struggle to influence urban development continued in Europe and during the first decades of the twentieth century a new city model, the garden city, was invented. This development is characteristic of European cities, and Bagnasco and Le Galès are correct in emphasizing this. The use and legitimacy of town planning also distinguish European cities from American and Asian cities (Haila 1999). Although there are differences among European countries – such as the UK following the tradition of planning applications which give landowners and developers the right to draw up plans, and Germany and Finland accepting plans as laws – the tradition of town planning and the idea that public intervention in land use is legitimate have an enduring influence and can still be read in the pattern of European cities today.

Connected to town planning is public ownership of land, which has enabled European cities to have an important role in land-use decisions. The fact that cities owned large areas of land has made it easy for them to implement plans and use the sites in their possession for social and public utility purposes. Because of extensive public landownership, ideal city models were not left ideal, but were implemented in European cities (2281, 6462, 2439, 6501). Therefore, a characteristic of European cities, which distinguishes them from cities in America and Asia, is an extensive public realm and space, created and protected by planners, local politicians, and the urban public (4978, 4189, 2118, 4204, 0919).

The impact of town planning and public landownership in European cities is affected by the delicate relationship between the state and the city. We will take Helsinki as an example, but similar stories can be found, for example in Germany and the Netherlands. In Finland, the king donated the land to cities when they were established (this is the origin of the large city landownership in old towns), and the city further gave the sites to "good burghers" (this is how burghers got their possessions). Cities began drawing up detailed plans as early as the seventeenth century. In 1931, the state of Finland intervened and passed the Detailed Planning Law, which was applicable to the whole nation. Until the 1931 Detailed Planning Law, cities could draw up plans only for the land in their possession. Since 1931, cities can also plan private lands. This involved an extension of the regulatory ideology; cities were not only managing their own properties but planning the city as a whole. The Planning Law of 1958 further reinforced this regulationist ideology by introducing the idea of a hierarchy of plans; the point of the general plan was to take care of the interests of the whole city and guide detailed planning and development. The purpose of these planning laws was to give the power to plan to public authorities and to introduce the idea of a collective interest. In the Finnish vocabulary this is called "the planning monopoly of municipalities." Belief in the collective interest and town planners as legitimate representatives of this interest began fading away simultaneously with the passing of a new Land Use and Construction Law in 1999. This law provided more opportunities for citizens to participate.

Very similar observations can be made in Germany, where between 1918 and 1970 a continuous body of planning laws had been developed, granting the municipalities rights for regulating and intervening in the process of urban development. Since the 1960s, public participation rights have been expanded simultaneously. France, for a long time a very centralist state, has started to decentralize and to empower local administrations since the 1990s. In Spain, Barcelona has witnessed phenomenal change in its degree of autonomy since the end of the Franco regime.

The legacy of the burghers

Connected to town planning and public landownership is the question of burghers, a significant landowner group in European cities. The *Stadtbürger* in Weber's time was an owner of a building and, at the same time, the user of the building. The bourgeois city houses had shops on the street level and offices and living rooms on the upper floors. The site formed a social and economic unit. When the businesses of the burghers prospered, the economy of the city prospered. This coincidence of private and collective interests also guaranteed the social integration of the city, based on the patriarchal system of caring for dependants.

The enlightened bourgeoisie played a part as the harbinger of humanist urban development. Civilized burghers opposed market-led urban development which was seen as responsible for the deep social contradictions and inhuman living conditions of the lower classes in cities. Naturally, the Left was also concerned about the inhuman effects of market-led urban development as Friedrich Engels' famous report on English cities shows.

The portrait of the European city as a city where land use is regulated by public authorities, town planning is important, cities and burghers own land, and private and collective interests coincide is a true picture of old European cities. However, is it also true of cities in contemporary Europe where industrialization has ended the bourgeoisie's landownership and where real estate in the city center is owned by financial institutions; where users and owners of buildings are no longer one and the same person; where cities have begun selling their landed properties; where public regulation of land use has given way to new methods of control, like contracts and public–private partnerships that are more interested in separate projects (and whose performance is assessed by the success of the projects) (Häussermann and Kapphan 2000; Moulaert et al. 2003) than in planning the whole city in the interest of the whole city, and where political power is dispersed to various project organizations and ad hoc elite clubs? Do these changes make the concept of the European city based on landowning burghers obsolete? Is the neo-Weberian approach, postulating public landownership, collective interest and burghers' participation, relevant in analyzing contemporary cities that seem to be so very different from the cities in Weber's time?

To answer these questions we will discuss the example of Vuosaari, a neighborhood of Helsinki (5180, 3098, 3209). The Vuosaari Office was the first separate project organization in Helsinki. It was separated from the City Planning Office in 1989 and had a duty to draw up a general plan for Vuosaari. The plan the Vuosaari Office proposed would have increased the density of Vuosaari by drawing more inhabitants to the neighborhood. Citizens living in Vuosaari organized themselves to oppose the plan. Citizens were not the only group that did not like the plan drawn up by the town planners. In the center of Vuosaari there was a coffee factory, owned by Paulig, the largest coffee trading house in Finland. Paulig learned from a newspaper that its industrial site was zoned for housing. This zoning regulation turned the coffee company into a developer. Paulig wanted to keep its coffee factory in Vuosaari and to draw up its own plan for its large landed property in the area. The plan promoted a mixed-use development, including housing, offices, and a shopping center (4157, 4160, 3191, 3196). Paulig was not just acting as a developer and trying to make money through its real estate, but acted as a town planner devising a plan for a whole neighborhood. What is interesting is that the citizens of Vuosaari found an ally in the private coffee corporation, not in the city planning office that was supposed to defend the interests of citizens.

To explain the Vuosaari case we find the neo-Weberian framework useful. It is true that the city, in allowing a private owner to plan and by accepting the plan drawn up by Paulig, gave away its rights to determine the development, conceding its "planning monopoly." One might take this as evidence of the American model of private urban development. However, the reason why citizens allied themselves with the private coffee corporation rather than the city planning office was that Paulig was acting as a town planner interested in the whole neighborhood, and not simply speculating with real estate. In this Paulig took on the role of the old European landowning bourgeoisie that was concerned with the collective interest of the neighborhood and felt social responsibilities connected to that ownership.

Cities or metropolises

One of the main claims Bagnasco and Le Galès make to support their neo-Weberian approach is that cities in contemporary Europe have regained some of the autonomy they lost to the rising nation-states. It is true that in some respects cities have become more autonomous. For example, states have shifted the burden of provision of social services to cities. However, it is also true that in the era of globalization some cities have grown beyond their administrative borders and this has undermined the power of the central city. Population growth has spilled over from the old core city to suburban municipalities, and people's daily lives are stretching across city limits. The users and the inhabitants of cities are not one and the same (see Chapter 4; Martinotti 1999). Do these trends make the concept of the city as a political unit inapplicable?

To defend the usefulness of the neo-Weberian concept of autonomous cities we will take our example again from Helsinki. The Organization for Economic Cooperation and Development (OECD) decided to draw-up a series of reports analyzing the problems in forming metropolitan governances. The report analyzing the Helsinki metropolitan region was the first report it published in November 2002 (Helsingin Metropolikatsaus 2002). The report suggested that the autonomous cities that form the

Helsinki metropolitan region – Helsinki, Espoo, Vantaa and Kauniainen (whose autonomy is guaranteed by Constitution), with their different political traditions and practices – should increase their cooperation. All these cities disagreed with the OECD report. The strong resistance of cities to any form of metropolitan governance is rather surprising. Cities forming functional economic regions would surely find it beneficial to cooperate in order to compete in the global world. Helsinki, with half a million people and located on the edge of Europe, needs partners to compete in the global world. However, the resistance of the cities in the Helsinki metropolitan region becomes a little more understandable if we recall the long tradition of autonomy of cities in Europe. Similar examples could be presented from Germany, where the relationships in territories no longer coincide with the juridical borders and where attempts to form regional governments are contested by local politicians and inhabitants (Salet et al. 2003). The autonomy of European cities seems to be far from dead, just as the neo-Weberian framework suggests.

Private or public services

Bagnasco and Le Galès mention the public provision of services as an important characteristic of European cities. Indeed, a typical feature of European cities was the development of an urban regime that made a compromise between particular economic interests and the interest of the city as a whole. Citizens and decision-makers felt social responsibilities and developed programs for social housing, public health, poverty alleviation, and public education. It is important to remember that it was European municipalities that introduced social policies long before the nation-states started their programs of social insurance, healthcare, and public education. Today it is the cities again that are responsible for the welfare of citizens because of the cuts in state subsidies. However, both the state and the city, in the neoliberal era, have reconsidered their provision of public services and become less generous.

In spring 2002, the City of Helsinki decided to cut its welfare spending and announced its intention to close down some libraries and day-care centers. When the city made known its plans, the citizens of Helsinki came out on the street to demonstrate and defend their city's public services. The city had no alternative but to cancel the cuts. These spontaneous and immediate protests show that citizens in Helsinki still conceptualize their city as one with public provision of services. They defended their European city and upheld their right to public services. In Cologne, also, the local parliament resisted the privatization of the municipal housing associations. In Finland, in their manifestos for the parliamentary

elections in March 2003, some political parties promised to cut taxes
(which are heavy in countries with extensive welfare states). Interestingly,
the polls repeatedly showed that people prefer public services to lower taxes.
They are willing to pay high taxes if they get public services. Europeaness
is here understood as a normative category, like Göran Therborn (2001)
understands it, as a collection of civic ideals such as democracy, progress,
equality, and human rights (Soysal 2002: 274). The depiction of Helsinki
as a city with public provision of services and citizens identifying themselves as citizens entitled to public services is an apt description. In this
sense Helsinki is a European city, just as the neo-Weberian framework
describes. And this applies – to different degrees – to other European
cities as well.

Conclusions

Max Weber contrasted "Occidental" cities in Europe and "Oriental" cities in Asia. Bagnasco and Le Galès contrast European and US cities. This
change of reference point is understandable for two reasons: first, in terms
of urban development American cities have long been a source of influence; and, second, the comparison between European and American
cities implies a criticism of the narrow view that American urban studies
sometimes have in neglecting the institutional and cultural differences
among cities in different parts of the world. In this second sense the neo-
Weberian framework is proposing a new paradigm for urban analysis.

In this chapter we have so far argued that despite the trends in European cities making them resemble American cities, public landownership,
town planning, the political role of cities, public services, and an apprecia-
tion of urban culture are still important in European cities, and therefore
the Weberian categories are still useful for analyzing European cities.
By way of conclusion we will discuss two points – slums and the physical
layout of cities – that are important topics in urban studies and urban
practices in Europe and the USA.

Traditionally, slums have been viewed as a problem affecting US cities.
Now many urban scholars, together with city mayors and the European
Union, warn about the danger of the emergence of slums in Europe and
the increasing segregation in European cities. Instead of focusing on the
outcome, for example judging whether male unemployment rates and
concentrations of immigrants in some European neighborhoods are high
enough to make such neighborhoods slums, we would like to focus on the
processes and discuss the question of slums from this perspective. The
national and local social policies in Europe since the late nineteenth century
have attempted to prevent the deterioration of neighborhoods. Urban

renewal programs, which in the USA and Asia displaced the urban poor, were carried out differently in Europe. It was never doubted that "the city" as a whole should feel responsible for the living conditions of the people in inner-city areas. The development of the inner city was never left completely dictated by capitalist interests. The passion with which the European Union today emphasizes antipolarization strategies in its agenda for European urban policy (see Chapters 11 and 14), or the enthusiasm with which some cities, like Helsinki, which is among the most homogenous cities in the world, launch their strategies to fight, in advance, against the threat of polarization (Haila 2001), show that the spirit to fight against slums is still alive in Europe.

The second issue we would like to discuss concerns the role of economic interests and the physical layout of cities. Both American and European cities have CBDs, suburbs and a tendency to shift consumption from the CBD to suburban shopping malls. Behind these similarities, however, there are differences. In Europe, although there are market-led and speculative projects, there is still a remarkable share of public housing, and land is used for public utility functions. Neighborhoods are more mixed and less segregated than in the USA (Préteceille 2000). State subsidies and regional policies protect cities from economic cycles. The variety of policies in Europe (see Oberti 2000) shows the importance of local traditions. Suburban shopping malls, although emerging in Europe, are also contested in many European cities – in fact their development has been almost stopped in Germany because of local planning regulations and in Finland because of new national laws. The new urbanism in the USA, which some take as a sign of convergence between American and European cities, is just imitating the European design, simulating the "community," and does not reflect the social content and urban way of life of European cities.

Those who argue that there is a convergence between European and American cities mistake the physical appearance for social and political forces. Behind the similar physical appearances are different policies, different kinds of cities as political actors. The convergence, if any, is superficial. The power of the category of the European city is that it guides us to focus on social and political processes instead of seeing the city as a physical layout, or prevents us from privileging economic forces as political economists and global city scholars have done. European cities function as collective actors, and it will depend on the national power relations how far the process of deregulation and privatization will go.

The contribution of the neo-Weberian framework is to disclose the good qualities of European cities and to emphasize the political role of cities, together with the political role and responsibilities of citizens. In other words, the neo-Weberian framework is a conceptual framework as well as a normative one.

REFERENCES

Alonso, W. (1964) *Location and Land Use: Towards a General Theory of Land Rent.* Cambridge University Press, Cambridge.

Bagnasco, A. and Le Galès, P. (2000) European societies and collective actors? In: Bagnasco, A. and Le Galès, P. (eds.) *Cities in Contemporary Europe.* Cambridge University Press, Cambridge.

Berry, B.J.L. (1973) *The Human Consequences of Urbanisation.* St Martin's Press, London–New York.

Burgers, J. and Musterd, S. (2002) Understanding urban inequality: a model based on existing theories and an empirical illustration. *International Journal of Urban and Regional Research,* 26 (2): 403–413.

Castells, M. (1977) Is there an urban sociology? Theory and ideology in urban sociology. In: Pickvance, C. (ed.) *Urban Sociology, Critical Essays.* Tavistock, London.

Döblin, A. (1929) *Berlin Alexanderplatz. Die Geschichte vom Franz Biberkopf.* S. Fischer Vlg., Berlin.

Engels, F. (1845) [1972 edn.] *Die Lage der arbeitenden Klassen in England.* In: Marx, K. and Engels, F. *Werke,* Band 2, Dietz Verlag, Berlin/DDR.

Gottdiener, M. (1985) *The Social Production of Urban Space.* University of Texas Press, Austin.

Haila, A. (1999) City building in the East and West: United States, Europe, Hong Kong and Singapore compared. *Cities,* 16: 159–267.

Haila, A. (2001) How to manage globalization: the case of Helsinki. *Helsinki Quarterly,* 3: 15–30.

Hamnett, C. (2003) *Unequal City: London in the Global Arena.* Routledge, London.

Harloe, M. (1995) *The People's Home? Social Rented Housing in Europe and America.* Blackwell, Oxford.

Harvey, D. (1973) *Social Justice and the City.* The Johns Hopkins University Press, Baltimore.

Harvey, D. (1985) Monument and myth: the building of the Basilica of the Sacred Heart. In: Harvey, D. (ed.) *The Urban Experience.* The Johns Hopkins University Press, Baltimore.

Häussermann, H. (2001) Die europäische Stadt. *Leviathan,* 29: 237–255.

Häussermann, H. and Kapphan, A. (2000) *Berlin: Von der Geteilten zur Gespaltenen Stadt?* Leske and Budrich, Opladen.

Helsingin Metropolikatsaus (2002) *OECD Territorial Reviews: Helsinki, Finland.* Raportin suomenkielinen epävirallinen tiivistelmä. Aluekeskus: ja kaupunkipolitiikan yhteistyöryhmän julkaisu, 2.

Kaelble, H. (2000) La ville européenne au XX siècle. *Revue Économique,* 51 (2): 385–400.

Le Galès, P. (2002) *European Cities.* Oxford University Press, Oxford.

Lehto, J. (2000) Different cities in different welfare states. In: Bagnasco, A. and Le Galès, P. (eds.) *Cities in Contemporary Europe.* Cambridge University Press, Cambridge.

Martinotti, G. (1999) A city for whom? Transients and public life in the second-generation metropolis. In: Beauregard, R.A. and Body-Gendrot, S. (eds.) *The Urban Moment*. Sage Publications, Thousand Oaks.

Moulaert, F., Rodriguez, A., and Swyngedouw, E. (eds.) (2003) *The Globalized City: Economic Restructuring and Social Polarization in European Cities*. Oxford University Press, Oxford.

Oberti, M. (2000) Diversity and complexity in local forms of anti-poverty strategies in Europe. *International Journal of Urban and Regional Research*, 24 (3): 536–553.

Préteceille, E. (2000) Segregation, class and politics in large cities. In: Bagnasco, A. and Le Galès, P. (eds.) *Cities in Contemporary Europe*. Cambridge University Press, Cambridge.

Salet, W., Thornley, A., and Kreukels, A. (eds.) (2003) *Metropolitan Governance and Spatial Planning*. Spon Press, London–New York.

Sassen, S. (1991) *The Global City: New York, London, Tokyo*. Princeton University Press, Princeton, NJ.

Saunders, P. (1981) *Social Theory and the Urban Question*. Holmes & Meyer, New York.

Savage, M., Warde, A., and Ward, K. (1993) *Urban Sociology, Capitalism and Modernity*. Palgrave Macmillan, New York.

Simmel, G. (1900) *Philosophie des Geldes*. Duncker & Humblot Verlag, Berlin.

Simmel, G. (1903) Die Großstädte und das Geistesleben. In: Simmel, G. (1995 edition) *Aufsätze und Abhandlungen 1901–1908* (Band I, Gesamtausgabe Band 7). Suhrkamp, Frankfurt am Main.

Smith, D. (1988) *The Chicago School: A Liberal Critique of Capitalism*. St. Martin's Press, New York.

Smith, N. (1997) Social justice and the new American urbanism: the revanchist city. In: Merrifield, A. and Swyngedouw, E. (eds.) *The Urbanisation of Injustice*. New York University Press, New York.

Soysal, Y. (2002) Locating Europe. *European Societies*, 4: 265–284.

Therborn, G. (2001) European modernity and European normativity: the EU in history and in social space. In: Andersen, S.S. (ed.) *Institutional Approaches to the European Union*. Proceedings from an Arena Workshop. ARENA Report, 3.

Weber, M. (2000) *Die Stadt*. (Studienausgabe der Max-Weber-Gesamtausgabe. Abt. I, Schriften und Reden, Bd. 22. Wirtschaft und Gesellschaft: die Wirtschaft und die gesellschaftlichen Ordnungen und Mächte; Teilband 5), Mohr Siebeck, Tübingen.

Wirth, L. (1938) Urbanism as a way of life. *American Journal of Sociology*, XLIV: 1–24.

Part I

The Changing Concept of European Cities

3

Urban Social Change: A Socio-Historical Framework of Analysis

Enzo Mingione

Introduction

In this chapter I will look at the problem of interpreting current urban social change starting from two theoretical and methodological assumptions. The first concerns the overall meaning of change viewed as a major transformation within a succession of long historical cycles (Pirenne 1948; Braudel 1977; Arrighi 1994). In interpreting the indicators of change, more importance is given to factors of discontinuity with respect to the preceding phase and the attempt is made to identify the rationale underlying the current historical cycle (post-industrial or global or fragmented capitalism) compared to the previous one (organized or welfare capitalism or, more commonly, Fordism) (Offe 1985; Lash and Urry 1987; Mingione 1991, 1997). The second assumption is that although it is characterized by similar trends on a global scale, social change is giving rise to different forms of adaptation in diverse contexts, both at the local and national level (Esping-Andersen 1990, 1999). The two assumptions can be subsumed within the hypothesis that we are moving from social regimes that are differentiated but all grounded in the goals and directives of welfare capitalism and standardized organizations, to ones which are still differentiated but centered on more unstable, fragmented, flexible, and non-standardized rationales.

Cities are windows on the transformation of social regimes. In fact, it is in cities that the trends of social change take place first, and in more intensive and visible forms. It is here that the tensions and difficulties of social integration and exclusion are predominantly localized and it is here that the complexity of the new organizational forms has its core (see Chapter 4; Sassen 1991, 1996; Martinotti 1993), independently of the population's residential distribution. Here we will focus mainly on West European cities with some comparative reference to US cases and with a few observations on the urban transition in East European countries. The trends of change operate on a global scale and so our capacity to understand phenomena on a partial scale is imperfect. However, the full story is too complex for a single piece of work and author. Contemporary change in other societies will remain in the background and be referred to only generically and sporadically.

In the following section, the main trends in social change are identified and interpreted as constitutive factors in the transition from one historical phase to another. The focus will be on the ways in which change is undermining the standardized welfare capitalism regimes[1] and how present-day urban societies are variously adapting to different social patterns. The third section focuses on the different configurations assumed in the diverse social contexts by the development of organizational features typical of the welfare capitalism phase (Esping-Andersen 1990), and on how different models and variants adapt to change in diverse ways. The conclusion opens discussion on how the current transition is being translated into the construction of varied models of fragmented societies (Mingione 1991). As this process is ongoing and still, at least in part, indecipherable, our conclusions will be open-ended and predominantly of a methodological nature: what needs to be looked at and what significance to attribute to the differences noted in current processes of change.

The Main Trends of Change

The 1970s were the years of the oil crises and consequent decline in the rate of economic growth in the industrialized countries, which in turn speeded up industrial restructuring and qualitative changes in productive organizations, consumer habits and technological innovation. The transformational trends began to erode the social regimes that had been consolidated in the "thirty glorious years" (*Trente Glorieuses*) following World War II (1945–75). At the nub of these regimes lay three dominant factors:

1   The diffusion (going some way towards full employment) of stable family-wage occupations for adult males (generally, permanent employee labor

contracts with legal and trade union guarantees, particularly in large manufacturing and service industries and predominantly located in large cities and metropolitan regions).

2   The centrality of the nuclear family with married parents, functioning as an institution for redistributing resources, rights, and duties.

3   The regulatory monopoly of the nation-state, committed to expanding forms of protection (welfare state) complementary to the balance between breadwinner and nuclear family and essential to developing high-productivity systems based on large organizations and economies of scale, as well as engaged in promoting social homogeneity and keeping local, regional, and particularistic divergences under control.

The synergy between the three areas of social regulation (stable breadwinner employment, standard nuclear family, and welfare-oriented nation-state) fashioned true social regimes, within which industrial growth, the expansion of public and private welfare programs, standardized consumerism structured on a class basis, gender role division, and female specialization in care activities fed on one another. Matching these welfare capitalism regimes, there were also specific territorial configurations and dynamics: an advanced phase of industrial urbanization with relatively segregated working-class quarters and shopping centers favoring standardized mass consumerism, and the intensifying of a culture revolving around the motor car, though within a transport system centered on working commuters (2281, 6625, 2790, 4518). It is the organized and divided metropolis at its height, both in the North American version delineated by the Chicago School (Park et al. 1925; Wirth 1928) and the European versions with their working-class peripheries, dormitory suburbs, *banlieues*, etc.[2]

From the 1970s on, the trends of change in employment, population and the state's regulatory capacity have undermined, though in different ways and time spans, the fundamental institutions of welfare capitalism. Let us briefly look at the most evident aspects of these trends.

On the employment front, permanent stable jobs with standard contracts have begun to diminish, first in large-scale manufacturing industry and subsequently also in the big organizations in the traditional tertiary sector (commerce, banking, insurance, etc.). What initially seemed to be a short-term trend later turned out to be a structural transformation. At the same time, there has been an increase in "flexible" forms of employment: temporary, part-time, homeworking, teleworking, external collaboration and consultancy, and self-employment in the leading-edge sectors. Even more importantly, this transformation is also based on the development of new technologies and what is called the knowledge-informational societies (Castells 1996, 1999).[3] This shift has particularly negative and discriminatory consequences for people lacking educational and professional skills. In this sense, while the Fordist cities were able to integrate, even if in a highly divided way, masses of unskilled male immigrant workers, and through them the members of their nuclear families, poorly educated and unskilled new migrants and children of minorities, are now at the center of social exclusion processes (Saraceno 2002). Furthermore, the number of married women in paid employment is rising everywhere. In the space of a generation, the typically Fordist coupling of the lifecycle and working career has been abandoned whereby most women stopped working on the birth of their first child and possibly started again when all the children had reached school age. However, this does not mean that the emphasis on the "maternal" and specialized quality of care work has been dropped, which had made possible the reproductive balance of a society based on high productivity. Women's involvement in work has moved in the direction of various contradictory combinations of paid employment and high care responsibilities, from the spread of part-time jobs to the division between working mothers and career-oriented women and to real forms of "double shift" work.

It is not a matter of the end of work (Rifkin 1995) or of a sharp decline in the centrality of work in social life – on the contrary, work is more important than ever in women's lives – but undoubtedly of a change such as to disrupt the social, cultural and ideological equilibrium of the welfare capitalism regimes. The level of long-term unemployment has been rising, above all because large numbers of young people are no longer able to find sufficiently stable and well-paid jobs to meet their needs and expectations. As we will see in the next section, the transformation in employment has different consequences in the different variants of contemporary industrialized societies and cities: unemployment and flexible jobs variously impacting the young or adults, men or women; new waves of migration in which immigrants, asylum seekers and discriminated-against minorities are the most vulnerable to job instability and hence to difficult life conditions and social insertion. In all cases, it is the employment cornerstone of the previous social order that is collapsing: stable standardized high-productivity jobs for low-skilled adult males that supported the lives of millions of working-class families and a generation of immigrants, and which triggered the large-scale social mobility and urbanization in Fordist societies. It is in this sense that Sennett (1999) speaks of corrosion of character and Castel (1995) of the crisis of the *salariat* (wage-earning class) regime.

Also in the 1970s, a new demographic transition set in (Lesthaeghe 1995) that, generally speaking, was barely noted nor, more importantly, was it properly linked with the other changes in society. The transition is made up of many different trends: increase in longevity, divorce, single-parent, separated and recomposed post-divorce families, births out of wedlock, and single-person households; decline in and delaying of marriages, and falling birth rates. All these trends are undermining the centrality of the married couple during the course of life and transforming the hegemony of the "nuclear family" ideology (the importance in life of having children and investing resources in their future) into increasingly self-centered forms of individualism.

These demographic changes are likewise distributed differently across the diverse urban contexts, but in all cases they are upsetting the redistributive balances of the standard nuclear family.[4] An ever longer period of an individual's life is spent outside of a nucleus of married parents with dependent minors, whereas previously for the overwhelming majority this family condition applied throughout three-quarters of a lifespan. As a result of increasing longevity, parents live on average for more than 30 years after their youngest child has reached adulthood. An effect of delaying the birth of offspring has been to lengthen considerably the period between cohabitation as minors in the family of origin and setting up one's own household with dependent children. Moreover, the share of the population without offspring has risen again and another part spends long periods in the passage from one nuclear family to another. Today, almost everyone spends only a relatively short period of their lives in a "traditional" nuclear family with dependent minors. However, the other equally important aspect is the fact that households with dependent minors are more and more heterogeneous. Single-parent and recomposed families are increasing in numbers and also those made up of married couples with their own or adopted children vary greatly in terms of age and number of children. The latter are today more likely to have relatively old parents (first child around the age of 35) and to be an only-child family, but there is no longer any social standard to which the majority conform as in the previous phase.

The combination of employment and demographic change is undermining all the variants of the breadwinner regime as regards available economic resources (the adult male family wage clearly predominant), responsibility for care within the family (the wife-mother is the one who does the housework and looks after members) and access to social rights directly or indirectly through the husband-father's working career. In this last respect, the question of the identity of individuals, which was chiefly constructed around the work of the adult male family head, is also becoming more complex. From this standpoint, the theory of the decline in the centrality of work is tenable: employment now no longer provides a reliable fixed reference point for the building of the adult male identity and, consequently, it is less and less likely that wives and offspring will refer to the husband-father's work in constructing their own identities.

The twin instability of work and family structure has spilled over onto the protection capacities of the welfare state, the fiscal crisis of the state being in the front line of discussion already in the 1970s (O'Connor 1973; Gough 1979). The transition has destroyed the synergy between rising public spending and economic growth in a situation in which the further expansion of welfare intervention has come up against a creeping historical crisis in the monopolistic regulation exercised by nation-states. This crisis is impacting on legitimacy, the availability of resources and, above all, the effectiveness of intervention and the capacity for control. It is worth summarizing briefly the rationale underlying these changes. The legitimation of public programs tends to diminish as the social fabric becomes more fragmented: class and charitable solidarity are replaced by positions aiming for an equitable relation between contributions to the state and a direct return in public services. The tax revolts in the USA in the 1980s are a clear sign of this trend, which, however, affects all social contexts in different ways. At the same time, globalization is siphoning off resources from the nation-states because economic interactions take place on an international financial scale and by computer link-ups that are too fast to control. The effectiveness of national public operations is conditioned by the global scale of the controlling financial markets and the local fragmentation of the population's needs and demands.

The wave of privatizations and neo-laissez-faire has not removed the basic welfare guarantees in any industrialized country (but in some cases, like in the UK, it has been particularly disruptive and created long-lasting difficulties in crucial sectors such as health, education and public transport); however, the era of the complementary relation between expanding public intervention and growth of the "organized" economy is over everywhere. In this case too, welfare reforms differ in the various contexts, as we will see shortly. Nonetheless, they all reflect the weakness of national regulation and growing specific and local structures in any attempt to deal with the heterogeneous situations of need. The decline in effective national regulation has revived the importance of regional and local differences that had been suppressed in the previous period by national standardization.

At the territorial level, the tendencies towards change are signaled by deurbanization (there is the beginning of a fall in the concentration of the resident population in the big urban areas of industrialized countries) and by global cities (the development of nodes of financial, cultural and ideological control on a global scale) (Sassen 1991; Beauregard and Body-Gendrot 1999; Castells 1999) (1542, 6282, 1221, 2758). What is most important is that urban social life is moving beyond the patterns and divisions typical of the industrial era. Beyond the classic tension between the specific interests of resident citizens and those of commuters, a crucial role is being assumed by the need to attract visitors, organize large-scale cultural and sporting events, be at the center of worldwide financial operations, promote vast economic innovations with a capacity for global control and, in any event, be inserted (in terms of rapid transportation and communication) in the major innovatory networks (1944, 4981). The maps of segregation, exclusion, and gentrification are becoming more and more complicated and unstable. On one side, forms of hyperghettoization (Marcuse 1996; Wacquant 1996) are appearing that no longer have much in common with the traditional working-class residential quarters and segregated locations for disadvantaged minorities (1613, 5728, 1608); on the other side, the neighborhoods where the rich and powerful reside are being continually and rapidly transformed, without the consolidation of specific and lasting traditions and residential styles (4133, 4983, 4201). The locations of standardized consumption are becoming less important and being shifted to the margins of social life (also because in this area of consumption it is easier to use computers in the home) in order to leave room for a new wave of specialized shops and restaurants, places of entertainment and technological centers (5979, 2450, 6291, 2586). The territory has an increasingly symbolic value[5] and under these conditions the industrial forms of social control and urban policies lose their effectiveness and significance. On the one hand, the link between nation-state and citizen is weakened, and on the other urban governance (instead of the clear hierarchical organizations of local governments) is tending to move beyond the patterns of control because the relation between population and territory is increasingly ambiguous (think of the homeless youth, the influx of illegal immigrants, but also businesspeople with many domiciles and consultants with several jobs), and the interplay of political interests and actors around the city increasingly complex.

At the time of the maturity of welfare capitalism regimes in the West, the Eastern European socialist societies were also pushing towards the development of high productivity in manufacturing but keeping under control consumerism and the expansion of mass consumer industries in favor of heavy industrial production, large collective infrastructures, and basic welfare services. In a way we could speak of a welfare socialist model centered on heavy industrialization, high employment rates at standardized low incomes and controlled levels of mass consumerism, and the diffusion of basic public provision of welfare services. In the cities this process meant a trend towards under-urbanization[6] (Szelenyi 1983), low investments in urban growth, concentrated in the expansion of social housing in new peripheries, and a less divided and dynamic city kept under control by the limitation imposed on the private housing market and on consumerism (2286, 2362, 5306). However, this asset was also overthrown by social change in the following decades and here, much more explicitly than in the West, the economic deadlock of socialist industrialization swept away the political regimes. Under these conditions, urban social change became turbulent and double-faced: on one side urban renaissance and dynamic expansion of consumerism and physical renovation of the cities (5319, 2965, 2366, 5350); on the other side the uncontrolled growth of social inequalities, poverty, unemployment, and homelessness (2461, 5426, 1574). As we shall see briefly in the conclusions, the two faces of the Eastern European transition have different aspects in different regions and cities and consequently also here social change is producing diversified itineraries of adaptation to the new trends of the fragmented global age.

Welfare Capitalism Regimes and Their Crises

The specific local social systems all differ from one another over time and space (as places with different cultural heritages and social and institutional path dependency systems) – it is impossible to find two that are similar and this also goes for the periods of greatest standardization. At the same time, it is true that in the last two centuries societies have "modernized" along similar lines of transformation and that it is now difficult to recognize a city from a photograph that is not of something very specific. In order to understand social change and interpret the diversities within this complicated interplay between similar trends and specific local cases (though regrouped in clusters of variants with similar characteristics), social models are constructed on the basis that cases with the same initial conditions develop during a specific historical phase their own features and differentiate themselves from other variants. We will not dwell on this issue here, but it is useful to recall in brief the specialized forms adopted by the welfare capitalism models and then to analyze the way the different models are reacting to the current transformation trends. We should also underline that this process of change is also complicated by the fact that while the age of welfare capitalism was highly homogeneous on the national scale and cities were only the main windows of a national social regime, now diversity goes much deeper on the local scale and cities, within the same country or even region, constitute different cases and may fall in different clusters (Saraceno 2002).

The development of the tendencies towards a capitalism of high productivity and standardization, centered on consumerism, economies of scale, and large durables' manufacturing groups, led to the formation of five different models of welfare capitalism during the thirty glorious years after World War II. The rationale behind the diversification of the models was that under the specific conditions (in large part produced by historical processes of path dependency) of each cluster of variants, different factors played a decisive part in the organization of society, the formulation of guaranteed protection against exposure to market competition, and the configuration of the breadwinner regime. These factors were:

1 The market under the control of powerful industrial conglomerates (the USA).
2 The market controlled by an interventionist state (the UK at the time of Beveridge and Marshall, and the variants of Canada, Australia, and New Zealand).
3 Systematic public regulation aimed at spreading universal services and social intervention (the Scandinavian model).
4 A complementary combination of strong legitimate public regulation and family responsibility (the countries of continental Europe).
5 The familial and kinship system as established in a sizeable number of small firms complementing a nation-state beset by the historical difficulty of facing persistent localism and particularism (the Southern European model).

To understand the rationales behind the variety of welfare capitalisms we need to look at the advanced industrial societies in the early 1970s when the new transition was just beginning.

The US model

The American welfare capitalism regime was founded on the combination of the economic and technological supremacy of the large vertically integrated industrial groups, promoting the expansion of standardized consumerism, and the complementary nature of immigrant ethnic economies. The organizational equilibrium was provided by a marked economic and geographic mobility driven by the expansion in manufacturing, which gradually permitted masses of unskilled immigrants and members of minorities to be selected and integrated into the system of large high-productivity enterprises providing family wages and guaranteed company welfare. Worldwide economic and technologic hegemony and huge investment in the military–industrial complex made it possible then to promote across-the-board forms of standardized consumerism through big credit-based incentives to acquire durable goods and growth of imports, offset by investment abroad and the resulting profits.

When the expansion of manufacturing in the 1970s came to a halt, giving way to industrial restructuring and vertical disintegration, standardized and generalized occasions of upward social mobility ceased and a process of polarization began to the detriment of the most disadvantaged minorities. In the USA, those affected most of all were African Americans and Puerto Ricans segregated in the large metropolitan ghettoes and the most recent immigrants from Central America confined to the most precarious and poorest paid work (Mac-jobs) in services (4621, 0985, 1623). In European cities, the same process affected mostly both the new migrants and the children of minority groups; the former became involved in the worst forms of precarious employment and the latter were severely hit by long-term unemployment (*The Netherlands Journal of Social Sciences* 2000). At the same time, in the USA the transition boosted the ethnic economies (4644, 4668, 4626) and gave rise to a new economic regime dominated by financial operations, informatics, and the new technologies (Castells 1999). Social inequalities very quickly eroded the balance-restoring effect of the blue- and white-collar middle classes who, less protected than elsewhere by strong trade union organizations and guarantees, felt the impact of the growing instability of employment and family life (Sennett 1999). The American economic system rapidly turned into a true job machine, which created a substantial number of new jobs but was also the focus of new forms of precarious and poorly protected work, while in Europe the welfare state slowed down employment growth and the level of unemployment shot up.

The liberal state

The liberal-statist model of welfare capitalism – only some features of the UK case will be mentioned here – combines the importance of a developed industrial market (centered on manufacturing groups oriented to high productivity and specializing in durables) with far-reaching state intervention in welfare. Compared to the US configuration of welfare capitalism, the more limited economic power of the industrial conglomerates and consequent impossibility of reaching an effective synergy between big enterprises (and private welfare), consumerism, and ethnic economies gave rise to an organizational balance resting on public intervention and the part played by the trade unions (linked to the Labour Party) and employer associations. The regime was therefore grounded on the high family wage, protected by wide-reaching legal and trade union guarantees and by the development of welfare intervention, not across the board as in the Scandinavian countries, but in selective ways complementary to the growth of manufacturing industry and to trade union and employer interests.

Under these circumstances, the deindustrialization of the 1970s (particularly virulent in the UK because it affected obsolete apparatuses and organizations fossilized by industrial conflict) had a devastating effect (Massey and Meegan 1978) (6110, 6292). Adult male heads of families were hit most by unemployment and industrial decline undermined the organizational role of the trade unions and industrialists' organizations. Married women entered the labor market on a massive scale but mainly in part-time jobs on wages too low to support dependent cohabiting members. Thus, the forms of impoverishment of single-parent families, of redundant workers and their families, the elderly on low incomes, and the low-skilled young gained a foothold. This was especially so if they belonged to disadvantaged ethnic minorities confined in the decaying districts of the rapidly declining old industrial cities (3139, 5739).

The British industrial cities adapted differently to the deindustrialization trends. To give only a few examples, Bristol quickly became one of the dynamic centers of the British high-tech compound, Manchester redeveloped around an advanced tertiary, financial, and information economy able to provide new occasions for at least a part of minority groups, while Liverpool suffered the devastation of job losses almost passively.

The Scandinavian model

The Scandinavian system of organized capitalism rests on the capacity to expand the system of services and universal public welfare by setting up a benign circuit linking the diffusion of public care services and female employment under special conditions: a high tolerance of absenteeism for family reasons counterbalanced by lower pay and fewer career possibilities than in the private sector, where the workers are predominantly male. This system has remained viable despite its high cost (and high taxation) because of the particular fact that these countries are small and socially homogeneous with markets relatively protected from international competition and that their economies are characterized by advanced specialization and control over small market niches. The breadwinner regime has assumed its particular shape because it is complemented both by massive public intervention and high and rising levels of female employment in welfare services.

At least in a first phase, up to the second half of the 1980s, the Scandinavian countries were spared the negative effects of the employment transition. Protection of the specialized industrial niches has continued under the new conditions of global competition, while the spread of public care services has curbed the expansion of flexible jobs in the tertiary sector. However, the regime was affected earlier by the demographic transition. A low birth rate, coupled with high rates of divorce and children born out of wedlock have reshaped the household structure since the

1970s. Combined with the financial impact of increased longevity on health service and pension costs, this process has caused the already high level of social spending to rise further. When some marginal welfare programs had to be cut, a malign circuit was activated, bringing about a rapid increase in unemployment (first in Finland and Denmark, then in Sweden, whereas Norway was less affected because of North Sea oil receipts), which in turn called for more public spending to subsidize the jobless and finance active employment policies. On the whole, however, the universalistic welfare specialization of the Scandinavian regime has permitted the employment transition to be anticipated and its negative effects to be attenuated by promoting socially protected forms of flexible work in both the public and private sectors (a path eventually also followed by the Netherlands starting from a different model of welfare capitalism). However, in these cases the social fabric is becoming less homogeneous and a social division between locals and immigrants is developing (3211, 2846) where the latter are increasingly trapped in forms of welfare support that are ill-suited for their social integration and cultural expectations, and biased (Friedman 2002; Saraceno 2002).

Continental Europe

The corporative model is fairly differentiated internally because in consolidating its forms of organized capitalism it has incorporated diverse cultural traditions and a relatively large amount of family businesses and self-employment. The breadwinner regime reflects a clearer division between care responsibilities falling to women (less active in the labor market) and public welfare programs built on rights acquired during the working careers of adult males. Social security, pensions, and health insurance developed quickly in the Bismarckian tradition but have remained segmented in line with job specialization. The synergy between very pronounced public intervention and the development of organized capitalism has, above all in the German-speaking countries, led to the construction of a dual regime of protection for citizens (especially through improvements to education, training, and insertion into better paid jobs and the professions) and guest workers. Family responsibility for care services has remained high and is supported by incentives to save, a choice made possible by the fact that economic growth in these countries has been driven more by exports than by the expansion in domestic demand. This has produced less consumerist cities with a more conservative attitude towards local traditions and history.

Under these conditions, change has had a different impact from the previously mentioned models, above all as regards the demographic transition and female participation in the labor market. The crisis in the centrality of the married couple (divorce and children born out of wedlock) is more limited and has progressed more slowly, as has the entry of married women into the labor market and the development of public and private childcare services.[7] The direct impact of deindustrialization has been more limited (3988, 6581), but the inability to foster a rapid expansion of public and private welfare services has been translated into a slower growth in job opportunities and, consequently, in higher unemployment. The increase in longevity combined with a strong tendency to early retirement has put a great economic strain on the health and pension systems. The decline in stable job opportunities in the big cities has exacerbated the unequal balance between citizens' life conditions and those of immigrants and naturalized minorities, in particular the young, born and educated in the host country under discriminating conditions, who can no longer find stable jobs in industry.

As anticipated, the political-social adaptation of these variants now differs also along regional lines.[8] What we have is a continuing historical process of increasingly differentiated modernization of societies overlaying a persistent culture rooted in the countryside to which the particular local diversities react after lying dormant for a certain time; this situation is even more manifest in the Southern European variants, as we shall see in more detail below.

Features and crisis of the Southern European welfare capitalism regime

The two main features of the Southern European model are, first, a high proportion of small firms and self-employed workers offset by a weaker proletarianization of the economic fabric and a low rate of female employment and, second, and more importantly, a large part of the responsibility for welfare services is delegated to the family system (which includes not only the cohabiting nuclear units but also kinship relations). This delegation of responsibility, however, occurs in conditions transformed by the need to increase industrial productivity and specialization in administrative, health, and education services. As Ferrera (1998: 82–3) notes, these features are reflected in a Bismarckian welfare, which is fragmented on an employment basis, typical of the continental European tradition, but without basic minimum protection and marked by widespread particularism and a large deficit in public services. These aspects of the configuration recall the specificity of weak statism, by which is meant a historical condition of weakness in building an alliance between the economic capitalist elite and the national political ruling class. This has resulted in a limited capacity to promote policies of homogenization and eliminate localism and particularism. It is the modalities of the institutional framework resulting from this historically weak alliance during the developmental stage of welfare institutions that have led to a model of welfare capitalism characterized by intermittently and arbitrarily effective state apparatuses, which encourage particularism and strong subsidiary features in respect of family, community, and the third sector (Mingione 2001a,b). This subsidiary development of the welfare mix maximizes family responsibilities and the recourse to voluntary provision; it thus becomes in a certain sense an alternative to the development of a structured network of basic protection and welfare services.

Within the current process of change, this model has demographic repercussions in the greater importance of kinship networks (they contribute to the welfare of non-cohabiting relations, thereby compensating for the reduction in multiple enlarged families), in the long cohabitation of parents and adult offspring until marriage (extended by the trend towards delaying marriage), and in the pronounced drop in the birth rate (combined also with a low propensity to have children outside wedlock). The lower incidence of forms of family instability is at the same time brought about and compensated for by an overburden of responsibilities on the head of the family (that is, women). It is this overburden, rather than the instability of married life, that tends to produce tensions in combination with increased longevity and the declining marriage and birth rates. This is particularly the case of a generation of women who find great difficulties in combining employment (mostly full-time because forms of part-time employment are particularly discouraged in these countries) with a very high burden of family care. Here, moreover, in many cases the burden is increased by the prolonged cohabitation of adult children with parents and the need to care for elderly parents living longer. A whole series of supports that were practicable for wide kinship networks, less beleaguered by subjects in serious difficulty (drug addicts, the long-term sick, the non-autonomous elderly, the young long-term unemployed, and so on), are problematic under present-day conditions.

Furthermore, the impact of this short-circuit between demographic changes and occupational transformations cannot be neglected; its negative consequences can be particularly serious where the unemployment crisis becomes chronic, as in Southern Italian cities. The capacity for protection in these variants depends on a combination of family, community and voluntary support and lasting employment of adult male breadwinners, and stable small firms. On the employee front, tertiarization and flexibilization are making male working careers more precarious, while educated women cohorts have great difficulty in finding employment and, when they do, in combining work with the overburden of responsibility for caring. Employment opportunities are scarce also because of the limited expansion of public and private welfare services, and from this derives the clear tendency for the female, as well as the young, component of unemployment to predominate. The consequence is that in these variants there are few "atypical" cohabitations – single-parent, de facto, socially isolated singles – but many single-earner nuclear units that are vulnerable when the income is low and the family overburden is high in the absence of welfare services and when the typical contribution comes from non-cohabiting relations and voluntary services. On the small family business front, the fact that kinship networks are more sporadic is now a greater threat to the reproduction of micro-firm systems. This growing weakness is occurring in a period in which small enterprises and self-employment, at least in the innovative sectors, constitute an important resource of flexibility.

Welfare innovations are still more difficult than elsewhere for at least three reasons: they are costly because previous investment was low; they are politically implausible because political and bureaucratic legitimization from the center is weak; and they conflict with a consolidated cultural model of solidarity inside the family (and in the informal, community, and voluntary sphere), which modernization has conveniently adapted to the new social conditions.

Nevertheless, it is precisely in this area, where large regional differences existed also in the phase of organized capitalism, that the transition generated strong tendencies towards regional divergence. The regions with dynamic industrial districts (in Northern Italy and in some parts of Spain, Portugal and Greece) are producing a particular model of flexibilization based on the combination of flexibility in self-employment and in the new forms of employment in small enterprises (the development of networks of firms and the extensive use of local social capital for innovative entrepreneurship), modernization of the family system and development of governance on a local scale (0912, 6066). Other regions, like Southern Italy (see Chapter 13), are in contrast persistently dogged by high levels of joblessness and poverty, a rigid dependence on interventionist aid from the central state and the inability to engender locally and autonomously innovatory social and economic processes (Gallie and Paugam 2000) (1486, 1489, 1383).

The urban transitional scenario of Southern Europe may appear, paradoxically, at the same time the most conservative and the most innovative. On the one hand, the importance of family and kinship protection, local social capital and network organization of firms discourages high waves of mobility out of the traditional system of cities and towns. In other words, recent trends of change have further reinforced local identity and loyalty. On the other hand, the arrival on a massive scale of immigrants from developing countries is here a new phenomenon, while in other cities a substantial presence of foreign immigrants and ethnic minorities is deeply rooted in the manufacturing past. The combination of strong local identities and completely new waves of immigration helps to explain the feeling of insecurity and invasion generated in the local population by a relatively small presence of foreign migrants (maximum 5 percent of the resident population against much higher levels in other European and American cities) (3094, 2069).

It is true, however, that everywhere the ethnic/migration urban scenario has changed considerably from that in the manufacturing age. The employment transformation confines large groups of migrants (particularly illegal immigrants and asylum seekers waiting for residence permits) in an assortment of service and informal jobs that are badly paid, unstable, isolated socially and extremely difficult to protect through union organizations.[9] This provides a strong foothold for a vicious circle of social discrimination and exclusion, which in the worst cases has led to new forms of racism. This same phenomenon in the deindustrializing cities with a tradition of foreign immigration (or ethnic minorities in the USA, UK, and France, particularly) has negatively affected the employment opportunities of the children of immigrants and minorities that settled in the cities during the periods of manufacturing expansion (Cole and Dale 1999; Saraceno 2002). Also in this case the map of urban social disadvantage is becoming more varied and fragmented. In Southern Europe there is a new division between economically dynamic areas that attract more immigrants who are well inserted in employment but highly discriminated against in urban social life, while in the less dynamic areas the immigrants are fewer and more often unauthorized; they frequently become employed in the black labor market but, with an apparent paradox, they are more accepted and better integrated (3724, 5000). In Eastern European cities, there are fewer immigrants and some communities have adapted well to the transition in the market economy, as in the case of people of Vietnamese origin in the industrial East German city of Halle (Saraceno 2002). However, traditional minorities, particularly Roma groups in Hungary and Romania, are highly penalized and discriminated against within the transition to a market economy (Ladanyi and Szelenyi 2000) (5417, 5433, 5381).

Conclusions: Lines of Diversification in the Fragmented Societies

The debate on the outcomes of the transition has concentrated on the opposition between two alternative models: the liberal one, exemplified above all by the USA and in Europe by the UK, which favors flexibilization and promotes new opportunities without creating forms of compensation for the concomitant increase in inequality (and social exclusion) and instability; and the welfarist model, which moves in the very opposite direction, even at the cost of limiting new opportunities. The quotation below from Jonathan Gershuny (taken from Scase and Pahl 1999: 11) refers to a version of this opposition, one based on the idea that the second model is superior to the first and therefore critical of the theory of sclerotic Europe[10] and the inability of welfare societies to face the challenges posed by globalization.

> The first is what I have called the *Wild West* – unregulated long hours of paid work, no family leave, ungenerous retirement – gender segregated paid and unpaid work roles – class type polarization between work (and money) rich time–poor households on the one hand and the new servant/Mac-job class on the other. People behaving entirely rationally, but in the context of the unregulated market mechanism, leads to the irrational collective outcome of a polarized stressed out society.
>
> The second is the *Nice North*, with regulated shorter hours, generous family leave – and other measures intended to reduce the culture of long hours in the work place. There is a decrease in gender segregation, class convergence, households looking after themselves, work sharing and a sensible social distribution of leisure.

The opposition identified by Gershuny is simplistic, but it helps to highlight a reality that has already been pointed out and is today confirmed by the data on low unemployment, high economic flexibility, welfare innovation, and dynamic local systems in certain regions. Contrary to how things appeared in the early 1990s, those countries (though as we have seen, it would now be more correct to adopt a local and regional scale) with a welfare culture have managed to combine flexibilization of labor and promotion of opportunities with new forms of social protection. At present, a large number of regions in continental Europe are recording levels of flexibility and economic competitiveness as high as those in the USA, and low rates of unemployment and negative social repercussions – from the "corrosion of character" to social exclusion and polarization. The latter are kept in check by innovative forms of social protection, ranging from permanent education to work insertion policies, subsidized leaves of absence and programs of social protection for people in need, and by the development of intervention on the part of voluntary organizations and the third sector. As noted recently by Storper (2001), the transition is producing everywhere new tensions and an increase in economic inequality, but the real question is how these trends are matched by different arrangements of social protection.

What the setting in opposition of the two models of adaptation does not discern is the complex articulation of the ways of reacting to the transition and the fact that the process needs to be viewed over the long term and thus from subsequently adjusted perspectives. For instance, 10 years ago the *Nice North* appeared doomed to an inevitable decline. By way of conclusion and at the same time to open the debate, let us briefly consider what the possible articulations and historical itineraries are within the processes of adaptation to fragmented capitalism. As will be seen, one of the central elements in this final task – making it even more complicated – is that as a consequence of the decline in the regulatory monopoly of the nation-state, the models of fragmented capitalism are increasingly shaped within local and regional moulds and difficult to both analyze (comparative data are almost always national) and piece together.

First of all, I have indicated that there is another reality different from neo-laissez-faire and welfare innovation; that which puts the emphasis on using local and family networks to foster flexible and innovative competitiveness, above all in self-employment and in small and medium-sized enterprises. This reality comes up against the problem of overloading responsibilities onto family and kin. It is a trajectory typically found in some regions of Southern Europe, in many parts of France and Germany and, under different conditions, in the most dynamic parts of Eastern Europe (where urban and economic renaissance prevails over the negative aspects of the transition to the market economy), areas that now have low rates of joblessness and poverty and high levels of economic success. Their prospects are tied to the ability to inject a growing share of resources into local initiatives so as to lessen the burden on family networks (introducing public and private social programs for those most vulnerable to lifecycle and work transitions), attenuate the negative impacts of an aging population and the low birth rate, and activate the effective social insertion of a high proportion of immigrants, which serves to boost dynamic economies suffocated by the scarcity of labor in personal services and in many "dirty" but crucial areas of manufacturing. However, the new feature of economic insertion of immigrants and minorities often generates a vicious circle of discrimination and fear of insecurity: migrants are welcome in the jobs that are less acceptable to local residents (4074, 2317, 2852) but then they are feared in the everyday life of the city and held responsible for the increasing rates of street crime (3051, 2928). In reality, the resources are there, especially of the private kind if we count the innovative potential of the third sector, but this does not mean that all the different contexts are able to use them in equally efficient ways. This could be a third model of adaptation, structured by many regional variants, and include regions moving away from the corporative (parts of France and Germany), familistic (parts of Italy and Spain) and liberal-statist (Ireland and parts of Canada and Oceania) variants of welfare capitalism, and even parts of Eastern Europe (the Czech Republic, the Budapest region, parts of Poland, and the Baltic republics).

At present, other regions in Southern and continental Europe, such as Southern Italy and parts of Spain, Portugal and Greece, Eastern Germany, and a large part of Eastern Europe, are in a more difficult situation with chronically high rates of unemployment and poverty and little capacity to attract investment and foster innovation (5327, 1756). If there are no substantially new developments,[11] this fourth model may turn out to be worse than the social polarization encouraged by neoliberal policies. However, in a long process of adaptation it would be wrong to foreshadow outcomes that cannot be predicted. Also, as regards the fate of the neo-laissez-faire variants, it cannot be taken for granted that the combination of the maximization of opportunities and increasing instability will persist in long-term social polarization and exclusion.

The importance of cities (and differences among them) is not declining with the age of industrial decentralization, vertical disintegration of firms, global financial control, and information technology (Castells 1999). On the contrary, urban social life, and not only in global cities, is more and more at the center of our attention and concerns. Social exclusion, insecurity and criminality, the risks of pollution and environmental tragedies on the negative front, welfare reforms and policy experiments and innovations, new coalitions of actors and new forms of mobilization together with great opportunities for self-fulfillment on the positive front, are all predominantly located in cities (Musterd and Ostendorf 1998; Marcuse and van Kempen 2000, 2002). As we have seen, cities are the first to follow in the wake of the general trends of change but they persistently show important differences; the distribution of positive and negative features is extremely variable.

Cities, even more than national societies, are characterized by common problems with different configurations. Both the urban social problems – from the social and economic regeneration dynamics to cultural and tourist attractiveness on the positive side, to the spread of insecurity and intolerance, precarious jobs and long-term unemployment, poverty and social exclusion on the negative side – and the construction of policy responses to such problems – from the development of new agencies of the third sector to the innovative programs of the local authorities – are variously distributed in different urban contexts and change fast over time (Mingione and Oberti 2003). In line with the arguments put forward here, what is now seen to be new is that the location of a city in a specific country, that is, within a specific model of welfare capitalism in the past and within a more articulated set of fragmented clusters today, is less a pointer to its social reality than it was in the age of standardized manufacturing expansion. The literature on local regulation and on urban governance (see Chapter 11; Bagnasco and Le Galès 2000; Le Galès 2002; Pichierri 2002) contributes a framework through which the diversity of urban welfare regimes can find an initial stage of interpretation, but in order to understand the local trajectories of change we have to face the hard task of international comparative analysis.

NOTES

1 By welfare capitalism regime I mean a set of rules and practices that regulate social integration, inequalities, and conflicts during the Fordist age, particularly at its peak in the thirty years after World War II, in industrially advanced countries (see, among others, Esping-Andersen 1990; Mingione 1997).

2 In the European cases, socio-spatial inequalities and segregation tend generally to coincide with the expulsion towards the periphery of less well-off and discriminated-against populations (mainly new immigrant workers). This process has resulted in variously heated and persistent forms of segregation, even in cities located in the same country and with a similar industrial vocation, as exemplified by the difference between Milan (less segregated) and Turin (more divided and segregated) in Italy (see Saraceno 2002, chapter 2).

3 By "informational societies" Castells means in particular three (simultaneous) social and economic trends that are restructuring urban space:

   (a) The reinforcement of metropolitan areas as nodal centers through the use of information technology.
   (b) The decline of Fordist regions that, once dominant industrial centers, were not able to make a successful transition to the informational economy.
   (c) The emergence of new dynamic regions with informational capacity and networks to major metropolitan centers of international importance.

4 Fordism produced a social construction of the household based on the institution of the nuclear family relying on the redistributive capacity of the male breadwinner. Nowadays, comparative research on the transformation of welfare capitalism is showing that the ever growing instability of both work and family structure is undermining precisely such redistributive capacity; as a result, "non-traditional" households, such as singles, single-parents and families with many children, are becoming the most vulnerable (Saraceno 2002).

5 By way of example we could mention the exponential value increase of residential areas in the center of Paris, in Barcelona after the urban restructuring for the 1992 Olympic Games and, more recently, in the "fashion city" area of Milan. All these areas are experiencing a process of gentrification: skyrocketing rent, evictions of former residents and shopkeepers, new well-off residents.

6 By suburbanization is meant mainly a complex process through which urban growth is discouraged and a large number of new industrial and service

workers employed in the expanding urban industries are forced by social and economic constrictions to continue to live in traditional rural villages and small towns and commute to work.

7 In this respect France is the exception, also because of a historical vocation to compensate for a low birth rate throughout the nineteenth century with adequate social policies.

8 The diversity is also becoming more and more pronounced on city lines but, as we experienced in trying to elaborate city clusters for comparative European research on social assistance involving only 13 cities (Saraceno 2002, chapter 2), this kind of operation is extremely complicated.

9 As indicated in recent comparative research on social assistance dynamics in Europe (Saraceno 2002), foreign immigrants constitute a majority of the local poor. The new waves of recent immigrants, and asylum seekers in particular, are facing social insertion problems aggravated by the difficulties arising from insecure employment and lack of affordable housing.

10 By sclerotic Europe we mean a welfare culture that precludes innovation and flexible solutions to organizational and economic drawbacks.

11 Naples is a remarkable and positive example. After a long decline it is once again a major capital city of European culture and a center attracting attention and tourism. This change was possible thanks to a new flow of resources whose beneficiaries, constraints, and rules are different from those funded by the central government in Rome through patronage and the control of political party machines. It could well be an opportunity to set in motion a Neapolitan "miracle" in the wake of those in the Third Italy, Holland, Ireland, Catalonia, and others.

REFERENCES

Arrighi, G. (1994) *The Long XX Century*. Verso, London.

Bagnasco, A. and Le Galès, P. (2000) *Cities in Europe*. Cambridge University Press, Cambridge.

Beauregard, R.A. and Body-Gendrot, S. (eds.) (1999) *The Urban Moment*. Sage, London.

Braudel, F. (1977) *Afterthoughts on Material Civilization and Capitalism*. Johns Hopkins University Press, Baltimore, MD.

Castel, R. (1995) *Les métamorphoses de la question sociale: Une chronique du salariat*. Fayard, Paris.

Castells, M. (1996) *The Informational City*. Blackwell Publishers, Oxford.

Castells, M. (1999) *End of Millenium, The Information Age: Economy, Society and Culture*. Blackwell Publishers, Oxford.

Cole, M. and Dale, G. (1999) *The European Union and Migrant Labour*. Berg Publishers, Oxford.

Esping-Andersen, G. (1990) *The Three Worlds of Welfare Capitalism*. Polity Press, Cambridge.

Esping-Andersen, G. (1999) *Social Foundations of Postindustrial Economies*. Oxford University Press, Oxford.

Ferrera, M. (1998) *Le trappole del welfare*. Il Mulino, Bologna.

Friedman, J. (ed.) (2002) *Globalization, the State, and Violence*. Altamira Press, Walnut Creek, CA.

Gallie, D. and Paugam, S. (eds.) (2000) *Welfare Regimes and Experience of Unemployment in Europe*. Oxford University Press, Oxford.

Gough, I. (1979) *Political Economy of the Welfare State*. MacMillan, London.

Ladanyi, J. and Szelenyi, I. (2000) Poverty and social structure in transitional society. Unpublished Paper. Center for Comparative Research, Yale University.

Lash, S. and Urry, J. (1987) *The End of Organized Capitalism*. Polity Press, Cambridge.

Le Galès, P. (2002) *European Cities (European Societies)*. Oxford University Press, Oxford.

Lesthaeghe, R. (1995) The second demographic transition in Western countries: an interpretation. In: Oppenheim Mason, K., and Jensen, A.M. (eds.) *Gender and Family Change in Western Countries*. Clarendon Press, Oxford.

Marcuse, P. (1996) Space and race in the post-Fordist city: the outcast ghetto and advanced homelessness in the United States today. In: Mingione E. (ed.) *Urban Poverty and the Underclass: A Reader*. Blackwell Publishers, Oxford.

Marcuse, P. and van Kempen, R. (2000) *Globalizing Cities*. Blackwell Publishers, Oxford.

Marcuse, P. and van Kempen, R. (2002) *Of States and Cities*. Oxford University Press, Oxford.

Martinotti, G. (1993) *Metropoli*. Il Mulino, Bologna.

Massey, D. and Meegan, R. (1978) *The Anatomy of Job Loss: The How, Why and Where of Employment Decline*. Methuen, London.

Mingione, E. (1991) *Fragmented Societies: A Sociology of Economic Life Beyond the Market Paradigm*. Blackwell Publishers, Oxford.

Mingione, E. (1997) *Sociologia della vita economica*. Carocci, Rome.

Mingione, E. (2001a) Il lato oscuro del welfare: trasformazione delle biografie, strategie familiari e sistemi di garanzia. In: *Atti del Convegno "Tecnologia e Società"*. Accademia dei Lincei, Roma.

Mingione, E. (2001b) The Southern European welfare model and the fight against poverty and social exclusion. In: *Encyclopedia of Life Support Systems*. Unesco, Paris.

Mingione, E. and Oberti, M. (2003) The struggle against social exclusion at the local level: diversity and convergence in European cities. *European Journal of Spatial Development*, Vol. 1.

Musterd, S. and Ostendorf, W. (eds.) (1998) *Urban Segregation and the Welfare State: Inequality and Exclusion in Western Cities*. Routledge, London–New York.

The Netherlands Journal of Social Sciences (2000) Debate: immigrants and assimilation. 2 (2): 117–175.

O'Connor, J. (1973) *The Fiscal Crisis of The State*. St Martin's Press, New York.

Offe, C. (1985) *Disorganized Capitalism: Contemporary Transformations of Work and Politics*. Polity Press, Cambridge.

Park, R.E., Burgess, E.W., and McKenzie, R.D. (1925) *The City*. Chicago University Press, Chicago.

Pichierri, A. (2002) Concertation and local development. *International Journal of Urban and Regional Research*, 26 (4): 689–706.

Pirenne, H. (1948) Les périodes de l'histoire sociale du capitalisme: pensée et action, Bruxelles. Italian translation: Pirenne H. (1953) Le fasi della storia sociale del capitalismo. In: Bendix, R. and Lipset, S. (eds.) *Classe, potere, status: Teorie della struttura di classe*, Marsilio Editori.

Rifkin, J. (1995) *The End of Work: The Decline of Global Labor Force and the Dawn of the Post Market Era*. G.P. Putnams Sons, New York.

Saraceno, C. (ed.) (2002) *Social Assistance Dynamics in Europe: National and Local Poverty Regimes*. Policy Press, Bristol.

Sassen, S. (1991) *The Global City: New York, London, and Tokyo*. Princeton University Press, Princeton.

Sassen, S. (1996) Service employment regimes and the new inequality. In: Mingione E. (ed.) *Urban Poverty and the Underclass: A Reader*. Blackwell Publishers, Oxford.

Scase, J. and Pahl, R. (1999) *The Millennium Papers: Future Works and Life Styles*. Age Concern, London.

Sennett, R. (1999) *The Corrosion of Character*. Norton and Company, New York–London.

Storper, M. (2001) Lived effects of the contemporary economy: globalization, inequality, and consumer Society. *Public Culture*, 12 (2; special issue on millennial capitalism).

Szelenyi, I. (1983) *Urban Inequalities under State Socialism*. Oxford University Press, Oxford.

Wacquant, L. (1996) Red belt, black belt: racial division, class inequality and the state in the French urban periphery and the American ghetto. In: E. Mingione (ed.). *Urban Poverty and the Underclass: A Reader*. Blackwell Publishers, Oxford.

Wirth, L. (1928) *The Ghetto*. University of Chicago Press, Chicago.

4

Social Morphology and Governance in the New Metropolis

Guido Martinotti

Introduction

Contemporary urbanites are confused. While walking – or driving – in the new urban terrain, they feel nostalgia for a disappearing city, or muse about the "city of the future" without recognizing that such a city is probably already there. The task of the scholar is to help them find their way by making them aware of the revolution in which they are living, and by giving them the right lenses to look at the new urban reality, already vastly different from the one imprinted in their hearts or minds, with all its similarities and differences.

While the changes are undoubtedly deep and radical, one must not expect to see the old city crumbling down as in a disaster movie.[1] The city, says Giddens, "displays a specious continuity with pre-existing social orders" (1990: 6). Despite converging trends, path dependency (still) continues to structure differences among cities, and the pace of change, however fast, is still one that can be gauged only by historical standards.

A number of signs suggest that we are facing change of a deep *structural* nature, affecting the contemporary city both in the more developed and in the less developed areas of the world, albeit with remarkable differences in the various situations.

On one hand we notice the interruption and even the inversion of urbanization trends of secular breadth. On the other, the interest of scholars, local elites and the public in the urban question is growing disproportionately. In great cities the mundane problems of daily life, from traffic congestion to the quality of air and water, are the object of uninterrupted attention and discussion. Equally crucial are the problems of control of the urban social environment, manifesting themselves in widespread episodes of violence and criminality (and in related anxieties), the growing difficulties of providing collective urban services, and the various forms of local financial crises. The quality of air, the very medium absolutely essential for the physical survival of living organisms, is being monitored in real time in a growing number of urban areas, from Milan to Barcelona to Hamburg.

All these phenomena are occurring both in the USA and in Europe – showing a certain degree of convergence – but the models of governance and regulation and the founding patterns of the urban setting are quite different. Urban planning and the regulation of urban systems are far more binding in Europe than in the USA. This clearly influences the degree of control on future trends. In other words, despite converging macro-processes, outcomes and impacts depend very much on the local arrangements.

At the same time, governing elites of all major and minor centers are increasingly enthralled by the idea of *city marketing*: the advertisement of the mix of competitive localization advantages any given city can boast. The unabashed commodification of cities as sellable objects has become a matter of course only in very recent years, and can be easily dated to the early 1990s (Ashworth and Voogd 1990). Witness the strenuous fights between cities to attract important events such as the Olympic Games, soccer world championships, festivals, jubilees, and exhibitions. The main cities of the world get together in "clubs" and "lobbies," while a growing number of daily newspapers have specific sections dedicated to metropolitan issues. The enticing images of the new technologies blend with the subtle anxieties of daily life and with the morbid visions of an incipient urban Middle Age, *à la Gotham City*.

These visions have become highly intermeshed with the Adventist mood brought about in the last decade first by the approaching end of the old millennium, then by the devastating anxiety of the new one. Every generation, particularly in our change-conscious era, wants to be at the watershed of history, and the twentieth century has provided a bounty of symbolic turning points. Among the plethora of millennial signs, a particularly significant one tends to be forgotten. Around the turn of the century, more than half of the inhabitants of the planet have come to live in the social and physical context created by humanity for itself some 60–100 centuries back: the metropolis. This context will be vastly different, not only from the "original," but also from that of a few decades ago, in large part precisely because of the growing number of people involved.

In this chapter I sketch the conceptual tools needed to stimulate a growing awareness of the processes involved and their social consequences, showing some similarities and differences between US and West European cities emerging in this process. I add my contribution to an increasing body of literature on contemporary urbanization,[2] and I will do so in three steps. First, I will highlight some of the unresolved questions that arise from the observation of current urban trends. Second, I will suggest some answers based on a heuristic scheme proposed in my previous work.[3] Third, I will identify the consequences of the emerging social morphology for the governance of the contemporary urban world, particularly for the fate of public spaces. I will finally conclude by raising a couple of basic questions on the ways we observe the city.

Metropolitan Development and Population: The Paradox of Deurbanization

As is well known, during the second half of the 1970s and the following decade, and in almost all countries with advanced economies, urban growth underwent an abrupt and unforeseen slowdown. Before the end of the 1970s, urban development seemed universally bound to never end. In the following decade, the slowing down became evident. At the same time, the much popularized images of the crisis in all great industrial metropolises, from Glasgow to Milan or Turin in Europe or Detroit in the USA, set the stage for an inversion of previous prophecies of growth.

In the preceding decades, cities were depicted as "exploding," or as some sort of poisonous growth enveloping the planet; now the doomsayers have started to talk about the "death of the city," deurbanization and even about an implausible "return to the countryside." True, the death of the city has been heralded on various occasions in the past,[4] but this time the theoretical elaborations seemed to be supported by incontestable data. From the beginning of the industrial revolution, urban populations had grown following the rule that "the larger the center, the faster its growth." After 1971, this rule began to be challenged. In the intercensual decade 1971–81, the USA saw its non-metropolitan population grow faster than the metropolitan one. Similar trends were recorded in many European countries, although to varying degrees and in successive waves. These results were relayed to the public with great emphasis by the media and by scholars who shared the excitement of the discovery of such a downturn.

It was a mistake. Trends observed so far in most of the advanced economies indicate that cities are not disappearing but are undergoing a profound transformation, the full consequences of which are still to be fathomed.[5] If we do not recast rather radically our thinking about cities, it will be impossible to forecast even approximately future developments, despite the flood of symposia, special issues, research projects, and other discursive enterprises. Our concepts continue to be shaped according to an analytical model of the city embodying a static urban structure, while in today's metropolises the concept of "flow" would be more adequate to describe the new developments tied to current macroeconomic changes. It is to a certain extent fairly easy (too easy) to list all the theoretically possible conditions that will make cities liveable places in the future, from clean air to social peace and well-organized and abundant social services. However, without a clear idea of what is actually happening in the urban world, such a list will be little more than an exercise in futility.

I would like to contribute to the many efforts currently underway in this direction with an attempt to analyze urban changes, evading the straightjacket of strict social ecologic thinking and class analysis, based on the simple concept of *population*: namely, an aggregate of individuals defined by one or more simple common traits. Contrary to the kind of theoretic assumptions we need in order to analyze classes, movements, groups or organizations, it is possible to talk about populations without any strong assumption about their collective rationality. A population has simply some common traits and to explain its behavior we do not need to assume that it is aware of the collective rationale behind it.

An Analytical Framework for Understanding the Changing City

In current urban analyses many functions are considered, but the residential one is greatly overstated. Simple evidence of this lies in the fact that most statistics about cities are based on residential patterns and residential units of observation. On the other hand, it is quite evident that the new form of urban morphology is largely the product of the progressive individuation of several populations gravitating towards metropolitan centers, and in particular of four populations, increasingly differentiated from one another: inhabitants, commuters, city users, and metropolitan businesspeople. We can define these four populations by using three dichotomous variables: where the population lives, where it works and where it consumes (see Table 4.1).

As can be seen, apart from the technical difficulty in collecting data, measurement of these variables is conceptually neat, and labels are needed only for discursive purposes. In order to identify various types of urban morphologies, in the following paragraphs I will be using a simple combination of the four populations, differentiating between successive phases – generations – of metropolitan development.

Guido Martinotti

Table 4.1 The four urban populations and their characteristics

	Live	*Work*	*Consume*
A Inhabitants	Yes	Yes/No	Yes
B Commuters	No	Yes	(Yes)
C City users	No	No	Yes
D Metropolitan businesspeople	No	Yes	Yes

From the traditional city to the first generation metropolis

In the traditional town, on which all the current thinking about urban life is still largely based, the inhabitants, or the population living in the city, largely coincided with the population working in the city, especially if considering European cities from their Middle Ages' patterns onwards, as Max Weber (1922) and Pirenne (1925), among others, have shown with great clarity. City limits encompassed both these populations in one territory or spatial unit for millennia, until very recently encircled by walls and neatly separated from the rest of the land (5015, 6107). The additional population of market-goers, visitors, pilgrims or suppliers, while not irrelevant numerically or functionally, did not deeply affect the social and ecologic structure of the city. Until relatively few decades ago, city walls, even when they had lost their military relevance, retained administrative significance: tolls were paid at the entrance and doors were closed at night.

The industrial revolution did not greatly affect this situation, because production of goods in the secondary sector requires mostly the shifting of raw materials, manufactured goods and financial assets, while workers and entrepreneurs remain largely concentrated in urban areas, once the great transformation that has brought them there is completed. One important aspect of this traditional urban structure has to do with the structure of local government. This is based on the autonomy and franchise of inhabitants all over the world, and especially so in countries such as Italy, and several other European city systems, where the basic political patterns of local government (as well as the finely meshed network of settlements on the land) can be derived directly from original medieval (or earlier) characters (Lichtenberger 1976: 81–107).

The early metropolitan development that took place in the USA from the 1920s, and after World War II also in Europe (5859, 6230, 2790), can essentially be seen as a growing differentiation of two populations: the inhabitants and the workers. One can think of this early metropolitan development as two circles progressively separating from each other while they both grow in diameter, as in a Venn diagram. While a sizeable portion of the diagram remains overlapping, the two circles come increasingly apart. Commuting is the consequence of this process. From the sociologic point of view, the class structure of the commuting population is quite different and actually almost symmetrical in the USA and in Europe (people commuting from urban fringes in the USA generally belong to middle-class suburbs, while in Europe they generally belong to the working-class periphery) (5956, 2655, 6082). This is a result of a basic difference in city growth in the two systems. In Europe, contemporary cities grew around a medieval (or Roman) kernel. This kernel contains portions of land that are non-marketable: the cathedral and the *Rathaus* or the royal palace and their adjoining squares and other services (2426, 0274, 1995). This provided substantial stability, attraction for the elites, and overall ballast for the functions of the central core. In the USA, the original kernel of the city is usually functional: a harbor or a crossing railroad node, and no portion of the land is subtracted from the market. Thus, the central business district (CBD) is subject to the dynamics of change, competition, and succession so well described by the Chicago School. Not that the occasional developer would shy away from turning the Duomo, the Coliseum or the Parthenon into a multiplex or some other nice place; it is simply out of the question. However, Times Square or the Rockefeller Plaza, which have a comparable degree of sacredness for the New York population, are on sale. Despite the two different structures, the overall core-ring pattern is similar, and the urban morphology produced by this differentiation is the same (4518, 6551, 3544). The result is what I call the *first generation* (or *early*) *metropolis*, largely based on Functional Urban Regions (FURs) or commuting basins, and embodied in the concept of metropolitan area.

This new pattern introduced great changes in the organization of both US and European cities, but it was not totally disruptive of their original structures. Fordist features are embedded in planning traditions, growth chances, and development lines. For one thing, the commuter population spent most of the time in the central city secluded in working organizations and largely separated from the rest of the city population. Changes were indirect, affecting the socio-economic traits of urban regions and creating problems in the superimposition of new functional entities on existing administrative subdivisions. Difficulties were more acute in areas where the contrast was sharper. For instance, in the USA, the largely middle-class character of suburbs contributed to the fiscal crisis of central cities through the well-known phenomena of spillovers and free-riding, but on the other hand the flexibility of territorial administrative units like the county allowed fair degrees of adaptation. In general, European cities, where the fiscal system is largely centralized, work according to sophisticated compensation mechanisms or, most importantly, where middle classes until very recently remained in central cities (1375, 2439), the fiscal crisis did not take the same proportions registered in the USA (Martinotti 1981). On the other hand, the more rigid network of communal or municipal institutions delayed, and has actually so far prevented, administrative adaptation to an urban morphology having an increasingly metropolitan – if not regional – dimension that is far more composite and larger than the traditional European idea of "city" as the walled spatial unit mentioned above (Martinotti 1993; Rotelli 1999). All in all, however, early metropolitanization did coexist with the traditional urban structure to a fair degree.

No doubt what has been called a *standard metropolitan area*, following a considerable amount of studies culminating in the late 1960s, brought about the need to think of the changes in contemporary urbanization as an evolutionary process, provided, of course, that we purge this term of its linear implications. During the twentieth century, the urban form has undergone, and is still undergoing, profound changes. If we avoid the predicted apocalypses highlighting explosions or implosions, it is not difficult to recognize that the phases of this process trace the contour of an extraordinary evolutionary process in which the developments of one phase provide support for the next. In other words, this process has proven to be sustainable, which does not mean it is ideal or costless. It only means that the trend toward increasing urbanism has accelerated during the century, and it shows no signs of slowing down. Rather, indications are that powerful forces are still at work shaping our urban world in a consistent way, as suggested by the convergence theory put forward by Cohen (1996: 25–38). For these reasons, I speak of different *generations* of metropolises, distinguishable one from the other by considering the subsequent emerging mixes of populations identifiable with the simple analytical tools I have put forward.

City users, and the second generation metropolis

Early metropolitanization, based on the emergence of the commuter population, coexisted with traditional urban structures to a fairly large degree. However, the increased mobility of individuals, combined with higher income levels and greater leisure, allowed the differentiation of a third population: the population of city users – a population composed of persons going to a city mainly to use its private and public services, from shopping, to movies, to museums, to restaurants, to health and educational services. This is a swelling population that is having radical effects on the structure of cities and actually uses localities in a rather uncontrolled way. There are cities that have a very small population of inhabitants, a slightly larger population of commuters, but a vast population of users. Venice is a typical case. It has a resident population (shrinking) of approximately 70,000, a working population almost entirely composed of commuters, and on certain days it is visited by a population of visitors as large as its resident population. The density of people becomes so high that Venice is probably the only city in the world to have pedestrian traffic lights. Venice is an extreme special case, but many other cities in the world, and not only the so-called "cities of art," experience this phenomenon (2403, 2063, 6294).

London's airports handle more than 60 million people every year, and are expected to double this population in the next few years. A large chunk of this mass, numerically equivalent not to the inhabitants of London or any of the world metropolises, but to entire nations such as Italy or the UK, is composed of city users, coming and going and increasingly contributing to the economy of London, or of any other major metropolitan city.

In fact, because their economy increasingly depends on these non-resident populations, most contemporary cities of all sizes want to attract their share of city users (2961, 4978, 2657). Unlike the commuters, the users make use of, and sometimes abuse, the public areas of the city, more often than not in a rather barbaric way. Not surprisingly, at the end of 1989 the mayor of West Berlin declared that he was not worried about disposing of *Die Mauer* "because tourists will take it away."

The size of this population is growing but it is difficult to assess, precisely because all our collective cognitive apparatus is geared to a traditional city that is undergoing a profound mutation, and statistics still deal mainly with inhabitants, to a smaller degree with commuters, but practically in no way with users. Huge traffic clogs in central cities now no longer occur only in the rush hours – to a degree foreseeable and resolvable with public transportation systems – but during shopping sprees, and coinciding with great symbolic leisure moments. In Italy by far the most consistent boost to urban development in recent years came from the world soccer championship in 1990 and from the *Jubilaeum* in 2000. Competition for hosting the Olympic Games witnesses the increasing crucial importance attached to the city user population by local elites (2480, 2478).

Sociologically, the population of users is difficult to define, for the very lack of statistics just mentioned. An educated guess would assess it as being fairly differentiated, from hinterland kids roaming and cruising on evenings and weekends, to middle-class tourists and shoppers of all ages, to special groups like soccer fans or concert- and exhibition-goers. A theatre such as La Scala, traditionally the artistic and social temple of the Milanese population, is increasingly taken up, years in advance, by city users coming from faraway countries.

This phenomenon is far from being limited to tourist cities or to Western countries. Cities such as Singapore have more visitors than inhabitants and are entirely geared to consumption. They are not different, in many ways, from New York (5774), London (5545, 5547, 2434), or Milan, where, for instance, every year 300,000 Japanese visitors religiously visit the Last Supper as well as the fashion golden triangle. Amsterdam meets an increasingly serious problem of incoming temporary populations, particularly from England (0242, 0239).

However, differences between European and US cities subsist, even in relation to the above-mentioned changes existing in all Western economies. For instance, the city-building process (consisting in the creation of highly concentrated quarters for city users' needs) is a widespread form of city marketing in the USA, evoking the idea of a CBD typical of North American cities. In Europe this idea bumps into resistances for many reasons, partly outlined above. Planning in Europe is often oriented to balanced development, while mono-functional areas are seen as unfair for creating dweller-unfriendly and empty "holes" in the urban fabric; gentrification, not infrequently linked with the city-building process, meets stronger resistance than in the USA because heavy transformations of districts with their own history, identity, and traditions cause tensions with former inhabitants, who are not so happy to move away (see Chapter 10). Important socio-ecologic changes are at work also in the USA. A recent work by the Brookings Institution points to the intercensual dramatic decline of the number of US neighborhoods with a high poverty rate, but the prospect is that poverty migrated to the inner-ring suburbs (Jargowsky 2003). Summing up, urban policy on city marketing in Europe is less market-oriented, so that capitalistic competition is interwoven with other aspects having a social more than economic background (Kee and Molotch 2000).

Although direct competition or conflict between users and inhabitants is not evident, indirect competition (in the sense in which classic social ecology uses this term) is taking place. The user population is not attracted by purely residential areas, except when the latter fall into the category of "picturesque" (4069, 4958, 5019), but it heavily affects the spatial composition of central cities and of some specialized suburbs. Commercial and leisure areas of the city are most affected with increasingly profound impacts on the global social structure of the city. Areas such as the Parisian *Quartier Latin* (6001) or parts of Rome, London, New York, or scores of other cities teeming with discount stores, jeans shops, fast-food, and the omnipresent signs of the *rags multinational*, tend to selectively filter out the original population of the neighborhood, even when it initially constituted the local attraction in the first place. The same is happening in top commercial strips such as Rodeo Drive, Faubourg Saint Honoré or via Montenapoleone (6493, 2405, 2506). However, the population of city users is not limited to leisure or shopping. The city provides other services that can be used; for instance, those connected with mass education or health. In many cities around colleges and universities, students cause housing conflicts, particularly in neighborhoods (and on their fringes) called "college-towns" (2014, 3564, 2490, 1205). Even large cities nowadays have significant educational economies; as Tom Bender (1998) pointed out, the role of universities in shaping New York has been paramount. The type of metropolis that is growing out of the heightened gravitation of *city users* is the one we live in nowadays, with its strong tendencies towards homogenization and strong resilience by European cities. It is very different from the city we are accustomed to dealing with in popular and scientific terms and can be defined as the *second generation* (or *mature*) *metropolis*.

The third generation metropolis

In recent years, a fourth metropolitan population is differentiating itself. This is a small but growing and highly specialized population of metropolitan businesspeople – people who come into central cities to do business and establish professional contacts: visiting high level customers, convention-goers, consultants, and international managers. This fourth population is characterized by having a considerable availability of both private and corporate money. It typically stays for only a few days, sometimes for more extended periods, but it is not a permanent population. It spends part of the time doing business and part using the city, although at relatively high levels of consumption. This is a population of expert urbanites; individuals composing it tend to know their way around and to be very selective in terms of shopping and hotel and restaurant use, as well as in the use of top cultural amenities such as concerts, exhibitions, museums, but also saunas and gyms. Increasingly, business and top-level tourism go together (2996, 0292, 2733).

Both the city users and the metropolitan businesspeople are a product of the service industry. One little-explored sociologic aspect of the service industry is the fact that while secondary-type industries shift goods, *services* in large part require the shifting of population. There is no doubt that tourism, and urban tourism in particular, is a powerful driving force in this process of change, as Judd and Fainstein (1999) have shown in their illuminating book.

Despite a growing portion of services that can be delivered online, most of the services need face-to-face contacts, even when the partners are not terminal consumers, as in the important area of services to firms.

Consulting, public relations, marketing, and the like, but also teaching, acting, healing: all these activities require intense and in most cases repeated face-to-face interaction. For a moment, the prophets of the New Economy maintained that all these activities would rapidly go online. This did occur, but to nowhere near the extent anticipated and after a while it became clear that Amazon.com cannot thrive without UPS-type organizations, so service activities still attract people as well as virtual consumers. As for the future, very little can be said that does not run the danger of being challenged in a very short time.

The fourth population increasingly constitutes a transnational middle class, living not in *a* city, but in *cities*, or *between* cities.[6] This affects the morphology and functions of all large cities well beyond the group's numerical weight. For the sake of classificatory completeness, we can call this still-emerging metropolis the *third generation* (or *late*) *metropolis*.

The growth of the fourth population, the metropolitan businesspeople, signals another very important phenomenon: the internationalization or globalization of metropolitan centers. In Europe this trend has been to a degree broken by the strength of national urban cultures. For centuries the top-ranking cities of European urban systems embodied the specificity of local culture and traditions. Nineteenth century European national and regional capitals symbolized the climax of this dynamic: Vienna, Paris, London, Berlin, Milan, and Florence each offered themselves to the learned traveler as a unique city, with distinct languages, architecture, cultural institutions, and social mores, proudly displaying the best of their respective national or regional character. The facade of this identity is still standing (2426, 6239, 0860, 2441, 0516), despite World War II destruction and post-war oftentimes destructive reconstruction, but the homogenization is at work. The London skyline displays vividly the superimposition of the old and new architectural patterns (6280). The fight against fast-food shops in several European capitals (4762, 6484, 3161, 2136), Rome and Paris in particular, far from being a marginal episode, is a nodal indicator of the conflict between the traditional national and urban identity immanent in European cities, which includes the culinary culture, and one of the most aggressive modern multinationals whose commercial success is precisely based on an extremely fastidious imposition of product and labor-force standardization.

Reference to fast-food is also more than anecdotal. In fact, as the city users' population increases, fast-food and catering in general become a growing strategic economic urban function in metropolitan centers, adding a new angle to the emerging class structure. Catering and related industries are actually the portion of the labor market that overwhelmingly attracts another growing segment of the new metropolitan population: low-level foreign workers from developing countries. The services required by city users[7] and metropolitan businesspeople are largely furnished by marginal workers. It would be preposterous to extend the argument to the point of seeing here a new class conflict reproducing the traditional one between the factory owner and the factory worker, but there is no doubt, to my mind, that the incipient class polarization, noted by several studies, is largely connected with the impact of the new populations of metropolitan *users* as opposed to *dwellers* or *workers*. Saskia Sassen has shown very clearly that there is a relation between the economy of the global city and the "vast supply of low-wage jobs required by high-income gentrification in both its residential and commercial sectors" (1991: 9).

The above analysis receives additional insights in the frame of Giddens' concept of "disembedding" as a trait constituent of what he calls "radical modernity," a concept that I found more illuminating and analytically powerful than the current cult term of postmodernity (Giddens 1990). The concept highlights the importance of knowledge allocation and conflict control; in a disembedded society, relations are stretched in the spatial and time dimensions to the point where the local framework of reference fades away. There, many people lose full control over their own actions, which can be heavily influenced by unknown and distant persons operating in the global scenario.

Class structure in the new metropolis

Positing of these *four populations* does not imply that more traditional class relations and conflicts have disappeared, but there is little doubt that they are undergoing deep transformations that undermine some of the classic socio-ecologic factors of urban class conflict. The strength of the industrial urban proletariat was to a large degree, as has been noted repeatedly since Marx, a function of its territorial organization. Working-class districts reinforced and projected on the urban plane the class solidarity, so to speak, created in the factory, while the organization of traditional working-class parties and movements relied heavily on the urban ecologic niches in which subcultural factors created an extraordinary synergy of economic, social, and political interactions (1949, 6334, 2794). Much of the lore about industrial cities and early metropolitan areas are centered on these essential components of the urban landscape, which tend to wane in the present-day metropolis. In purely numerical terms, the *inhabitants* are probably the most disfavored of the four populations by the overall dynamic. However, *commuters* are also probably shrinking or, more specifically, changing to more circumferential trajectories vis-à-vis center–peripheral ones. In fact, often even top-level coordination functions tend to move to the periphery of large conurbations. All in all then, the traditional class cleavages and solidarities, while by all means still existing and perceivable, give way to new cleavages and group realignments.

The glittering image of the city of consumers seems at odds with the growth of visibly impoverished populations in most cities of the world. The answer to this apparent paradox is that all four populations are stratified, albeit at a slanted angle,[8] from which we can see the entire class structure changing in an interactive way. Limiting ourselves to the class structure of the industrial city, we can say that with the rise of industrialism, cities became ugly places of toil, human misery, and social and physical ills: unhealthy houses, insalubrious streets, but also unbreathable air ("*mala aria urbana*" in the original meaning of malaria), were common aspects of urban life in nineteenth century metropolises (6383, 0519, 1637). The emergence of the welfare state and the Fordist direction taken by industrial development eased the filling of the gap, so that some scholars began talking about the death of social classes, "dissolved" in the great container constituted by the middle class. Nowadays, the decline of Fordism and the subsequent macro-economic perturbations in the service economy, together with the fiscal crisis of nation-states (which led to the end of the golden age of the welfare state and its redistributive policies), originated new forms of stratification and new risk areas which made polarizing tendencies emerge again.

The reader will find accounts of the bottom end of this polarization in many chapters in the second part of this book. As for the top end, the French sociologist Denis Duclos has introduced the concept of *Hyperbourgeoisie* (1998), which has several points of contact with what I have in mind in referring to the population of the metropolitan business world. Despite the fact that I find it too highly politically loaded (not surprisingly in view of the orientation of the journal where it appeared), and more evocative than analytical, I find the concept very interesting and pointing in the right direction for additional research. A theoretically stronger work in the same direction is *The Transnational Capitalist Class* by Leslie Sklair (2001).

This social group is fairly varied, but it is increasingly identifiable:[9] managers of multilocal enterprises, both private *and* public, such as the large number of international organizations (UN, ILO, UNESCO, OECD, etc.) and the growing family of European governmental bodies – businesspeople, international consultants, academics, performers, sports personalities, and the like. This population requires fairly similar services all over the world: hotels, offices, and meeting places, restaurants, shopping centers, and so on (2353, 2070, 2741, 6621). The result is already visible in large sectors of several world cities (in Europe, for instance London, Brussels . . .). Among the postcards that the traveler can buy in any airport news-stand, there is one that can be bought the world over, reproducing the local skyline. Increasingly, these skylines, as well as the urban areas they depict, tend to look alike (6303, 4679, 3034, 2339). This is not surprising, because increasingly these areas are not the product of national economies, but a segmental unit of a larger entity (Friedmann and Wolff 1982). Hotels, offices, and commercial centers, built by the same companies in many cities, go together with the standardization of local shops interested in catering to an increasingly homogeneous trans-national population of urban travelers.

Consequences for the Urban Sciences

In all respectable scientific enterprises, including the sciences of the city, namely the various "urbanologic" enterprises from city history to city planning, knowledge is based on the quality of observational tools. Much can be said in favor of direct observation of city life. The city is an eminently visible phenomenon, although literary and occasional onlookers tend to be misled by what they can see in the open. A large part of the total social life takes place out of view. Valuable as it may be, direct observation only tells a partial story about urban society. Society, after all, is literally invisible and can only be inferred by the traces it leaves. The bulk of our knowledge of the social or invisible aspects of the city comes from the large body of systematic data collection that we call "statistics." In all countries, the majority of the "statistics" pertaining to cities is com-posed of census-type data. These data are universally used by planners, local administrators, newspeople and scholars, all of whom consider them to be endowed with a high degree of validity. Undoubtedly, they appear as data of a "harder" nature than the "soft" sample survey data. However, census-type data are not observational data at all, but recordings of indi-vidual verbal behavior, with all the limitations that affect survey results and a few additional ones. The quality of the individual data collection is not very high. The advantage to the researcher is that census-type data are by definition exhaustive of a given population, and therefore can be used to construct ecologically based maps or tables. Better coverage and, in some cases, even more reliable data, come from "process-produced data", such as the various population registers or the growing number of organizational databases. These are the traces that people leave during their passage through the bureaucratic maze. As I have indicated else-where (Martinotti 1993), and as every urban scholar knows very well, these traces, which are part of the organizational knowledge of our times, are often extremely useful and reliable.

Both primary data for urban research, such as census-derived data, and process-produced data, in addition to their well-known technical limitations, have a further weakness deriving from the changes in urban social structure outlined in this chapter. Census data, as well as process-produced data based on administrative records, are collected at the place in which people live. Census schedules are very specific about this; their instructions call for the identification of the persons who are in a given location "at midnight" of the census tallying day. This means that these data provide an image of the *dormant city*. Thus, the immense variety of thematic maps of social aspects of the city – which scholars have been using to draw their social models of cities ever since the Chicago School and even earlier, starting at least from John Graunt (1662) and Sir William Petty in the seventeenth century – produce snapshots of the urban population *asleep*.

In the past, the *sleeping city* and the *active* one overlapped to a very large degree. The map of the sleeping city would not differ considerably from that of the working city, if the unit of observation was the block or the neighborhood. With the rise of the first generation metropolis, and increasingly with the growth of the city users' populations, the difference between the two becomes progressively more significant. While the non-resident populations become more and more visible on the streets, they are invisible in the statistics. Of course, these populations are tallied in one way or another, for example through directories, airports, hotels, exhibition checkpoints and rosters, and credit reports. There is no systematic or public way, however, in which these new populations are measured, or even estimated exhaustively. Quite apart from the fact that most of these data are patently beyond the reach of social scientists – who, by the way, would be much more careful and innocuous users of data of this kind than the snoopers who currently get their hands on them – what is really damaging for the knowledge of urban phenomena is the quantitative disparity between these and the more traditional data. It is fair to say that inhabitants account for the great majority of available data, commuters for a very small proportion, and the remaining populations very little indeed. Data about the users' population may be sometimes, but not very often, of high quality (top-level survey data on travelers, hotel and exhibition guests, for example) but they are *scattered* data. This means that we are looking at today's city with biased eyes and this is no minor problem.

Conclusions

The deep transformation that urban systems in advanced economies are undergoing brought about cities in which at least three urban formations are intermeshed in the territorial reality (this is particularly true of regions with millenary urban history such as Europe):

1   The traditional town (with all its historical variations) that can be defined as an entity in which the commune, or its institutional and physical morphology, coincides with a community, a sociological entity defined by interactions among individuals, groups, classes, and organizations.

2   The mid-twentieth century metropolis embodied in the idea of the metropolitan area – an entity less easily definable than the traditional city, but still fairly interpretable by a functional system, large, but limited in area (albeit with uncertain borders) and dominated by a center (core)–periphery (fringes) morphology with strong homogenization tendencies.

3   A new entity that is still difficult to grasp and that has been variously defined as an open network with no central places, or with a plurality of "nodes," not necessarily arranged in a clear hierarchical order.

The latter entity is rather harder to map on the territory, and has borders varying by many orders of magnitude, depending on the particular "net" we decide to make reference to. We can call this entity second generation metropolis or world city or global city, depending on the analytical framework we choose. No matter what precise definitions we accept for the new urban form, many of the social problems of contemporary metropolitan societies depend on the coexistence and superimposition of these three "urban layers." The first generation metropolis has not totally substituted the traditional towns, and the network city still contains towns and metropolitan areas. The highly intertwined new urban form poses problems for its conceptual definition, its empirical description (the above-mentioned problem of data) and its governance. In the latter issue, the European heritage plays an important part in defining the frame within which social consequences will be dealt with: European urban history feeds a "path dependent" resistance to standardization, so that spontaneous overwhelming changes in macro-dimensions of social life encounter a higher informal and institutional resilience than in North American metropolises. However, it is not clear to what degree local specificities will in the end constitute clear-cut differences from the development of the "European city model" advocated by Jacques Delors (1994), or whether macrovariables will in the end prevail to give birth to a more homogeneous type of twenty-first century metropolis.

NOTES

1   Although disasters of all sorts, from earthquakes to technological glitches to violent acts, are looming, and this should be a sobering thought.

2   The list is long, but not as long as one would expect. In my opinion, only recently have social scientists started to delineate the contours of the new urbanization in a way not hampered by mental categories founded on disused urban forms (i.e. works making a deliberate effort to look at the emerging urban form by connecting changes in the economy with technological innovation and social change). Among the most important ones, in addition to the initial work of John Friedmann and Goetz Wolff (1982) and Friedmann (1986), I would list Bagnasco (1986) Bianchini and Parkinson (1993), Castells and Hall (1994), Castells (1996), Logan and Molotch (1987), Masser et al. (1992), Pumain and Godard (1996), Sorkin (1994), Sudjic (1993) and, most prominently, Sassen (1991, 1995). On the European specificities see Bagnasco and Le Galès (2000) and Le Galès (2002). Recently, the work of Richard Florida (2002) has added an important angle to the comprehension of urban dynamics.

3   Originally in *Metropoli* (Martinotti 1993). Further versions can be found in Martinotti (1996, 1997). I give credit to the European Foundation in Dublin and the EU Commission for permission to reprint and revise parts of the English version of the report. Parts are published also in Beauregard and Body-Gendrot (1999).

4   See the interesting comment on this theme in Harvey's introduction to his work on postmodernity (1989: 4–9).

5   An excellent and early attempt to understand the parable of US cities from the "Verge of Catastrophe" to "Arising from the Ashes" can be found in Beauregard (1993).

6   I thank the late Roy Drewett for this formulation. Easy for him, who was an outstanding member of this new population.

7   With this term I do not refer to the distinction between use value and exchange value of the city, such as adopted by Logan and Molotch (1987), although a good deal of my reasoning seems to go in the same direction.

8   The issue of the relation of these populations with the migration dynamics has been treated in an earlier work (Martinotti 1993) but needs further clarification. Migrants are by definition persons changing abode from one place to another. Whether the change is stable, as in most traditional migration, or temporary, as in the case of vagrant populations, is mostly a question of legal definition. In all cases, migration affects mostly the composition of the inhabitants' population. Unfortunately, even scientific writings tend to use the word "immigrant" to mean "poor immigrants," as well as to think of "temporary" populations as homeless or hobos or marginal populations. This habit is highly misleading and should be carefully avoided. Some of the more derelict populations in contemporary cities are elderly long-term residents, while temporary populations of metropolitan businesspersons can be very rich. An albeit cognate but separate issue is the class structure of the four populations. These issues have been explored in depth by Giampaolo Nuvolati (2002) and it is useful to talk of all the populations that do not inhabit a given city as non-resident populations (NRPs).

9   There is very little research conducted on this population, at least to my knowledge, and even less so by urban sociologists. See, however, the interesting book by Jane Marceau (1989) or Sklair (2001).

REFERENCES

Ashworth, G.J. and Voogd, H. (1990) *Selling the City: Marketing Approaches in Public Sector Urban Planning*. Belhaven Press, New York.

Bagnasco, A. (1986) *Torino: Un profilo sociologico*. Einaudi, Torino.

Bagnasco, A. and Le Galès, P. (eds.) (2000) *Cities in Contemporary Europe*. Cambridge University Press, Cambridge.

Beauregard, R.A. (1993) *Voices of Decline*. Blackwell, Cambridge, MA.

Beauregard, R.A. and Body-Gendrot, S. (eds.) (1999) *The Urban Moment*. Sage, London.

Bender, T. (ed.) (1988) *The University and the City: From Medieval Origins to the Present*. Oxford University Press, Oxford.

Bianchini, F. and Parkinson, M. (eds.) (1993) *Cultural Policy and Urban Regeneration: The West European Experience*. Manchester University Press, Manchester.

Castells, M. (1996) *The Information Age: Economy, Society and Culture*. Vol. I, *The Rise of the Network Society*. Blackwell, Oxford.

Castells, M. and Hall, P. (1994) *Technopoles of the World: The Making of the 21st Century Industrial Complexes*. Routledge, London.

Cohen, M.A. (1996) The hypothesis of urban convergence: are cities in the North and South becoming more alike in an age of globalization? In: Cohen, M.A., Aruble, B., Tulchin, J.S., and Garland, A.M. (eds.) *Preparing for the Urban Future: Global Pressures and Local Forces*. Johns Hopkins University Press, Baltimore.

Delors, J. (ed.) (1994) *En quête d'Europe*. Éditions Apogée, Rennes.

Duclos, D. (1998) La naissance de l'hyperbourgeoisie. *Le Monde Diplomatique*, August, 16–17.

Florida, R. (2002) *The Rise of the Creative Class*. Basic Books, New York.

Friedmann, J. (1986) The world city hypothesis. *Development and Change*, 17: 69–84.

Friedmann, J. and Wolff, G. (1982) World city formation: an agenda for research and action. *International Journal of Urban and Regional Research*, 6 (3): 309–344.

Giddens, A. (1990) *The Consequences of Modernity*. Stanford University Press, Stanford.

Graunt, J. (1662) Natural and political observations on the bills of mortality. (http://www.ac.wwu.edu/~stephan/Graunt/bills.html)

Harvey, D. (1989) *The Condition of Postmodernity*. Basil Blackwell, Oxford.

Jargowsky, P.A. (2003) *Stunning Progress, Hidden Problems: The Dramatic Decline of Concentrated Poverty in the 1990s*. The Brookings Institution (May).

Judd, D.R. and Fainstein, S. (1999) *The Tourist City*. Yale University Press, New Haven.

Kee, W. and Molotch, H. (2000) *Building Rules: How Local Controls Shape Community Environments and Economies*. Westview, Boulder.

Le Galés, P. (2002) *European Cities: Social Conflicts and Governance*. Oxford University Press, Oxford.

Lichtenberger, E. (1976) The changing nature of European urbanization. In: Berry, B.J.L. (ed.) *Urbanization and Counter-urbanization*. Urban Affairs Annual Review No 11. Sage, Beverly Hills.

Logan, J.R. and Molotch, H. (1987) *Urban Fortunes: Making Place in the City*. University of California Press, Berkeley.

Marceau, J. (1989) *A Family Business? The Making of an International Business Elite.* Cambridge University Press, Cambridge.

Martinotti, G. (1981) The illusive autonomy: central control and decentralisation in the Italian local financial system. In: Sharpe, L.J. (ed.) *The Local Fiscal Crisis in Western Europe.* Sage Publications, London.

Martinotti, G. (1993) *Metropoli: La nuova morfologia sociale della città.* Il Mulino, Bologna.

Martinotti, G. (1996) Four populations: human settlements and social morphology in contemporary metropolis. *European Review,* 4 (1): 3–23.

Martinotti, G. (1997) *Perceiving, Conceiving, Achieving the Sustainable City: A Synthesis Report.* European Foundation for the Improvement of Living and Working Conditions, Loughlingstown, Dublin.

Masser, I., Sviden, O., and Wegener, M. (1992) *The Geography of Europe's Futures.* Belhaven Press, London.

Nuvolati, G. (2002) *Popolazioni in movimento, città in trasformazione: Abitanti, pendolari, city users, uomini d'affari e flâneurs.* Il Mulino, Bologna.

Pirenne, H. (1925) *Medieval Cities.* Princeton University Press, New Jersey.

Pumain, D. and Godard, F. (1996) *Données urbaines.* Anthropos, Paris.

Rotelli, E. (1999) Le aree metropolitane in Italia. In: Martinotti, G. (ed.) *La dimensione metropolitana.* Il Mulino, Bologna.

Sassen, S. (1991) *The Global City: New York, London, Tokyo.* Princeton University Press, Princeton, NJ.

Sassen, S. (1995) *Losing Control: Sovereignity in an Age of Globalisation.* Columbia University Press, New York.

Sklair, L. (2001) *The Transnational Capitalist Class.* Blackwell, Oxford.

Sorkin, M. (ed.) (1994) *Variations on a Theme Park: The New American City and the End of Public Space.* Noonday, New York.

Sudjic, D. (1993) *The 100 Mile City.* Flamingo, London.

Weber, M. (1922) *Wirtschaft und Gesellschaft: Grundriss der Verstehenden Soziologie.* Mohr, Tübingen.

5

Capitalism and the City: Globalization, Flexibility, and Indifference

Richard Sennett

Introduction

Urban life has a peculiar cultural value that makes it worthwhile to live in cities, even in decaying urban areas. In particular, two urban virtues define the urban context. The first one relates to sociability; a city is a place where people can learn to live with strangers. The practice of modern democracy demands that citizens learn how to enter into the experience and interests of unfamiliar lives. Society progresses when people's experience is not just limited to those who resemble them in class, race, or ways of life. Sameness stultifies the mind, diversity stimulates and expands it. Cities are places where learning to live with strangers can happen directly, bodily, physically, on the ground.

The size, density, and diversity of urban populations make this sensate contact possible – but not inevitable. One of the key issues in urban life, and in urban studies, is how to make the complexities a city contains actually interact. If contact occurs, and people can make a life with those who are not like themselves, a cosmopolitan setting rises.

The second urban virtue derives directly from the first and relates to subjectivity. The experience of urban life can teach people how to live with multiplicity within themselves. The experience of complexity is not just an external event, it reflects back on individuals' sense of themselves. People can develop multiple images of their own identities, knowing that who they are shifts, depending upon who they are with. Moreover, complex social systems tend to be open-ended rather than tightly closed; they are incomplete ways of living that can reflect back into the subjective realm, as lessons about human limits and the irresolvable and necessarily incomplete character of experience.

In principle, of course, everyone can have a complex inner life – apart from the place one lives – but the urban milieu furnishes a fundamental feature, i.e. the concrete materials for developing that consciousness. Again, this is a possibility rather than inevitability; the specific conditions of a particular city might prompt people to shut out that evidence, treat the crowded street as a space of fear rather than a space of self-knowledge.

Levinas (1991) asserts that when a person's experience is so complex as to become multiply defined or open-ended, he or she has need of others – others whom he or she does not know. Levinas calls this "the neighborliness of strangers" (*proximité des inconnus*) – a definition aptly capturing the aspiration city planners ought to have in designing cities. This *confession de foi* sets the stage for other less spiritual themes, which will be the focus of this chapter. The virtues of urban sociability and subjectivity were played out a century ago, when urban studies began, in terms of a dialectic between rigidity and strangeness; today they are played out in terms of a dialectic between flexibility and indifference.

My argument, which I will try to sum up below, is that a great change in capitalism has transformed the context of urban cultural values.

Rigidity and Strangeness

To understand this duality, we need to recall that although cities are as ancient as human civilization, the discipline of urban studies is only a century old. It took root first in sociology and geography, then spread to economics, political science and, more recently, anthropology. In sociology, we owe to German writers such as Weber and Simmel the first modern analyses of cities; this "Berlin School" at the turn of the century inspired in some of its American students a desire to work more collaboratively, and they did so at the University of Chicago from the 1910s to the 1940s.

Both the Berlin and Chicago Schools took form in an age of bureaucratic stabilization. Nineteenth century capitalism was frequently anarchic and disorganized, but unwillingly so. In Germany, the Bismarckian era saw an effort to remedy these crises through consolidating the relations between the state and private enterprise; government was to supply the rule the free market lacked. In the USA, the massive formation of monopolies by Rockefeller, Gould, and Carnegie similarly sought to escape the competitive eruptions of the market. The "search for order" as the historian Robert Wiebe (1967) put it, bred enterprises on an ever larger scale, and with ever more internally complex bureaucratic structures. In turn, this arduous history affected cities, and what urbanists could say about them.

For the moment, I want to delay discussing how that happened, and focus on its opposite, the other side of the urban dialectic: the importance accorded to strangers and strangeness. This was Georg Simmel's subject par excellence. In a letter he wrote to a friend about Potzdammerplatz in Berlin, he evoked the cacophony of languages he heard, the strange costumes of the people in the great square. As he would later write, "the urbanite is a stranger" (Simmel 1903, 1908). By this, he meant to describe – in modern jargon – a condition of alterity rather than of difference: not a fixed classificatory scheme of identity but rather the unknown other, marked by strangeness. Alterity is a provoker, a force of anxiety, because you do not know what the other will do, how he or she might behave – and each of us bears this power to provoke unease in a crowd.

The power of strangeness makes sense in the conditions of Simmel's time. Berlin (0526, 0516) was in the midst of rural-to-urban migration, and these migrants came not just from Prussia, but from Poland, Hungary, and the Balkans; speaking languages other than German, the rural cultures they brought with them were not at all of a piece. Equally important at this stage of capitalism, there was as yet no culture of mass consumption that unified people as social subjects in the city; the consolidation of production preceded the standardization of consumption, so that desire, taste and lifestyles were discontinuous and puzzling. We could as easily cite parallel material phenomena in New York in 1900 (0250, 0249); the complex world of immigrants on the lower East Side squeezing hard south against Wall Street, north against the bourgeois WASP residential neighborhood around Washington Square. Alterity was the material condition of urban culture.

At that time, patterns of urban change were similar both in Europe and America. Both were a kind of *agora*, a meeting ground where differences get in touch in a mixed social space. However, American cities developed in a distinctive way, which would influence the structure of public life, the spatial narratives and the forms of power.

Strangeness as alterity is a force that Simmel celebrated in cities. Like Joyce or Proust, Simmel believed the stranger was the bearer of a new freedom. To give an American example of what the German sociologist meant, we can instance Willa Cather. When she finally arrived in New York's Greenwich Village in 1906, Cather, who had been haunted in small-town America that her lesbianism would be discovered, wrote to a friend, "at last, in this indecipherable place, I can breathe." Simmel's own labors aimed at specifying just how, on crowded streets and squares, the freedom of strangeness, the freedom of alterity, played itself out. In public, the urbanite dons an impassive mask, acts cool and indifferent to others on the street; in private, however, he or she is aroused by these strange contacts, disturbed and reactive. Certainties are shaken in the presence of others: subjective life seethes behind the protective mask (Simmel 1903).

In itself, this is a highly Romantic view of the city, but it acquires weight precisely because the subjective stimulation of strangeness is depicted in exactly the same places ruled by the emerging forces of bureaucratic rigidity. Bureaucratic rigidity was the great theme of Max Weber (1922), Simmel's colleague and protector. In the Berlin of their time, you would only have to look at the insurance companies, banks and railroad corporations housed in structures meant to resemble Egyptian temples or Renaissance palaces to see the realization of the desire for economic stability in stone.

We owe to Simmel's student Robert Park, and to Park's student Louis Wirth, an analysis of how the organizational consolidation of capitalization could be related to the territory of a city, rather than just to its architecture. Though Park (1926) remained loyal to Simmel's insights into urban subjectivity, which the young American rephrased as the "moral order" of the city, when Park returned to Chicago he had to take up the other side of the coin. Both Park and Wirth sought to depict an ecologic division of land based on the division of labor in modern capitalism. The most interesting maps the Chicago School produced of the city were maps of where different functions occurred in the city; you can find them, for instance, in a book with a resoundingly dull title, *One Hundred Years of Chicago Land Values*, written by Homer Hoyt (1933). Louis Wirth tied directly these data on the functional articulation of urban space to the phenomenon of bureaucratization.

How is it possible then, to relate the ecology of the city to the figure of the stranger and the freedom of alterity? How is it possible, as Park put it, that the city is both a "place on the map" and a "moral order"? The Chicago urbanists responded by imagining the urbanite as a permanent internal migrant traveling through the city's ecology. Wirth (1938), for instance, depicted the city as a mosaic of different roles in different places – what he called "segmented roles" – but he argued that the subject transcends each of his or her roles in space. The idea of a subject superior to his or her surroundings is familiar to us in the writings of Wirth's contemporary Walter Benjamin (1936) – specifically in Benjamin's figure of the *flaneur*. Less imaginative, Wirth was interested in the examples of second generation immigrants in Chicago and the city's nascent black bourgeoisie. Both groups seemed to him at the same time located in an ever more defined urban ecology and mobile across fixed territories. In their lack of a single definition, in their multiple identities, lay their freedom.

The dialectic between strangeness and rigidity defined the "mental compass" of modern urban studies when it first began. Like any serious version of culture, it both embodied and addressed contradictions. In the visual realm, for instance, the urban design of this time sought both to flee the anxiety of strangeness of the city yet preserve the freedom of the urbanite. This is the great drama in Daniel Burnham's plan of 1909 for Chicago, at once an attempt to impose a rigidly functional order on the city, yet in each of the city's zones to mix the different classes and immigrant groups in the city. German and Viennese city planners were attracted by the healthy qualities of the Garden City movement of Ebenezer Howard (1902) in Britain and simultaneously repelled by its infantile simplicities (2574, 2577, 5597).

Today, many of the material conditions that formed the first era of urban studies a century ago still continue: the flood of immigrants into cities, for example. And we continue – as indeed we should – to think of alterity as a social condition that holds out the promise of subjective freedom, freedom from arbitrary definition and identification. However, the larger conditions of capitalism have taken a new turn, and this change in political economy has altered both the nature of the city itself and the intellectual tools we need to understand our own times.

Flexibility and Indifference

When we talk about a new stage in capitalism, we are really pointing at two phenomena. One is the globalization of labor and capital flows. The other consists of a transformation in production, that is, a change in institutions and bureaucracies so that people can work more flexibly and less rigidly.

The word "new" instantly arouses suspicion, because it belongs to the realm of advertising. Labor migration and multinational finance are long-established in the capitalist economy, but in the last generation they have been reformulated. Banks no longer trade within national constraints; labor migrants have found new international routes; changes in workplaces have similarly not been conjured out of thin air. Anarco-syndicalists have long argued for less rigid workplaces, an argument that, by a rich irony, modern capitalists have taken to heart.

As the bureaucratic revolution that had made capitalism flexible is a less topical and mediatic subject than globalization, I will start with it.

Max Weber's (1922) description of rational bureaucracy was founded on an analogy between military and business organization. His image for both was the bureaucratic triangle: the more the rational division of labor progressed, the more slots opened up unequally; the need for different kinds of soldiers or workers expanded far more rapidly than the need for more generals or bosses. The chain of command within this triangle operated on the principle that each niche had a distinctive function; efficiency dictated that there is as little duplication as possible. The general can thus strategically control platoons far from his command post; the corporation executive can determine how the assembly line or back office functions.

In industrial production, Weber's triangle became embodied in the phenomenon of Fordism, a kind of military micro-management of a worker's time and effort which a few experts could dictate from the top. It was graphically illustrated by General Motors' Willow Run auto plant in America – a mile long, quarter mile wide edifice in which raw iron and glass entered, as it were, at one end and a finished car exited at the other. Only a strict, controlling work regime could coordinate production on this giant scale. In the white-collar world, the strict controls of corporations such as IBM in the 1960s mirrored this industrial process.

A generation ago businesses began to revolt against the Weberian triangle. They sought to "de-layer" organizations, to remove levels of bureaucracy, making use of new information technologies in place of bureaucrats. They sought to destroy the practice of fixed-function work, substituting instead teams that work short-term on specific tasks – teams that are shuffled when the organization embarks on new projects. Just as these techniques enabled businesses to respond externally to new market opportunities, the organizations sought to create internal markets. In this new business strategy, teams compete against one another, trying to re-spond effectively as quickly as possible to goals set by the top. Internal markets mean that the old Weberian logic of efficiency is overthrown; instead of each person doing his or her own particular bit in a defined chain of command, there is duplication of function, many different teams compete to do the same task fastest, best. All these practices are meant to make corporations flexible, able to change quickly within in response to rapidly changing conditions without.

The apologists for this new world of work claim it is more democratic than the military-style organization of the past, but in reality that is not the case. In place of the Weberian triangle, an image of the new realm of power might be a circle with a dot in the center. At the center, a small number of managers rule, make decisions, set tasks, judge results. The information revolution has given it more instantaneous control over the corporation's workings than in the old system, where orders often modulated and evolved as they passed down the chain of command. The teams working on the periphery of the circle are left free to respond to output targets set by the center, free to devise means of executing tasks in competition with one another, but are not free to decide what those tasks are.

In the Weberian triangle of bureaucracy, rewards came for doing one's job as best one could; in the dotted circle, they come to teams winning over other teams – which the economists Frank and Cook (1996) call winner-take-all organization; sheer effort no longer produces reward. This bureaucratic reformulation, Frank and Cook argue, contributes to the great inequalities of pay and perks in flexible organizations: in short, the material realities of inequality and workplace democracy are absolutely poles apart.

To understand the effect of this new form of organization on the urban places in which people live, we have to specify one further characteristic of flexibility: its time dimension. The mantra of the flexible workplace is "no long term." The short-term dimensions of time are evident in the replacement of clear career paths within fixed organizations by jobs – jobs that consist of specific and limited tasks; when the task ends, often the job is over. In the high-tech sector in Silicon Valley, the average length of employment is now approximately 8 months. The re-engineering of corporations often leads to abrupt, involuntary job change; in the shifting world of flexible work – as in advertising, the media, and financial services – voluntary job change follows an erratic path, people tending to make lateral, ambiguous moves. Finally, within a given corporation, the emphasis on tying teams to tasks means that people are constantly changing their working associates – modern management theory argues the "shelf life" of a team ought to be a year at most.

These changes in institutional time, I want to make clear, do not dominate the workplace at present, no more than global finance is the dominant mode of finance. Rather, they represent a leading edge of change, an aspiration of what businesses ought to become: no one is going to start a new organization based on the principle of permanent jobs.

To turn back to corporations, just as the space of power in the flexible organization is not democratic, so the time dimension of these institutions promotes neither loyalty nor fraternity. Business leaders who were once enthusiasts for constant corporation reinvention are beginning, as it were, to sober up. It is hard to feel committed to a corporation that has no defined character, hard to act loyally to an unstable institution that shows no loyalties to you. Lack of commitment translates into poor productivity, and to an unwillingness to keep a corporation's secrets.

The lack of fraternity bred by "no long term" is rather more subtle. Task-work puts people under enormous stress; on losing teams, recrimination tends to mark the final stages of working together. Again, trust of an informal sort takes time to develop; you have to get to know people, which team break-ups short circuit. The experience of being only temporarily in an organization prompts people to keep loose, not to get involved, because they are going to exit soon. Practically, this lack of mutual engagement is one of the reasons it is so hard for labor unions to organize workers in flexible industries or businesses, from Mac-job workers to call-center employees and developers. The sense of fraternity as a shared fate, a durable set of common interests, has been weakened. Socially, the short-term regime produces a paradox: people work intensely, under great pressure, but their relations to others remain curiously superficial. This is not a world in which getting deeply involved with other people makes much sense in the long run.

My argument is precisely that flexible capitalism has the same effects on the city as in the workplace itself. Just as flexible production produces more superficial, short-term relations at work, this capitalism creates a regime of superficial and disengaged relations in the city. This dialectic of flexibility and indifference is a challenge both to those who live in cities and those who study them. In this case, the difference between European and American cities often fades and is jeopardized. Other more transversal differences become important, like the one between globalized and non-globalized cities, which create a map of areas that are largely interchangeable.

The dialectic of flexibility and indifference appears in three forms. The first is expressed in physical attachment to the city; the second expressed in the standardization of the urban environment; the third in relations between family and urban work.

The issue of physical attachment to place is perhaps the most self-evident of the three. Rates of geographic mobility are very high for flexible workers. Service temp-workers are a good example – and temp-work is the single fastest-growing sector of the labor market. Temp-work nurses are, for instance, eight times more likely to move house in a 2-year period as single-employer nurses; mainframe servicemen are 11 times more likely than their single-employer mates. Lack of fixed work means less attachment to place.

In the higher reaches of the economy, executives in the past frequently moved as much as in the present, but the movement was different in kind; they remained within the groove of a company, and the company defined their "place," the turf of their lives, no matter where they were on the map. It is just that institutional thread which the new workplace breaks. Some urbanists, such as Sharon Zukin (1982), have argued, intriguingly, that for this elite certain zones in the modern city – gentrified, filled with sleek restaurants and specialized services – have replaced the corporation as an anchor (5630, 2896, 2415); this new elite has become more attached to their style of life in the city than their jobs. That argument looks a little different, however, if we consider the other effects of the flexible realm on cities.

Standardization of the environment results from the economy of impermanence, and standardization begets indifference. I can make this dictum clear, perhaps, by describing a personal experience. A few years ago I took the head of a large, new economy corporation on a tour of New York's Chanin Building, an art deco palace with elaborate offices and splendid public spaces. "It would never suit us," the executive remarked, "people might become too attached to their offices, they might think they belong here."

The flexible office is not meant to be a place where you nestle in. The office architecture of flexible firms requires a physical environment that can be quickly reconfigured – at the extreme the "office" becomes just a computer terminal. The neutrality of new buildings also results from their global currency as investment units; for someone in Manila it is easy to buy or sell a hundred thousand square feet of office space in London: the space itself needs the uniformity, the transparency, of money.

This is why the style elements of new economy buildings become what Ada Louise Huxtable (1997) calls "skin architecture," the surface of the building dolled-up with design, its innards ever more neutral, standard and capable of instant reconfiguration (3539, 6279, 4681).

Another phenomenon in the modern city reinforces "skin architecture": the standardization of public consumption – a global network of shops selling the same commodities in the same kinds of spaces whether they are located in Manila, Mexico City or London (6493, 2506, 6601, 5289). This standardization forms a stark contrast to the conditions of Simmel's Berlin. There, a century ago, though institutional coherence was the economy's aim, consumption remained erratic in form and mostly small scale in the city's economy. Today, institutional coherence is coming apart, but the consumable results of production and services are becoming more uniform in the network of world globalized cities. The same is true for the spatial impact of these processes. For instance, in certain parts of gentrified Berlin you can be in London, you can be even in New York (2271, 5624, 5886, 1439). Gentrification has acquired a certain kind of standardization, which shows that cities often stop setting alterity stimula.

It is hard to become attached to a particular Gap or Banana Republic; standardization begets indifference. From another point of view, the problem of institutional loyalties in the workplace, now beginning to sober up managers once blindly enthusiastic about endless corporate re-engineering, finds its parallel in the urban public realm of consumption; attachment and engagement with specific places is dispelled under the aegis of this new regime. Benjamin's image of the *flaneur* gets a new meaning in a world of Starbucks and Niketowns. No longer is the urban *flaneur* someone who can discover – at least in the new public realm – the strange, the unexpected, or the arousing. Alterity is missing. Equally, the accumulation of shared history (and so of collective memory) diminishes in these neutral public spaces. The space of public consumption attacks local meanings in the same way the new workplace attacks "ingrown" shared histories among workers.

This is, visually, one way to interpret the relation between flexibility and indifference. I do not mean to invoke clichés of urban "alienation" or argue that the impulse to seek stimulus in the city has died. Rather, the visual economy of modern capitalism has put up new barriers to the experience of complexity on the city's streets.

Socially, the coupling of flexibility and indifference produces a conflict less visible to the eye. High-pressure flexible work profoundly disorients family life. The phenomena of "latch-key childhood", of adult stress or of geographic uprooting – so often cited in the press – do not quite get at the heart of this disorientation. It is rather that the codes of conduct that rule the modern work world would shatter families if such commandments were taken home from the office: do not commit, do not get involved, think short term. The assertion of "family values" by the public and by politicians has a more than right-wing resonance; it is a reaction, often inchoate but strongly felt, of the threats to family solidarity in the new economy. Christopher Lasch's (1977) image of the family as a "haven in a heartless world" takes on a particular urgency when work becomes at once more unpredictable and more demanding of adult time. One result of this conflict, by now well-documented, on middle-aged employees, is that adults withdraw from civic participation in the struggle to solidify and organize family life; the civic becomes yet another demand on time and energies in short supply at home. I introduce this third element because "indifference" can seem only moralistic and pejorative. Withdrawal from the civic realm – neglect of it – can be something to which people are driven by the contrary demands of family and work.

In summary, when a society's organizational, bureaucratic forms alter, both the experience of time and space alters. This conjoined alteration in the time of labor and the space of cities is what we are living through today, expressed in geographic impermanence, the effects of impermanence on standardization in the public realm, and conflicts between work and family, office, and home.

I want to say less about the effects of globalization on cities, because they are the subject of many other critiques. I only wish to take up the issue posed by Sharon Zukin (1982) about the peculiar home the new global elite has made for itself in cities such as New York, London and Chicago. Here we would do better to focus on politics than on lofts and trendy restaurants. This is an economic elite avoiding the urban political realm. It wants to operate in the city but not to rule it; it composes a regime of power without responsibility (see also Chapter 4).

Let me give an example. In Wirth's Chicago, in 1925, political and economic power were coextensive; presidents of the city's top 80 corporations sat on 142 hospital boards and composed 70 percent of trustees of colleges and universities. Political machines were deeply linked to business; tax revenues from 18 national corporations in Chicago formed 23 percent of the city's municipal budget. By contrast, in New York now – with London the world's most globalized city – political and economic power are not coextensive in this way. Big players in the global economy located in the city are absent from civic enterprises – hospitals, libraries, universities, and schools. Few CEOs of global firms in New York, for instance, are trustees of its educational institutions; none sit on the boards of its hospitals. The network of the bourgeois "great and the good" is no more international in London, despite the fact that the City of London is Europe's financial capital.

The reason for this change is that the global economy is not rooted in the city in the sense of depending on control of the city as a whole. It is instead an island economy, literally so within the island of Manhattan in New York (4679), architecturally so in places such as Canary Wharf in London (6303), which resemble the imperial compounds of an earlier era. As John Mollenkopf and Manuel Castells (1991) have shown, this global wealth does not trickle down, leech out, very far beyond the global enclave – which is why Mollenkopf and Castells' speak of global cities as "dual cities".

Again, as when reflecting about the new forms of work, I do not assert that those are the dominant patterns in urban areas; rather, this is one of the development directions taken by the globalized cities across the world. Most parts of cities, especially European ones, are more rooted, but sensible to and torn by those kinds of changes in fact, like the history of former industrial cities (Manchester, Leeds, Sheffield and partly also in Turin . . .) shows (2746, 6028, 2223, 4095).

Indeed, the politics of the global enclave cultivates a kind of indifference vis-à-vis the city, which Marcel Proust, in an entirely different context, calls the "passive beloved" phenomenon in *À la recherche du temps perdu* (1919–27). Threatening to leave, go anywhere in the world, the global firm is given enormous tax breaks to stay, a profitable seduction made possible by the firm appearing indifferent to the places where it touches down.

In other words, globalization poses a problem of citizenship in cities as well as nations. I remarked that the conflicting demands of family and work are now diminishing civic participation. There is another, less sympathetic form of civic indifference, particularly urgent at the top of global organizations. Cities cannot tap into the wealth of these corporations, and the corporations take little responsibility for their own presence in the city. The threat of absence, of leaving, makes possible this avoidance of responsibility; we lack correspondingly the political mechanisms to make unstable flexible institutions contribute fairly for the privileges they enjoy in the city.

For all these reasons, I want to argue that the dialectics of flexibility and indifference pose three new dilemmas for cities: a dilemma of citizenship; of arousal in the public realm, because the impermanence/standardization connection leaves people indifferent to public places; and, finally, the dilemma of sheer, durable attachment to the city.

The political economy of a century ago posed the problem of how to cut free from rigidity. The city embodied that rigidity in its ecology, but paradoxically, in the newness and rawness of the urban population, the very concentration of strangers seemed also to promise an escape from rigidity, from Weber's iron cage: a promise of freedom (*"die Stadtluft macht Frei,"* Weber 1922).

We now have cities of globally mobile corporations, flexible workers, a dynamic capitalism bent on erasing routine. Paradoxically, in the city this restless economy produces political disengagement, a standardization of the physical realm, new pressures to withdraw into the private sphere.

Conclusions: The Fate of the Urban Virtues

I would like to conclude this chapter by investigating what this new kind of city life implies about the two ethical values that the city durably stands for.

About the sociability of living with strangers: the mark of the civic realm now is mutual accommodation through dissociation. That means the truce of letting one another alone, the peace of mutual indifference. In the language of cultural studies, identity has taken the place of alterity in urban life (2049, 3409, 2827). This is one reason why, on the positive side, the modern city is like an accordion, easily able to expand to accommodate new waves of migrants; the pockets of difference are sealed. On the negative side, mutual accommodation through dissociation spells the end of citizenship practices that require understanding of divergent interests, as well as marking a loss of simple human curiosity about the Other.

About subjectivity: personal experience of the incomplete seems achieved by this new capitalist time. Flexible time is serial, rather than cumulative; the spaces of flexible time are unmarked, neutral. However, there is no Levinasian bridge, no sense that because some time seems missing in my own life, I should turn outward to others, toward the "neighborliness of strangers." This very problem of capitalist time, however, suggests something about the art of making better cities today.

We want to overlay different activities in the same space, as, for example, created by family activity in working space. The incompleteness of capitalist time returns us to the issue that marked the very emergence of the industrial city, a city that broke apart the *domus* – that spatial relation which had, before the coming of industrial capitalism, combined family, work, ceremonial public spaces, and more informal social spaces. In fact, flexible capitalism has been territorialized in a way that makes an unholy marriage between placeless work and a kind of mono-functional space – a disaggregation that draws people from each other.

Summing up, individualization and territorial separation are, in different ways, two sides of the same coin. That is one of the peculiarities of flexible capitalism, that it is increasing Fordist place, it is producing highly segmented mono-functional (and economically functional) spaces. Today, we need to repair the collectivity of space to combat the serial time of modern labor.

The art of making a city is not, I believe, like rocket science. Almost none of the good city builders of the past possessed a comprehensive theory of the city; but equally, they did more than just represent the existing economic and political conditions of their times. They sought to interpret and so to transmute the material conditions of the political economy through the expressive medium of walls and windows, volumes and perspectives – an art that concentrated on details, compounded specific discoveries about space into an urban whole. The art of urban design is a craft-work.

Today's capitalism imposes on us a specific task: creating complexity and mutual attachment in a city that tends to difference rather than alterity, a city in which people withdraw behind the walls of difference. We need to discover the craft-work that answers to this particular challenge.

In European cities there is a comparative advantage for that. Their rootedness and history provide the building blocks for a more adequate answer. Will they resist the standardization trends?

REFERENCES

Benjamin, W. (1936) [1991 edn.] Paris, die Hauptstadt des XIX Jahrhunderts. In: Benjamin, W. (ed.) *Das Passagen-Werk. Gesammelte Schriften*, Vol. 1. Suhrkamp, Frankfurt am Main.

Frank, R.H. and Cook, P.J. (1996) *The Winner-Take-All Society*. Penguin, London.

Hoyt, H. (1933) *One Hundred Years of Chicago Land Values*. University of Chicago Press, Chicago.

Howard, E. (1902) *Garden Cities of Tomorrow*. Swan, Sonnenschein, London.

Huxtable, A.L. (1997) *The Unreal America: Architecture and Illusion*. New Press, New York.

Lasch, C. (1977) *Haven in a Heartless World: The Family Besieged.* Basic Books, New York.

Levinas, E. (1991) *Entre nous: Essais sur le penser-à l'autre.* Grasset, Paris.

Mollenkopf, J. and Castells, M. (1991) *Dual City: Restructuring New York.* Russell Sage Foundation, New York.

Park, R.E. (1926) The urban community as a spatial pattern and moral order. In: Park, R.E. (ed.) (1952) *Human Communities.* The Free Press, Glencoe.

Proust, M. (1919–27) *À la recherche du temps perdu.* Gallimard, Paris.

Sennett, R. (1990) *The Conscience of the Eye.* Faber and Faber, London.

Simmel, G. (1903) Die Grosstädte und das Geistesleben. *Jahrbuch der Gehestiftung,* 9: 185–206.

Simmel, G. (1908) *Soziologie Untersuchungen über die Formen der Vergesellschaftung.* Duncker & Humblot, Berlin.

Weber, M. (1922) *Wirtschaft und Gesellschaft: Grundriss der Verstehenden Soziologie.* Mohr, Tübingen.

Wiebe, R. (1967) *The Search for Order 1877–1920.* Hill and Wang, New York.

Wirth, L. (1938) Urbanism as a way of life. *American Journal of Sociology,* 44 (1): 1–24.

Zukin, S. (1982) *Loft Living Culture and Capital in Urban Change.* Johns Hopkins University Press, Baltimore.

6

Urban Socio-Spatial Configurations and the Future of European Cities

Christian Kesteloot

Introduction

The conspicuous social and spatial changes in European cities have common roots in the economic crisis of the 1970s, with a strong deindustrialization process and the advent of structural unemployment in the wave of globalization that followed (Marcuse and van Kempen 2000). Everywhere, social exclusion and its spatial concentration are related to three types of problems:

1 Absence of stable integration in the labor market.
2 Problematic participation in the benefits of state redistribution.
3 Weakening of traditional social bonds and networks related to processes of individualization and changes in household structures (see Chapter 3; Mingione 1996).

Globalization has exacerbated social polarization between rich and poor. It has also intensified interurban competition for investments, employment and the purchasing power of the middle class, which, in contrast to the impoverished working class, is more and more seen as the guarantor of a sound economic, social, and fiscal basis for each urban or regional entity. In this competition process, cities have restructured their spatial arrangements and equipped themselves with new infrastructure and amenities (Harvey 1985). When necessary, they have driven the poor away from neighborhoods that can attract investments or middle-class residents and, as a consequence, the residual poor neighborhoods have been further stigmatized.[1]

The same changes in the economic realm have created new categories of rich people, whose wealth is derived from the new economic activities and their international embeddedness. Among them are the transnational elite (Friedmann and Wolff 1982), but also the highly skilled workers in the new technology firms and advanced producer services (Sassen 1994).

However, this general picture does not take the same forms in all European cities. In a very general way, one can distinguish the European cities of the economic and demographic core of the continent from the others. This core is known as the "blue banana" of Europe after it was so described by a French geographer, Roger Brunet (1989).[2] It corresponds quite well to the main trajectory of diffusion of the nineteenth century industrial revolution in Europe. Therefore, the banana has a north–south historical gradient, which is also important when looking at European urban diversity.

The social issues at stake in urban Europe may be very similar, but the differences in the socio-spatial arrangements of the cities, broadly corresponding to the core–periphery contrast on the continent, could have quite different effects on the way these issues are dealt with. They could shape different futures for different European cities. This chapter is both about the origin and the explanation of these differentiated socio-spatial arrangements and about how they could affect the future, especially in terms of social relations within the urban communities.

In the first part, we attempt to grasp the logic of socio-spatial arrangements through a geologic metaphor. Indeed, the organization of urban residential space results from social processes on a much longer timescale than the changes mentioned in this introduction, because the spatial organization of society involves strong inertia forces related to the lifetime of the built environment. Therefore, just as past physical geographic conditions can be inferred from the study of geologic layers, the spatial organization of the city in previous periods can be understood from the study of the different residential environments. The industrial revolution and the related waves of urbanization are crucial to understanding the differences in arrangements between the core and the periphery of urban Europe, although, as we will see, still other elements explain the diversity in more detail.

The second part endeavors to explore the future of the cities in relation to this socio-spatial diversity. In order to take a fruitful analytic stance, the urban diversity is reduced to a dual model of cities, with the poor in the inner city and rich in the suburbs on the one hand (reflecting the cities in the European core), and cities with the contrary arrangement on the other (the cities in Europe's peripheries). The future of the urban communities emerges from the interplay between poor inhabitants, rich inhabitants and city users. The spatial position of the poor in relation to the city center appears to be a particularly crucial factor in this respect.

European Socio-Spatial Configurations

Cities offer a mosaic of socio-spatial configurations. We mean by these different types of residential environments associated, at least in terms of their origins, with a precise social group in the city. At a purely abstract level, socio-spatial configurations can be conceived as the material environment in which the related social group reproduces itself. When the social structure of the urban population changes in line with economic development, new social configurations appear. Thus, the mosaic, or the socio-spatial structure of the city, results from historic processes. The period in which these environments were created and the organization of the economy and conditions of class struggle at the time are reflected in the type of housing, the material and institutional modes of organization for collective consumption, and the spatial arrangement of the area.

Taking the industrial revolution as a starting point, the nineteenth century working-class areas, epitomized by Engels' famous description of Manchester (1892), are probably the most striking new configuration (5511, 4073, 1949, 5173). Before that, the separation between residential and workplace was less developed and the functional division of urban space, each area focusing on a different craft, overrode social divisions (Sjoberg 1960; Vance 1977). Before the appearance of large concentrations of waged workers, micro-segregation at the level of street blocks and vertical segregation was prevalent, lingering on in some cities until today (a good example is Naples, where today the top floors, giving access to terraces and views over the bay, are systematically occupied by a literally upper class) (5021, 1375, 1487). The new presence of a "dangerous" working class in the cities triggered a reaction of spatial distanciation by the rich. In order to avoid epidemics and the socio-political threat that the poor represented, they started building castles and manors at a distance from the city. However, this distanciation also generated a backlash, usually termed "Haussmannization". Haussmann was the prefect of the Seine Department who planned the large boulevards with luxury apartment buildings in central Paris in the third quarter of the nineteenth century (Reau et al. 1954) (2439, 0703). This offered an opportunity for the upper classes to stay in the inner city. Haussmann's example was followed in many European cities, but usually on a much reduced scale (5305, 1379). Often, the densified medieval urban tissue was cut by a prestigious lane linking the railway station at the edge of the old city with the city center. Since then, the socio-spatial history of European cities has been character-ized by tensions between centrifugal and centripetal forces that, for the sake of simplicity, can be termed suburbanization and gentrification.

The working class was compelled to live in over-densified, centrally located neighborhoods because long working hours and low wages im-peded any significant journey to work (4989, 6383, 5206, 2590, 5556). Similarly, job insecurity, with labor being hired on a daily or weekly basis, forced the workers to live close to potential sources of employment. This was also the inner city, except when production sites depended on the location of raw material, as in mining or the early steel industry. The consequences of these centripetal forces, appalling living conditions in working-class neighborhoods, triggered centrifugal reactions. However, the first attempts to solve the housing problem, which had resulted in a severe shortage of healthy workers in the cities, were developed on the spot as long as the workers' time and money were too short for decentral-ized housing. They mainly comprised architectural forms devised to in-crease access to air and light in the dwellings (4435, 4250). The Mulhouse housing type, with four houses joined together to form an apparently larger detached dwelling is famous in that respect (4427, 4297). The thrust to the countryside is embodied in the garden cities concept, proposed by Ebenezer Howard (1902). The first garden city, built in Letchworth, 50 km north of London, served as an example for many garden cities throughout the world (2577, 2580, 2582, 2950, 5595, 0697). The aim was to create an ideal environment as a response to the miserable living conditions of the working class in industrial cities. Therefore, workers had to be located in new places, which would be a synthesis between wealthy towns and healthy countryside. The garden city movement was paradoxically very often sup-ported both by the bourgeoisie, because it appeared to be a means to counter socialism, and by the workers' movement, because it promised a definitive solution to improve the living conditions of the working class. However, garden cities rapidly shrank to garden neighborhoods located outside the contemporary city limits, linked with it through public trans-portation lines (4428, 5871, 0693, 5087).

Another solution to the working-class neighborhood problems in the inner city is best exemplified by the Paris *banlieues pavillonnaires* (Bastié 1964). The better off among the workers and the petty middle class were encouraged to build their own small bungalows on cheap and poorly serviced estates on the contemporary city fringe, giving rise to an impres-sive sprawl of low-quality single-family dwellings (2790).

Homer Hoyt (1939) signaled in his work the return of wealthy people to the central city in prestigious apartment buildings. These people sought the advantages of a central urban location and avoided the trouble and expense of traveling to the city and maintaining a large villa or manor on the periphery. The same phenomenon appeared in European cities. The Brussels International Press Center, for instance, was built in the 1920s under the name *Résidence Palace* and offered in its premises not only all the services one would obtain from domestic servants in the suburbs, such as cleaning and catering, but also shops, barbers, a theater, and a swimming pool. High-rise building and reliable elevators were crucial to this development (4032).

After World War II, squatter settlements, very much like those found in the cities of developing countries, appeared in some European cities. Among them the *bidonvilles* in Paris (see, for example, Sayad 1995; Volovitch-Tavares 1995), the *coree* in many Italian cities (1687), the *chabolas* in Spain and the *barracas* in and around Porto and Lisbon (Barata Salgueiro 1995). In all cases these squatter settlements reflected a shortage of housing brought about by war destruction, insufficient construction activity and population increase, mainly through immigration. They formed a much less enduring socio-spatial configuration than the others. However, their imprint in urban space is still reflected in the rapidly built high-rise social housing estates that replaced them, in which very often new housing problems appear because of the poor architectural design and construction quality of these buildings (2664, 2638, 2662, 1685, 4553, 4548).

Thus, squatter settlements were one of the origins of another configuration, the high-rise peripheral social housing estates. However, not all these estates were built under strong housing pressure. Particularly in the 1960s, urban developers and decision-makers were convinced that high-rise mass housing with lots of open space between the buildings and a sharp separation of housing, work, leisure, and traffic would provide ideal living environments for modern citizens. These ideas also originated in the responses to the problems of the nineteenth century industrial city, but incorporated the new phenomenon of automobility. They were codified by Le Corbusier and the Congrès Internationaux d'Architecture Moderne in the Charter of Athens (1943). In Europe, the Bijlmermeer in Amsterdam was probably the most fully developed example of this new configuration (2071, 1315). Although demographic pressure was high in the Netherlands at that time, Bijlmermeer was conceived as a "city for the future" for the Amsterdam middle class. The few high-rise social housing estates built in Belgian cities (6497, 6381, 1884) also correspond to this modern experimental configuration (De Kooning and Strauven 2000). However, everywhere in Europe high-rise estates became associated with social problems from the 1980s on, even the good quality, experimental ones (Power 1997).

The most important post-war configuration in terms of people and space were the middle-class suburbs around the cities. They reflect changes in the social division of labor and economic growth, as these suburbs accommodated a rapidly increasing middle class in owner-occupied dwellings. This type of suburbanization appears as the spatial embodiment of the consumer society upon which Fordist economic growth is founded. The long period of growth resulted from sustained improvements in productivity. Wealth was divided into profits to invest in new rounds of productivity increase and higher wages. The increase of purchase power, together with full employment and the general spreading of credit, supported access to owner-occupation outside the cities. This new residential environment compelled households to enter into a consumption spiral of durable consumption goods, chiefly the car and home appliances. The resulting continuous expansion of the sales of these goods promoted economic growth (Harvey 1985). However, these suburbs vary significantly from country to country, the most important difference being between estate and individual building. The former is usually related to planning, the strongest examples being the *New Towns*, especially around London (the first one being Stevenage, started in 1946) (5608, 5605), and later Paris (e.g., Marne-la-Vallée, Créteil) (5960, 5956, 5965, 5959) and the Randstad (e.g., Lelystad, Almere) (Merlin 1972) (2671, 2672, 2670). The latter produces a sprawl of many diversified detached houses (5859, 5360). Fragmentation or consolidation of the land market, the real estate sector and its financing, and the construction industry, but also planning traditions, class-related housing politics and ideology, explain the contrasts between Belgium and Southern Europe on the one hand (4117, 4119, 4084, 4522), and the UK, the Netherlands and Northern Europe on the other (5175, 6152, 6230, 3237, 1257). France and Germany present more complex situations (Barlow and Duncan 1994). In the Netherlands and Germany, suburbanization has been contained, and urban environments adapted to the needs of a growing middle class were created, even if many of these inhabitants would have preferred a suburban way of life. In Germany this happened through the post-war reconstruction programs; in the Netherlands through urban renewal, especially during the 1970s.

Suburbanization, especially in the European core, entailed the import of foreign unskilled workers to fill the gaps left by the upward social mobility of the autochthonous population in the labor and housing markets. This brought about the transformation of nineteenth century working-class neighborhoods into ethnic neighborhoods (4156, 3139). Elsewhere, because of the absence of such nineteenth century configurations, these immigrants, usually arriving later in the cities, filled the already described *bidonvilles* or peripheral social housing estates (3209, 5127, 2071, 3707, 5381). When, as a reaction to the economic crisis, the economic buoyancy of these neighborhoods is based on local initiative and ethnic entrepreneurship (5663, 5841, 2481, 2868, 4883), one speaks about ethnic enclaves (Marcuse 1997).

The most recent configurations, initiated in the USA just like the middle-class suburbs, are the gated communities (0708, 1494, 0194, 5348, 5350) and the gentrified areas in the city (2883, 0300, 2366, 0898, 1439), configurations that we will consider in more detail in the second part of the chapter.

The temporality of urban social space

The actual spatial arrangement can be thought of as a geologic metaphor, transposing to urban social geography the ideas Massey (1979) explored in her work on spatial divisions of labor. In short, Massey argues that economic growth goes with rounds of investments that create new spatial divisions of labor. These spatial patterns overlay and combine with patterns produced in previous periods. The effects of the combination of successive layers vary over space and give rise to regional variation in the conditions of production, which are the spatial basis for the next round of investment. This spatial basis is crucial, because investments make use of spatial variations in order to maximize profits (see Warde 1985 for a critical discussion of Massey's contribution and probably the first reference to geology to describe her conception).

The rounds of investments define the temporality of economic geography. This brings us to the literature on economic cycles. Although economic cycles have been detected at different timescales, the long waves, or the Kondratiev cycles, are the relevant ones in this case, because the shorter ones, like business cycles, do not involve qualitative changes in production and consumption patterns involving geographic change. Because of this, exactly the same periods are at stake when transposing the geologic metaphor to urban social geography. Basically, Kondratiev, a Russian Marxist economist, empirically demonstrated synchronic patterns of economic development in capitalist countries since the late eighteenth century. The Kondratiev cycles typically involve periods of approximately 50 years, with a phase of rapid growth followed by stagnation (Mandel 1980). Each phase of growth is reliant on a set of successful products and technologies, such as coal and steel in the late nineteenth century, chemicals and electricity in the interwar period, consumer durables in the postwar period, or ICT and new materials in the present day. Stagnation phases are related to the exhaustion of the growth potential of these products and technologies, and are periods in which weaker competitors on the market are eliminated and new technologies are sought.

During the last period of stagnation, French economists tried to understand the reasons for the previous long period of sustained economic growth. This French regulation school (Boyer 1986) showed sustained

growth to rest on the maintenance of a delicate balance between production organization, forms of competition, social and spatial divisions of
labor, modes of consumption, and state intervention. Regulationists distinguish accumulation regimes, the economic relations generating growth,
and corresponding modes of regulation, the social, political and cultural
institutions and relations necessary for holding up an accumulation regime.
Spatial patterns appear as powerful elements in stabilizing an accumulation regime, but their fix hampers in turn the passage to a new regime in
periods of stagnation.

In casting the socio-spatial configurations of the cities in such a geologic
metaphor, much attention has to be paid to the wage relation or, more
precisely, how the balance of power between employers and workers within
the context of capitalist economies determines wage levels and wage
variations. These levels and variations command the reproduction of the
labor force: the consumption processes and domestic work that enable
the daily regeneration of one's labor capacity and the maintenance of the
labor force over generations by procreation. Housing is the place where
this reproduction process is organized and where most of the related
activities take place. Socio-spatial configurations will reflect this social
reproduction process. Each accumulation regime goes with its own spatial
division of the reproduction of the labor force. Since changes in the division of labor imply changes in the social structure of the urban population, each accumulation regime creates a different spatial pattern,
determined by this social structure and the level of consumption or reproduction assigned to each social group through the wage relation. The
wage relation is also strongly mediated by the state, through taxation and
social security contributions and their redistribution under the form of
indirect wages and collective consumption. As a matter of fact, much of
this collective consumption relates to housing policies and the provision
of social infrastructure in residential space. Finally, the wage relation
balances necessarily between the tendency to minimize wages in order to
increase profits and the possibility of increasing demand for consumption
goods and thus creating capacity for economic growth with higher wages.
In this way, the social reproduction of the labor force and the role of
consumption in the economic cycle are intimately related. The urban
socio-spatial configurations will necessarily express these two aspects of
social reproduction (Kesteloot 1986).

Socio-spatial configurations as a geologic metaphor

The regulation school, in its effort to understand the long post-war period
of growth and its crisis, distinguished originally only two regimes: extensive

and intensive accumulation, or Fordism. The regulation school concepts are very fruitful to unveil the social and economic logic of the layers of socio-spatial configurations in European cities. However, as we can expect as many layers as Kondratiev cycles, we must try to describe each Kondratiev cycle in terms of an accumulation regime and its mode of regulation. We therefore distinguish a laisser-faire or competitive accumulation regime in the second half of the nineteenth century from the extensive accumulation regime during the interwar period and add flexible accumulation, a term proposed to grasp the contours of new economic growth in the early 1980s (Harvey 1989), also called post-Fordism.

The era of competitive accumulation is characterized by the absence of state intervention in the reproduction of the labor force, strong competition between many capitalist producers, and fluctuating wages depending on supply and demand of the labor force. Expansion of the proletariat and extraction of absolute surplus value (by extending the working time) were the main sources of accumulation. Under such conditions, housing for the workers was limited to a mere shelter function. The conditions of reproduction of the labor force caused poverty, illness, accidents and addictions, threatening the availability of the workforce in the long term.

Extensive accumulation resulted from the stronger position of the working class after the Great Depression of the last quarter of the nineteenth century and the concentration of capital. Under the pressure of the working class, the state issued the first significant social laws, among them the first social housing policies. Real wages had risen as a result of the growing organization of workers into trade unions and were stabilized in order to absorb a significant amount of capitalist-produced consumption goods. Accumulation was to a much greater extent achieved through relative surplus value (increases in productivity), by incorporating more technology into the production process. Thus, the working class was diversifying according to a more complex division of labor. Housing was accordingly diversified and tailored to a healthy reproduction of the labor force.

Fordism, or intensive accumulation, is the response to the exhaustion of the former accumulation regime. Higher productivity yielded more products, which could not be sold once all other outlets had been exploited without increasing the purchase power of the working class. The new regime is termed intensive because it incorporates consumption in the growth mechanism. Continuous productivity improvements are the core of the growth mechanism, but state intervention and social regulation of the wages assure a matching development of consumption. In this era, the middle class swells considerably along with the expanding activities of the state. Housing develops into a consumption machine and suburbanization becomes the spatial expression of the expansion of mass consumption.

The wave of globalization, the introduction of flexibility into production, distribution and consumption processes, social polarization as the expression of accumulation strategies bearing on both absolute and relative surplus value, and a state-supported neoliberalism are the ingredients of the flexible accumulation regime that emerged from the restructuring efforts after the crisis of the 1970s. These four periods are used as a fundamental historic framework to understand socio-spatial configurations. A synoptic presentation of these configurations invites an analysis of their temporal and spatial dynamics (see Figure 6.1).

Each configuration reflects the reproduction processes of the social group affected by it and the concomitant organization of urban residential space as long as the corresponding accumulation regime exists. For instance, the nineteenth century working-class neighborhoods reflect the very bad reproduction conditions of the working class as a result of the exploitation processes in competitive accumulation and the central location of these neighborhoods is crucial to this.

Clearly, as shown by the complex interplay between social classes around wages, profit and productivity progress, there is an increasing complexity of class structure over time. Alongside the persistence of past socio-spatial configurations, their change over time and the appearance of new configurations result in a growing complexity of the urban socio-spatial structure. Thus, the social structure can be reduced to two social classes to understand the structuration of residential space during the competitive accumulation period, but in the following periods, one has to deal with an increasingly complex social structure in order to explain the appearance of new socio-spatial configurations.

The simple conception of urban space as a center with its periphery[3] reveals suburbanization and gentrification to be centrifugal and centripetal forces, which, in relation to the social groups involved, appear as processes of distanciation (from other social groups) or reconquest (of lost positions in urban space). These movements between center and periphery are repeated through urban history and, because they imply each time the transfer of a social group from one environment to another, they create new socio-spatial configurations. However, the forces behind these spatial movements and the socio-economic motives behind them are different for each accumulation regime (among others, the danger of the city and its control in competitive accumulation, healthy environments for the reproduction of the labor force in extensive accumulation, mass consumption in intensive accumulation).

When a city enters into a new accumulation regime, configurations can change in three possible ways. In some cases, there is simply a persistence

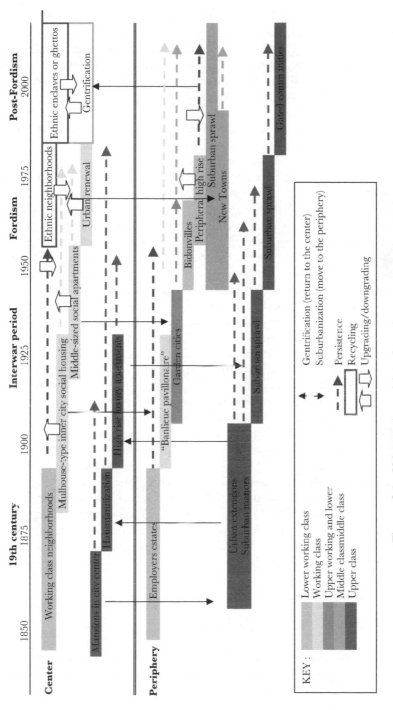

Figure 6.1 Urban socio-spatial configurations as a geologic metaphor

of the configuration, with broadly the same social group attached to it. This is the case, for instance, in the inner-city working-class area until the Fordist period. One can find neighborhoods that remained popular and housed workers from the same origin for nearly a century (e.g., the East End, the Jordaan, and the Marolles in London, Amsterdam, and Brussels, respectively) (5739, 5511, 0637, 4002).

In other cases, the configuration houses a new social group. We therefore label such a transformation of a configuration "recycling." This change is often realized by a gentrification movement. It can also result from the appearance of a new social group in the city. The transformation of inner-city working-class areas in immigrant neighborhoods is a strong example of the last sort, because the new group is physically constituted outside the city and appears in the urban social structure through international immigration. To a certain extent, the association of yuppies with gentrification (which certainly does not cover all the social groups involved in the process – see later in this chapter) combines both situations in the sense that movement towards the center is related to the changing composition of the middle class. When the appearance of new social groups generates centrifugal movements or suburbanization, it usually involves the creation of a brand new socio-spatial configuration and city expansion.

Finally, it happens that socio-spatial configurations retain their initial social group, and that downgrading or upgrading processes appear as a result of the new accumulation regime. Downgrading means that the configuration slowly loses its function of social reproduction for the social group concerned, because the group is rejected from the urban economy. Such configurations turn into areas concentrating population groups with integration problems in the urban community. Such areas, improperly called ghettos, at least in the European context, appear both in the inner city (the deprived ethnic neighborhoods) and in the periphery (the large-scale high-rise social housing estates). The downgrading of the configuration concerns both its inhabitants and its built environment (5728, 4572, 2645, 1888). Of course, the reverse movement of upgrading is also possible, when the configuration is transformed by the improvement of the environment and the possible upward mobility of its same inhabitants. This is clearly the aim of social urban renewal projects (6501, 5226, 2794).

European diversity

Although much refinement would be possible, figure 6.1 combines the most important socio-spatial configurations present in the European cities.[4]

Evidently, these configurations are not all present in each city. If we try to understand why, four factors emerge:

1 There is the moment in which the cities enter into the logic of modern industrial or tertiary development. This determines the number of accumulation regimes that will shape the modern city. If one were to develop a geography of nineteenth century working-class areas all over Europe, the diffusion trajectory of the industrial revolution, or the "blue banana," would surely appear as a significant concentration of cities with such a configuration. Moreover, the earlier the industrial revolution, the more important this configuration will be relative to the others in a single city. One would expect the north–south gradient in the banana to be relevant in this respect.

2 There are the national – and in some cases regional – welfare states, which codetermine the social structure of the urban population, the wage levels, the modes of consumption, urban planning, and the level of amenities present in each socio-spatial configuration, to name but a few (Esping-Andersen 1990). Those interventions in the production of spaces of social reproduction are particularly important and will often depend on the balance of power between the workers' movement and the employers (Power 1993). Thus, social housing, corresponding to precise configurations, represents only a small proportion of the housing stock in Southern European countries, but nearly 40 percent in the Netherlands.

3 The regional economic context in which the city is embedded evidently influences its class composition and the impact of each accumulation regime. Obviously, the social structure will be quite different between manufacturing and service cities or between cities situated in a declining and a growing region.

4 City size sometimes explains the presence or absence of scale-related configurations (e.g., no ethnic neighborhoods will appear if the number of immigrants remains small).

Each of these four influencing factors also affects demographic change that commands the pressures on the housing market and, through the mediation of education and qualifications, the labor market. Demographic pressure depends on the stage of the region in the demographic transition, migration and urbanization policies, which again are all accumulation regime and policy dependent. All these elements individualize each city and determine the presence or absence of each possible configuration (for a social atlas of a set of European cities in which such differences clearly appear, see Vandermotten et al. 1999).

Most European cities will, according to their position in the European space and the interplay of the factors just discussed, display a dominance of center–periphery contrasts. North and south of the European core, including its south end with relatively late industrialization, one still finds a significant presence of the upper- and middle-income classes in the inner cities. Despite suburbanization, cities such as Stockholm (Borgegard and Murdie 1994) or Milan (Kazepov 1995) still present a broadly concentric socio-spatial structure, with the rich residing in the center and the poor in the periphery (4550, 4537, 2010). In Paris (2439, 2790, 2801, 1914, 2864), a similar structure has been achieved through the effects of Hausmannization, which forced the creation of the "red belt" around the center. The demographic and immigration pressure after the war have extended this red belt with the *bidonvilles* and the subsequent "*Grands Ensembles*," large peripheral social housing estates (Vieillard-Baron 1996). Urban renewal and municipality-led gentrification reinforced the position of the rich in the inner city during the 1980s (Carpenter et al. 1994). In Belgium (4133, 4073, 3996, 6625), cities look very like US ones, with immigrants in the former nineteenth century working-class areas and the middle class sprawled in the suburbs. The prolonged absence of planning, the corporatist support of Christian Democrats for the self-promotion of owner-occupied, detached, single-family dwellings, and the related poor development of social housing, a strong post-war welfare state backing the growth of the middle class, and the absence of severe pressures on the housing market are among the explanatory factors (Kesteloot 2000).

In some cases, one can find rich and poor configurations in both the center and the periphery. A good example is Naples (1487, 5898, 6040, 2975), which still has a pre-industrial environment in the inner city where rich and poor are fairly mixed, suburban developments for the upper-income class on the western hills along the coast and very problematic high-rise social housing estates in the north (Morlicchio 2001). In Scandinavian cities (5143, 3046, 5152), strong egalitarian principles and the fully developed welfare state have kept socio-economic differentiation to a minimum and this translates into configurations more characterized by their epoch than by the social groups they house. In Dutch cities (1213, 3350, 3568, 2110), ethnic neighborhoods are not fixed, but move from the inner city towards the periphery. In terms of our geologic metaphor, the neighborhoods successively recycle younger socio-spatial configurations. Today, ethnic minorities are concentrated in post-war garden neighborhoods. The explanation lies in the family reunification of immigrants and the strength of state intervention in the housing sector. Immigrants are displaced to larger dwellings according to their family size, and housing allocations help to bridge the gap between income and housing prices (Kesteloot and Cortie 1998).

Socio-Spatial Configurations and the Urban Future

When conceiving of the city as a mosaic of socio-spatial configurations, the role of spatial arrangements in the reproduction of the social structure becomes clear. Both the elements of separation and confinement to a particular residential environment contribute to the persistence of social differentiation and inequalities. But what about the functioning of the city as an urban community? How far do these separations hamper the necessary relations between the groups to make the city, to govern it and to give it a future? These are complex questions, involving many aspects (see Le Galès 2002 for a rather optimistic political approach). In this chapter we will limit ourselves to a partial exploration of the problem in terms of socio-spatial groups and their position in urban residential space. We also limit the analysis to our abstract dual model of the European city, involving rich and poor, center and periphery. Relating this to real world cities would mean that the case with the poor in the center and the rich in the periphery is more relevant to the cities in the northern part of the European core and the reverse case elsewhere. Within this framework, the question becomes how the relations between rich and poor are mediated by these spatial arrangements of the cities.

Dramatic versus topological cities

Until the economic crisis of the 1970s, the city could be conceived as the arena in which social classes faced each other. Even if segregation between rich and poor has been rapidly organized (be it through early suburbanization of the bourgeoisie, or the creation of wealthy areas in the inner city through Haussmannization), the positions of each group in urban space form the bases from which they confronted each other, through which they built up consciousness of their antagonist interests and from where they organized themselves to defend their interests, be it in an openly conflictual way (an interpretation of Haussmannization, backed by the events of the Paris Commune in 1870) or by negotiation. The city was not only the concentration of employment, through which labor conflicts necessarily became urban conflicts, it was in essence the public forum where demonstrations could develop in their full sense. Urban public space was thus a common space where both conflicts and the need to maintain an urban community were expressed. The key social question of the nineteenth and twentieth century, the division of income from capitalist production into profits and wages – the distribution of prosperity between social classes – has been developed and clarified in urban industrial Europe, and yielded

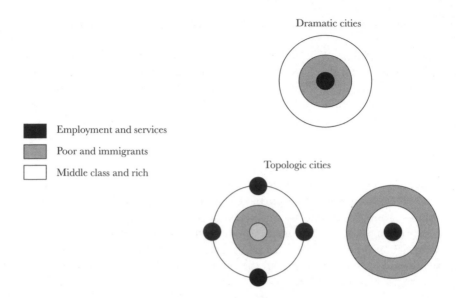

Figure 6.2   Dramatic and topologic cities

in the end a huge improvement in the living conditions of the working class and more social justice in Western societies. Geographically, the social question is an urban question, linked to the original confinement of the workers in their inner-city nineteenth century spatial concentrations and the places of potential jobs and services (see Figure 6.2).

Donzelot and Jaillet (1997) call the city as the focus of this social question the "dramatic city." They thus emphasize the actors of the social question and their interactions in order to contrast them with present-day tendencies. Indeed, this dramatic character of the city, based on difference and confrontation, seems to have faded away. Social fragmentation has taken its place. These changes are firmly expressed in the socio-spatial configurations related to the flexible accumulation regime. They first appeared in the USA and unleashed many debates on their presence in European cities. On the one hand, there is the gated community that symbolizes the secession of the rich from the rest of society (Blakely and Snyder 1997; for Europe, see Aalbers 2001); and on the other hand, the hyperghetto, the place where the socially excluded are systematically driven to and where only those who are able to climb up the social ladder have a chance to escape from (Wilson 1997; for a useful comparison between the USA and France, see Wacquant, 1996). Donzelot and Jaillet talk about topology rather than fragmentation, because it more clearly emphasizes the contrast with the dramatic city. A topologic city is characterized by the disappearance of interactions. Each class is confined in its own place, hence the topologic character of the city. There is no confrontation, no dialogue between the social groups and not even social conflict. However, there can be much urban violence, as an expression of exclusion and the impossibility of fighting for social change, but this never turns into social struggle. The topologic city brings the class struggle to a gloomy end, because inequalities and opposing interests still exist, albeit that part of the former urban actors are now socially excluded. They are still in the city but out of society.

At first glance, a topologic situation would be unexpected in the American city, because the ghettos are located in the inner city and they should be confronted by the middle class and the rich who use the inner city. However, the rich population has stopped using and appropriating the inner city where the ghettos are located. The concept of the edge city (Garreau 1991) clearly indicates the extent to which suburbanites live with their backs to the city and fulfill all their needs within the suburban ring.

The new dramatic city: the performance of three socio-spatial groups

Suburban living is very widespread as the ideal residential arrangement outside North America and the danger of the topologic city therefore also threatens Europe. The report of the British Urban Task Force (1999), for instance, is a brilliant essay on avoiding the fatal combination of urban sprawl and ghettos. However, the more diverse and complex socio-spatial structure of European cities leads to several situations. If we consider again the simple models of rich center and poor periphery and its contrary, other forms of urban topology and drama emerge.

The cities outside the diffusion track of the industrial revolution usually display a socio-spatial pattern contrary to the one that leads to the American topologic city. There are still rich people choosing to live in the inner city and enjoying the advantages of urban centrality. The poor, on the other hand, are often confined to high-rise social housing estates in the urban periphery. As long as the poor were integrated in the urban economy, this could not be equated to a topologic situation. Indeed, the very construction of these social housing estates can be seen as a result of social confrontation and change. However, when these relations are jeopardized by the restructuring of the labor market under global competition and by the curtailing of the welfare state, rich and poor no longer have any direct or indirect intercourse and a European topologic city could emerge (see figure 6.2). The poor from the *banlieue* do not have equal access to the inner city (5965, 5963, 2655, 5383), its jobs and services and, within the context of deindustrialization, the rich do not need them any more (5355, 5488).

■ Jobs

▨ Poor and immigrants

☐ Middle class and rich

— Urban administrative limits

1 = Inner city population, poor and politically weak
2 = Other city population, politically directly represented
3 = City users, politically indirectly represented

Figure 6.3   The three socio-spatial groups in the new dramatic city

By contrast, in the cities of the European core there is still a chance to develop a new kind of dramatic city. However, it no longer involves confrontation between the social classes as stakeholders of the old social question, but social groups defined by the socio-spatial configurations they occupy. Three socio-spatial groups appear in this new urban question (see Figure 6.3).

First, there are the poor, who are increasingly urban newcomers. Among them are the immigrant workers of the 1960s and 1970s, the continuous flow of immigrants generated through family reunification and marriage migration, and the new immigration of economic and political refugees from many different developing countries and all sorts of poor nationals looking for better life chances in the city. They render visible the global character of present-day cities. Both the continuous character of immigration and the concomitant structural weakness of the political representation of these groups at the city level, force this inner-city socio-spatial category into the weakest position in the urban arena. However, they hold the strategic advantage of occupying the central city, still necessary to the other inhabitants and users of the city. While this provides sufficient grounds to consider these people as one socio-spatial group within the city, they show increasing differentiation along two lines. On the one hand, there is a slowly growing vanguard of politicized immigrants, who have gained political rights, and therefore political consciousness, through adopting the nationality of their country of residence or from the extension of democratic rights. They could play an important part in the struggle to maintain the combination of diversity and confrontation in European cities or, in terms of our argument, in maintaining the dramatic capacity of the cities. They must therefore gain awareness of the strategic character of their socio-spatial position in the city centers and develop as advocates of the inner city rather than defenders of their own ethnic group. On the other hand, most forms of gentrification have brought new groups of young urbanites into the city. Except for the large top-level global cities, these are not fortunate yuppies aggressively transforming part of the city to their needs, but young middle and lower middle-class people who do not want or cannot opt for a suburban way of life (van Criekingen 2003). They could also represent a promising prospect for the city, in so as far as they engage in a solidary defense of the interests of all the inner-city dwellers, rather than associating themselves with the other socio-spatial groups that are closest to them in terms of social class.[5]

The second socio-spatial group lives in the next ring of the city. It is composed of the autochthonous population and newcomers from the regional immigration field of the city. This group derives from the vigorous post-war upward social mobility and therefore belongs mainly to the middle class. As a matter of fact, large parts of the autochthonous working class have disappeared because of this social mobility, but also because of deindustrialization. These inhabitants contrast sharply with the inner-city poor, in terms of social class, ethnicity and even, to a large extent, demographic characteristics. They form the major electoral group and also provide the majority of the political actors of the city. As a consequence, much of the city policy will reflect their visions and interests, which can run counter to those of the inner-city dwellers. Most evidently, they need space and security in the inner city because they use it for work, education, and leisure. Achieving these needs very often implies displacement or control of the inner-city inhabitants.

Depending on the magnitude of suburbanization and its overflow outside the urban administrative limits, there is an often forgotten third urban socio-spatial group: the city users (Martinotti 1999). These inhabitants of the outer suburbs and the commuter zones are in some cases even the largest of the three socio-spatial groups in the city. Although the urban fiscal systems can be very different in Europe, this group enjoys the urban amenities without paying for (all) the costs they generate in doing so. This is, for instance, particularly the case in Belgium, where a large share of the local public finance is fuelled by income taxes from the residents and land taxes. The rest comes from national and regional tax redistribution. In the Netherlands, municipalities are financed by the national state and thus even non-city users help to finance the urban local governments. France has the soundest financing system: city users contribute to the costs they generate in the municipalities where they work, because their local income tax is divided between the municipality of residence and the municipality of work (De Brabander et al. 1992).

At first sight this group is not represented at the urban political level, because it has no representation in the relevant political institutions. However, city users draw an underestimated indirect political power from two other sources. The first is their representation at the regional and national political levels. Local urban policies are profoundly affected by the legal frameworks laid down by regional and/or national political bodies, by their control of the local authorities and also by regional and/or national urban policies. The other source of power is represented by political parties, which develop their own ideas about urban policies (both local and at the other scales). Parties try to interpret the interests of their electorate and, because most of them target the middle class, they will defend political points of view that quite strongly serve this third socio-spatial group, among whom, because of the socially selective process of suburbanization, the middle class is well represented. Consequently, the ideologies of the main parties and their programs regarding urban problems are rather convergent. The latter are very often thought about from the point of view of the urban periphery, rather than the perspective of the urban center. Finally, city users influence the political attitude of politicians elected in the cities. This explains the apparently paradoxical phenomenon of city policies in favor of the city users and against the interests of the city inhabitants (especially frequent in the sectors of mobility and real estate).

Repressive city versus negotiated city

As long as these city users and the urban middle class need the central city, they are confronted with the poor inner-city socio-spatial group. Analytically, such a confrontation can develop in two opposite ways, although in reality they are sometimes found together.

The first development leads to the repressive city and emerges from the political non-recognition of the poor occupants of the inner city.[6] This poverty takes the form of post-Fordist social exclusion and generates fear and insecurity. This is even more the case when it is associated with immigration and thus strangeness. It is precisely this double otherness, socio-economic and ethnic, that is used as a justification for the rejection of this socio-spatial group. Very often this rejection takes the form of spatial displacement and concentration. Inner-city restructuring and gentrification are usually conceived in this way, and they involve social and spatial repression of the poor (Smith 1996). In a first step, social repression is used to lower poverty-related criminality in the target areas in order to reassure potential investors (5308, 2928, 2069). In a second step, the poor are displaced to residual areas in order to free space for the middle class, which is a spatial form of repression (4995, 4077, 1861). Concentration of the poor in a few zones of the city eases control and containment of their social discontent.[7]

As long as displacement and concentration are not completely fulfilled or are successfully countered by the poor, central areas where rich and poor confront each other in the city will remain. In that situation, the security of the city users is organized at the expense of the poor inhabitants. Such a secure city is achieved by social repression through heavy police presence and zero tolerance. According to this logic, poverty is dangerous and must be kept under control so that the users of the central city can access it without having to face the consequences of poverty. Depending on the fiscal arrangements of the cities, there are some cases where the poor pay for their own repression because they finance the urban police protecting the rich suburbanites in the city center.[8]

Evidently, tensions can only increase in a repressive city and conflicts are inevitable. Inner-city riots cause much more concern to city politicians than the suburban violence in a topologic city. They can direct urban policy towards even more repression or, on the contrary, preventive measures. In many cases, short-term measures of the former are combined with long-term measures of the latter and, hopefully, this could lead to the other development – the negotiated city.

A negotiated city implies a lasting institutionalization of all three socio-spatial groups that make up the city. It is materialized in a common urban project. This can only be achieved if the three groups recognize each other as equal partners in the city and if negotiation institutions are created for this purpose. This development implies important changes compared to the present-day set of territorial, fiscal and electoral arrangements that make up the city as a local state (Terhorst and van de Ven 1997). The first of these is the empowerment of the inner-city socio-spatial group. In many countries, immigrants still do not have political rights, and the continuous immigration from the rest of the world into European cities means that there is a lasting shortage of democratic representation that has to be compensated by new forms of democracy. One way of doing this would be to redesign the territorial arrangements inside the city so as to give more autonomy and greater political visibility to those areas in the city where the politically weak inner-city inhabitants are concentrated. In more general terms, this means that the territorial partition of the city should correspond to its socio-spatial configurations (an interesting example is Saint-Josse-ten-Node, the poorest Brussels municipality with a majority of foreigners in its population; Dassetto 1991).

An additional way to counter this democratic deficit would be to introduce new forms of urban democracy besides representative democracy. Many local problems and issues within today's European cities cannot be properly addressed by representative democracy because it is too slow and inflexible. Ad hoc public participation in local decisions and territorially sensitive decisions at the city level (such as local planning and design arrangements, and budget decisions; see the Porto Alegre model) are interesting instances of participative democracy that could be developed in this direction. Finally, in many cases, fiscal arrangements can be revised in order to reverse the flows caused by city users paying their taxes outside the city and not contributing to the collective costs they create by using the city center.

The other main problem is to involve the city users in a more accountable way with the future of the city. Again, participative democracy at the local level offers some opportunities. City users can be associated with city inhabitants in taking decisions on matters concerning the neighborhoods in which they work, study or consume. This right to intervene in a territory other than the one in which they are politically represented could be the means to turn them away from the lure of a repressive city. This would be easily justified if their contribution to the costs of the city became more effective and visible. This idea emerged from the rejection in the Netherlands of the amalgamation of urban metropolitan areas by the population. While amalgamation would have been a way to make the suburban city users contribute to the city, it reinforces the political weight of the middle class in urban politics, at the expense of the urban poor. Nowadays, extra-territorial financial and political participation is under debate, with the proposal of a part-time citizenship for city users (Musterd et al. 1997).

Conclusions

Real European cities are much more complex than the simple models presented here. However, the models help us to grasp what is at stake for their future. If the analysis seizes enough of the European urban reality, it would mean that the future of the city is no longer strongly dependent on the relations between social classes, which created several layers of socio-spatial configurations in the past, but on the very socio-spatial groups they give rise to in the present context. The deep causes of this shift from social classes to territorial groups is related to the way urban residential space was organized for the social reproduction of social classes and capital. On the one hand, the spatial separation of the middle class from the working class in the city has created the necessary spatial distanciation between classes to create territorial interests. In the cities of Europe's urban core, this separation is mainly achieved by the extraction of the middle class from the city itself and its dispersion into the suburbs. In the other cities, the creation of a "red belt" around them has achieved the same distanciation. On the other hand, the social integration of the lower income classes was taken apart by the restructuring of the economy and the welfare state, transforming them into a territorial group from which the others want to distance themselves.

In many cities, the spatial arrangement of this double distanciation combines elements of the topologic and the dramatic cities, crucially depending on the presence or absence of the different socio-spatial configurations. In all cities, the issue is the inclusion or exclusion of the weakest socio-spatial group in the city. As far as the future is made by the aspiration for inclusion, the central location of the poor in Europe's urban core cities is a strong advantage compared to the other European and the American cities. By developing the negotiated city, they could pave the way for new forms of societal arrangements, responding to the challenges of post-Fordism.

NOTES

1   This process is a hot discussion theme in American literature. For Europe, see Atkinson (2000); van Weesep and Musterd (1991).
2   The banana refers to the shape of the core; the color was given to it by an illustrator in *Le Nouvel Observateur*.
3   This is a simplification in the sense that many cities also display sectoral patterns, the rich locating in the directions of attractive environments and convenient communication lines with the city center and the poor along industrial axes. This model was proposed by Hoyt (1939) in a study of American cities, but the feature is also present in Europe. However, even within the sectors, the center–periphery contrast remains an important differentiating factor and the subsequent analysis is not refuted by this qualification.
4   One important element has not been considered for the sake of clarity, namely population movements between configurations related to the household life-cycle and, more generally, demographic changes (Rossi 1980).
5   In Brussels, the Green Party has the strongest urban profile (in the sense of fostering diversity and confrontation) and is gaining influence. Interestingly, its strongholds are in the inner city and not in the middle-class suburbs. An analysis of the residence of their political members shows a quasi systematic concentration in gentrification pockets. The party also has the largest number of elected members of immigrant origin (De Borman et al. 2001).
6   A similar tendency towards the repressive city can be expected in cities outside the European core as new immigrant concentration areas appear in the inner cities.
7   A remarkable strategy of the poor to resist this type of development on the housing market has been emergency buying. Immigrants bought cheap and low-quality houses in their original concentration area. They were thus protected from further increases in housing costs and from being displaced from the neighborhoods in which they had their vital social networks and ethnic infrastructure (Kesteloot et al. 1997).
8   This is the case in Belgium, where the local police is largely paid by the municipalities.

REFERENCES

Aalbers, M. (2001) *The Double Function of the Gate: Social Inclusion and Exclusion in Gated Communities and Security Zones*. Eurex paper (http://www.shakti.uniurb.it/eurex/library/Albers-Gated Communities.pdf).

Atkinson, R. (2000) The hidden costs of gentrification: displacement in Central London. *Journal of Housing and the Built Environment*, 15: 307–326.

Barata Salgueiro, T. (1995) La pauvreté urbaine dans la région de Lisbonne. *Espace-Populations-Sociétés*, 3: 341–348.

Barlow, J. and Duncan, S. (1994) *Success and Failure in Housing Provision: European Systems Compared*. Pergamon, Oxford.

Bastié, J. (1964) *La croissance de la banlieue Parisienne*. Presses Universitaires de France, Paris.

Blakely, E.J. and Snyder, M.G. (1997) *Fortress America, Gated Communities in the United States*. Brookings Institution Press, Washington D.C.

Borgegard, L. and Murdie, R. (1994) Social polarisation and the crisis of the welfare state: the case of Stockholm. *Built Environment*, 20: 254–268.

Boyer, R. (1986) *La théorie de la régulation: Une analyse critique*. La Découverte, Paris.

Brunet, R. (1989) *Les Villes Européennes*. Datar, Paris.

Carpenter, J., Chauvire, Y., and White, P. (1994) Marginalization, polarization and planning in Paris. *Built Environment*, 20: 218–230

Dassetto F. (1991) *Immigrés et communes, équilibres difficiles: Le cas de Saint-Josse-ten-Noode*. Sybidi Papers No 12, Academia, Louvain-la-Neuve.

De Borman, L., Dobruszkes, F., and Marissal P. (2001) Analyse socio-spatiale du lieu de résidence des élus communaux à Bruxelles. *Belgeo*, 1: 63–76.

De Brabander, G., Vervoort, L., and Witlox, F. (1992) *Metropolis, over mensen, steden en centen*. Kritak, Leuven.

De Kooning, M. and Strauven, I. (2000) Bruxelles 1945–1970: espoirs et illusions. In: Jacqmin, Y. and Vander Brugghen, B. (eds.) *Un siècle d'architecture et d'urbanisme 1900–2000*. Mardaga, Sprimont.

Donzelot, J. and Jaillet, M.C. (1997) *Deprived Urban Areas, Summary Report of the Pilot Study*. North Atlantic Treaty Organization, Committee on the Challenges of Modern Society, Report No 215.

Engels, F. (1892) *The Condition of the Working-Class in England in 1844*. Swan Sonnenschein, London.

Esping-Andersen, G. (1990) *The Three Welfare States Of Capitalism*. Polity Press, Cambridge.

Friedmann, J. and Wolff, G. (1982) World city formation: an agenda for research and action. *International Journal of Urban and Regional Research*, 6: 309–344.

Garreau, J. (1991) *Edge City: Living on the New Frontier*. Anchor Books, New York.

Harvey, D. (1985) *The Urbanization of Capital*. Blackwell, Oxford.

Harvey, D. (1989) *The Conditions of Postmodernity: An Enquiry into the Origins of Cultural Change*. Blackwell, Oxford.

Howard, E. (1902) *Garden Cities of Tomorrow*. Sonnenschein, London.

Hoyt, H. (1939) *The Structure and Growth of Residential Neighborhoods in American Cities*. Federal Housing Administration, Washington D.C.

Kazepov, Y. (1995) Urban poverty patterns in Italy: the case of Milan. *Espace-Populations-Sociétés*, 3: 329–340.

Kesteloot, C. (1986) Les dimensions historique et structurelle de la différenciation sociale de l'espace urbain, l'exemple bruxellois. *Espace-Populations-Sociétés*, 1: 15–30.

Kesteloot, C. (2000) Brussels: post-Fordist polarization in a Fordist spatial canvas. In: Marcuse, P. and van Kempen, R. (eds.) *Globalizing Cities: A New Urban Spatial Order?* Blackwell, London.

Kesteloot, C. and Cortie, C. (1998) Housing Turks and Moroccans in Brussels and Amsterdam: the difference between private and public housing markets, *Urban Studies*, 10: 1835–1853.

Kesteloot C., de Decker, P., and Manço, A. (1997) Turks and housing in Belgium, with special reference to Brussels, Ghent and Visé. In: Özüekren, A.S. and van Kempen, R. (eds.) *Turks in European Cities: Housing and Urban Segregation.* European Research Centre on Migration and Ethnic Relations, Utrecht University, Utrecht.

Le Galès, P. (2002) *European Cities, Social Conflicts and Governance.* Oxford University Press, Oxford.

Mandel, E. (1980) *Long Waves of Capitalist Development.* Cambridge University Press, Cambridge.

Marcuse, P. (1997) The enclave, the citadel and the ghetto: what has changed in the post-Fordist US city? *Urban Affairs Review*, 33: 228–264.

Marcuse, P. and van Kempen, R. (eds.) (2000) *Globalizing Cities: A New Urban Spatial Order?* Blackwell, Oxford.

Martinotti, G. (1999) A city for whom? Transients and public life in the second generation metropolis. In: Beauregard, R.A. and Body-Gendrot, S. (eds.) *The Urban Moment: Cosmopolitan Essays on the Late 20th Century City.* Sage, London.

Massey, D. (1979) In what sense a regional problem? *Regional Studies*, 13: 233–243.

Merlin, P. (1972) *Les villes nouvelles: Urbanisme régional et aménagement.* Presses Universitaires de France, Paris.

Mingione, E. (ed.) (1996) *Urban Poverty and the Underclass: A Reader.* Basil Blackwell, Oxford.

Morlicchio, E. (ed.) (2001) *Spatial Dimensions of Urban Social Exclusion and Integration: The Case of Naples.* URBEX No 17, AME, Amsterdam.

Musterd, S., De Klerk, L., Boomkens, R., Yap Hong, S., van der Wouden, R., and van Delden, B. (1997) *Stad zonder horizon: Stadspolitiek en stedelijke ontwikkeling in Nederland.* Van Gennep/Nederlands Gesprek Centrum, Amsterdam.

Power, A. (1993) *Hovels to High Rise: State Housing in Europe since 1850.* Routledge, London–New York.

Power, A. (1997) *Estates on the Edge: The Social Consequences of Mass Housing in Northern Europe.* MacMillan, London.

Reau, L., Lavedan, P., Plouin, R., Hugueney, J., and Auzelle, R. (1954) *L'oeuvre du Baron Haussmann, Préfet de la Seine (1853–1870).* Presses Universitaires de France, Paris.

Rossi, P.H. (1980) *Why Families Move.* Sage, Beverly Hills.

Sassen, S. (1994) *Cities in a World Economy.* Pine Forge Press, Thousand Oaks, CA.

Sayad, A. (1995) *Un nanterre Algérien, terre de bidonvilles.* Autrement, Paris.

Sjoberg, G. (1960) *The Preindustrial City, Past and Present.* Free Press, New York.
Smith N. (1996) *The New Urban Frontier: Gentrification and the Revanchist City.* Routledge, New York.
Terhorst, P.J.F. and van de Ven, J.C.L. (1997) *Fragmented Brussels and Consolidated Amsterdam: A Comparative Study of the Spatial Organization of Property Rights.* Netherlands Geographical Studies, No 223, Netherlands Geographical Society, Amsterdam.
Urban Task Force (1999) *Towards Urban Renaissance.* Department of Environment, Transport and the Regions, London.
Vance, J.E. (1977) *This Scene of Man: The Role and Structure of the City in the Geography of Western Civilization.* Harper, New York.
van Criekingen, M. (2003) *Revisiting the Diversity of Gentrification: Neighbourhood Renewal Processes in Brussels and Montréal.* (http://www.gla.ac.uk/departments/urbanstudies/gentpaps/mc.doc)
van Weesep, J. and Musterd, S. (eds.) (1991) *Urban Housing for the Better-Off: Gentrification in Europe.* Stedelijke Netwerken, Utrecht.
Vandermotten, C., Vermoesen, F., De Lannoy, W., and De Corte, S. (1999) Villes européennes, cartographie comparée. *Bulletin du Crédit Communal,* 207–208: 1–408.
Vieillard-Baron, H. (1996) *Les banlieues.* Éditions Flammarion, Paris.
Volovitch-Tavares, M.C. (1995) *Portugais à Champigny, le temps des baraques.* Autrement, Paris.
Wacquant, L. (1996) Red belt, black belt: racial division, class inequality, and the state in the French urban periphery and the American Ghetto. In: Mingione, E. (ed.) *Urban Poverty and the "Underclass": A Reader.* Blackwell, Oxford.
Warde, A. (1985) Spatial change, politics and the division of labour. In: Gregory, D. and Urry, J. (eds.) *Social Relations and Spatial Structures.* Macmillan, London.
Wilson, W.J. (1997) *When Work Disappears: The World of the New Urban Poor.* Knopf, New York.

Part II

The Spatial Impact of Ongoing Transformation Processes

7

The Dynamics of Social Exclusion and Neighborhood Decline: Welfare Regimes, Decommodification, Housing, and Urban Inequality

Alan Murie

Introduction

The term "social exclusion" represents more than just a new fashion in debates about poverty and social inequality. New patterns of social deprivation have emerged in post-Fordist cities associated with the uneven development of their economies and changes in their organization and structure. These patterns have been analyzed from different perspectives. Some American contributions have focused on the emergence of an underclass and a new poverty, associated with higher unemployment and the growth of insecure employment. This creates new poverty groups, essentially from a distributional perspective, in which the lack of income is related to individual problems and consequences of market change.

The European debate has developed differently. While residential segregation is the principal organizational feature of American society and provides the structural conditions for the development of an underclass, segregation is less marked in European cities and European welfare states retain safety nets that further limit the potential for development of an underclass.

Social exclusion represents a different tradition in debates about poverty and a change of focus from distributional issues to relational issues (van Kempen 2002). Low income is not regarded as a sufficient cause for being poor and issues of membership, access and belonging are also at stake – inadequate social participation, lack of social integration and lack of power. This builds on the social rights identified by Marshall (1963) as the key element in post-war welfare states and turns the attention to the concept of social citizenship and social exclusion. It reflects the different perspectives on urban inequalities and policies in Europe and in North America. Rather than a new poverty focus on the underclass, the European focus on social exclusion refers to participation, redistribution, and rights. While the different European approach arises partly because of more generous welfare systems, it also leads to a critical examination of the welfare state and decommodified services.

This chapter argues that the emergence of the term "social exclusion" as the focus of debate requires a critical analysis of welfare institutions. While this can fit with a neoliberal agenda, which sees public services as inherently flawed, it also connects with previous research agendas that highlighted the inequalities associated with the way that decommodified services are operated. After discussing the concept of social exclusion, the chapter connects this with debates about welfare regimes and decommodification and uses examples from housing to raise questions about the operation of decommodified services. Where services are not provided through the market and access is not determined simply by ability to pay and a price mechanism, it is important that we do not assume that problems of exclusion, access, and inequality no longer exist or that services are distributed simply according to need.

Social Exclusion: Different Perspectives

Levitas (1998) has explored the different meanings of social exclusion and how these have shaped current government thinking and policy. She views the term social exclusion as problematic because it divides society into two groups: the excluded and the included. In policy terms, this might seem a valuable distinction because it facilitates targeting of resources. However, it can lead to a static view of who the excluded are and neglect people at the margins. Levitas argues that by dividing society into two groups, issues of inequality become less important and minimalist solutions are easier to adopt: "What results is an overly homogeneous and consensual image of society . . . in which inequality and poverty are pathological and residual, rather than endemic" (1998: 6).

Levitas identifies three competing approaches to understanding and implementing policies on social exclusion:

1 An "underclass" approach.
2 A "poverty" approach.
3 An "integrationist" approach.

In an "underclass" approach, the excluded are blamed for their poverty. The term underclass was originally coined over 30 years ago with reference to the emergence of structural unemployment in the USA at the beginning of the 1960s (Myrdal 1963). At that time, the rediscovery of poverty led to speculation that the rise in unemployment and failure of the welfare state to end poverty would have serious implications for the development of an isolated section of society outside the mainstream. The term has come into fashion in the past decade through Murray (1990). Core arguments concerning the persistence of an underclass have been based on the intergenerational transmission of inadequacy and poverty, focusing upon hereditary psychological and pathological traits within the working class and the importance of learnt behavior that is perpetuated, from generation to generation, because of its effects on children (e.g., Lewis 1964, 1966).

The recurring emphasis in this underclass approach is that a section of the population is detached from the rest of society and does not share the same culture or values. Revival of the concept started in the USA where the underclass has been associated with issues of "race" and has a distinctly spatial dimension. The most developed account focuses upon outcomes of social deprivation and increased dependency within black communities (Wilson 1987). Wilson's thesis, from empirical research into America's poor black neighborhoods, rests on his observation of increased social mobility for middle-class blacks. The "concentration effect" of social drift led Wilson to conclude that an increasingly marginalized group of poor people become left behind and unable to identify or emulate successful role models (Wilson 1987). This fulfills the conditions for the emergence of an underclass. While Wilson recognizes structural factors affecting poverty, including the deindustrialization of North American cities, Murray argues that the underclass is an emerging form of moral and social behavior and attitudes, stimulated by an expansion of welfare, which promotes short-term economic rationalism and results in increased dependency upon the state (Murray 1990).

Each of these underclass approaches has been vigorously contested in America and elsewhere. The evidence of intergenerational transmission has been challenged and it has been argued that short-term coping strategies and behavior associated with poor diet and lack of opportunity have been mistakenly identified as habitual and cultural. In Europe, more generous welfare states may also make the model inappropriate. As Musterd and Ostendorf (1998) have argued, European cities do not show the same degree of social and ethnic segregation as the USA and polarization is less associated with ethnicity than with class. For example, they note Massey and Denton's view (1993: 9) that in America residential segregation is the principal organizational feature of society responsible for the creation of the urban underclass. Segregation creates the structural conditions for the development of a kind of counter-culture in which a job, good education and strong relations between people are no longer part of the prevailing system of values and norms (Musterd and Ostendorf 1998: 5). This perspective builds into those associated with an underclass. The concentration of poverty generates attitudes, behaviors, and values that impede the ability of residents to grasp whatever opportunities exist for social mobility.

Friedrichs' (1998) summary of the American literature accounting for segregation suggests that spatial segregation of two social groups increases with the degree of income inequality in a city, the degree of inequality of education (years of schooling in a city), the percentage of minorities in the total urban population, and the size of the total population in the city. The omission of housing from this list is explicable because housing is provided almost exclusively through the market and access is directly determined by income. In European cities, housing is significantly decommodified and access to high-quality housing in the not-for-profit sector may be based on other factors not always correlated with income. Although there is concern about the development of ghettos in European cities, the actual situation is still far from that reality (Musterd and Ostendorf 1998: 3).

European cities do not have the same levels of segregation or the same organizational arrangements determining processes of segregation and, in this context, it would seem that Levitas' (1998) "poverty" and "integrationist" alternatives for the term social exclusion are more relevant.

In a "poverty" approach, the causes of exclusion are related to low income and resources. The poverty approach is strongly associated with Townsend's (1979) research which involved a wide-ranging survey of individuals' and households' incomes, savings, material possessions, investments, and lifestyles.

In an "integrationist" approach, the excluded have no jobs and need to be reintegrated through paid employment. In discussing this approach, Levitas draws heavily upon policy literature from the European Commission including key documents on social policy (Levitas 1998: 19).

When the term "social exclusion" is used essentially to refer to exclusion from the labor market, it represents a much more limited notion than relative deprivation. It neglects low pay, poverty among people who would not be expected to be employed, and those in unpaid work. It focuses attention disproportionately upon access to employment and employability. This is too narrow an approach for many commentators and justifies too narrow a policy focus on employment and training activities. Some commentators have largely dismissed the notion of social exclusion, either because of this narrow base or because of the lack of precision of definition and the flexibility of the notion.

Accepting these problems and cautions, it is possible to use the term "social exclusion" in a different way and this chapter seeks to build upon a more constructive view of the notion of social exclusion. This view first of all emphasizes the continuities between notions of social exclusion and the notion of relative poverty developed in particular by Townsend. Relative poverty is about the measurement of "participation standards" accepted as normal by society. The measurement of participation involves measuring income, resources, consumption, and entitlement: "Individuals, families and groups can be said to be in poverty when . . . their resources are so seriously below those commanded by the average individual or family that they are, in effect, excluded from the ordinary living patterns, customs and activities" (Townsend 1979: 32).

This approach links to the work of Marshall (1963) in the sense that participation standards are seen as a measurement of citizenship. To be full citizens individuals need incomes, resources and access to facilities in order to meet their economic and social obligations.

Townsend sought to develop a deprivation standard of poverty that related to people's participation in society. Rather than poverty being based on a relative income standard such as average income or a certain percentile of average income, poverty should take account of people's ability to fully participate in the activities regarded as normal by others in that society. This dynamic concept of poverty acknowledged that subsistence minima or other poverty levels established at one period of time needed to be adjusted in the light of changing expectations and opportunities in society. Townsend argued that households could be ranked according to income and according to the types of deprivation they experienced.

The key conclusion from Townsend's work was that as income diminishes from the highest levels, so deprivation steadily increases, but at a certain trigger point deprivation begins to increase swiftly. This indicates a point below which incomes could be regarded as insufficient to enable people to fully participate in society.

An approach that builds on ideas of relative deprivation can go beyond Townsend's to recognize material deprivation and lack of income but also focus on the processes and dynamics that cause material disadvantage. This approach relates to the contrast made between what Room refers to as an "Anglo-Saxon" approach whereby poverty involves measurement of the outcome of a process (measured by the distribution of resources and incomes) and social exclusion involves analysis of the process and the interaction between different elements that lead to exclusion (Room 1995a,b). These elements are measured by inadequate social participation, lack of social integration and lack of power. Room identifies four aspects of social exclusion:

1 Concentration of disadvantage on population groups or areas.
2 Persistence of disadvantage over time.
3 The compound nature of disadvantage.
4 Resistance of problems to existing or traditional policy solutions.

The definition emerging from the debate on social exclusion is one that embraces more than traditional household and individual measures of poverty and has a spatial dimension. Social exclusion has increasingly come to be used to refer to a dynamic process that shuts people off from the benefits enjoyed by full citizens (Walker 1997: 8; Saraceno 2002).

Measurement or Process

Different approaches to social exclusion involve different assumptions and are open to different criticisms. Much of the caution about the term social exclusion arises from caution over measurement and implied divisions between the excluded and included. The implications are that, rather than precise measurement and a focus on households, understanding social exclusion requires methods that are sensitive to a range of different deprivations and which focus on the processes of exclusion. This implies the use of qualitative as well as quantitative methods and a focus on agencies and individuals that "do the excluding" rather than solely on those at the receiving end. In this way, a constructive use of the term social exclusion refers to more than paid work or the household or income poverty.

The shift away from measurement of outcomes will mean that reference is made to the circumstances and strategies of households experiencing different processes and combinations of circumstances. This is important in view of what we know about the changing circumstances of households. Changes in incomes may mean that households move in and out of poverty – if we were preoccupied with measuring poverty outcomes they would be included at one stage but excluded at another and the understanding of dynamics and trajectories is undermined.

An example of this can be provided from Britain. The British Household Panel indicates that 29 percent of people who leave poverty return within a year and that just under one-fifth of lone parents and unemployed recipients of income support reclaim benefit within 6 months. Short and repeated spells of poverty are much more common than the persistent or permanent poverty implied by traditional class-based approaches. Only 4 percent of people were income poor in each of the first 4 years of the British Household Panel study. This represents only 14 percent of those who were poor at any time between 1990/1 and 1993/4 (Jarvis and Jenkins 1996). Similar results are reported in other European countries (Leisering and Leibfried 1999; Saraceno 2002).

The British Household Panel Survey showed that among the poorest 10 percent of individuals, approximately half moved off the bottom rung of the ladder within a year. Some fall back quickly but most do not move very far. The groups most likely to move back down the income ladder are lone parents and pensioners living alone. Walker argues that a longer time frame for looking at numbers in poverty reduces the numbers counted as poor than when taking a snapshot. A reduction of the accounting period from 12 months to 1 month, for example, increases the official US poverty rate by almost one-quarter (Walker 1995: 105).

Although attention has tended to focus on persistent poverty, it is also important to refer to recurrent poverty. People who need assistance to cover a single short-term contingency or occasional users claiming once, or for very short spells, are not obviously subject to the same exclusions as sporadic users who require assistance on several occasions. The literature on poverty in Europe indicates that the events that trigger poverty include reductions in work, divorce and relationship breakdown, job loss, and the termination of insurance (Walker 1997; Saraceno 2002). Routes out of poverty are associated with similar events: remarriage, social insurance begins, job begins, more work. In Britain, family changes appear to have a minor role and indeed stability in household composition may have a benign influence. Most scholars analyzing economic exclusion, social exclusion, interpersonal and civic exclusion state that, just as poverty does not necessarily result in exclusion, any one form of exclusion does not always predicate another. In conclusion, Walker (1997), Leisering and Leibfried (1999) as well as Saraceno (2002) state that reconceptualizing poverty and exclusion as processes rather than states will result in a better understanding of the nature of the problems to be addressed. It also brings to the fore policy strategies that are proactive and preventive rather than reactive and ameliorative.

A constructive approach to social exclusion emphasizes factors other than income. It emphasizes process and enables us to avoid an artificial dualism that refers to households that are excluded and those that are included. It begins to open up the fact that households at different stages in their lives and in different circumstances are affected by different processes of exclusion and experience social exclusion to different extents and in different ways. It focuses much more upon the factors contributing to exclusion and involves questioning whether everything is solved by income: whether access to services is ultimately dependent upon income status. Through this it opens up questions about the operation of the welfare state.

Integration, Welfare States, and the Production of Exclusion

Social exclusion, as set out above, does not lend itself to precise measurement and if the differences between this concept and poverty are to be real the approach to measurement has to be different. In developing alternative approaches a wider framework is suggested in the literature. This refers to different ways in which households access resources – through the market and payment for work, through transfer payments and services provided by the state and other bodies where access is not based on ability to pay and where payment is not at the point of consumption, and through reciprocal and other non-market transactions based on family, community, and other affiliations. A broader concept of social exclusion involves explicit reference not simply to material deprivation but also reference to access and use of a wide range of services and participation in social, economic, political, and community life.

A number of the key contributions in this area have built upon Polanyi (1944) and ideas of decommodification and the extent to which resources are available to households independent of market participation. For example, Mingione (1991) and Kesteloot et al. (1997) refer to overlapping spheres of social integration. These are those of the market (employment), redistribution (the welfare state) and reciprocity (affiliation). Just as these are spheres of integration providing the mechanisms for inclusion and participation, so they are the sources of exclusion. A dynamic approach concerned to identify the ways in which exclusion is produced would refer to these same spheres. A narrow view of social exclusion might regard the market and the labor market as the key source of barriers to full social participation and a naïve view might assume that the welfare state necessarily operates to reduce such barriers. One of the key elements in a broader approach to exclusion would be to avoid such assumptions.

The most widely used literature on welfare states and the evolution of welfare states since the mid-twentieth century is also based on ideas of decommodification. Esping-Andersen (1990: 37) refers to decommodification as the degree to which individuals or families can uphold a socially acceptable standard of living independently of market participation and identifies three welfare regime types referring to the "combined interdependent way in which welfare is produced and allocated between state, market and family" (Esping-Andersen 1999: 34–5). A number of criticisms have been leveled at Esping-Andersen's operationalization of this perspective (see Leibfried 1992; Castles and Mitchell 1993; Alber 1995; Castles 1996; Ferrera 1996; Gough et al. 1997; Room 2000). He has recognized that his initial categorization makes too little reference to gender differences and the analysis of the family but has largely defended his classification of countries into regime types. For this chapter, two particular dimensions of the approach adopted by Esping-Andersen (1990) are questionable. First, the reference to social security and transfer payments is consistent with the focus on national arrangements related to income and employment. It either assumes that income buys other services (including, for example, housing, education, and health), or that questions about the distribution of these services are unimportant (perhaps that they are equitably distributed). In some welfare systems this approach may be appropriate; for example, access to health services may be based upon insurance contributions and the key issue is whether people can afford to maintain insurance contributions. The extent to which social security systems support income to enable people to maintain their health insurance is then critical in determining their access to health. The same may apply where access to education involves some payment at the point of consumption or, for example, housing services are priced at market levels or basic benefits are intended wholly or partly to meet housing costs.

Even in these circumstances, there are questions over how far equal access to services is purely dependent upon the ability to pay and the neglect of the local administration and operation and rationing of decommodified services is a weakness (Saraceno 2002). It could be inferred that decommodified services operate on the basis of need or merit when in practice they may not. Undoubtedly, this concern is greatest where access to services is strongly determined by local bureaucratic processes and where the social security system is not the only system ensuring the delivery of equal access. For example, the British welfare state, categorized quite rightly by Esping-Andersen as ungenerous in terms of social security provision, is much more generous in terms of health, education, and housing (Murie 1997). The National Health Service is a universal service that involves some charges at the point of consumption but there is no insurance test for access. There is no link between social security status and access to health provision. Similarly, primary and secondary education is a universal service which is free and compulsory for children up to the age of 16. Again, there is no requirement to make contributions through income and the processes of determining access to different qualities of education are separate from those related to social security.

In relation to housing, the British system, as with most Western and Northern European countries, includes a very large social rented sector (at its peak in the 1970s one in three of all properties). Access to public sector housing has never been determined by income. Rents in this sector have not been based solely on market processes and general subsidies have meant that rents are significantly below market levels. A means-tested subsidy operates alongside mainstream social security provisions and can meet 100 percent of rent (because there is no element in other social security payments to contribute towards rent). This subsidy (housing benefit) embraces a much higher proportion of the tenant population than its equivalents in many other countries (Kemp 1997).

Put crudely, the British welfare state involves a range of processes of access to different decommodified services, and households may experience very different treatment in relation to different services. While the social security system is ungenerous, decommodified health, education and housing services have, in the past, been inclusive and generous. However, their operation is fragmented, services are intrinsically varied in quality (based in part on age of infrastructure, condition, reputation and funding over time) and delivery is affected by various factors. Where services are applied for affects whether and when they will be received; the quality of service varies in a way that does not apply to nationally determined social security payments. We need to look beyond employment and income transfers and also look at access to services in kind if we are to understand how the welfare state contributes to and alleviates exclusion.

This relates to a second dimension which is not fully addressed in Esping-Andersen's work: a critical evaluation of how decommodified services operate. One possibility is that we are left with an idealized picture of decommodified services. Thus, the argument runs that decommodification means that households are able to access certain services in a way that they could not do if access was determined simply by position in the processes of production and the income generated through employment and market processes. As a result of decommodification, households with limited bargaining power in the labor market or limited skills and employability are able to access certain crucial services on a basis more equal with that of people with greater employment opportunities and resources in the labor market. However, we need to move the debate one step further to consider how decommodified services operate, what processes of stratification exist within them and what inequalities are associated with non-market processes. The inclusiveness of decommodified welfare state systems is not adequately measured by the range of services and generosity of benefit levels in Esping-Andersen's analysis. We should not accept the framework of decommodified welfare provision based on the analysis of welfare regimes carried out by Esping-Andersen as the last word in the debate. The questions raised by concerns about social exclusion require us to focus much more closely on the operation of other decommodified services that are being provided.

Classes of Welfare in Decommodified Housing

In the final part of this chapter it is helpful to give some illustrations of the kind of issues that arise in relation to the operation of decommodified welfare state services. The primary example referred to in this chapter relates to the operation of decommodified housing provision. There is a literature from different countries that suggests that access and bargaining power in relation to decommodified housing services is not simply based upon need. Access is not based upon income but other resources are brought into play so that some households get a better deal than others.

The fundamental issue in relation to housing is that the quality of properties is not uniform. In all public or decommodified housing systems there are more desirable and less desirable properties (2231, 5728, 4990, 2687); there are larger properties and smaller properties; there are properties in better condition, in better locations, and so on. Against this background there is a familiar analysis of the previous operation of decommodified housing systems in Eastern European countries (2286, 2284, 5338, 5336). This has indicated that party membership and the sector of the economy worked in affected the likelihood of accessing the best properties (Simmie 1991). There is a clear stratification that was not based upon income or economic position alone but which privileges certain groups rather than others. The effects of this have been carried through into privatization processes operated in these economies. Those who are in the best properties have benefitted most from privatization and groups that were regarded as most crucial to earlier political regimes, and were rewarded by them, benefit from subsequent reorganization. The processes do not operate the same as in the market, but they do involve unequal access, exclusion and inclusion and this extends to the effects of privatization.

White (1998) has developed a discussion of social exclusion in France drawing heavily on processes relating to public sector housing. He emphasizes the importance of power and ideology in exclusionary processes: "To exclude someone or something is to prohibit access to some form of resource: the exclusion mechanisms therefore relate to the interests of those who are instrumental in creating such exclusion for others" (1998: 149).

The mechanism of exclusion, groups excluded, and the reasons for exclusions depend on the material, political, and societal circumstances at a certain place, at a certain time. Exclusion is likely to be contested and will therefore generally be unstable and evolutionary in nature, with societal boundaries shifting in response to tensions built up through existing mechanisms. The resources that are subject to exclusion include jobs, welfare services, education, housing, territory, political legitimacy, and citizenship, and the mechanisms include coercive practices backed by the use of judicial powers, the operation of free market forces, as well as the more conciliatory position of closure through persuasion and ideology.

White emphasizes processes through which the residents of *grand ensembles* have changed and become excluded in Paris. These large estates were built for skilled working-class and lower middle-class residents rather than for the poorest elements in French society. However, over time these more affluent groups have moved into the growing owner-occupied sector leaving their social rented apartments to those who have less ability to buy properties: immigrants, those without stable employment prospects, single parent families, and young households (5934, 1914, 5971). The changing reputation and perception of these estates was increased by a series of disturbances in the early 1980s and their identification as target projects for neighborhood rehabilitation (5942, 5939, 5929, 5945). The areas became seen as problem areas; their residents were subject to social exclusion because of where they lived and also because of where there were young people. Exclusion in the Paris area was concentrated in the inner suburbs and in large social housing estates in particular. Accessing decommodified social housing meant increased exposure to social exclusion. Processing by the state confirmed the status and labeled individuals and households rather than being redistributive.

Research related to access to council housing in Britain shows a similar pattern (see Henderson and Karn 1987; Malpass and Murie 1999). It highlights the extent to which access to housing is not based purely upon need in a decommodified system. In certain respects decommodified council housing operates as a market. The differential bargaining power that is brought to bear relates to need and formal prioritization, but also relates to understanding of what is available and the ability to wait. Ability to wait relates to the severity and unsustainability of existing housing arrangements. At the same time, the process of matching applicants with properties involves a process of social stereotyping that reflects underlying processes within the society. Applicants are likely to be stereotyped as "rough" or "respectable", or "deserving" or "undeserving", and the opportunities they are afforded through bureaucratic allocation processes will be different. The outcome of all of this is that there is unequal treatment initially between two broad categories. The first category is those who have priority but are able to wait (because they can cope with their present situation for longer) and are classified as potentially good tenants or respectable households. These households are more likely to access the better quality housing. The second category of applicants are regarded as "rough" or "undeserving" (or perhaps the homeless) and those who have little capacity to wait until a better offer arises (again, including the worst housed and the homeless) will be more likely to be channeled towards poorer quality housing (6141). These processes are not official or transparent and relate to the ways in which managers within the public sector seek to cope with the different pressures upon themselves (including pressure to let the least attractive dwellings) (2559, 2560, 5725, 5736). They are also associated with processes of institutional racism.

The question that this analysis raises is whether similar processes of stratification operate within all welfare regimes (6477, 1885). For example, in Sweden, Sahlin (1995) has argued that there are very explicit processes of exclusion, which mean that the equivalent of the British "undeserving poor" or "rough" households are excluded from mainstream decommodified housing. They are more likely to be left in the privately rented sector in a market sector of poorer quality and dependent on benefit payments to maintain their position in the housing market.

These examples refer to housing but there is a wider literature that suggests that the same issues arise in relation to other decommodified services. In the British context, there is a growing analysis of performance indicators for the quality of local welfare state services and there is substantial variation in the quality of services between local authority administrations and between neighborhoods. There are schools that perform at a very high level and schools that perform at a much lower level. There are areas with very good services for elderly or for young people and those with very poor services. The variation in quality of services is explained by a range of financial, political, and other factors, but there is very little evidence that it relates at all to differences in patterns of need. Differences in expenditure on services that are provided in kind do not relate to differences in patterns of need measured by demographic or social and economic variables (Bramley et al. 1998). Consequently, decommodified services for lower income neighborhoods are often worse than in higher income areas (0782, 5954).

The implication of this is that, depending upon where you live, you are likely to access different qualities of service. In relation to schools, you may live in an area where the local school is a dilapidated older building, there is a high turnover of teaching staff, and poor-quality facilities. The population mix in the school may be limited and the amount of specialist activities may also be limited. In another area, you may be able to access a local school that is newly built with modern facilities, a range of specialist programs available to children, and a high degree of social mix where peer group pressure may be more significant in achieving better examination results and where the pupil population is much more stable (1698, 4156, 4280).

It would be wrong to imply that children who live in a neighborhood that can access the better school will necessarily get a better education. However, there continue to be some striking connections between educational achievement and social class or income or ethnicity and these are at least in part explained by the quality of local facilities. As with the discussion of housing, we can begin to identify neighborhood as one of the important factors affecting the quality of decommodified provision.

Neighborhood Disadvantage

European welfare states are all presented with challenges by declining inner-city or peripheral neighborhoods, whether they are of decommodified housing, private housing or mixed ownerships. As certain areas and parts of the market become more strongly associated with poor people and represent poor social environments, those with choice in the housing system are less likely to move to such areas. As a result, the social and income mix in these areas is further eroded (5946, 4208). The common features of these households – relating to incomes and expenditure patterns and lack of access to information networks, and other resources that could change household circumstances in the short term – exacerbates problems for residents and affects the reputation of areas. The stigma and reputation of areas further affects residents in seeking jobs and in a variety of other contexts. Households living in areas with limited resources are likely to be disproportionately dependent on local facilities – shops, schools, health services, transport services, jobs, and training (1867, 5963, 3135). Yet, these are areas that tend to be deprived in terms of the key local services.

For example, Taylor (1995) suggests that there is a downward spiral that reinforces the disadvantage faced by households on deprived estates. Concentrations of low-income households result from limited access to jobs, incomes, and lack of choice in the housing market. They contribute in turn to a lack of political clout, no market to attract quality goods and services, overstretched public services, the stereotypes that reinforce isolation and lack of access to jobs, and capital, poor health, low self-esteem, and crime (3469, 4246, 2639, 5713, 2714, 5023).

The spiral of decline is only one side of the picture. The alternative view emphasizes the resilience of communities, families, and social groups, and the minority behavior that is used to stereotype the characteristics of a neighborhood. This comes close to what Wacquant and Wilson (1993) referred to as the organized or institutional ghetto of mid-twentieth century American cities where "activities are . . . structured around an internal and relatively autonomous social space that duplicates the institutional structure of the larger society and provides basic minimal resources for social mobility" (Wacquant and Wilson 1993: 32).

Although responding to unfavorable circumstances, segregation then has a positive function, increasing security and avoiding contact with dominant groups. Under this argument, concentrations of poverty may be highly functional for the group or groups who are segregated (4000, 4882, 5663, 5722). The position becomes a complicated one. It is not as simple as a discussion about whether segregation is voluntary or involuntary because it is likely to be dynamic and changing over time and it may have elements of advantage as well as disadvantage at the same time. Environments that contribute to the maintenance of ethnic cultures may also contribute to the protection of majority culture and may reduce or minimize the electoral or political threat. As Castles (1993, quoted in Boal 1998: 97) claims, segregation may be contradictory and migrants:

May be socially disadvantaged by concentration in areas with poor housing and social amenities but they frequently want to be together in order to enjoy mutual support, rebuild family and neighborhood networks, and maintain their languages and cultures. Ethnic neighborhoods allow the establishment of small businesses and agencies which cater to migrants' needs, as well as the formation of associations of all kinds. Residential segregation is thus a pre-condition for and result of community formation.

The discussion of these issues can be taken further through the results from a study of the neighborhood dimension of social exclusion in 11 European cities (Amsterdam, Rotterdam, Antwerp, Brussels, Berlin, Hamburg, London, Birmingham, Paris, Milan, Naples) (Musterd and Murie 2001). The experience of households most exposed to processes of social exclusion (lone parents, black and minority ethnic groups, young unemployed people) in these cities is not the same. Households in the same income, socio-economic or poverty category have different local resources on which they can draw. Where people live affects the experience of poverty and consequently is a key element in social exclusion. Their experience is affected by the nature of national political and social rights and social security systems but also by the resources provided in neighborhoods. For example, the older private sector neighborhoods in Berlin, Birmingham, Brussels, and Rotterdam all provide different opportunities and resources from each other but also from the more modern planned peripheral neighborhoods in the same cities. Nor is one type of neighborhood consistently "better" than the other type. In Berlin, it is the peripheral public sector estate of Marzahn that has provided relative safety and security to new migrants to the city, while it is inner-city Sparkbrook that has come to have a similar role for Asian households in Birmingham (Musterd and Murie 2001). What is evident from both of these cases is that the effect is not simply one of the neighborhood impact on its population. Neighborhood resources partly relate to physical form, history and local policies but they are also generated by their residents and the history of residence. There is a two-way interaction in which residents shape the neighborhood and the character of the neighborhood affects household decisions to stay, move to, and move on from the neighborhood. This perspective resonates with Wacquant and Wilson (1993) and the discussion above.

The dynamics of social exclusion both affect neighborhoods and are affected by them, and the understanding of deprivation and exclusion is sterile without reference to neighborhood and place as key elements in the production and experience of exclusion. Such reference includes aspects of the local welfare state and rebalances accounts that neglect the welfare state altogether or are selective about what they include. Some neighborhoods are better placed to access jobs and training; some have a greater diversity of public, voluntary and community services – more acceptable to a mixed faith and diverse population. Others are less diverse. The perceptions and realities of opportunity, security, and safety relate to all of these and are important aspects of the experience of exclusion.

Conclusions

Current debates about social differences in cities and neighborhoods have moved beyond the literature concerned purely with income poverty. While the cautions about the vagueness of the term "social exclusion" are wholly justified, this chapter has argued that the term "social exclusion" connects with the concern to identify different resources that households draw upon and which determine their life chances. The term "social exclusion" enables us to take a wider and more critical view of resources other than income and those generated through employment.

This chapter has argued that this enables us to focus upon the way in which services provided in kind, or below market price, are accessed. Rather than assuming that such decommodified services are of unvarying quality and are distributed according to need, it is more realistic to recognize that they are highly variable in their quality and that there are systematic differences in ability to access different qualities of services. Even if these differences conformed with position in the labor market, the processes that determine this differentiation would not be market processes, but ones that relate to bureaucratic means of access.

The patterns of stratification are not the same as in the market but decommodified services privilege households with certain non-market-related attributes and general processes of social and racial stereotyping mean that households with the same or similar levels of need experience unequal treatment in bureaucratic systems.

The final element in the argument is that where people live is a significant factor in this process of differential access to services. This arises because where you live is an important element in stereotyping (sometimes referred to as postcode stereotyping), but also because the quality of local services varies. The two things also reinforce each other. Areas with poor services (housing, schools, and a range of other public services) are less likely to be regarded as areas of choice by those who have sufficient bargaining power to exercise choice. They are much more likely to become the areas of last resort with a greater predominance of households with the least bargaining power. Areas where schools and houses are better are more sought after and households that have the capacity to wait and have bargaining power will be more likely to move to them. The areas of last resort will be marked by a higher degree of churning and turnover of population, which affects the extent to which social cohesion and community develops and also affects the extent to which social programs can be effectively targeted. It is difficult to target highly mobile communities and to improve their employability, education and training.

A constructive approach to social exclusion raises questions about the operation of decommodified services. The existence of decommodified services that are widely accessible is not consistent with notions of an underclass but is consistent with stratification in relation to welfare state provision. Whether services are decommodified or provided through the market, they will privilege some groups and some groups will be able to access better quality services more easily. There is little reason to start from a position that assumes that decommodified services are even in their quality, and are distributed purely on the basis of need. The likelihood is that they will contribute to inequalities. This does not mean that decommodified services operate in the same way as market processes, nor does it mean that they are less effective than market processes. However, a realistic starting point is to assume that they reward and exclude households on different grounds and through different processes and with different impacts. The empirical questions are about the precise patterns of stratification or differences in bargaining power and differences in quality of services. The implication is that if we are to understand processes of social exclusion we need to have evidence about more than income and the generosity of social security systems. We need to refer to neighborhood resources and local welfare state services and to understand how decommodified systems are working and what inequalities they generate as well as reduce.

REFERENCES

Alber, J. (1995) A framework for the comparative study of social services. *Journal of European Social Policy*, 5 (2): 131–149.

Boal, F.W. (1998) Exclusion and inclusion: segregation and deprivation in Belfast. In: Musterd, S. and Ostendorf, W. (eds.) (1998) *Urban Segregation and the Welfare State*. Routledge, London.

Bramley, G., Evans, M., and Atkins, J. (1998) *Where Does Public Spending Go?* DETR, London.

Castles, F. (1996) Needs-based strategies of social protection in Australia and New Zealand. In: Esping-Andersen, G. (ed.) *Welfare States in Transition*. Sage, London.

Castles, F. and Mitchell, D. (1993) Worlds of welfare and families of nations. In Castles, F. (ed.) *Families of Nations: Patterns of Public Policy in Western Democracies*. Dartmouth, Aldershot.

Esping-Andersen, G. (1990) *The Three Worlds of Welfare Capitalism*. Polity Press, Cambridge.

Esping-Andersen, G. (1999) *Social Foundations of Postindustrial Economies*. Oxford University Press, Oxford.

Ferrera, M. (1996) The Southern model of welfare. *Journal of European Social Policy*, 6: 17–37.

Friedrichs, J. (1998) Social inequality, segregation and urban conflict. In: Musterd, S. and Ostendorf, W. (eds.) (1998) *Urban Segregation and the Welfare State*. Routledge, London.

Gough, I., Bradshow, J., Ditch, J., Eardley, T., and Whiteford, T. (1997) Social assistance in OECD countries. *Journal of European Social Policy*, 7 (1): 17–43.

Henderson, J. and Karn, V. (1987) *Race, Class and State Housing*. Gower, London.

Jarvis, S. and Jenkins, S.P. (1996) *Do the Poor Stay Poor?* ESRC – Research Centre on Micro-Social Change, University of Essex, Colchester.

Jordan, B. (1997) *A Theory of Poverty and Social Exclusion*. Polity Press, Cambridge.

Kemp, P. (1997) *A Comparative Study of Housing Allowances*. HMSO, London.

Kesteloot, C., Meert, H., Mistiaen, P., Savenberg, S., and van der Haegen, H. (1997) *De geografische dimensie van de dualisering in de maatschappij, overleveningsstrategieen in twee Brusselse wijken Federale Diensten voor Weten schappelijke*. Technische en Culterele Aangelegenheden, Programma Maatschappelijk Onderzoek, Brussels.

Leibfried, S. (1992) Towards a European welfare state: on integrating poverty regimes in the European Community. In: Ferge, Z. and Kolberg, J.E. (eds.) *Social Policy in a Changing Europe*. Campus Verlag, Frankfurt.

Leisering, L. and Leibfried, S. (1999) *Time and Poverty in Western Welfare States*. Cambridge University Press, Cambridge.

Levitas, R. (1998) *The Inclusive Society: Social Exclusion and New Labour*. Macmillan, London.

Lewis, O. (1964) *The Children of Sanchez*. Penguin, London.

Lewis, O. (1966) The culture of poverty. *Scientific American*, 215 (4): 19–22.

Malpass, P. and Murie, A. (1999) *Housing Policy and Practice*, 5th edn. Macmillan, London.

Marshall, T.H. (1963) *Citizenship and Social Class in Sociology at the Crossroads*. Heinemann, London.

Massey, D.S. and Denton, N.A. (1993) *American Apartheid: Segregation and the Making of the Underclass*. Harvard University Press, Cambridge.

Mingione, E. (1991) *Fragmented Societies*. Blackwell, Oxford.

Murie, A. (1997) The social rented sector, housing and the welfare state in the UK. *Housing Studies*, 12 (4): 437–461.

Murray, C. (1990) *The Emerging British Underclass*. Institute of Economic Affairs, London.

Musterd, S. and Murie, A. (2001) *A Comparative Report on Social Exclusion and Integration in Neighbourhoods in 11 Cities in 6 European Countries*. Urbex Paper No. 20, Amsterdam (available at http://gp.fmg.uva.nl/urbex/menureps.htm) (accessed 29/08/2003).

Musterd, S. and Ostendorf, W. (eds.) (1998) *Urban Segregation and the Welfare State*. Routledge, London.

Myrdal, G. (1963) *Challenge to Affluence*. Pantheon Books, New York.

Polanyi, K. (1944) *The Great Transformation.* Rinehart, New York.

Room, G. (1995a) Poverty in Europe: competing paradigms of analysis. *Policy and Politics,* 23 (2): 103–113.

Room, G. (ed.) (1995b) *Beyond the Threshold: The Measurement and Analysis of Social Exclusion.* Policy Press, Bristol.

Room, G. (2000) Commodification and decommodification: a developmental critique. *Policy and Politics,* 28 (3): 331–351.

Sahlin, I. (1995) Strategies for exclusion from social housing. *Housing Studies,* 10 (3): 381–404.

Saraceno, C. (ed.) (2002) *Social Assistance Dynamics in Europe: International and Local Poverty Regimes.* Polity Press, Bristol–London.

Simmie, J. (1991) Housing inequality under state socialism: an analysis of Yugoslavia. *Housing Studies,* 6 (3): 172–181.

Taylor, M. (1995) *Unleashing the Potential.* Joseph Rowntree Foundation, York.

Townsend, P. (1979) *Poverty in the UK.* Penguin, London.

van Kempen, E. (2002) "Poverty pockets" and social exclusion: on the role of place in shaping social inequality. In: Marcuse, P. and van Kempen, R. (eds.) *Of States and Cities.* Oxford University Press, Oxford.

Wacquant, L. and Wilson, W.J. (1993) The cost of racial and class exclusion in the inner city. In: Wilson, W.J. (ed.) *The Ghetto Underclass: Social Science Perspectives.* Sage, London.

Walker, R. (1995) The dynamics of poverty and social exclusion. In: Room, G. (ed.) *Beyond the Threshold: The Measurement and Analysis of Social Exclusion.* Policy Press, Bristol.

Walker, A. (1997) *Britain Divided: The Growth of Social Exclusion in the 1980s and 1990s.* CPAG, London.

White, P. (1998) Ideologies, social exclusion and spatial segregation in Paris. In: Musterd, S. and Ostendorf, W. (eds.) (1998) *Urban Segregation and the Welfare State.* Routledge, London.

Wilson, W.J. (1987) *The Truly Disadvantaged: The Inner City, the Underclass, and Public Policy.* University of Chicago Press, Chicago.

8

Social Exclusion, Segregation, and Neighborhood Effects

Sako Musterd and Wim Ostendorf

Introduction

Segregation, social polarization, and social exclusion have been central concepts in urban debates for quite some time now (Wilson 1987; Sassen 1991; Fainstein et al. 1992; Massey and Denton 1993; Hamnett 1994; Marcuse 1996; O'Loughlin and Friedrichs 1996; Musterd and Ostendorf 1998; Marcuse and van Kempen 2000). These debates are about inequality, separation, apartheid, estrangement, isolation, ghettos, "income-neighborhoods," and how people are affected by them both in social terms and in terms of other characteristics, such as ethnic origin. Cities in the Western world reflect the socio-spatial outcomes of polarization, segregation, and exclusion processes. The outcomes vary according to the character and intensity of social processes. In their turn, these social processes depend upon a wider range of factors and developments. The economic structure of a city and the kind of restructuring that is taking place are frequently regarded to be among the most powerful forces behind social fragmentation and integration in the urban realm. However, state regimes, the state's attitudes towards inequality and redistribution, the quality of the social welfare systems, housing subsidy schemes, pension systems, and current changes in welfare provisions (cutbacks) are also thought to be highly important. There are indications that the more liberal welfare states, which are characterized by more modest social welfare programs and moderate state intervention in housing and a variety of social spheres, will "produce" more social inequality, polarization, and perhaps also social exclusion compared with the strong redistributive welfare states (van der Wusten and Musterd 1998; Domburg-De Rooij and Musterd 2002). That would explain, for example, why levels of segregation and levels of social and socio-spatial inequality are higher in contexts such as the USA than in many European countries, such as Sweden, the Netherlands and Germany. Other – related – factors are frequently mentioned too, such as racial or ethnic divisions in society, which are associated with different levels of economic, social, and cultural capital, and also the reinforcing effect of socio-spatial and ethnic segregation itself: the neighborhood effect.

This chapter focuses on the ongoing process of segregation and social exclusion, and the potentially reinforcing role of the spatial clustering of socially excluded people. In the next section, the discussion starts with a brief introduction to the concepts we are going to apply, followed by an overview of the dimensions that are considered central in the theoretical debates about the forces behind the urban social processes affecting segregation and exclusion. The third section focuses on the debate about neighborhood effects and provides some empirical evidence that may be helpful to understand the magnitude of the effects. Some conclusions are drawn in the fourth section.

Analytical Dimensions of Segregation and Exclusion

Strictly speaking, the concept of segregation refers to spatial distinctions and the spatial separation of different population or demographic categories. With regard to people, the segregation and exclusion debate usually focuses on socio-economic distinctions, on ethnic distinctions and – albeit infrequently – on household type or other demographic distinctions. Thus, we may talk about socio-spatial inequality, ethnic neighborhoods or even ethnic ghettos, or about lifestyle-related neighborhoods: neighborhoods appealing to the young or the childless, to family households, careerists, etc.

As far as the concept of exclusion is concerned, we must think of the access people have to various parts of life in society. The debate on exclusion is also a debate about inclusion, participation, and integration in society. People may become socially excluded because they do not participate in the labor market and so cannot raise sufficient income to actively participate in society. They also miss out on direct interactions with colleagues. It is assumed that the socio-spatial composition of the population is a relevant factor in this respect (Wilson 1987; Musterd and De Winter 1998; Robson et al. 2000; Galster 2002). People may become ethnically excluded when there are strict ethnic divisions, both in society and spatially. The extreme example of institutional ethnic exclusion was the situation of apartheid in South Africa. Such strict divisions prevent the development of interactions between ethnic groups, reducing participation in society. Finally, demographic exclusion is also possible, and potentially harmful, as in the case of age generation conflicts. The population composition in neighborhoods in terms of different age groups or different lifestyles may account for exclusion or inclusion processes.

It is important to be aware of the fact that segregation and exclusion processes will differ between different places, both within states and – probably more significantly – between states.

Having outlined what we regard to be the most important elements in the concepts of segregation and exclusion, we turn now to the dimensions that are considered relevant to understand the variations in levels of segregation and exclusion. In the remaining part of this section, we will discuss those dimensions that appear to be most central in the theoretical debate.

Economic restructuring

Over the past decade, the advanced industrial countries in the world have experienced an economic restructuring process that is considered to be strongly associated with the process of globalization. Improved technological conditions have led to a growing interconnectedness and internationalization of firms, economic processes, and people. This is expressed in the rapid growth of flows of people, money, and goods across the world. Among the characteristics of these changes is a growth in the demand for services and thus for service jobs for which high-skilled labor in particular is required. However, the global economic restructuring process also brings a demand for low-skilled or unskilled jobs, and where new labor demand and old labor supply fail to match unemployment may be the outcome. According to some, the outcome of the restructuring process will be increased social polarization, that is, growth at the bottom and top end of the socio-economic distribution. For example, an increase in the share of households with moderate skills or with a low income (not uncommonly immigrants) and at the same time an increase in the share of people who are highly skilled or households with a high income (e.g., Sassen 1991). Increased social inequality and social division will result in social inclusion of one part of society and social exclusion of another part. The excluded will lose the opportunities, means, and finally the ability to participate in society, which will be expressed by a lack of labor market participation, moderate school participation, a weak position in the housing market, low or extreme-wing political participation, and few signs of socio-cultural integration. The divisions will be reflected in spatial patterns. Separate residential concentrations of wealthy people in gated communities (5350, 0194, 0205) and of poorer households in "ghetto-like" neighborhoods (2685, 5713, 6143, 5378): socio-economic spatial segregation will result.

Saskia Sassen has expressed this viewpoint most clearly over the past decades. She contends that we are witnessing a new phase in an ongoing process of "internationalization". This new phase consists of the internationalization of production sites through foreign investment. This process also explains at least part of the growing international migration. Countries of origin and destination of migratory flows are directly related in one way or another and international investment is an important link in this respect. The process of economic globalization, Sassen argues, presupposes locations that operate as loci of control: "global cities." These cities are important production sites for a vast array of specialized services needed for the management and control functions they fulfill. At the same time, global cities are key destinations of migrants. The most important reason for migrants to settle in global cities is that the particular economy of these cities generates both high-level specialized jobs and low-wage jobs. The presence of specialized services and corporate headquarters where the attractive jobs are to be found is an important source of low-wage jobs. Because of this peculiar occupational structure, global cities are "dual cities," polarized or divided basically along ethnic and social lines.

A second major theory on economic restructuring and social inequality is known as the "mismatch theory." The basic line of reasoning is that a post-industrial society needs more highly educated workers. The labor market will therefore be subject to a process of continuous upgrading instead of a tendency towards polarization. As for inequality, the problem is the emergence of a potential underclass, which consists of people living in inner cities who are too poorly educated to match the increasing qualifications demanded by a post-industrial economy. Apart from their lack of education, these people face the problem that they live in (inner) cities, where, more than in other locations, employment that they would qualify for – unskilled industrial work – has decreased, resulting in a spatial mismatch as well. These processes create "the truly disadvantaged" (Wilson 1987). There are clear differences here compared with Sassen's theory: no polarization in the labor market, but upgrading; and people at the bottom of the social hierarchy are not exploited – working in poorly paid, unattractive jobs, the working poor – but excluded: unemployed. In reality, mixed forms will be shown: upgrading and polarization; and working poor and unemployed.

The welfare state

Economic restructuring may result in polarization between those who have the right skills and get a good job, and those whose skills do not fit the requirements and have to take one or two very low-paid jobs: the working rich versus the working poor. However, economic restructuring may also result in less polarization. Much depends on the organization of the wider welfare state in which cities operate.[1] Some countries developed very extensive welfare systems in which substantial redistribution of the bargaining power was established. Progressive and high income taxes, the development of high minimum-wage levels, the provision of relatively generous benefits in situations of old age, illness, unemployment, and disability, extensive systems to redistribute the costs and the benefits in the sphere of housing (brick and mortar subsidies, individual rent subsidies); all of these types of state involvement were made part of the system of care in many countries. Countries such as the Netherlands, Scandinavian countries, the UK, France, Germany, and Belgium experienced tremendous welfare expansion between 1945 and the mid-1970s.

Many support the idea that there is a strong relationship between the extent to which the welfare states have developed their social security and welfare systems and the levels of social polarization, socio-spatial segregation, and social exclusion in urban areas. In general, there is a belief that well-developed welfare states have thus far been largely successful at shielding certain population categories from social deprivation and isolation (Musterd and Ostendorf 1998). Unlike the "laissez-faire" situation in the USA, the interventions in many North and West European countries have reduced the levels of polarization. However, the reduced polarization levels may result in higher levels of unemployment in these well-developed welfare states if there is a structural or conjunctural mismatch in the labor market. This is because in order to survive, inhabitants in these states will not be forced to accept low-paid jobs when their skills no longer match the requirements of the market. This is not only because of the lack of such jobs as a result of the high minimum-wage levels set by law, but also because many people will be permitted to enjoy relatively generous unemployment or social benefits while waiting for other labor market opportunities to come along. Temporarily, the unemployment levels can become rather high. Currently they are very high in Germany; however, they are lower in strong welfare states such as Denmark, Sweden and the Netherlands.

Yet, it is not only the structure of the welfare state we should look at. The restructuring that occurs over time should also be addressed. After the first (1973) and particularly after the second (1979) oil crisis, many Western countries were faced with relative economic decline alongside economic restructuring processes, often parallel with rising social problems. High structural unemployment in the large cities, among immigrants in particular, and exploding state budget deficits laid the basis for the revision of welfare states. Many of them moved in a more liberal direction. A general atmosphere was created in which all initiatives were pushed into more market-led and deregulated directions, with new keywords such as: tax reduction, no universal welfare benefits, a reduction of redistribution, deregulation, subsidy cuts, and easier access to and exit from the labor market. It is now a widely shared view that these revisions will result in an increase in individual employment opportunities, but will at the same time result in an increase in social polarization and sociospatial segregation in urban areas (cf. *Built Environment* 1994). However, when prosperity increases once more, the edges will again be taken off the cutback programs.

One of the interesting and crucial elements in today's theoretical debate about segregation and exclusion is the question of the relationship between global economic restructuring processes and the role of the (welfare) state (Mishra 2001). The key hypothesis that the globalization process almost inevitably results in an increase in the power of "the market" (private firms) and big international organizations, such as the International Monetary Fund (IMF), the Organization for Economic Cooperation and Development (OECD) and the World Bank, and a loss of power and opportunities – though not necessarily a loss of activity – of local and national governments has received wide support. Peter Marcuse (1996: 40) expressed this idea when he looked at the new role of the state and said: "They rather shift direction, from a social and redistributive to an economic and growth or profit-supporting purpose. At the same time, they shift from a public, in the sense of a democratic or popular, instrument, to an instrument of private business purpose." However, this hypothesis has also been challenged. Because of globalization processes, some factors may lead to convergence, but others may result in divergence. Place-specific characteristics appear to become more important as unique selling points in a consumption-oriented society, and the new expressions of regional identities may also push the convergence ideas aside (see below). One might even go one step beyond that and think of state interference as a much more independent factor, with effects upon the social structures that support certain economic structures, but not others. Welfare states impact upon the labor market structures, and also upon the levels of inequality and levels of participation in the labor market. Therefore, the global economy does not dictate the structure or the participation rate in the labor markets of the advanced economies. Consequently, the social consequences of globalization differ according to differences in institutional contexts or, more specifically, different types of welfare states (Musterd and Ostendorf 1998; Saraceno 2002).

Cultural capital

The polarization and mismatch theories have also been severely criticized for other reasons. Jack Burgers and Sako Musterd (2002) referred to the sociologist Roger Waldinger (1996), who has argued that Wilson's theory does not take into account ethnic differentiation, which is clearly visible in American urban labor markets. He wondered how it is possible that African Americans have become the victims of deindustrialization if they have always been under-represented in that sector in the first place? If the African Americans who live in the inner cities are unemployed because of a fatal combination of educational level and geographic location, why do Hispanics and Asians with the same level of education and living in the same inner cities find jobs? A similar criticism is possible regarding Sassen's theory. If there is such a need for unskilled labor in the labor market of "global cities," why has this need to be fulfilled by immigrants from other continents (Asia, Latin America), while just around the corner many unskilled and unemployed African Americans are available? Both Sassen and Wilson have a dominant focus on the supply side of the labor market (jobs); they neglect the (differentiation of the) demand side (different groups of workers). According to Waldinger, the mix of their cultural capital and the vacancies in the labor market at the time they arrived in their country and city of destination determines the position of immigrants in the labor market.

Ethnic segregation in European cities is much lower than in American cities. The Index of Segregation (IS)[2] for Surinamese residents versus the rest of the population in Amsterdam is 34; Moroccans in Frankfurt 21; people from the Indian Subcontinent in London 49; but blacks in Detroit 85, in New York 82, in Chicago 81. Consequently, Wacquant (1993), Rhein (1996) and Musterd et al. (1998) note that although many Europeans are worried about the development of ghettos in European cities, the actual situation is still far from that reality. Yet Waldinger's ideas also seem applicable to many European cities. In many cities, different migrant categories, with similar levels of skills, clearly show different levels of participation in the labor market, as was shown, for example, in the European URBEX research program (Musterd and Murie 2002). In Amsterdam, in 1998, for example, the unemployment rates of Turks (18 percent) and Moroccans (20 percent) were clearly higher than for Surinamese (10 percent) and the "native" Dutch population (4 percent).

Path dependency and place-specific identity

Some authors (Scott 1997; Storper 1992) have argued that instead of lead-ing to homogeneity of geographic locations, globalization rather deepens differences between locations. The basic argument here is the paradox that in an age of rapidly increasing mobility, "place" becomes more in-stead of less important: "place matters." Comparative advantages of places are to be sought in unique characteristics, which are hard to copy else-where. This could be a historically grown social or economic structure (population compositions, economic complexes), a historically grown welfare state structure (with widely accepted redistributing mechanisms), or historically grown physical structures (cultural monuments or highly valued architecture) (Musterd and van Zelm 2001). Economic develop-ment may predominantly be triggered by place-specific historically grown social, cultural, economic, and political structures, which will be to some extent interrelated and result in fairly unique "local models" (e.g., the "Dutch *polder* model," which includes a style of governance in which consensus-building is extremely important; see Beck 2000). Consequently, the "place-specificity" thesis can be interpreted as a divergence thesis. Each location, each city, will have its own place-specific characteristics and may be able to use these characteristics to attract certain economic activities and people. The differentiating effects of local specificity may also result in dissimilar social and socio-spatial structures.

Many European cities have a rather rich historical profile in terms of the length of their paths. This has contributed to the diversity among European cities, and also diversified their urban economic structures (Le Galès 2002). Whereas some show rather narrow economic profiles, others reveal multilayered economic structures with ample opportunities to attract new economic activities. Awareness of diversity seems crucial to understanding the variety of socio-spatial and social inequalities.

Thus, social inequality, or polarization, is not the unavoidable result of globalization. In some places this is the case, in others not. Local or regional conditions, both institutional and historically grown, as well as "cultural" factors, may result in different social inequality situations and a variety of socio-spatial patterns in cities.

An independent effect of spatial segregation: the neighborhood effect?

Apart from the mutual relationships that are expected to exist between economic restructuring, the welfare state, cultural capital, and place-specific histories on the one hand, and social polarization, socio-spatial

segregation, and social exclusion on the other hand, it is also assumed that
the socio-spatial or ethnic segregation patterns of the population that were
developed in the past are a potentially major and independent cause of
ongoing social problems of individual households in cities. However, much
thinking in this field seems to be inspired by images and perceptions that
originate from specific but relatively special cases; specific cities in the
USA where social polarization and social and ethnic segregation are reaching very high levels. In these circumstances, one can imagine that segregation or even "hypersegregation" may easily become a factor in its own
right (Massey and Denton 1993: 9). The "opportunity structures" available in local and social networks and the support of the state would be
insufficient to help people escape from their situation (see, for example,
Galster 2002). Segregation, then, might create the structural conditions
for the development of a kind of counter-culture in which a job, a good
education, and solid relations between people are no longer part of the
prevailing system of values and norms. Geography-oriented sociologists
too believe that segregation in American cities is producing and aggravating social problems (Wilson 1987).

However, we have to bear in mind that the ethnic and socio-economic
spatial segregation of the population in American cities is generally more
rigid compared with the segregation encountered in many other Western
cities, those of Europe in particular. If it is true that the continental
European, so-called "redistributing welfare states" – which are different in
social, political and ethnic-cultural terms too – have produced cities that
are only moderately segregated in the first place, it is questionable whether
these moderately segregated areas have any effect on social integration or
exclusion processes at all.

Even though many European politicians repeatedly express their fears
about exclusion through segregation, many (though not all) scholars continue to express their doubts (see the special issue of *Housing Studies* 2002
for a recent discussion). In the Netherlands, Hans van Amersfoort (1992)
has repeatedly shown the weak relationship between residential segregation, labor market participation, educational attainment, and income
position. In a recent essay on *Ethnicity and the Multicultural City*, Ash Amin
(2002) referred to research in which equally segregated cities in the UK
(Leicester and Bradford) show very different levels of social problems.
These are just examples to illustrate that the impact of so-called neighborhood effects may not be as strong as many people think.

It is our aim for the remainder of this chapter to contribute to the
understanding of the relationship between segregation and social exclusion by showing some recent findings of research that was carried out in
the Netherlands and the large Dutch cities, and which focused on the
neighborhood effect.

We will show the levels of segregation, both ethnic and socio-economic, and then focus on the empirical results of a longitudinal research project carried out at individual level, through which we were able to follow the social position of individuals over a period of 5 years, controlling for relevant individual characteristics. We were also able to ascertain the direct social environment – the social composition of the neighborhood individuals were living in. This provided opportunities for a detailed analysis of the effect of the neighborhood upon an individual's social chances.

Spatial Segregation and Neighborhood Effects on Social Exclusion

Segregation

We have already referred to the rather moderate levels of ethnic segregation in European cities, compared with US cities. This is certainly true for large Dutch cities, where the IS for immigration categories turns out to be moderate, perhaps with the exception of Turks and Moroccans in The Hague (Table 8.1). These low levels are confirmed by in-depth studies of the spatial distribution of these populations. Research carried out in Amsterdam by Deurloo and Musterd (1998) revealed that there are many ethnic concentration areas[3] of small size. In 1996, 72 separate concentration areas of at least 2.5 hectares could be discerned. In these areas there lived 85,000 so-called foreigners (Turks, Moroccans, Surinamese, Antilleans, and people from other non-industrialized countries), comprising 39 percent of all foreign residents in Amsterdam. There were only two larger areas (at least 40 hectares) with at least 50 percent foreign residents (a statistically weak proportion, because the share of selected foreigners in Amsterdam, according to the definition, is already 30 percent). Applying a more realistic criterion of, say, 75 percent, would reveal that only 10 areas of at least 2.5 hectares would be left, together comprising 7.3 percent of

Table 8.1 Index of segregation for various immigrant categories in the four large Dutch cities, 1998

	Turks	Moroccans	Surinamese	Antilleans
Amsterdam	42	41	34	35
Rotterdam	50	44	26	26
Den Haag	53	49	39	26
Utrecht	43	45	23	20

Source: van Kempen et al. (2000).

the foreign population. Only two areas of at least 10 hectares could be found. So, only two significant, but still small, concentrations of foreign residents can be found, but only if five population categories are taken together. The majority of Surinamese, Antilleans, Turks, and Moroccans did not live in so-called concentration areas of their own ethnic group. Furthermore, levels of concentration in these areas were not very high. Maps of concentration areas of Surinamese and Moroccans (the two largest immigrant groups from non-industrialized countries) confirm these statements (see Figures 8.1 and 8.2, included on the CD-Rom). So far it is obvious that the Dutch welfare state has prevented the rise of persistent and extreme concentrations of ethnic immigrants. International comparative studies that have been carried out reveal that similar statements can be made for many other European cities, such as Frankfurt, Stockholm, Milan, Oslo, Munich and Vienna (see also Domburg-de Rooij and Musterd 2002).

The story about the socio-economic ghetto, or the lack of it, must be put into a similar framework. This is partly because of the moderate share of poor people in Dutch cities. If we apply a strict definition of poverty, only low percentages can be found. In Amsterdam, we were able to analyze a large random sample of the urban population of 18 years and older (in 1994). Based on 4085 responses we could estimate that, applying a strict definition of poverty as "low-educated and unemployed, without a partner with a job" only 4.5 percent of the population could be labeled "poor." Large concentrations of poverty could not be found; only some small "pockets of poverty" could be discovered. In these pockets, the percentage of poor people remained low (under 25 percent).

The moderate level of socio-economic segregation is also reflected in the low scores on the IS of poor households, as measured by the Central Bureau of Statistics. They used a definition of poor households based on income. If a household's income does not surpass the level of social welfare benefits, the household is labeled "poor." According to this definition, in 1998, 11 percent of Dutch households were poor. In the Amsterdam agglomeration the figure was almost 16 percent. The IS, which was calculated for poor households relative to the rest of the households, based on information available at a 500-m grid system of the city and the metropolitan area, revealed rather moderate spatial inequality (Table 8.2).

The neighborhood effect

On the basis of the moderate spatial differences, it is not, in fact, to be expected that major neighborhood effects on the social position of individuals and households will develop. Yet, as said, the idea that there are

Table 8.2 Segregation of low-income households in the municipalities and agglomerations of the four large Dutch cities, 1998

	Municipality	Agglomeration
Amsterdam	19	27
Rotterdam	24	30
Den Haag	28	31
Utrecht	21	27

Source: CBS (1998).

important neighborhood effects on the social mobility opportunities of individuals and households is still strong in Europe, and also in the Netherlands. As a matter of fact, we should not rule out the possibility that even small spatial differences between population categories could already result in significant differences in terms of social opportunities. It therefore makes sense to test the assumption about the relationship between neighborhood composition and social mobility opportunities. Here, we will confine the analysis to the socio-economic dimension.

It should be noted that the neighborhood effect assumption is hard to test, because rich datasets are required which are not always available. Ideally, huge sets of longitudinal data with large numbers of variables and proper geographic information should be present at the individual level. This would provide the required individual social development data, and also give the opportunity to control for individual characteristics that may have impacted upon an individual's social career when analyzing the effects of the social composition of the neighborhood on individual careers. We were fortunate to have had access to such a dataset.

The empirical study aimed to investigate the association between segregation and social mobility (Musterd et al. 2001). The data available contained a 16 percent sample of the income tax forms of the entire Dutch population. Data for 1994 were assembled and the individual level 1989 information was coupled with that. Variables available at the individual level included age, ethnicity, the six-digit postal code, income, and socio-economic position, including information such as being on welfare or not.

The operationalization of social mobility (upward social mobility is regarded as diminishing the risk of becoming socially excluded; downward social mobility is regarded as increasing the risk) was formed by the socio-economic position of each household in 1994 compared with its position in 1989. The socio-economic position of a household was determined according to one of the following three categories:

1   Households who depend solely on unemployment or disability benefits (weak position).
2   Households among whom at least one member is receiving a pension.
3   Households with at least one member who has a paid job.

The postal code information was used to construct "environments" or neighborhoods for each individual. For each household it was possible to determine the social composition of the environment. We calculated the percentage of households in 1989 that depended solely on unemployment or disability benefits, i.e. the share of households with a weak socioeconomic position. The size of the areas analyzed was set at a radius of 250 m surrounding each household (with a minimum of 100 households). In short, what we did was to consider persons with a fixed – a weak – socio-economic position in 1989; then we calculated the social level of their environments (the percentages of people on welfare); and finally looked at their socio-economic position in 1994. Tables 8.3 and 8.4 reveal

Table 8.3 Households in 1989 who solely live on benefits according to their situation in 1994, and differentiated for social composition of the environment in 1989 with a radius of 250 m

"Weak" households in the environment in 1989 (%)	Number of households	Situation in 1994 In relation to all households			In relation to households not belonging to "at least a pension" in 1994
		Solely benefits	At least a pension	At least a paid job	Solely benefits
0–2	760	34.7	27.3	38.0	47.7
2–4	3603	42.6	25.5	31.9	57.2
4–6	6751	45.8	22.6	31.6	59.2
6–8	8485	46.8	22.0	31.2	60.0
8–10	9139	48.9	19.3	31.8	60.6
10–12	9212	49.9	18.3	31.8	61.1
12–14	8940	51.1	16.9	32.0	61.5
14–16	8638	51.8	14.7	33.5	60.7
16–20	13,366	53.5	13.4	33.1	61.8
20–30	21,777	57.0	8.8	34.2	62.5
30–40	7654	60.4	6.0	33.6	64.3
40–50	667	67.4	4.5	28.1	70.6
50–75	380	90.0	7.9	2.0	97.8
75–100	464	96.8	2.9	0.4	99.6
TOTAL	99,836	52.9	14.7	32.4	62.0

Source: CBS (1994, 1989).

Table 8.4 Households in 1989 who at least have a paid job according to their situation in 1994, and differentiated for the social composition of the environment in 1989 with a radius of 250 m

"Weak" households in the environment in 1989 (%)	Number of households	Situation in 1994 In relation to all households			In relation to households not belonging to "at least a pension" in 1994
		Solely benefits	At least a pension	At least a paid job	Solely benefits
0–2	61,603	5.6	7.1	87.4	6.0
2–4	112,071	6.4	7.8	85.8	7.0
4–6	121,544	7.2	7.9	84.9	7.9
6–8	107,966	8.2	8.1	83.8	8.9
8–10	86,573	9.4	8.1	82.5	10.2
10–12	69,301	10.4	8.2	81.4	11.3
12–14	53,045	11.4	7.9	80.7	12.4
14–16	41,713	12.4	8.1	79.5	13.5
16–20	53,510	13.6	7.7	78.7	14.7
20–30	57,997	17.8	6.1	76.1	19.0
30–40	13,583	23.5	4.7	71.8	24.7
40–50	762	23.3	4.7	72.0	24.5
50–75	217	19.6	11.3	69.0	22.1
75–100	90	35.5	0.0	64.5	35.5
TOTAL	779,975	9.9	7.7	82.4	10.8

Source: CBS (1994, 1989).

the outcomes for people who were on benefits in 1989 and for those who had a job in 1989, respectively. Conclusions were as follows:

- A very weak relationship was found between the social environment and the individual social mobility of socio-economically weak households (solely dependent on unemployment and disability benefits; table 8.3).
- The contextual effect tends to be much stronger for households who in 1989 had at least one job (Table 8.4).
- Controlling for age and the number of persons per household with a paid job did not reveal a more pronounced contextual effect.
- Controlling for education did not suggest that this dimension is fully explanatory for the contextual effects found.

These findings are remarkable. In general, when in the literature attention is paid to the effects of the social environment on social mobility, this is usually confined to the category of the population that is already in a "weak" socio-economic position (for instance only those who are dependent on benefits). They would spend more time in the direct environment of the dwelling (the neighborhood) and therefore would be more sensitive to all the negative influences that could come from that environment. Two interpretative theories are often referred to when people try to explain the negative results. The first is the theory of stigmatization of a neighborhood, through which certain employers exclude people for instance. The second is the type of theory in which the effects of negative role models are predominant: socialization theory. According to these theories, individuals who live in a weak environment will be negatively influenced and therefore encounter more problems in escaping from their own individual weak position.

However, the results of our analyzes seem to suggest that the social composition of the environment hardly has any effect on those who are already in a weak position; instead there is a possible neighborhood effect for the category of population that is not (yet) in a "clearly weak" socio-economic position. We also carried out these analyzes for each of the large Dutch cities, and came to similar conclusions.

It is difficult to explain these differences. An explanation for the lack of neighborhood effect in Dutch cities would be easiest, because we have already pointed out the relatively moderate levels of spatial segregation. This implies that those who are a little bit mobile can easily get in touch with "the other" and still have the opportunity to participate in society and to socialize. In fact, the pockets of poverty are simply too small to prevent that from happening. However, what may be more important is that the Dutch welfare state is putting a fair amount of resources into those who are defined as in need of help. Special programs are available to raise their education level and to improve their access to the labor market. This is often done without taking the social composition of the neighborhood into account. However, not all welfare policies are universal; there are area-based policies as well and we may hypothesize that poor people in poor neighborhoods who are considered to be in need of support, especially the long-term unemployed, will receive more attention from the welfare state than less poor people, such as those who have had a job but have recently become unemployed. That would imply that a neighborhood effect exists both for the clearly poor (long-term unemployed) and for the less poor (formerly employed, but recently unemployed), but that this effect is neutralized for the clearly poor by welfare state interventions, whereas it is not neutralized for the less poor. The latter have to take care of themselves until they get into serious trouble. It may also be true that the somewhat stronger households who lose their jobs are already those who are living in downgrading areas. The changes that occur in the neighborhood should, therefore, also be taken into account. This could not be properly carried out in our research project.

However, the findings we have presented have some far-reaching implications and repercussions for policies with regard to "weaker neighborhoods." The area-based policies, which have become increasingly important in European cities, may have very negative effects upon those who are in a somewhat stronger position (those who initially had a job, but lost that job during the course of the period we researched). In particular, the proposals for "mixed housing policies" that have been developed over the past decade in many European countries could have negative, instead of positive effects. It may indeed be true that for all households the social composition of the neighborhood has effects upon their social mobility opportunities. It may also be true that the negative effects upon weaker households are counterbalanced by strong welfare state interventions; these interventions may also be stronger in weaker environments and targeted to individuals in need in a more direct way. Those who are not defined as being "in need" do not receive that support, whereas the negative impacts of the neighborhood composition could be detrimental to them as well. The mixed-neighborhood policy then, might have negative results in total. When people with a job are more or less forced to accept a change of their neighborhood from a homogeneous neighborhood, where having a job and a stable social position was the norm, towards a mixed situation in which many unemployed are also living, they may run a greater risk of bearing the strong negative consequences of that policy, while there are fewer positive consequences (in terms of the probability of escaping from unemployment) for those who already are in a weak social position.

Conclusions

Segregation and exclusion are two extremely difficult concepts, with many connotations. There is a large variety of theoretical viewpoints, and the motivations for applying the concepts are wide-ranging too. In this chapter we discussed the possible interpretations of the various forms of segregation (and exclusion) and elaborated on several explanatory dimensions that are frequently addressed in the literature. We also considered the criticism linked to these. We have discussed the contrast between the levels of segregation and exclusion in European cities and US cities. Finally, we have tried to contribute to the debate about the so-called "neighborhood effect" on social exclusion.

We argued that there is a big difference between the USA and many European states and cities. In the latter contexts, the economic restructuring processes and their impacts upon social structures seem to be modified by relatively extensive state interventions, but also their impacts seem to be modified by a larger variety of historic legacies of cities; some have rich histories that have given them a strong position in today's dynamic changes towards a consumption- and service-oriented society, whereas others do not. The European variety seems to be larger than can be found in North America, which is because of a much longer urban history in Europe. Welfare states and urban histories may thus make a big difference as to how cities can develop and what kind of social structures will be part of that process. In general, one could say that in the USA there is usually a strong relationship between a person's employment position and other social indicators, such as income, education, and housing situation. If someone becomes unemployed, he or she will soon be confronted with a low income, and be forced to move to a marginal segment of the housing market in a separated area of the city. The spatial segregation of the population will then be a reflection of the social participation in other spheres. In many European cities, particularly those that are embedded in strong and relatively generous welfare states, the relationship or association between residential segregation, employment, income, and education is much weaker. Not only is the distance between poor and rich smaller, as is the association between an individual's position in the housing and labor market and their socio-economic position, but also there are no, or hardly any, ghettos.

In European cities, urban life is still characterized by fairly moderate levels of social and ethnic segregation. It appears that these moderate levels do not produce tremendous negative neighborhood effects in terms of the negative influence of weak social environments on the social opportunities of people who live in these environments. However, these effects may not be totally absent, as we have illustrated with Dutch longitudinal research results aimed at understanding the relationship between the social composition of the neighborhood and the social mobility (or exclusion) of individual households. If these effects are there, they may, surprisingly, have greater negative impacts upon the lives of those who are in a somewhat stronger position (those who had a job at the beginning of our research period), compared with those who are in a weaker position (those who were unemployed from the start). We hypothesized that these diverse impacts may be caused by the interventions of welfare states in many (other) spheres of life, whereby specific programs are offered to those who are regarded to be in need of social assistance and not to those who are not considered in need of help. The combined result may be that those who have a somewhat stronger social position, but live in a weak social environment, may experience more negative effects than those who are in a weak position and are living in a weak social environment. If this hypothesis receives substantial support, it will have major repercussions for today's area-based and mixed-neighborhood policies. The implication and recommendation would be to stop intervening in the socio-spatial mix, but widen the individual targeting of those who are in need. For the moment, this seems to be a too revolutionary change in urban policy.

What certainly would not be the right response would be a withdrawal of the welfare state, and the stimulation of market processes in the arrangement of housing and social spheres. That could only create sharper divisions, and the social, ethnic, and household inequalities would increase instead of decrease. Because liveable cities are becoming an increasingly important asset of modern consumption and service- and culture-oriented cities, it is crucial to avoid the development of "hard cities." The welfare state may help to reduce that risk and thus become an economic asset in its own right.

NOTES

1   Local welfare arrangements may, of course, also be relevant; however, it is beyond the scope of this contribution to go into the details of these local welfare interventions.
2   The index runs from 0–100; 100 implies absolute spatial segregation; 0 implies equal distributions across the city. A level under 40 is regarded to reflect moderate or low levels of segregation; 80 or higher reflects high levels of segregation.
3   A concentration area has been defined as an area in which the percentage of the category involved is at least two standard deviations above the mean. Adjacent areas have been taken together. The lowest level is the six-digit postal code area. Only areas with at least 100 inhabitants have been shown.

REFERENCES

Amin, A. (2002) *Ethnicity and the Multicultural City: Living with Diversity*. ESRC, London.

Beck, N. (2000) The Netherlands, a model for macro-economic development. *Social Science*, 410 (November): 1–14.

Built Environment (1994) Special issue on "A Rising European Underclass?", 20 (3).

Burgers, J. and Musterd, S. (2002) Understanding urban inequality: a model based on existing theories and an empirical illustration. *International Journal of Urban and Regional Research*, 26 (2): 403–413.

Central Bureau of Statistics (CBS) (1989) *Regionaal Inkomens Onderzoek*. CBS, Voorburg.

Central Bureau of Statistics (CBS) (1994) *Regionaal Inkomens Onderzoek.* CBS, Voorburg.

Central Bureau of Statistics (CBS) (1998) *Regionaal Inkomens Onderzoek.* CBS, Voorburg.

Deurloo, M.C. and Musterd, S. (1998) Ethnic clusters in Amsterdam, 1994–96: a micro-area analysis. *Urban Studies,* 35 (3): 385–396.

Domburg-de Rooij, T. and Musterd, S. (2002) Ethnic segregation and the welfare state. In: Schnell, I. and Ostendorf, W. (eds.) *Studies in Segregation and Desegregation.* Aldershot, Ashgate, 107–131.

Fainstein, S.S., Gordon, I., and Harloe, M. (eds.) (1992) *Divided Cities, New York and London in the Contemporary World.* Blackwell, Oxford–Cambridge, MA.

Galster, G. (2002) Trans-Atlantic perspectives on opportunity, deprivation and the housing nexus. *Housing Studies,* 17 (1): 5–10.

Hamnett, C. (1994) Social polarization in global cities: theory and evidence. *Urban Studies,* 31 (3): 401–424.

Housing Studies (2002) Special issue on "Trans-Atlantic perspectives on opportunity, deprivation and the housing nexus," 17 (1).

Le Galès, P. (2002) *Cities in Europe.* Oxford University Press, Oxford.

Marcuse, P. (1996) *Is Australia Different? Globalization and the New Urban Poverty.* Occasional Paper 3, Australian Housing and Urban Research Institute, Melbourne.

Marcuse, P. and van Kempen, R. (eds.) (2000) *Globalizing Cities: A New Spatial Order?* Blackwell, Oxford.

Massey, D.S. and Denton, N.A. (1993) *American Apartheid.* Harvard University Press, Cambridge.

Mishra, R. (2001) *Globalization and the Welfare State.* Edward Elgar, Cheltenham.

Musterd, S. and Murie, A. (eds.) (2002) *The Spatial Dimensions of Urban Social Exclusion and Integration* (Final Report). URBEX Series 22, AME, Amsterdam.

Musterd, S. and Ostendorf, W. (eds.) (1998) *Urban Segregation and the Welfare State: Inequality and Exclusion in Western Cities.* Routledge, London.

Musterd, S. and de Winter, M. (1998) Conditions for spatial segregation: some European perspectives. *International Journal of Urban and Regional Research,* 22 (4): 665–673.

Musterd, S. and van Zelm, I. (2001) Polycentricity, households and the identity of places. *Urban Studies,* 38 (4): 679–696.

Musterd, S., Ostendorf, W., and Breebaart, M. (1998) *Multi-Ethnic Metropolis: Patterns and Policies.* Kluwer, Dordrecht–London–Boston.

Musterd, S., Ostendorf, W., and De Vos, S. (2001) *Armoedeconcentraties en sociale effecten in dynamisch perspectief.* AME, Amsterdam.

O'Loughlin, J. and Friedrichs, J. (1996) Polarization in post-industrial societies: social and economic roots and consequences. In: O'Loughlin, J. and Friedrichs, J. (eds.) *Social Polarization in Post-Industrial Metropolises.* Walter de Gruyter, Berlin–New York.

Rhein, C. (1996) Social segmentation and spatial polarization in Greater Paris. In: O'Loughlin, J. and Friedrichs, J. (eds.) *Social Polarization in Post-Industrial Metropolises.* Walter de Gruyter, Berlin–New York.

Robson, B., Parkinson, M., Boddy, M., and Maclennan, D. (2000) *The State of English Cities*. Department of the Environment, Transport and the Regions, London.

Saraceno, C. (ed.) (2002) *Social Assistance Dynamics in Europe*. Policy Press, Bristol.

Sassen, S. (1991) *The Global City: New York, London, Tokyo*. Princeton University Press, Princeton, NJ.

Scott, A.J. (1997) The cultural economy of cities. *International Journal of Urban and Regional Research*, 21: 323–339.

Storper, M. (1992) The limits to globalization: technology districts and international trade. *Economic Geography*, 68: 60–93.

van Amersfoort, H. (1992) Ethnic residential patterns in a welfare state: lessons from Amsterdam, 1970–1990. *New Community*, 18 (3): 439–456.

van der Wusten, H. and Musterd, S. (1998) Welfare state effects on inequality and segregation: concluding remarks. In: Musterd, S. and Ostendorf, W. (eds.) (1998) *Urban Segregation and the Welfare State: Inequality and Exclusion in Western Cities*. Routledge, London.

van Kempen, R., Hooimeijer, P., Bolt, G., Burgers, J., Musterd, S., Ostendorf, W., and Sncl, E. (2000) *Segregatie en concentratie in Nederlandse Steden: Mogelijke Effecten en Mogelijk Beleid*. Van Gorcum, Assen.

Wacquant, L. (1993) Urban outcasts: stigma and division in the Black American ghetto and the French urban periphery. *International Journal of Urban and Regional Research*, 17 (3): 366–383.

Waldinger, R. (1996) *Still the Promised City? African-Americans and New Immigrants in Postindustrial New York*. Harvard University Press, Cambridge.

Wilson, W.J. (1987) *The Truly Disadvantaged: The Inner City, The Underclass and Public Policy*. University of Chicago Press, Chicago–London.

Figure 8.1 Amsterdam: concentrations of Surinamese, 2002.
(Concentrations: >2 SD above the mean; based on six-digit postcode data, produced with Mapinfo GIS.)
Source: Onderzoek en Statistiek, gemeente Amsterdam and Department of Geography and Planning, Universiteit van Amsterdam

Figure 8.2 Amsterdam: concentrations of Moroccans, 2002.
(Concentrations: >2 SD above the mean; based on six-digit postcode data, produced with Mapinfo GIS.)
Source: Onderzoek en Statistiek, gemeente Amsterdam and Department of Geography and Planning, Universiteit van Amsterdam

9

Segregation and Housing Conditions of Immigrants in Western European Cities

Ronald van Kempen

Introduction

European cities have been characterized by a mixed population with respect to origin for centuries. Fryer (1984, cited in Phillips 1998) relates that clusters of Africans and Indians lived in port cities such as London, Liverpool, and Cardiff as early as the 1800s. Cities have attracted migrants for numerous reasons, such as the availability of jobs, protection from robbers, the closeness to power, and the availability of housing. More recently, cities have become attractive, at least for some people, because of their leisure opportunities. Cities have attracted rich and poor migrants, young and old, men and women, individuals and families.

From the late 1950s through to the 1970s, many countries in Western Europe experienced a thriving economy and consequently a shortage of labor. Labor had to be imported because a national labor reserve was no longer available and, in order to keep the economy running, people from Southern European countries were invited to work temporarily in Western European industries. They were eager to come as the situation in their countries was not so prosperous, and became the first generation of guest workers.

In the 1970s, the host countries were forced to look to countries further away for an additional guest worker labor force. Because the economy in countries such as Spain, Portugal, Italy, and Yugoslavia started to improve, the recruitment of new guest workers became more difficult and countries such as Morocco and Turkey became the new recruitment grounds.

At the same time, other groups were migrating to Western European countries. People from former colonies in particular were attracted for various reasons; for example, Algerians to France, Surinamese to the Netherlands, and people from Pakistan, India, and the West Indies to Britain. Refugees and asylum seekers added to the number of immigrants in almost all European countries.

Many guest workers decided to stay in the host countries and started to bring their families over. In a number of countries this was made possible in the 1970s. Circumstances, economic as well as others (such as education facilities), were considered better in the host countries compared with the home countries of the guest workers. Large numbers of guest workers did return to their home countries, but many others decided to settle. The host countries slowly started to realize that they had become immigration countries and that they had to take care of a multicultural society.

Several economic crises, already appearing at the beginning of the 1970s, accompanied by structural economic reforms, resulted in rising unemployment in Western European countries. Within these countries, cities and immigrants were hit especially hard. Unemployment among the former guest workers rose steeply and became structural.

In the housing market, opportunities for immigrants and their descendants were limited for several reasons. In some countries they did not have access to social housing at the beginning of their stay, forcing them to live in the private rented sector or to buy an often derelict dwelling. In most of the countries, they simply did not have enough money to afford a decent house. Allocation procedures sometimes resulted in concentrations in specific blocks or segments, while in some cases people apparently deliberately chose to live close together. Because of these factors, spatial concentrations of migrants in cities became the normal picture.

Now, at the beginning of a new millennium, the housing conditions of (former) migrants are on average still worse than those of nationals, and spatial concentrations still prevail. In this chapter we focus on these aspects. More specifically, we try to answer the question: how can the segregation patterns of immigrant groups in Western European cities be characterized and explained? The basic aim of the chapter is to discern some broad patterns in selected countries and cities and to mention some general threads of explanations for these patterns. It is not our intention to detail and explain small differences.

In the next section we describe the extent of segregation in a number of large European cities and draw some general conclusions. Because data on segregation are not available for every city in Europe, we have to rely on figures for a small number of large cities. These cities have therefore not been selected on the basis of hard criteria, but simply on the basis of availability of data. We briefly outline the housing situation of some immigrant groups. We focus specifically on Turks, because for this population category more information is available than for other groups. We then turn to the explanations of the patterns found. Here we offer an explanatory framework that can be used when evaluating patterns of segregation and spatial concentration in European cities in general. We do not believe that these European explanations can be readily transposed to the US situation. In the USA, a factor such as racism is much more pervasive, while the role of the public sector is minimal compared with European welfare states (see, e.g., Marcuse and van Kempen 2000).

Segregation Patterns in Western European Cities

Comparing patterns of segregation between cities is a hazardous task. First and foremost, this has to do with the availability and comparability of data. The definition of immigrant groups may differ between countries. In some countries, a certain group may be defined on the basis of nationality, in other countries on the basis of birthplace, and elsewhere the birthplace of the father and/or the mother may even be taken into account. In some countries, ethnic groups define themselves; the British census, for example, uses self-definitions.

When measuring segregation, two of the most frequently used measures are the Index of Dissimilarity (ID)[1] and the Index of Segregation (IS).[2] The main advantage of both these measures is that they can be interpreted very easily. When there is maximal segregation their value is 100, and when there is no segregation their value is zero. The values indicate what percentage of a category should move to other districts in order to end up with a spatial distribution similar to the group with which the segregation pattern is compared (Duncan and Duncan 1955; Lieberson 1981). The problem, however, is that the size of the ID and IS is not only dependent on the pattern of segregation per se, but also on the size of the areas used in the calculation of these indices. The larger the area in terms of population (and the fewer the number of areas), the smaller the chance of an ID or IS with a high value (Woods 1976). This means that cities where the calculation is based on a large number of small areas are more likely to display a high ID or IS value than cities where the calculations are based on only a small number of relatively large areas. It will be clear that this limitation seriously impedes comparability between cities within a country and between countries. Comparisons over time in the same cities are, however, relatively unproblematic (if the spatial delimitations within a city have not changed).

On the other hand, differences in IS and ID values may indicate real differences. Giffinger (1998) has shown three values of the IS for Turks in Vienna. For census districts (the largest areas), the value of the IS is 41.7, for census areas it is 50.8 and for housing blocks (the smallest areas) the IS value is 62.9. Giffinger concludes that this may mean that the spatial separation of this group is more evident at the most disaggregated spatial level of housing blocks. For most cities, these comparative figures are not possible because data are only available for one spatial level.

The question of which spatial level is the most appropriate to investig-ate patterns of spatial segregation is not easily answered as it depends on the aim of the research. When the aim is to find out the relation between neighborly contacts and patterns of segregation, it is useful to work with figures on street or block level (but at the same time these data are almost never available – see Musterd and Deurloo 2002 for an exception). Figures on neighborhood level (areas with approximately 2000–10,000 dwellings) are more often used. In this case, figures still refer to the more or less direct living environment of an individual or household. Daily shopping often takes place in the neighborhood and young children go to primary school there. In other words, this level of analysis is appropriate for determining the relation between more or less routine daily activities and patterns of segregation. Figures on a district level (larger areas, which may number from 20,000 to as many as 100,000 people) are in general not very relevant, because these figures often hide enormous differentiation within areas.

Despite these limitations, we show some segregation figures (Table 9.1) that have been selected from recently published articles and books. The figures presented here do not represent the whole body of knowledge in this field but are selected for the following reasons:

1   A comparison can be made between different groups in cities.
2   A comparison can be made between cities in the same country.
3   A comparison can be made over time.

As can be seen from Table 9.1, not every selection conforms to all three criteria.

What can be inferred from this presentation of indices of segregation? First and foremost, the simple conclusion must be drawn that segregation exists in all selected cities. Although this might sound like a platitude, it is important to start with this conclusion. It indicates that in terms of spatial segregation, immigrants and their descendants are still far from a situation of complete dispersal. Apparently this holds for every category and for every city.

Second, it is clear that in the course of time the values of the ID do not always decline. In some cases they have even slightly increased (e.g., for

Table 9.1 Segregation indices of selected groups in selected European cities

Amsterdam (NL)	1986	1994	1998
Turks	38.8	40.0	42.3
Moroccans	36.9	38.6	41.2
Surinamese	33.7	34.8	34.2
Southern Europeans	24.1	15.9	
The Hague (NL)	1986	1992	1998
Turks	65.1	60.4	53.0
Moroccans	57.3	53.1	48.6
Surinamese	46.4	42.0	38.7
Southern Europeans	20.9	16.7	
Brussels (B)	1991		
Moroccans	59.0		
London (UK)	1991		
Bangladeshis	75.0		
Indians	51.0		
Black African	41.0		
Birmingham (UK)	1991		
Bangladeshis	79.0		
Indians	56.0		
Cologne (D)	1984	1989	1994
Turks	33.7	34.2	32.7
Yugoslavs	24.9	25.0	25.7
Italians	30.9	29.5	27.0
Frankfurt (D)	1994		
Turks	18.8		
Yugoslavs	32.3		
Düsseldorf (D)	1983	1993	
Turks	29.5	29.5	
Yugoslavs	25.9	26.9	
Berlin (D)	1982	1991	
Foreigners	34.9	32.1	
Vienna (A)	1990		
Turks	41.7		
Yugoslavs	33.7		

Sources: De Winter and Musterd (1998); Friedrichs (1998); Giffinger (1998); Kemper (1998); Musterd et al. (1998); Peach (1998); Bolt et al. (2002).

the Turks and Moroccans in Amsterdam). In many cases they remain more or less at the same level (e.g., the Turks and Yugoslavs in Cologne). This again indicates that immigrants are not distributed evenly in cities and that also in a period of 10 or more years no considerable changes can be detected. This is an interesting conclusion, because the expectation might have been that in the course of time the different groups would have become more dispersed over the city. That expectation might fit the hypothesis that immigrants generally start their housing careers in their host country in some highly selective neighborhoods (e.g., in those areas where a large number of their fellow countrymen already live; see Dahya 1974), but after a while they change residence as a consequence of a better position in the labor market. However, the figures presented give no evidence at all of individual housing careers. It might well be the case that a number of former immigrants have indeed dispersed over the city, while at the same time a number of new people have moved to the city. In this way, the value of the ID might stay the same. Another possibility is that complete concentrations have moved. The ID only indicates an average measure of segregation and does not measure where the segregation takes place (we will come back to this later).

A third conclusion is that big differences exist between the same groups in different countries (e.g., compare the Turks in The Hague, Vienna, and Cologne). This might be a strong indication that cultural variables (ethnic choice) do not play a decisive part in the explanation of patterns of segregation, but that other factors (such as the availability of housing and allocation procedures) are more important, a point to which we will return. Another possibility might be that different cities house different subgroups of the same group. For example, Turks in The Hague might come from more rural areas, while Turks in Vienna might originate from more urban areas. Unfortunately, no evidence is available here.

There are big differences between different groups within cities (e.g., between Turks and Yugoslavs in Vienna, between Bangladeshis and Indians in London and Birmingham, between Southern Europeans and Moroccans in the Dutch cities). Although Southern Europeans generally show a lower level of segregation than more recent immigrants (but see Cologne for an exception), it would be rash to conclude that it is just a matter of time before segregation starts to decline. Circumstances (economic, political, etc.) might have changed, leading to fewer opportunities to move to other parts of the cities.

Finally, while big differences exist between countries and groups, equal (or sometimes even larger) differences exist between cities within one country. This can be the result of using different area sizes, but in some cases these within-country differences can also be explained in other ways (see below). The differences indicate that even for a single ethnic category (e.g., Turks) different spatial patterns may emerge. Within the Nether-lands, for example, Turks and Moroccans are clearly more segregated in The Hague than in Amsterdam. This is a result of the fact that in Amster-dam Turks and Moroccans are more or less dispersed over a large number of pre-World War II neighborhoods and many areas built in the period 1945–60 (3593, 3601, 1977). In The Hague, this influx into post-World War II areas has only started very recently. Here the Turks and Moroccans used to live only in the pre-war areas so were much more concentrated than in Amsterdam (see also van Kempen and van Weesep 1998).

It is important to add to these conclusions that explanations of the patterns and processes of segregation may be different for different groups, different cities and different countries. Equal IS values may hide an enormous variation in concentration patterns and may point to very differ-ent backgrounds. Later in the chapter we will come back to this, but one example might illustrate this point here. The extent of segregation of Turks is very much the same in Amsterdam as in Vienna. This does not mean, however, that they live in the same kinds of areas. In Amsterdam Turks can mainly be found in areas of social rented housing, while in Vienna many Turks live in areas of private rented dwellings. Moreover, in explaining the segregation patterns in these cities, discrimination should be stressed in Austria (Giffinger and Reeger 1997; Giffinger 1998; Giffinger and Wimmer 2002), while allocation processes and demographic variables should form the main components of the explanation in the Dutch situ-ation (Bolt et al. 2002). British researchers have discovered that in many cities in the UK many immigrant groups have high scores on the IS, suggesting similar spatial concentration patterns. Looking at patterns of concentration, however, it can be seen that the location pattern of, for example, black Africans is totally different from that of black Caribbeans (Daley 1998), while both groups are characterized by low incomes (see also Peach 1998). Their locational patterns differ strikingly from those of migrants from North America, Australasia, and Europe (White 1998), but this difference can largely be explained by income. Because the migrants from these more Western countries generally have higher incomes, they are better able to make choices between dwellings and between neigh-borhoods. Having a lower income generally limits choice for households on the housing market.

Housing Conditions

To arrive at a good interpretation of patterns of spatial concentration and segregation, it is necessary to say something about housing conditions in the countries and cities of the groups under consideration. Detailed information about the housing conditions of immigrants and their descendants has been provided in earlier publications (see van Kempen and Özüekren 1998a, 2002) so we only present a brief summary here. The aim of this summary is to give a general characterization of the housing situation of the groups considered. For several reasons this is not easy:

1 Recent and reliable data on housing situations are not universally available.
2 Data are not always comparable, because of different definitions.
3 Data limitations generally do not allow for breakdowns by, for example, income.
4 It is virtually impossible to obtain information on the subjective aspect of the housing situation (the opinions of the immigrants themselves about their own housing conditions).

Minority ethnic groups generally concentrate in the rental sector, while they are under-represented in the owner-occupied sector. For example, in Denmark and the Netherlands 92 percent of the Turkish households are tenants, while in Sweden and the German city of Düsseldorf the figure is as high as 98 percent. In Belgium and France 85 percent of the Turks are tenants. This pattern is to a large extent a consequence of their low and insecure incomes (van Kempen and Özüekren 1998a). In many countries, such as Belgium, France, and Germany, there is a clear increase in owner-occupation among minority ethnic groups (De Villanova 1997; Glebe 1997; Kesteloot et al. 1997). In the Belgian city of Ghent, the vast majority of Turks are now owner-occupiers.

Minority ethnic households often have to make do with less space per person in the dwelling compared with native households (see, e.g., Friedrichs 1998 for Germany). Figures on overcrowding are striking in some countries (6559, 4572). Of all the Turkish households in Sweden, more than 40 percent live in overcrowded situations. For native Swedes this figure is lower than 4 percent (Özüekren and Magnusson 1997).

Many minority ethnic households live in low-rent dwellings built before the 1960s (3592, 2537, 3996, 5066), but as a consequence they often pay a smaller part of their income towards rent than non-immigrants. For example, the mean rent quota for Turks in the Netherlands is 15 percent of income, compared with 18 percent for non-immigrants. In Sweden, immigrants (many of them Turks) are concentrated in the newer segments of the housing stock, generally built between 1965 and 1974 (as a result of the so-called "million dwellings program"). Consequently, they pay higher rents compared with non-immigrants who live in private rented housing, which is on average older and less expensive than the municipal housing stock (Özüekren and Magnusson 1997). In Germany, foreign-born renters also pay more rent than German renters. Despite this, they have fewer rooms per person and are concentrated in buildings built before 1918 (Friedrichs 1998).

In general, minority ethnic groups live in lower quality housing (6572, 5387, 1575, 4568). This holds for such countries as the Netherlands (Bolt et al. 2002), Belgium (Kesteloot et al. 1997), and Austria (Giffinger and Reeger 1997). In Sweden, the rented dwellings occupied by Turks are generally of a high standard and do not show significant differences from those occupied by nationals (Özüekren and Magnusson 1997).

Explanations of Segregation and Housing Conditions

We may conclude that in large European cities:

1   Minority ethnic groups are highly concentrated in some urban areas and less concentrated or even do not live at all in other urban areas.
2   The housing conditions of minority ethnic households are for the most part worse than those of nationals.
3   Minority ethnic households can mainly be found in the more undesirable parts of the housing stock.

Which factors can help to explain these patterns?

The role of resources

Income can be seen as a major determinant of patterns of segregation and housing conditions because those who have more money can more easily put their preferences into reality. Key to the income position of the household is the labor market position. People with a relatively good labor market position are better poised to take an advantageous position in other markets, including the housing market. Because many immigrants in Western Europe entered the country in response to demand at the bottom of the occupational structure, they usually end up in housing and locations that are generally less desirable (4825, 6581, 5739). In addition to the level of income, income security can be a major factor when the household is thinking about buying a home. Access to owner-occupied housing is easier for persons with incomes that are both stable and high. To become a homeowner may be more difficult for immigrants, whose incomes are generally low and more precarious as a result of their skill levels.

Resources can, of course, take other forms. Cognitive resources include education, skills, and knowledge of the housing market. Knowledge of the local housing market is an important cognitive resource that may enable one to reach a desired housing situation in the housing market. People who are not proficient in the language may not understand allocation rules. Özüekren, for instance, showed that none of the Turkish interviewees in a Stockholm neighborhood belonging to the million dwellings program knew that private rental flats existed (cited in van Kempen and Özüekren 1998b).

Political resources reflect the possibility of attaining and defending formal rights in society, which may enable people to achieve important aims in life. Giffinger and Wimmer (2002) note that foreigners in Austria have no access to social housing.

The concept of social resources, or social capital, refers to direct or indirect access to "important" persons or groups and to membership of social networks. These social networks can have important functions in social integration, in society as a whole or within subgroups (see also Friedrichs 1998). They can also help people to find solutions in significant areas of life to achieve important aims, and to attain positions in the labor market and the housing market. The role of information is crucial in this respect. Dahya's (1974) research in the English city of Bradford has demonstrated that the concentration of Pakistanis in certain neighborhoods can largely be explained with reference to networks of fellow countrymen.

The question of preferences and the ethnic-cultural approach

Many of the disadvantaged positions in the housing market can be explained by the low incomes of ethnic minority households, but other household factors may also have a role. Preferences, perceptions, and the decision-making of the individual refer to the demand side of the housing market. Choices of households can directly be linked to positions and events in the family lifecycle (see, e.g., Clark and Dieleman 1996). Household characteristics, particularly the age of the head of the household and household composition, are major determinants of housing (and locational) preferences (see, e.g., Clark et al. 1986). Age intersects with the household formation cycle: establishing a durable relationship, starting a family (children are born), contraction of the family (children leave home), and the death of a partner. These are all situations that influence the household's size and its preferred type of dwelling (Rossi 1955; Speare et al. 1975; Stapleton 1980). Explanations that stress these kinds of factors are generally subsumed under the behavioral approach. The ethnic-cultural approach can be seen as a variant of the behavioral approach.

The general argument within this approach runs as follows: housing conditions and residential patterns differ between groups, and these differences can be attributed to cultural differences between these groups. As in the behavioral approach, there is a clear element of "choice" in this approach, although the ethnic-cultural approach allows for the inclusion of constraints in the explanation. The choice of owner-occupied dwellings, for example, can be seen as a cultural preference, but also as a defensive reaction against racist practices of landlords (e.g., Cater and Jones 1987; Bowes et al. 1990). Implicitly, or sometimes even explicitly, this approach is used by those who try to explain spatial concentrations of certain groups by referring to the wish to live together in one area. However, there are only a few indications that this kind of explanation is valuable.

Ceri Peach (1998) explains the divergent patterns of different immigrant groups in London (see above) by referring to elements of choice. His idea is that if income is the most important factor for the explanation of segregation, then the poor groups would be more mixed. Their strong concentration in different parts of the city indicates that they have been able to do something with their (ethnic) preferences. Immigrants establish localities where they become the characteristic symbolic groups and this cannot be a coincidence: "The importance of this point is that it illustrates the operation of choice within the constraints to which the minorities are subject" (Peach 1998: 1667).

Peach does, however, recognize the book by Sarre et al. (1989) as an important contribution to the discussion of the role of choice and constraints. One of their most significant arguments is that minority groups might internalize external constraints so that they choose only realizable options. In this reasoning, people might cluster together, not because they specifically want to be and to live together, but because they know that other places are unattractive; for example, because of (real or perceived) discrimination or racist attitudes by white people. In other words, people opt for those areas that are known to them and that are considered more or less attractive or safe.

If this reasoning is valid, it may also explain why the influx of immigrants into neighborhoods often originates in adjacent neighborhoods. A pattern like this has been recognized in Brussels (Kesteloot et al. 1997) and in the UK (Phillips 1998). Apparently, it is easier to obtain information about areas that are close.[3] On the other hand, moving to an adjacent area may also be the result of the wish to stay close to fellow countrymen.

A focus on the supply side

Contrary to the USA, in many West European countries the state has had a strong influence on housing markets. Particularly in countries such as the Netherlands and Sweden, the number of social rented dwellings has been very important in the supply of housing. By providing social rented dwellings, the state ensures that low-income households have the opportunity to live in decent housing. In other countries – for example, the UK (2561, 2549) – the social rented sector has either been declining very rapidly (Meusen and van Kempen 1995; Murie and Musterd 1996) or has never been very large (as in Belgium; see Kesteloot et al. 1997) (6577, 4250). In a retreating welfare state, the number of affordable rented dwellings will almost inevitably decline, especially in the newly built stock. This has happened in most West European countries since the second half of the 1980s (Özüekren and van Kempen 1997).

The availability of certain types of housing can explain different spatial patterns. Differences in spatial patterns between Brussels and Amsterdam, for example, have been attributed to the location of housing alternatives. Because of the lack of a social rented sector in Brussels, Turks and Moroccans are dependent on the private rented sector, which is concentrated in an area west of the city center (1903, 3996). The same groups in Amsterdam can rely on the social rented sector (3545, 2115) that can be found in many parts of the city (Kesteloot and Cortie 1998).

It is not only the quantity, but also the quality of housing that matters. Public housing in the USA, for instance, is known for its very low quality and only houses those who have no alternative (0192, 1962, 1583). More or less automatically this results in spatial concentrations of the poor, often in ghettos (see, e.g., Marcuse 2002). Social housing in the Netherlands, however, is generally of high quality (van Kempen and Priemus 2002) and therefore seen as an attractive place to live (1898, 1973, 0208). While social housing is in principle only allocated to low-income households, residents are entitled to stay in their dwelling if their income increases. Many households have opted to do this, resulting in a mix of different income groups in social housing areas.

The retreat of the welfare state has an obvious effect on the income position of households of all kinds. When governments pursue a policy of cutting budgets, everyone who depends on the state (e.g., pensioners, the unemployed, the disabled) will inevitably feel the pinch. Austerity programs may lead to lower subsidies for housing. Consequently, fewer affordable dwellings might be built or less maintenance may be carried out on the existing stock.

Alternatively, new types of grants may be introduced, resulting in upgrading of urban areas. In the Netherlands, for example, a new policy of urban restructuring will result in a larger number of more expensive dwellings in areas that used to be characterized by an overwhelming majority of inexpensive social rented housing (van Kempen and Priemus 2002). This means that patterns of segregation may change: the expectation is that low-income ethnic minority households will have to move to other areas, which might very well result in larger values of segregation indices because they will be forced to concentrate in fewer areas (1220, 3439).

The role of the state and the supply of dwellings are also important in a totally different context. Kemper (1998) points to the situation of Berlin after the fall of the Iron Curtain. In Berlin, an increase of foreigners in the eastern part of the city can be detected since the beginning of the 1990s and a concomitant decrease in the IS since the fall of the Wall. The political circumstances leading to the disappearance of the Iron Curtain can be seen as a trigger but most important was the available stock of inexpensive flats (many of them in large unattractive slab-blocks) in the eastern part of the city. Still, however, the percentage of foreigners is not very impressive. For example, only 2 percent of the total Turkish population in Berlin resides in the eastern part of the city. Kemper offers a cultural explanation for this (Turks prefer residential areas with a social network and infrastructure of their own group), but he also points to the possible fear of discrimination: many East Germans have prejudiced attitudes towards foreigners. Finally, Kemper suggests that many Turks may not be looking for a cheap flat at all.

The role of the individual in the supply side

Local government or housing associations might decide to allocate dwellings in a certain neighborhood exclusively to non-immigrants. Housing association officers can indirectly refuse to register immigrant families by claiming that no large dwellings are currently vacant or by asking high registration fees (van Kempen and van Weesep 1998). Allocation procedures are often a combination of formal rules and the application of such rules by individuals. The influence of these people has been stressed in the work of Pahl (1975), who examined the role of the housing officer in the allocation of resources (see also Lipsky 1980; van Kempen and Özüekren 2002). Pahl suggests that these social gatekeepers can allocate resources according to their own implicit goals, values, assumptions and ideologies. This means that stereotypes and racism can influence their decisions, as has occurred in the UK (Tomlins 1997). Discriminatory practices can be encountered among private landlords as well as among the intermediaries between landlords and prospective buyers or tenants. Landlords might offer a vacancy to a national rather than rent it to an ethnic household. In the UK, again, exclusionary policies of local authorities and private landlords have forced ethnic minorities into owner-occupation, even, or especially, at an early stage of their housing careers (Phillips and Karn 1992). Consequently, ethnic households may be more or less forced to rent or buy a substandard dwelling and to live in neighborhoods where accessible housing is available (e.g., Ward and Sims 1981) (3139, 2536, 5739). For the Netherlands this has been documented by van Hoorn and van Ginkel (1986). Unfortunately, not much is known about other European countries and cities, which means that no general pattern can be discerned. Some studies from Canada indicate that particular ethnic patterns may result from the specific actions of real estate agents: they only look in certain neighborhoods for particular groups (Teixeira 1995).

A wider perspective: the macro-context

Housing conditions are basically the result of the interrelation between the resources and preferences of households, and the availability and accessibility of dwellings. This interaction does not take place in a vacuum but in a context of economic, demographic, and political structures, including the character of the welfare state (in some cases, such as the Netherlands, redistributive elements are still strong, while in other countries, such as Belgium and the UK and particularly the USA, redistribution barely plays a part, while the role of the market is much stronger). Context may differ from one country to the next, sometimes even between regions within countries. Moreover, these elements may change through time. Seen in this way, local differences and historic developments set the stage for the current housing conditions of all households that operate within a housing market. Therefore, a study of (individual) housing conditions and housing market positions should pay attention to an analysis of (aggregate) contextual developments. We will point out only three of the possible relations between macro-developments and housing conditions and spatial divisions.

The global restructuring of the economy and the consequent transfer of manufacturing to newly industrializing nations leads to higher unemployment among manual workers in West European countries. The post-industrial transformation of the economy in the late twentieth century has affected the economic backbone of the cities; the traditional goods processing industries. These industries in particular provided entry-level employment opportunities for the lesser skilled, among them immigrants, but, because of the transformation, employment opportunities in these industries are being decimated. As a result, their household incomes tend to decline, which limits their possibilities of neighborhood choice (van Kempen and Özüekren 1998b). However, Harloe and Fainstein (1992) have also warned us against making too deterministic links between economic change and its consequences for the population.

The number and type of households looking for a home is an important factor. Fierce competition may result if households are looking for the same kind of dwelling in the same area, resulting in the displacement of the weakest groups.

Within many cities there is ongoing talk about growing social polarization and increasing inequality between groups. While the discussion on the exact definition and operationalization of these concepts is already a difficult one, the problem is worse when the translation from the social to the spatial has to be made. Polarization does not necessarily have to lead to spatial segregation. The spatial structure of the city is important here: in cities with a clear mixture of housing types within neighborhoods the chance for segregation is much less (van Kempen 2002) (5127, 3048). The relatively low segregation figures in the Netherlands are a consequence of this mixture of housing types within urban areas (see Chapter 8) (3180).

More macro-developments may be influential in explaining patterns of segregation in different societies. The role of racism and discrimination, the influence of changing values and norms with respect to the dwelling and the housing environment, attitudes towards sustainable development, the changing demographic structure as a consequence of aging, births and deaths, are just a few examples. It will always be difficult to make links between these kinds of developments and individual housing conditions and places where individual households live, but our idea is that these contextual factors should always be taken into account when housing conditions and spatial patterns have to be explained. On the one hand, this does also mean that each case, each city, is unique; everywhere unique combinations of explanatory factors will emerge. On the other hand, this does not mean that finding general patterns will be impossible. In every country, the combination of income and the availability of housing will be crucial in determining patterns of segregation and concentration. The point is that merely recognizing the fact that "globalization is important" or "racism has a role" are statements that are too general for a relevant analysis of a local situation. It should be determined in which ways and through which intricate combination of variables and developments all kinds of factors interact with each other. This chapter only offers the ingredients.

Conclusions

Comparing patterns of segregation between countries, as well as the housing conditions of immigrants and their descendants, is a difficult task. Scant availability of data along with differences in the data themselves prevent a thorough analysis. Even more difficult is the explanation of the patterns and processes of segregation and the housing conditions of these groups. Many factors are important; many factors interact. Moreover, in different spatial contexts the importance of explanatory factors may be different. The enormous influence of racism has been briefly mentioned as an important factor in the USA while being of relatively less importance in Western Europe.

A lack of social rented housing in Belgium largely explains the concentration patterns of Turks in the city of Brussels, and the location and accessibility of social housing in the Netherlands could be the principal explanatory factor in Dutch cities. Discriminatory regulations have a very important role in Austria, while patterns of "choice" might be more important for different groups in the UK. These examples highlight the important role of welfare systems/regimes and of policies in general.

Despite these difficulties, some important conclusions can be drawn:

* Immigrants and their descendants generally do not live in the same circumstances as nationals. On average, they can still be found more often in distressed neighborhoods, dilapidated housing, and in overcrowded dwellings. Despite the fact that many of them have been in the host country for many years and even decades, many barriers still have to be removed.
* In the case of minority ethnic households, explanations that stress the importance of income, the supply of dwellings and the accessibility of these dwellings are generally more fruitful than explanations that emphasize the preferences and choices of individuals and households. However, it should also be noted that there is increasing diversity within minority ethnic groups in terms of experience, needs, and aspirations (see also Somerville and Steele 2002).
* Macro-developments should be taken into account. They can at least sketch the backdrop of the changes on the supply and demand side of the housing market. They can also help in identifying trends for the future.

One additional point should be mentioned. While immigrants in Western European cities are generally worse off than nationals, the discussion in this chapter has not helped us to answer the question of where, in which countries and cities, they are better off. For example, being worse off in Vienna is probably quite different from being worse off in Amsterdam. The situation of American ghettos is probably incomparable to the situation of any neighborhood in Europe.

For the future it is easy to sketch a bleak perspective for immigrants and their descendants (see also van Kempen and van Weesep 1998). The restructuring of the economy, leading to still fewer jobs for which a low education is needed, probably means increasing unemployment figures for members of immigrant groups. Increasing numbers of households may enhance the competition for housing. Declining welfare states may have negative effects on the incomes of the unemployed (and still dispropor- tionate numbers of ethnic minorities are unemployed) and may diminish the role of the social rented sector in the housing market, leading, in combination, to fewer possibilities for the low-income ethnic minority households.

We will, however, end on a positive note. In some countries, such as Germany and Belgium, ethnic minorities have started to enter the owner- occupied sector in rather large numbers (see, e.g., Glebe 1997; Kesteloot et al. 1997). This might be an indication of rising incomes for at least some of these households. In the labor market we should not forget that not every (former) immigrant is unemployed. The increasing wealth of some households (particularly young households with two career-oriented earners) may increasingly feel the need to use the services of people for tasks for which they cannot find the time (e.g., cleaning, child care). Increasing emphasis on the construction of more expensive dwellings in the market sector may lead to a movement of nationals out of the social rented sector, thereby making room for people who cannot afford to live anywhere else.

NOTES

1 The Index of Dissimilarity measures the concentration of a group relative to another group. It relates the number of individuals belonging to a certain group in a small area (e.g., a neighborhood) to the total number of that group in a larger area (e.g., a city) and to a reference group.
2 The difference between the ID and the IS is that in the case of the IS the reference group comprises all other people in the area under investigation. In the case of the ID the reference group is just one other group (e.g., Moroccans). There are many other measures that can be used to determine the extent of spatial segregation, but the ID and the IS are generally seen as the ones that are most easy to interpret.
3 This has already been recognized by Brown and Moore (1970). They intro- duced the concept of "awareness space" to indicate an area that people, directly or indirectly, have knowledge of.

REFERENCES

Bolt, G., Hooimeijer, P., and van Kempen, R. (2002) Ethnic segregation in the Netherlands: new patterns, new policies? *Tijdschrift voor Economische en Sociale Geografie*, 93 (2): 214–220.

Bowes, A., McCluskey, J., and Sim, D. (1990) Ethnic minorities and council housing. *New Community*, 16: 523–532.

Brown, L.A. and Moore, E.G. (1970) The intra-urban migration process: a perspective. *Geografiska Annaler*, 52B: 1–13.

Cater, J. and Jones, T. (1987) Asian ethnicity and home-ownership. In: Jackson P. (ed.) *Race and Racism: Essays in Social Geography*. Allen and Unwin, London.

Clark, W.A.V. and Dieleman, F.M. (1996) *Households and Housing: Choice and Outcomes in the Housing Market*. Center for Urban Policy Research, New Brunswick.

Clark, W.A.V., Deurloo, M.C., and Dieleman, F.M. (1986) Residential mobility in Dutch housing markets. *Environment and Planning A*, 18: 763–788.

Dahya, B. (1974) The nature of Pakistani ethnicity in industrial cities in Britain. In: Cohen A. (ed.) *Urban Ethnicity*. Tavistock, London.

Daley, P.O. (1998) Black Africans in Great Britain: spatial concentration and segregation. *Urban Studies*, 35: 1703–1724.

De Villanova, R. (1997) Turkish housing conditions in France: from tenant to owner. In: Özüekren, A.S. and van Kempen, R. (eds.) *Turks in European Cities: Housing and Urban Segregation*. European Research Centre on Migration and Ethnic Relations, Utrecht.

De Winter, M. and Musterd, S. (1998) *Towards Undivided Cities in Western Europe: New Challenges for Urban Policy. Part 4: Brussels*. Delft University Press, Delft.

Duncan, O.D. and Duncan, B. (1955) Residential distribution and occupational stratification. *American Journal of Sociology*, 60: 493–503.

Friedrichs, J. (1998) Ethnic segregation in Cologne, Germany, 1984–94. *Urban Studies*, 35: 1745–1763.

Fryer, P. (1984) *Staying Power*. Pluto, London.

Giffinger, R. (1998) Segregation in Vienna: impacts of market barriers and rent regulations. *Urban Studies*, 35: 1791–1812.

Giffinger, R. and Reeger, U. (1997) Turks in Austria: backgrounds, geographical distribution and housing conditions. In: Özüekren, A.S. and van Kempen, R. (eds.) *Turks in European Cities: Housing and Urban Segregation*. European Research Centre on Migration and Ethnic Relations, Utrecht.

Giffinger, R. and Wimmer, H. (2003) Segregation and integration: public discrimination as a decisive element of housing policy in Vienna. Paper presented at the ENHR-conference on "Housing Cultures", Vienna, July 1–5.

Glebe, G. (1997) Housing and segregation of Turks in Germany. In: Özüekren, A.S. and van Kempen, R. (eds.) *Turks in European Cities: Housing and Urban Segregation*. European Research Centre on Migration and Ethnic Relations, Utrecht.

Harloe, M. and Fainstein, S.S. (1992) Conclusion: the divided cities. In: Fainstein, S.S., Gordon, I., and Harloe, M. (eds.) *Divided Cities: New York and London in the Contemporary World*. Blackwell, Oxford.

Kemper, F-J. (1998) Restructuring of housing and ethnic segregation: recent developments in Berlin. *Urban Studies*, 35: 1765–1789.

Kesteloot, C. and Cortie, C. (1998) Housing Turks and Moroccans in Brussels and Amsterdam: the difference between private and public markets. *Urban Studies*, 35: 1835–1853.

Kesteloot, C., De Decker, P., and Manço, A. (1997) Turks and housing in Belgium, with special reference to Brussels, Ghent and Visé. In: Özüekren, A.S. and van Kempen, R. (eds.) *Turks in European Cities: Housing and Urban Segregation.* European Research Centre on Migration and Ethnic Relations, Utrecht.

Lieberson, S. (1981) An asymmetrical approach to segregation. In: Peach, C., Robinson, V., and Smith, S. (eds.) *Ethnic Segregation in Cities.* Croom Helm, London.

Lipsky, M. (1980) *Street-Level Bureaucracy: Dilemmas of the Individual in Public Services.* Russell Sage, New York.

Marcuse, P. (2002) The shifting meaning of the black ghetto in the United States. In: Marcuse, P. and van Kempen, R. (eds.) *Of States and Cities: The Partitioning of Urban Space.* Oxford University Press, Oxford.

Marcuse, P. and van Kempen, R. (2000) Introduction. In: Marcuse, P. and van Kempen, R. (eds.) *Globalizing Cities: A New Spatial Order?* Blackwell, Oxford.

Meusen, H. and van Kempen, R. (1995) Towards residual housing? A comparison of Britain and the Netherlands. *Netherlands Journal of Housing and the Built Environment* 10: 239–258.

Murie, A. and Musterd, S. (1996) Social segregation, housing tenure and social change in Dutch cities in the late 1980s. *Urban Studies,* 33: 495–516.

Musterd, S. and Deurloo, R. (2002) Unstable immigrant concentrations in Amsterdam: spatial segregation and integration of newcomers. *Housing Studies,* 17: 487–503.

Musterd, S., Ostendorf, W., and Breebaart, M. (1998) *Multi-ethnic Metropolis: Patterns and Policies.* Kluwer Academic, Dordrecht.

Özüekren, A.S. and Magnusson, L. (1997) Housing conditions of Turks in Sweden. In: Özüekren, A.S. and van Kempen, R. (eds.) *Turks in European Cities: Housing and Urban Segregation.* European Research Centre on Migration and Ethnic Relations, Utrecht.

Özüekren, A.S. and van Kempen, R. (eds.) (1997) *Turks in European Cities: Housing and Urban Segregation.* European Research Centre on Migration and Ethnic Relations, Utrecht.

Pahl, R. (1975) *Whose City?* Penguin, Harmondsworth.

Peach, C. (1998) South Asian and Caribbean ethnic minority housing choice in Britain. *Urban Studies,* 35: 1657–1680.

Phillips, D. (1998) Black minority ethnic concentration, segregation and dispersal in Britain. *Urban Studies,* 35: 1681–1702.

Phillips, D. and Karn, V. (1992) Race and housing in a property owning democracy. *New Community,* 18: 355–369.

Rossi, P.H. (1955) *Why Families Move: A Study in the Social Psychology of Urban Residential Mobility.* The Free Press, Glencoe.

Sarre, P., Phillips, D., and Skellington, R. (1989) *Ethnic Minority Housing: Explanations and Policies.* Avebury, Aldershot.

Somerville, P. and Steele, A. (2002) Conclusion. In: Somerville P. and Steele A. (eds.) *Race: Housing and Social Exclusion.* Jessica Kingsley, London.

Speare, A., Goldstein, S., and Frey, W.H. (1975) *Residential Mobility, Migration and Metropolitan Change.* Ballinger, Cambridge.

Stapleton, C.M. (1980) Reformulation of the family life-cycle concept: implications for residential mobility. *Environment and Planning A,* 12: 1103–1118.

Teixeira, C. (1995) Ethnicity, housing search, and the role of the real estate agent: a study of Portuguese and non-Portuguese real estate agents in Toronto. *Professional Geographer*, 47: 176–183.

Tomlins, R. (1997) Officer discretion and minority ethnic housing provision. *Netherlands Journal of Housing and the Built Environment*, 12: 179–197.

van Hoorn, F.J.J.H. and van Ginkel, J.A. (1986) Racial leapfrogging in a controlled housing market: the case of the Mediterranean minority in Utrecht, the Netherlands. *Tijdschrift voor Economische en Sociale Geografie*, 77: 187–196.

van Kempen, R. (2002) The academic formulations: explanations for the partitioned city. In: Marcuse, P. and van Kempen, R. (eds.) *Of States and Cities: The Partitioning of Urban Space*. Oxford University Press, Oxford.

van Kempen, R. and Priemus, H. (2002) Revolution in social housing in the Netherlands: possible effects of new housing policies. *Urban Studies*, 39 (2): 265–282.

van Kempen, R. and Özüekren, A.S. (1998a) Ethnic minority housing in the European Union: a case study of Turks. *Tijdschrift voor Economische en Sociale Geografie*, 89: 459–464.

van Kempen, R. and Özückren, A.S. (1998b) Ethnic segregation in cities: new forms and explanations in a dynamic world. *Urban Studies*, 35: 1631–1656.

van Kempen, R. and Özüekren, A.S. (2002) The housing experiences of minority ethnic groups in Western European welfare states. In Somerville, P. and Steele. A. (eds.) *Race: Housing and Social Exclusion*. Jessica Kingsley, London.

van Kempen, R. and van Weesep, J. (1998) Ethnic residential patterns in Dutch cities: backgrounds, shifts and consequences. *Urban Studies*, 35: 1813–1833.

Ward, R. and Sims, R. (1981) Social status, the market and ethnic segregation. In: Peach C., Robinson, V., and Smith, S. (eds.) *Ethnic Segregation in Cities*. Croom Helm, London.

White, P. (1998) The settlement patterns of developed world migrants in London. *Urban Studies*, 35: 1725–1744.

Woods, R.I. (1976) Aspects of the scale problem in the calculation of segregation indices: London and Birmingham, 1961 and 1971. *Tijdschrift voor Economische en Sociale Geografie*, 67: 169–174.

10

Gentrification of Old Neighborhoods and Social Integration in Europe

Patrick Simon

Introduction

The emergence of post-Fordist capitalism not only triggered a reform of existing social systems – as Mingione highlights in Chapter 3 – but it thoroughly transformed at the same time the ways in which cities are organized.

Analyses of social change have not revealed any reduction of inequalities, any leveling out of social positions or, indeed, any reduction of uneven distribution in the various stratifications built on income, occupation, or localization (Martens and Vervaeke 1997). Rather, there is evidence that cities have encountered a new phase in the spread of inequalities: dual city (Mollenkopf and Castells 1991), global city (Sassen 1991), or divided city (Fainstein et al. 1992) are the concepts[1] used to describe these processes. The widening gap between affluent and poor areas is an indication that the relationship between space structures and socio-economic inequalities is a crucial one or, as Park et al. (1925) put it, is a reflection of the projection of social relationships on space.

The issue of social polarization tends, in the literature, to be grounded on the assumption of a leading role played by spatial segregation. The erosion of intermediate social groups – the middle class – because of heightened social inequalities, has produced direct consequences for urban territories. The deterioration of the social mix in neighborhoods, with a process of deprivation of poor areas on one side and a "piling-up" process in the affluent areas on the other, leads to a repartition of class into exclusive territories. The concentration of poor populations in depreciated areas is often considered to accelerate social exclusion (see Chapters 7 and 8). This view justifies new policies attempting to link up urban development and some economic insertion schemes (OECD 1996, 1998). Most European countries thus developed urban revitalization policies attempting to tackle both the social effects of economic restructuring and urban segregation: for example, Urban Development Policy in the UK, *Stedelijke Herstructurering* (Urban Restructuring) in the Netherlands, *Politique de la Ville et Développement Social des Quartiers* (City Policy and Neighborhood Social Improvement) in France (OECD 1998). To fight the adverse effects (or at least perceived as such) of the concentration of poverty, these policies encourage social mixing in deprived neighborhoods through settlement policies in cases where authorities have some control over public housing, or through a variety of incentives where the housing structure is private. The strategy followed to develop social mixing is to attract middle-class households to deprived neighborhoods by improving the infrastructures and amenities, and the quality of life, to make them more appealing.

An alternative strategy is to facilitate the mobility of deprived households to affluent neighborhoods. This policy has been developed in recent years in the USA and is known as the "Moving to Opportunity" (MTO) program (e.g., Rosenbaum 1995). Evaluation of this policy is still ongoing, but some results have already been gathered and have shown that there are no clear positive effects on the economic opportunities of deprived households. To quote Popkin et al. (2000: 928–9):

> There is no empirical evidence that it is even possible to artificially create a *community* where people interact rather than a development or neighborhood where people of different income levels simply share the same physical space. Nor . . . is there strong evidence that exposing low-income public housing tenants to higher income residents has any effects on their employment or educational outcomes.

The conclusions of the analysis of the MTO program confirm what major urban sociology surveys have already stated: spatial proximity does not necessarily help to reduce social distance (Chamboredon and Lemaire 1970). Evaluation of past attempts at social "requalification"[2] of neighborhoods by an influx of middle and upper-income class people has yielded results that are not very convincing. On the contrary, common residence in a single space tends to foster differentiation strategies among residents that tend to hamper cooperation, raising controversial questions about the advantages of social mixing. One can thus challenge the idealistic promotion of social mixing by placing greater weight on the resources that ethnically or socially homogeneous neighborhoods offer: solidarity, common values, social integration (Bolt et al. 1998).

Understood as an influx of middle and upper-income class residents into working-class or poor neighborhoods to the point where the resident population is partly taken over by the incoming population, gentrification is usually conceived as a spontaneous and willful process relying on the intervention of investors. In the case of public policies aiming to produce a social mix, one can talk of a deliberate gentrification process in order to change the attractiveness of poor neighborhoods. Gentrification is a very well-documented process. It has been defined by Hamnett (1991)[3] as a new phase in the structuring of urban space, a reflection in space of economic restructuring, or a strategic criterion for analyzing the building up of social groups and the links between the spatial position and the social position. Initially identified in North America, then in the UK and Northern European countries, the gentrification of old central neighborhoods is now a recognized fact in most European cities. It involves not only the operation of the housing market and the economy thereof, but also the characteristics and beliefs behind the attitude of the gentrifiers themselves and, lastly, the interrelationships between economic restructuring and the emergence of new social categories, new housing needs and a new mode of political expression in the struggle for the preservation of the environment. The gentrifiers comprise a new social group – even more a "new class" according to Ley (1996) – which can be defined by its economic position, political practices and cultural attitudes. The activity of its members brings major transformations to the social pattern of the city and to its physical makeup, because the renewal of neighborhoods is based on the possibility of selling or renting housing to more affluent households who may want to become residents in degraded neighborhoods.

This chapter aims to address the consequences of gentrification on a neighborhood's integration. If we understand "integration" as a process whereby social cohesion between different social and ethnic groups is achieved, we have to consider that the gentrification process implies a modification in the pattern of the integration process.[4] The purpose here is to reintroduce analysis of social interactions to the urban studies literature, focusing on the subtle forms of coexistence, complementarity and conflict that may emerge from a confrontation between dissimilar social or ethnic groups. After presenting the essential characteristics of gentrification and the various interpretive frameworks through which analyses of the phenomenon have been attempted, we take a more detailed look at the integration of those neighborhoods confronted with major transformations in the composition of their population. The main assumption behind gentrification is that it will requalify the social status of neighborhoods through improvements in housing, amenities and, most of all, the social profile of its residents. However, the consequences of the substitution of populations are a seldom-raised issue, and when it is, it is critical of the displacement of the working classes (Marcuse 1986).

I base my analysis on the situation of the Belleville neighborhood, which lies in the eastern part of Paris and is a typical case combining most parameters at work in a gentrification process. Whenever a source of information is available, moreover, I present data taken from similar experiments in other European cities. Case studies in London (Hamnett 1991; Lyons 1996), Berlin (Simons and Häussermann 2000), Hamburg (Alisch and zum Felde 1992; Dangschat and zum Felde 1992), Rotterdam (De Jong 1989; Burgers and Kloosterman 1996), Utrecht (van Kempen and van Weesep 1994), and in several French cities (Coing 1966; Ballain et al. 1990; Bidou-Zachariasen 1994; Simon 1995; Authier 2001) have yielded data that is introduced in the discussion of the Belleville case.

Urban Decline and Gentrification in European Cities

The concept of "urban decline" emerged in the mid-1970s to describe the transformations affecting most cities in industrial societies. After a period of economic prosperity and urban reorganization, the "slum" again became a looming figure in the image of the city. Clearly, then, new concentrations of poor populations once again emerged in distressed neighborhoods suffering from deteriorating housing, destitute public amenities and lack of commercial infrastructure (5717, 6144, 3469, 5424). Net job losses in most of these "distressed neighborhoods" did much to heighten existing population impoverishment, with a resulting degradation of social relationships in the community and greater segregation. The worsening plight of these "distressed neighborhoods" is not just because their inhabitants have become socially marginalized. What is even more crucial, in fuelling it, is the intensification of segregation mechanisms, which, by categorizing people according to their personal socio-economic residential profiles, tends to push those households living at the bottom of the social scale into the very areas affected by the crisis.

Urban decline first occurred in early industrialized town centers that were badly hit by the economic restructuring. Thus, as inhabitants with prospects for upward social mobility left and new populations with an increasingly precarious social situation arrived, old central neighborhoods were faced with "degeneration." The typical patterns approximately follow the phases outlined below. Of course, this schematic description may differ significantly according to the local context, but the case studies analyzed in the literature broadly conform to this common dynamic.

The economic *structure* of declining neighborhoods typically shows evidence of a movement of some activities towards territories with better geographic links to production and distribution networks, and traditional activities (artisan workshops, small industries) are unable to survive under the new production regime. Such transformations are part of a wider process of redistribution of activities and job opportunities inside the metropolitan areas. Not only is the local labor market in crisis, but the employability of the residents of declining neighborhoods also deteriorates as they work with low qualifications in industrial sectors undergoing total restructuring. Levels of unemployment and job insecurity are therefore particularly high among them.

The *housing situation* in old neighborhoods is quickly deteriorating (6559, 4995, 4570, 2645). With the waning of any solvent demand as more affluent groups leave for other neighborhoods, and especially for residential suburbs (suburbanization), old central areas are heavily affected by private and public under-investment. Originally substandard housing estates are no longer maintained by landlords who will not make any further investments in an area undergoing a transitional stage. As rental and property values drop, the neighborhood becomes affordable for the most marginalized populations. They tend to gather there, occupying the positions that have become available by the flight of former, more affluent residents.

A *population succession* process follows as confirmation of the decline of the neighborhood. This succession stage has historically coincided with the arrival of massive waves of immigrants in major European cities. In such a context, immigrants will serve as transitional households in order to make a greatly depreciated housing sector profitable. Housing segregation produces ethnic concentrations in old neighborhoods, and immigrant visibility then becomes the sign and the token of their "social dereliction" (Simon 1998). The dilapidation of the premises is paralleled by a sizable decrease in the animation of social life and in the relationships among residents. Community-based organizations lose their activists who, because they generally belong to the more affluent segments of the population, have moved to better neighborhoods. The emergence of local forms of delinquency, possibly including drug addiction and trafficking, then poses a severe threat to the security of the neighborhood and further contributes to its bad reputation.

It was in this context that the reverse move towards a requalification of city centers, or urban revitalization, took place (6141, 1861, 1624, 0194). For a long time, urban regeneration amounted to mere public fundraising which was intended for heavy renovation schemes (over the 1950–70 period). More recently, the latest stage in urban development has involved the emergence of new modes of urban governance bringing together public authorities and private investors for the building of high-profile facilities (cultural centers, major business facilities) (see Chapter 11). While these were meant to restore the attractiveness of declining areas and to revitalize the economic fabric, they were also policies that sought to retake – or "re-conquer," to use the concept used by the authorities implementing these policies[5] – the traditional centers from their poor inhabitants. In most cases, revitalization comes as a result of middle and upper-income class people "coming back" to the centers as a replacement for the working classes (2936). This "reconquest" move is a solidarity-based combination of a re-appreciation of housing and people according to a process that, however spontaneous it may appear, is nevertheless part of a move by gentrifiers towards restoring the prestigious functions of the center of the city. Gentrification is a major consequence of this reconquest process, as stated by Lyons (1996: 341): "Households of a high socio-economic status must displace households of low socio-economic status; previously devalorized housing must have been refurbished and revalorized; and this must have taken place in the inner city, generally in stages and often accompanied by changes in tenure."

Two types of interpretation are put forward to account for the mechanisms at work in the gentrification process. The first stresses specific reasons related to the real estate structure and the use value of housing. According to Smith (1986), whose view is shared by many others, inner-city depreciation as a result of suburbanization produced an artificial depressive bubble in the housing market. A so-called "rent gap" consequently emerged in the potential of depreciated neighborhoods. This differential in land value is attractive to investors as it may produce financial opportunities, albeit with some degree of risk. Smith disputes the impact of the choices made by the gentrifiers themselves. This, indeed, is the second type of interpretation of the phenomenon, placing more emphasis on the emergence of a "new class" with specific social preferences, as well as specific tastes, expectations, and consumer habits (Ley 1996). Members of this new class are supposedly the real protagonists of gentrification, not just because of the existing real estate or renting opportunities which would make inner-city investment worthwhile, but even more so because the economic, cultural and symbolic functions of these neighborhoods fit in with what the "new classes" are looking for. The fact that they own enough economic capital to afford their residential choices is indeed a key factor in this theory (Hamnett 1991). In a more recent article, Hamnett (2000: 333) puts forward an explanation that encapsulates the links between economic organization, social lifestyles and the property structure: "While gentrification clearly involves changes in the structure of the land and property market, it is better seen as a product of the shift from an industrial to a post-industrial society in particular cities and associated changes in class structure, particularly the growth of an expanded middle class and their social relations, cultural tastes and consumption practices."

Another limitation to the "rent gap" theory was voiced by Beauregard (1990: 856), who insisted on the potential for resistance to the gentrification process by "local communities": "The potential of gentrification is not simply equal to the rent gap. Rather, potential is both a function of accumulation opportunities and of the nature and the strength of the 'community' as historically produced. Where community is embedded and where neighborhood residents have captured control over accumulation through home ownership, for example, the potential for and the pace of gentrification might be correspondingly reduced." Even though he merely equates the local factor to the real estate structure, Beauregard raises here an essential dimension which I develop in the final part of this chapter. In my view, social organization on a local level produces determining effects on the very conditions of gentrification as well as on its consequences. A dynamic and local militant structure is thus in a position to influence the transformations of the local housing market: to control the increase in sale prices and rents, and also to control the social profile of gentrifiers by modifying the way the neighborhood is perceived.

Major variations appear in the pace and intensity of the phenomenon. There is no evidence that gentrification is a thorough and irreversible move: poor neighborhoods may not necessarily become fully fledged bourgeois neighborhoods at the end of the process. Intermediate situations are a common example wherein the process comes to a halt before working classes entirely and effectively leave the area. The duration of the process is also variable according to how flexible the housing market is. In this respect, the housing markets in North American cities are more flexible, which is in sharp contrast to the prevailing inertia in most European cities. In a matter of only a few years, the population makeup of a neighborhood in the USA or Canada may change dramatically. This is the reason behind the emergence of residential succession theories in urban ecology studies in the literature in the USA. The observation of micro-changes taking place in population settlement processes in order to identify what Duncan and Duncan (1965) called the "tipping point" – the transition from a "white" to a "black" neighborhood because of a steady influx of black dwellers and the departure of white people ("white flight") – would not be relevant (and many critics consider that it is not) if the conditions under which the market operates did not allow for such rapid changes. The context of the housing market is quite different in European cities where the weight of ownership in housing, the role of public investors and the lower residential mobility of households tend to slow down population changes. In her review of North American literature on urban revitalization, Dansereau (1985: 195) noted that mutations take place over a 2–5-year period in North American cities, while the same process often takes more than 10 years in Europe.

Major variations were also observed according to whether gentrification was a spontaneous process (resulting from the operation of the housing market, from the "remanufacturing" of cities, from the emergence of a new class) (5631, 4294, 1391) or a planned process (through public renewal, the setting up of market controls and rehabilitation devices, the building of social housing) (4065, 2864, 0901). The timetable for public renewal is often a considerably delayed one. When the decision to act is taken the local housing market is frozen, either as a result of a regulatory decision (pre-emptive measures allowing buildings to be withdrawn from the housing market) or as a result of insecurity (fears of buildings demolition policies with landlords waiting for the municipality to buy back their housing). The effects of public intervention in the renovation process tend to minimize, to some extent, the "rent gap." Indeed, Smith's (1986) central argument is valid when just taking into account the logic of speculation and profit, excluding any regulatory factors that are not market-related. In this respect, of course, any instance of urban planning – and an active one indeed in the case of Paris (Godard et al. 1973) – changes the whole picture of how gentrification is likely to take place. Similar and more recent situations can be discerned with large-scale urban development projects (UDPs) which combine economic revitalization and urban planning. In most European towns, UDPs are concerned with prestigious high-profile programs (6271, 5979, 0902) including spectacular project developments and economic revitalization of the area (URSPIC 2000).

Finally, any deliberate actions taken by the authorities produce reactions by residents on a more or less consistent collective level (grassroots mobilizations, opposition to or participation in the renewal projects), whereas in cases when revalorization happens after private property developers or operators have been speculating, the conditions for collective action are made more difficult. In the case of Belleville or the Goutte d'Or neighborhood in Paris (Toubon and Messamah 1991), Het Oude Westen in Rotterdam (De Jong 1989) or in the squatting movement in the big German cities (Berlin, Hamburg, Frankfurt), the fact that a public entity motivated people to mobilize made it possible to influence urban planning projects (0897, 2118). Such mobilizations had significant impacts on the integration of the different population groups living in the neighborhoods undergoing gentrification, which can be viewed as a result of public intervention – a paradox that will be addressed in the next section.

Renovation and Social Change

The role of renovation in the recent history of European urban planning is a strategic one. Major operations have been the hallmark of the wave of real estate reconstruction in large towns since the 1950s (1579, 5946, 0658). These kinds of operation have led to massive demolition of "condemned housing blocks" and to the reconstruction of modern buildings, usually with radically new types of buildings and an equally radical change in the social makeup of the population. For public authorities, the struggle to overcome degenerating housing conditions and to modernize the real estate infrastructure provides an opportunity to plan the redistribution of functions and the redistribution of social groups in the city.

I mentioned earlier that gentrification may occur without direct public intervention, according to a mere market incentive and following the spontaneous mobility of the middle and upper-income classes of society. Urban renewal, however, speeds up social changes and reaches beyond the areas directly concerned. The reason why its impact can be perceived in wider areas than just those included in the operations, is simply because it announces a transformation of housing and a revalorization that is going to benefit the whole neighborhood, and this, in turn, justifies investments by property developers. I witnessed this specific instance of gentrification in Paris, in the Belleville neighborhood. This particular case serves as a valuable reference framework for our discussion on the relationship between gentrification and social integration. I will begin with a brief outline of the history of the neighborhood.

The Belleville quarter, one of Paris's former working-class neighborhoods, is located in the eastern part of the city. It was urbanized at the end of the nineteenth century and its architecture is typical of working-class areas, with artisan workshops and low-quality apartment buildings (6757). Those who first came to live in Belleville were the households evicted from the center of Paris during Haussmann's renovations in the 1860s. This population was socially homogeneous; for the most part skilled workers working in small artisan industries. In 1871, during the Paris Commune, this working-class identity was emphasized: the actions of revolutionaries from Belleville gave the neighborhood the reputation of a hotbed of rebellion, a reputation it has never really lost since. As a result, Belleville became a socially isolated area with a strong sense of its own identity. In the 1920s, Armenians, Greeks, and Polish Jews began to move in. During the 1920s and 1930s, Belleville became the social center of the Yiddish and Armenian communities: stores, workshops, cafés, places of religious worship or assembly, political newspapers, Zionist or Bundist discussion groups, common interest groups, Jewish or Armenian trade unions – a dense and dynamic network of community organizations (5980).

During the 1950s, the neighborhood's "Yiddish period" slowly became history, while a new era of immigration dawned with the arrival of massive contingents from Algeria; alongside them came the Tunisian Jews fleeing North Africa in the throes of decolonization. The settling of immigrants in

Belleville went through three phases: from 1954 to 1968, a massive wave of arrivals; from 1968 to 1975, a period of stability; from 1975 to 1982, the population of immigrants began to increase again because of the family reunion policy. The resulting diversity of origins is quite impressive. In 1990, the major groups were Algerians (15 percent of immigrants), Tunisians (15 percent), Sub-Saharan Africans (9 percent), Moroccans (8 percent), and former Yugoslavs (7 percent). Asians, Turks, and Sri Lankans complete the picture of Belleville as a global village (Simon 1993) (5991, 5987, 5983, 5981).

This brief history of Belleville's demographics is inseparable from the characteristics of the neighborhood's housing pattern and from its transformation throughout the urban renewal process. Having been identified as an *"îlot insalubre"*[6] as early as 1918, Belleville was to be renovated in several stages from 1956 onwards. In the space of 40 years six schemes were launched, during which almost 50 percent of the total neighborhood area was destroyed and rebuilt (5931). The slow pace of renovation works had tremendous effects in terms of population settlement. Unlike Paris as a whole, which has witnessed a steady increase in middle and upper-income class residents over the past 40 years, Belleville stayed mainly a working-class neighborhood until 1975. The development of "public renewal projects" produced paradoxical effects on the local housing market. Private investors and property developers left the areas to be developed. Landlords no longer maintained their buildings, which continued to deteriorate and eventually were left outside the housing market (6757). The metaphor of the "fallow urban area" gives a good description of the situation of the transition zones. In turn, the continuing presence of dilapidated buildings did much to develop Belleville's function as a working-class "reservation" in the French capital, while elsewhere former working-class territories were gradually losing all of their traditional populations. However, the population settlement of the neighborhood did not remain completely stable as French working-class households living in insalubrious premises started to leave for social housing projects being built in distant suburbs or in the peripheral areas of Paris. Those were quickly replaced by immigrants who were leaving their temporary accommodation or had just arrived from their home countries. Between 1954 and 1982, while the neighborhood's population density was dropping dramatically, the French population halved (from 45,263 to 24,654 inhabitants), while the foreign population doubled (from 4696 to 9740 inhabitants). As run-down areas received populations who had been rejected from gentrified neighborhoods in central Paris, renovated sections received more affluent new dwellers (1918). The percentage of blue-collar workers in Belleville's employed population thus went down from 51 to 25 percent between 1954 and 1990, while that of the professionals and middle and upper executives went up from 9 to 35 percent. This typical evolution remarkably coincided with the calendar of renewal operations. For instance, the proportion of workers in industrial jobs in an area that underwent a two-stage renovation went down from 60 percent in 1954 to 40 percent in 1968 (first stage), then reached 18 percent in 1982 (end of the renovation program). The clear divide between new buildings and deteriorated ones therefore appears as a territorial transcription of the social distance between new inhabitants and "indigenous" ones.

The gentrification process of the neighborhood's last genuinely working-class areas clearly testifies to the thorough transformation of Belleville's situation on the Parisian market. Even though the neighborhood is a peripheral one, it is well enough connected through a sizeable transportation network to be able to benefit from the attraction of being central. It appears as a new land open for conquest by those populations who have been forced to leave their traditional territories because of skyrocketing real estate prices. However, this major influx of middle and upper-income classes shows signs of some kind of sorting or selecting of destinations and settlement places, which provides an opportunity to refine the picture of this highly differentiated social group. Public sector executives, teachers, and scientists on the one hand, and media, arts, and show business professionals on the other, are the professions whose presence in Belleville increased most noticeably between 1982 and 1990 (increasing by 43 and 48 percent, respectively). Similarly, employees and intermediate professions in the public sector were also on the rise (increasing by 16 and 25 percent, respectively), which is very unlike the evolution in Paris (down 18 percent and up 2 percent, respectively) (1990 Census). Information, arts, and show business professionals doubled their effective presence as they went from a total of 352 to 720 people. Thus, groups that are only marginal in terms of sheer numbers, are gradually taking hold of local powers and are now playing an essential part as protagonists in Belleville.

The New Middle Classes and the "Multiculturals"

Most surveys of the phenomenon of gentrification have shown that gentrifiers are not a homogeneous social group who share common social positions or ideological representations, or similar forms of commitment or consumption patterns. If the initial "invaders" are termed gentrification "pioneers" and the following wave gentrification "actors", their differences span beyond issues of opportunity and are related rather to deeper divides in terms of projects and lifestyles. The pioneers often buy their housing and refurbish it themselves (self-rehabilitation), while the so-called actors tend to seize on real estate opportunities as offered by either private or public sector property developers and investors. Alisch and zum Felde (1992) showed how in Hamburg the pioneers were younger (less than 35 years old), with a better education, had no children, and had lower incomes than the actors, who were 10 years older on average, were professionals or employees with high positions and incomes three times higher than the pioneers, and very often owned their own housing.

However, there is more to the differences between gentrifiers than just the stages at which they settled down. They can also be analyzed against the different historic periods, thereby following the transformations of the "new class" itself: from counter-culture and political activism to conservatism, the NIMBY syndrome and defense of one's property. Lyons also noticed a significant change in the profile of gentrifiers in London between the mid-1970s and the mid-1980s, especially against the criterion of women's work (1996: 354). The evolution is probably not always so clear; furthermore, it is based on a series of stereotypes defining the "pioneers" and the "new class", as Lees pointed out in her study of representations of gentrification (1996). In the same way, Mayer (1997) is rather cautious about the interpretation of a depoliticization of urban social movements in the 1990s, pointing out that people fighting for a better living environment are not always supporting private interests and that grassroots mobilization may also have political outlets. The case of Belleville brings confirmation of these views.

Two groups become apparent among the new dwellers in the neighborhood. Although they comprise both middle and upper income class people, they do not share the same perception of the "old neighborhoods". I have suggested calling the former "multiculturals", meaning that they enjoy social and ethnic mixes, are looking for an atmosphere and are quite willing, a priori, to respect the neighborhood's social order (Simon 1995). The latter are, on the contrary, very distant with respect to old neighborhoods. The term "transplanted" is an apt way to describe them. In the case of Paris, where social housing receives a large proportion of middle-class households, the transplanted often find accommodation in the new social housing built after the renewal. They usually come simply because they were offered this housing, as they were mostly looking for a rather affordable and modern place in Paris. These characteristics define their motivations: comfort and a central location are the two major assets they expect from the place where they live. Nevertheless, they wish to find themselves in an environment matching their practices: relatively "neutral", offering a wide variety of services and shops and, most of all, widely accessible to a vast majority. Basically, Belleville is not the right place for this kind of expectation. On the contrary, the use of space is strictly codified by a population whose social and ethnic origins are very different from their own. This produces a high degree of dissatisfaction with the way of life in the neighborhood. They are not part of it, they try to avoid the noisy crowds, seldom meet other residents and redirect their social life into other neighborhoods.

The multiculturals are the model of those "marginal gentrifiers" described by Rose (1984). Most of them own their housing and their residential choice is embedded in a broader design of way of life. They live close to the degraded sections, in the most lively streets and near to the shops. They enjoy a high level of education and cultural consumption, and work in the intellectual, artistic, show business, information, education, social facilitation, and social work professions. Such occupational proximity makes for a quite homogeneous socio-cultural group with typically some degree of material affluence and access to some power circles even though they are not a part of the governing elite. In describing this "new class" (Gouldner 1979), Ley (1996) insisted on the importance of its relationship to aesthetics and consumption. "The constitutive basis of this new class is not only a community of language and ideological representations, it is also a capacity to organize the market in cultural capital of which this class is the owner" (Dagnaud 1981: 387). With its "critical and radical" approach, the new class is in a position to oppose the state apparatus in all fields of activity, and especially, as I will explain later, at the local level in the management of municipal affairs. The other characteristic feature of this new class is its fondness for transnational culture, which gives it the ability to take a universal interest in society.

These general features of the "new class" or, to echo Dagnaud's (1981) phrase, the "*classe d'alternative*," provide a quite accurate description of the profile of the new Belleville dwellers or those studied by Dangschat and zum Felde in Hamburg (1992). These new dwellers reject uniformity and try to escape the vicinity of those who, even though they share a common social status, are proponents of a totally different societal project. The antipathy between the multiculturals and those they refer to as "bourgeois" is especially visible with respect to residential selection criteria. The residential strategies of the multiculturals are first and foremost determined by the search for an environment that is not controlled by the "bourgeoisie." Several reasons can account for this quest for a new place to live, preferably in working-class neighborhoods in transition.

The first is economic. In bourgeois neighborhoods the cost of housing is often quite unaffordable for the multiculturals. From this point of view, market selection is perfectly efficient. In Paris, an exceptional surge in real estate prices brought radical transformations to the "ecology" of social groups. The fact that middle and upper-income classes moved to former working-class neighborhoods is a direct consequence of this speculative escalation in housing values. In a general move eastwards, the multiculturals were gradually rejected from the neighborhoods they formerly controlled. A cleavage then took place inside the "new class," between the multiculturals representing the lower income contingent and a comfortably established "intellectual bourgeoisie" in its central and prestigious neighborhoods.[7]

The second reason is ideological. As they have become economically unaffordable for the multiculturals, the neighborhoods of the intellectual bourgeoisie have lost their cultural attractiveness. Multiculturals will resort to the most scathing words to describe the demise of their former territories, calling them "dead," "uneventful," or "artificial." Consequently, they have to go further afield to find the kind of atmosphere they are yearning for, and popular neighborhoods on the verge of new mutations are a perfect place for this. Being ideologically supportive of working-class culture and natural advocates of its interests, the multiculturals admire the working-class way of life, or what they consider to be such, including such features as simplicity in social relationships, widespread exchange between individuals in terms of services rendered or conversations, widespread mutual insights, ongoing liveliness of public place. All these aspects make up a comprehensive, idealistic living environment in which multiculturals are willing to live (Piolle 1991). In addition, working-class neighborhoods have another advantage for multiculturals; alone as a group among immigrants and "workers," they rapidly become aware of their own cohesion. This relocation, which they undertake as if in a "missionary land," this sacrifice of sorts, acts as a selection process between the members of the "new class" and guarantees similarities of socio-cultural profiles. The conditions in which they settle down in Belleville become the essential criteria that bind them together. "Choosing" this very neighborhood, when it was old, insalubrious and poor, is constitutive of an adherence to a highly codified ideological and cultural construction. The optimal conditions for the establishment of a sense of community are then met.

It is clear, however, that such an exceptional situation will not last. Several waves of gentrification may often take place (Dangschaft and zum Felde 1992) and the "pioneers" are joined by more gentrifiers. When the image and the real estate potential of the neighborhood really improve, larger fractions of middle and upper-income class people arrive. A dynamics of invasion starts and, after a variable amount of time, the very notion of the selection that is contained in the perception of the neighborhood – as a poor, dilapidated place with immigrants – fades away. Gradually, the initial cohesion of the group dwindles as immigrants and workers leave and the local social order is swept away under pressure from the incoming, more affluent residents. At the end of the process, gentrification has irreversibly changed the social makeup of the neighborhood and the "pioneers" will leave in order to conquer new territories.[8]

Gentrification and Integration

The influx of a new population, when it is either socially or ethnically different from the former, changes significantly the atmosphere of any neighborhood undergoing a gentrification process. Classical analyses of population succession processes describe the relationships between former and incoming inhabitants according to different stages: hostility, competition, conflict, cooperation. Antagonisms are not systematically caused by mere ethnic or racial confrontations, they may also be the result of differences in class or generation positions. If we choose to look at things from a general perspective, as do Elias and Scotson (1965), any population change produces changes in the organization of "communities" and therefore requires some regulations, bearing in mind that the "outsider" status of the incomers makes them inferior to the former "established" inhabitants. However, in gentrified neighborhoods, the privilege that is attached to the anteriority of settlement is reduced because of the differences in social, economic, and cultural capital between the incomers and the traditional dwellers.

Conflicts between incoming and former inhabitants by and large focus on the control of power positions on the local scene: on the establishment of the rules according to which the "community" is meant to operate. They are the expression of diverging views concerning the use of premises, space appropriation and also the way the neighborhood is perceived.[9] Alisch and zum Felde (1992: 336) have even said that the "original inhabitants" of gentrified neighborhoods in Hamburg had a feeling of distress when confronted with the changing atmosphere and social life resulting from the arrival of new gentrifiers. The major population change faced by the neighborhood undergoing the gentrification process in turn weakens the local social order and reduces the influence of former inhabitants. In a context of "disorganization," the incomers have better intervention opportunities, especially if they have a community or lobbying network organization.

It was precisely this context of a disorganization of the social and political fabric at a local level that created the conditions for the Belleville "pioneers", the multiculturals, to take control of the local scene. Even though they had not been there for long, these relentless protagonists pervaded the neighborhood's political scene, thereby acquiring a special place for themselves in Belleville's social order. Their commitment to the preservation of their living environment provided the incentive for them to get in touch with the other groups on the local scene, through ways and means well known to the middle and upper classes: grassroots mobilization, media coverage, lobbying public authorities. For that matter, these "living environment militants" are far more pragmatic in their claims and in the achievement of their goals than the former groups who led the urban struggles of the 1970s (Cherkie and Mehl 1979). They did away with their predecessors' radical ideology and have developed instead a more management-oriented position based on expertise in urban matters. Let us take a look now at how they have changed the local social order (Suttles 1968) to see if they have improved or rather threatened the social integration of former inhabitants, immigrants or native French working classes.

In Belleville, the social order is a system of codes and values ensuring cohesion between the various groups that make up the local population and enabling them to coexist in the same space, both materially and symbolically speaking. The coexistence of these groups within a circum-scribed area has led to a division of the neighborhood into small clusters. To describe the spatial organization of the groups living in Belleville, the most accurate image is that of the mosaic, "separate and closed-in worlds which exist side by side but do not mix," to quote Park et al. (1925). Each urban segment has its own "local color" and the atmosphere can differ completely from one street to the next. These "micro-environments," in which urban functions, users, and specific practices are combined, are undoubtedly "quasi-communities" (Gans 1962). The division of space must not be interpreted as a sign of hostility between the different groups. Thanks to these borders, which are constantly shifting, a group can define itself in opposition to the "others," as pointed out by Barth (1969) in his seminal analysis of ethnic boundaries.

Such a system could not have existed without a tremendous effort to rewrite history and without the condensation of collective memory into what has become the "Belleville myth." This myth has made it possible for these groups to create a common area, open to all, and to transcend deeply ingrained cultural specificities. The Belleville myth is based on two assertions: Belleville is "an old working-class neighborhood" and "a neighborhood where immigrants first settled long ago." These two assertions are, of course, based on historical facts, but the latter has been modified in the spirit of what Roland Barthes called "the naturalization of history." The elements that constitute the Belleville myth are no doubt historically true, but, and it is in this sense that a myth has been created, they had neither the impact nor the importance they are believed to have had today. Thus, Belleville is not an *old* immigrant neighborhood. Quite the contrary, if one looks at the censuses from the first half of the twentieth century, Belleville then had the highest proportion of Parisian natives in the city. Immigrant presence in Belleville has never been as strong as it is today. Similarly, although Belleville was a working-class neighborhood up until the 1970s, this was no longer the case at the time the myth crystallized.

By inserting the immigrants into the neighborhood's collective memory, the myth acts as a "factory of nativity"; thus, ethnic conflicts cannot be based on the denial of the simple right to live among one's group, because everyone in Belleville equally belongs to the neighborhood (5999, 5995). In other words, using Elias and Scotson's (1965) paradigm, thanks to this myth, immigrants cease to be outsiders and can aspire to the more legitimate status of the established. Thanks to the contractual nature of the myth, attitudes of intolerance and rejection, which are often observed in situations where local residents emphasize their cultural specificity and their genuine right to define who is able to be integrated, become totally irrelevant. Concerning relations between social classes, the image created by the Belleville myth is rather unrealistic. However, by laying emphasis on the neighborhood's identity as working class, the myth aims to make up for the social inequalities that are reflected in the housing conditions. Acceptance of this myth represents, for the members of the middle and upper-income classes, a guarantee of their own integration into the neighborhood. Even more so, they have a significant role in creating and spreading the myth, in particular through the action of the association of local residents, *La Bellevilleuse*, devoted to fighting the neighborhood renovation program.

This association was created in 1988 by local residents wishing to weigh upon the decisions concerning the renovation program of the lower Belleville area. Today, the association has 500 members, mainly from the recently settled middle and upper-income classes. Their commitment to collective action, aimed at defending the right of immigrants and the working-class to remain in Belleville, can be interpreted on two levels.

By demanding that people be rehoused in the same neighborhood, the multiculturals are speculating on the transformation of the population of Belleville: they wish to prevent the too rapid gentrification of the neighborhood and preserve the atmosphere they came for in the first place. Thus, they have become the advocates of a working class identity that is not theirs, but for which they feel sympathy.[10] They are themselves often of working-class background, and participation in community action is a manner of "reparation." The aim is to promote, at the local level, a social model that has not taken shape at the national level. The commitment of the multiculturals has provided the working class with a new edge in power relations. Indeed, when dealing with the authorities, immigrants and French workers are usually deprived of means of applying pressure; the multiculturals are thus able to serve as mediators, which is the role they took in the neighborhood renovation program. On a wider scale, their role as mediators has enabled them to create a more positive image of a social world that so far had been perceived as impoverished and pernicious. Through their joint reaction of protest against the renewal program and the bureaucratic organization that supports it, the neighborhood's different groups were able to get together symbolically and to a certain extent, to come closer operationally. De Jong (1989) described a similar process in an old neighborhood of Rotterdam, Het Oude Westen, which resembles Belleville in many respects (3342, 3341). There, ethnic conflicts were overcome thanks to associations of local residents committed to preventing the deterioration of their neighborhood (3437, 3438).

A new collective cohesion emerged during the 1990s through opposition to the last renovation projects and participation in a neighborhood counter-project. The leaders of this dynamic were mostly to be found among some of the gentrifiers, who in Belleville, as for instance in the case of Kreuzberg (Berlin), used the power they derived from their high social and cultural capital resources to achieve their integration in the neighborhood while respecting the local social order. Renovation therefore produced a paradoxical effect – compared with the disintegration it had been encouraging so far – in that it has produced a new cohesion by establishing a link between new middle and upper-income class inhabitants, immigrants, and former working-class residents of Belleville. However, the second group of gentrifiers to settle in Belleville, the "transplanted," are not part of this dynamic at all. They resemble more closely the kind of gentrifiers described in most studies, who will enter into conflict with prior residents until they finally leave the neighborhood for good. In that kind of example, gentrification leads to the complete destruction of the former local social order.

Conclusions

The ideology of social mixing in city centers has a long history behind it which started in the early nineteenth century with the ideas of "utopian socialists" such as Charles Fourier or Victor Considérant, as opposed to Marx and Engels' "scientific socialism." As urban policies in Europe are confronted with the phenomenon of social exclusion, which also has a significant spatial dimension,[11] they are turning once again to this ideology and are trying to produce a social mix in their distressed neighborhoods. This strong political stance is of a voluntary nature and is based on the idea that an influx of residents with high social and economic resources will positively affect the opportunities of deprived persons. However, the results of studies in the field of urban sociology or geography provide clear evidence that interclass cooperation in conditions of coexistence in a single space is by no means an easy process. The studies have emphasized the necessary conditions for this cooperation to take place, in terms of both economic and urban patterns and also of social dynamics.

My decision to analyze gentrification was indeed to put it in this very perspective. In most recent case studies of gentrification, class relations are of a conflictive nature. Splits appeared that reflected not only social differences, they were also highly dependent on the status associated with seniority of residence and on the legitimacy of the local social order that it provides. It thus appears that the benefits for deprived populations of an influx of middle and upper-income class residents are fairly limited. Even more so, the resulting social mix eventually takes a heavy toll, with the final eviction of poorer residents after the neighborhood has gone through its requalification process and there has been a consequent rise in local real estate values.

In some instances, however, gentrification may be positively instrumental in achieving the social integration of deprived populations. As an example, I have studied the case of the Belleville neighborhood where an influx of "marginal gentrifiers" – the ones I have called the multiculturals – started a collective dynamic based on opposition to the urban renewal project and in the process reaffirmed local identity. The multiculturals found a position in neighborhood life by speaking in favor of the residents facing eviction, in an attitude combining the struggle for their personal interests and a form of political or social commitment. Similar instances of interclass collaboration have taken place in other European cities, which shed new light on the specific role of this fraction of the new middle class, acting as mediators between the spheres of business, politics, and social movements. Quantitatively, this *"classe d'alternative"* are a tiny minority who are no doubt a fundamental factor in resisting the social destruction that is part and parcel of the polarization of global cities.

ACKNOWLEDGMENTS

I would like to thank Yuri Kazepov, Richard van Deusen, and Manuel Aalberts for their comments and fruitful contribution to improving this chapter.

NOTES

1 Or metaphors, to quote the criticism made by Marcuse (1989) about the diffusion of the terminology of "dual city."
2 By requalification, we mean transformation of the reputation and the structure (e.g., amenities, accommodation, social composition of the population) of neighborhoods to bring about a more positive and attractive image.

3   For a more recent review see Lees (2000), and for a non-academic review see the homepage of Tom Slater (2002).

4   For a similar perspective, see Khakee et al. (1999).

5   Smith (1996) talks about the "revanchist city."

6   An *"ilôt insalubre"* refers to the lowest geographic level in the city, a block of buildings, which are derelict. A plan was drawn up in 1894, and a new one in 1918, to demolish entirely these derelict blocks. Most of these renovation programs were not implemented before 1955.

7   Bessy's (1988) typology of Paris neighborhoods contains data on the localization of social groups and, to some extent, on the processes whereby they are gaining their autonomy vis-à-vis one other. The distinction between bourgeois business neighborhoods, bourgeois intellectual neighborhoods, and tertiary renovation neighborhoods is a good example of how middle and upper-income classes were divided into separate residential clusters.

8   This mechanism has been well accounted for by Chalvon-Demersay (1984) in the case of the gentrification of the "Daguerre triangle" in the XIV arrondissement of Paris. After being a working-class neighborhood until the 1960s, the area was later conquered by Parisian artists and a bohemian style population and has now become completely gentrified.

9   Beauregard has analyzed the conflicts resulting from the recreation of a "community": "The formation of 'community' often leads to intraclass struggles as different groups attempt to establish the social bonds, public image, and norms of behavior that define the neighborhood as their home" (1990: 856).

10   The multiculturals can be depicted as real "organic intellectuals" with a working-class background, if I may adapt Gramsci's concept.

11   On the spatial dimension of social exclusion, see the outcomes of the URBEX project published by AME, Amsterdam University between 2000 and 2002. They are available online at the following URL: http://gp.fmg.uva.nl/urbex/menureps.htm (accessed 25 July 2003).

REFERENCES

Alisch, M. and zum Felde, W. (1992) Rénovation et embourgeoisement du centre-ville de Hambourg: détresse et réactions des résidents. In: Lelièvre, E. and Levy-Vroelant, C. (eds.) *La ville en mouvement: Habitat et habitants*. Collection Villes et Entreprises, L'Harmattan, Paris.

Authier, J-Y. (ed.) (2001) *Du domicile à la ville: Vivre en quartier ancien*. Anthropos, Paris.

Ballain, R., Jacquier, C., Darris, G. et al. (1990) *Sites urbains en mutation: Territoires et trajectoires*. L'Harmattan, Paris.

Barth, F. (1969) Introduction. In: Barth, F. (ed.) *Ethnic Groups and Boundaries: The Social Organization of Culture Difference*. Scandinavian University Books, Oslo–London.

Beauregard, R.A. (1990) Trajectories of neighbourhood change: the case of gentrification. *Environment and Planning A*, 22: 855–74.

Bessy, P. (1988) Les 80 quartiers de Paris en 6 types. *Regards sur l'Ile de France*, 1: 5–10.

Bidou-Zachariasen, C. (1994) Rénovation urbaine et stratégies familiales: une étude de cas. *Sociétés Contemporaines*, 17: 11–27.

Bolt, G., Burgers, J., and van Kempen, R. (1998) On the social significance of spatial location: spatial segregation and social inclusion. *Netherlands Journal of Housing and Built Environment*, 13 (1): 83–95.

Burgers, J. and Kloosterman, R. (1996) Dutch comfort: postindustrial transition and social exclusion in Spangen, Rotterdam. *Area*, 28 (4): 433–445.

Chalvon-Demersay, S. (1984) *Le triangle du xivème, des nouveaux habitants dans un vieux quartier de Paris.* Editions de la MSH, Paris.

Chamboredon, J.C and Lemaire, M. (1970) Proximité spatiale et distance sociale: les grands ensembles et leur peuplement. *Revue Française de Sociologie*, 11: 3–33.

Cherkie, E. and Mehl, D. (1979) *Les nouveaux embarras de Paris: de la révolte des usagers des transports aux mouvements de défense de l'environnement.* François Maspéro, Paris.

Coing, H. (1966) *Renovation urbaine et changement social.* Edition Ouvrières, Paris.

Dagnaud, M. (1981): La "classe d'alternative", réflexion sur les acteurs du changement social dans les sociétés modernes. *Sociologie du Travail*, 4: 384–405.

Dangschat, J.S and zum Felde, W. (1992) Embourgeoisement: la ségrégation résidentielle par les capitaux économiques, sociaux et culturels. In: Lelièvre, E. and Levy-Vroelant, C. (eds.) *La ville en mouvement: Habitat et habitants.* Collection Villes et Entreprises, L'Harmattan, Paris.

Dansereau, F. (1985) La réanimation urbaine et la reconquête des quartiers anciens par les couches moyennes: tour d'horizon de la littérature nord-américaine. *Sociologie du Travail*, 2: 191–205.

De Jong, W. (1989) The development of inter-ethnic relations in an old district of Rotterdam between 1970 and 1985. *Ethnic and Racial Studies*, 12 (2): 256–277.

Duncan, O.D. and Duncan, B. (1965) *The Negro Population of Chicago: A Study of Residential Succession.* University of Chicago Press, Chicago.

Elias, N. and Scotson, J.L. (1965) *The Established and the Outsiders: A Sociological Enquiry into Community Problems.* Frank Cass, London.

Fainstein, S., Gordon, I., and Harloe, M. (eds.) (1992) *Divided Cities: New York and London in a Contemporary World.* Blackwell, Oxford.

Gans, H.J. (1962) *The Urban Villagers: Group and Class in the Life of Italian Americans.* The Free Press, Glencoe.

Godard, F., Castells, M., Delayre, H., Dessane, C., and O'Callaghan, C. (1973) *La rénovation urbaine à Paris: Structure urbaine et logique de classe.* Mouton, Paris.

Gouldner, A. (1979) *The Future of Intellectuals and the Rise of the New Class.* Seabury Press, New York.

Hamnett, C. (1991) The blind men and the elephant: the explanation of gentrification. *Transactions of the Institute of British Geographers*, 16: 173–89.

Hamnett, C. (2000) Gentrification, post-industrialism and industrial and occupational restructuring in global cities. In: Bridge, G. and Watson, S. (eds.) *A Companion to the City.* Blackwell, London.

Khakee, A., Somma, P., and Thomas, H. (eds.) (1999) *Urban Renewal, Ethnicity and Social Exclusion in Europe*. Aldershot, Ashgate.

Lees, L. (1996) In the pursuit of difference: representations of gentrification. *Environment and Planning A*, 28: 453–470.

Lees, L. (2000) A re-appraisal of gentrification: towards a 'geography of gentrification'. *Progress in Human Geography*, 24: 389–408.

Ley, D. (1996) *The New Middle Class and the Remaking of the Central City*. Oxford University Press, Oxford.

Lyons, M. (1996) Employment, feminisation, and gentrification in London, 1981–93. *Environment and Planning A*, 28: 341–356.

Marcuse, P. (1986) Abandonment, gentrification and displacement: the linkages in New York City. In: Smith, N. and Williams P. (eds.) *Gentrification of the City*. Allen and Unwin, Winchester, MA.

Marcuse, P. (1989) Dual city: a muddy metaphor for a quartered city. *International Journal of Urban and Regional Research*, 13: 697–708.

Martens, A. and Vervaeke, M. (eds.) (1997) *La polarisation sociale des villes européennes*. Edition Anthropos-Economica, Paris.

Mayer, M. (1997) Les mouvements sociaux comme acteurs politiques dans les villes européennes: leur évolution entre les années 70 et 80. In: Bagnasco, A. and Le Galès, P. (eds.) *Villes en Europe*. La Découverte, Paris.

Mollenkopf, J. and Castells, M. (1991) *Dual City: Restructuring New York*. Russell Sage, New York.

Organization for Economic Cooperation and Development (OECD) (1996) *Strategies for Housing and Social Integration in Cities*. OECD, Paris.

Organization for Economic Cooperation and Development (OECD) (1998) *Integrating Distressed Urban Areas*. OECD, Paris.

Park, R.E., Burgess E., and McKenzie, R. (1925) *The City*. University of Chicago Press, Chicago.

Piolle, X. (1991) Proximité géographique et lien social, de nouvelles formes de territorialité? *L'Espace Géographique*, 4: 349–358.

Popkin, S.J., Buron, L.F., Levy, D.K., and Cunningham, M.K. (2000) The Gautreaux legacy: what might mixed-income and dispersal strategies mean for the poorest public housing tenants? *Housing Policy Debate*, 11 (4): 911–942.

Rose, D. (1984) Rethinking gentrification: beyond the uneven development of Marxist urban theory. *Environment and Planning D Society and Space*, 2: 47–74.

Rosenbaum, J.E. (1995) Changing the geography of opportunity by expanding residential choice: lessons from the Gautreaux program. *Housing Policy Debate*, 6 (1): 231–269.

Sassen, S. (1991) *The Global City: New York, London, Tokyo*. Princeton University Press, Princeton.

Simon, P. (1993) Les quartiers d'immigration: 'ports de première entrée' ou espaces de sédentarisation? L'exemple de Belleville. *Espace, Populations, Sociétés*, 2: 379–388.

Simon, P. (1995) La société partagée: relations interethniques et interclasses dans un quartier en rénovation, Belleville, Paris XXe. *Cahiers Internationaux de Sociologie*, 68: 161–190.

Simon, P. (1998) Ghettos, immigrants and integration: the French dilemma. *Netherlands Journal of Housing and the Built Environment*, 13 (1): 41–61.

Simons, K. and Häussermann, H. (2000) *The New Berlin: Growth Scenarios and Local Strategies*. URSPIC (http://www.ifresi.univ-lille1.fr/PagesHTML/URSPIC/Cases2/Berlin/BERLIN2.htm).

Smith, N. (1986) Gentrification, the frontier and the restructuring of urban space. In: Smith, N. and Williams, P. (eds.) *Gentrification of the City*. Unwin Hyman, London.

Smith, N. (1996) *The New Urban Frontier: Gentrification and the Revanchist City*. Routledge, London.

Slater, T. (2002) *Gentrification Web*. (http://members.lycos.co.uk/gentrification/index.html)

Suttles, G. (1968) *The Social Order of the Slum*. University of Chicago Press, Chicago.

Toubon, J-C. and Messamah, K. (1991) *Centralité immigrée: Le quartier de la Goutte d'Or*. L'Harmattan/CIEMI, Paris.

URSPIC (2000) *Urban Redevelopment and Social Polarisation in the City*. URSPIC (http://www.ifresi.univ-lille1.fr/PagesHTML/URSPIC).

van Kempen, R. and van Weesep, J. (1994) Gentrification and the urban poor: urban restructuring and housing policy in Utrecht. *Urban Studies*, 31 (7): 1043–1056.

Part III

Social Exclusion, Governance, and Social Cohesion in European Cities

11

Elusive Urban Policies in Europe

Patrick Le Galès

Introduction

What is happening to urban policies in Western Europe? Rumors and evid ence of retreat or even the death of urban policies have been documented in line with the restructuring of the nation-state, globalization processes, and the neoliberal turn of many public policies; large public investments in social housing are, for instance, at a low ebb (Harloe 1995). By contrast, urban policies seem to be everywhere; "new" urban policies in particular, whatever that means, seem to be flourishing even at the European Union (EU) level. Against the view that globalization is sweeping across every-thing and determining the fate of cities, a body of literature is attempting to show that states and cities still have a major say in the structuring and organization of cities, hence a role for politics and institutions in relation to social groups, and economic relations that are constrained and articu-lated by different sets of pressures (Jessop 2002; Le Galès 2002; Marcuse and van Kempen 2002; Moulaert 2002; Saraceno 2002).

The puzzle of contemporary European urban policies has to be studied in relation to two trends:

1 The development of European multilevel governance.
2 The current "urban moment" (Healey et al. 1995; Beauregard and Body-Gendrot 1999).

European cities are growing, gaining inhabitants (not everywhere, in particular not so much in Britain) and they are seen, for the time being, to be gaining momentum (also in Britain), becoming once more places of cultural innovation (2587, 2292, 2452, 2017), economic development (6279, 5081, 4294), places of different kinds of projects and attempts to implement new modes of governance of multiculturalism (5999, 2544).

However, there are tensions and fragmentation (see Chapter 6). The urban is as unsettled as ever – urban regions organized in networks, metropolitan areas, global cities, classic European cities, ever-expanding suburbs, towns, and neighborhoods may all be targeted by urban policies. They face all kinds of problems: new forms or renewed forms of inequality, poverty (2372, 5426, 6010), illegal immigration, extreme right-wing votes (5843, 2069, 5433), urban renewal issues, pollution, crime, suburbanization, health alerts, lack of social housing, the creation of gated communities, globalization, competition pressure.

For the time being, political, economic, cultural, and social questions are increasingly becoming urban questions under the current conditions of capitalism. A key symptom of this dynamism of cities, and the importance it represents for the nation-states, are the conflicts surrounding urban policy which have been part of the picture for the last decade – in Denmark, Germany, Italy, the Netherlands, France, Finland, and lately Britain, to name but a few. Associations among cities were organized to challenge national urban policies and to claim a growing share of resources in order both to deal with social problems and to manage the investments related to their new economic and cultural role. This is occurring at the expense of classic priorities of state regional policies, such as remote rural areas or support to small towns. Although not determinant, the urban–rural cleavage has gained new salience in Nordic countries (witnessed in the rise of agrarian parties) but also in Britain, Germany, and France. Urban policies have even emerged in centralized uniform welfarist states such as Sweden (in 1998 in Göteborg, Malmö, and Stockholm) and Finland, or in the South of Europe.

This chapter looks at urban policies in Europe. It complements other chapters on social justice, local income revenue, social housing, and policies against social exclusion. Urban policies were classically strongly linked to issues of poverty: controlling the poor, regulating them, or improving their conditions of life provided the basis upon which many urban policies and welfare policies were founded. However, urban policies are also instruments for powerful groups and interests who can use them to exclude other groups (0897, 6372).

This chapter provides an overview of what is covered nowadays by the label "urban policy" in Europe. It suggests that urban policy should be analyzed in relation to the restructuring of the nation-state and public policies.

What is Urban Policy in Europe? The Legacy

Urban policy is not new, and there is in Europe a long history related to the rise of medieval cities, communal government and the making of the nation-state. The bourgeois elite running medieval urban communes invented public policies to organize town planning, maintain social order, build housing, protect properties, and foster economic development, with the last being their main concern. The making of nation-states also had an urban policy dimension to dominate cities: states' elites created castles and fortresses to protect cities, symbolizing their power through public buildings and transport networks such as roads. Developing a prestigious capital was seen as an essential element of state-making. In many ways, over several hundred years, national urban policy was first and foremost about the transformation of the state capital with the support of state resources. London, Madrid, Paris, Vienna, Stockholm, Berlin, and Rome all benefitted from national programs designed to develop the capital – creating new buildings, lighting the streets, constructing avenues, developing a police system to control the poor.

In the modern sense, urban policies started during the nineteenth century, at the time of the making or the reinforcement of the modern nation-state using all the modern techniques of government. The European urban map was modified by the rise of industrial cities, mainly in Britain and Germany, and the coming of age of imperial capitals, Vienna, London, Paris, Berlin. In that context, both urban government elites and state elites had to face the consequences of rapid urban growth in terms of the need to build or organize streets, roads, sewerage, gas, and then electricity networks, transport, street lighting, refuse collection, fire stations, abattoirs, but also uncertainties associated with crowds, riots, mass epidemics, and cycles of unemployment. Embryonic urban public policies were then adopted at the national level because public health issues and social concerns formed the basis upon which political elites started to react and to implement programs such as vaccination and slum clearances. The fear of the working class and the threat it posed to the existing social and political order were also central in the "urban" policies of the time (Topalov 1990) (4435, 2439, 5597) as Harvey (1985) eloquently put it in the Paris case.[1]

The development of urban policies went hand in hand with the making of professions and international networks of professionals – planners in particular, but also social reformers more generally. In many ways, forms of Europeanization were strongly at play at the time, as city elites and urban professionals from different countries and cities were in close contact and influenced each other (2577, 5871, 0693, 5305, 2488) – policy transfers were common practice, including with the USA (Saunier 2001).

After the two World Wars, a new cycle of modern urbanization came into play. Decades of economic growth fed urbanization and city growth. During the time of economic and welfare growth, cities were rather an anonymous category within the nation-state. In Northern Europe, for instance, the rise of the universal welfare state tended to erase the social or economic distinctiveness of cities. In Britain, anti-urban elite values, or French Jacobin lack of trust towards cities, did not contribute to either the development of urban programs or the political rise of cities' elites. Urban policy was geared towards the development of welfare state programs and services, first in cities and then all over the country: schools, universities, hospitals, roads, railway stations, research and cultural centers, social housing in the Central and Northern part of Europe (1983, 4297, 5937, 5742).

However, specific cases of urban policies emerged. In the Netherlands, the ambitious social housing programs were the main vehicle contributing to the development of cities (0658, 3375, 1216). In Italy, there was no such thing as urban policy (and a limited amount of social housing) but gradually historic city centers became centers of interest. They needed to be restored and protected from cars and pollutions. "*Centro storico*" became a keyword and goal of urban policies to protect historic city centers all over Italy (1995, 6188, 3178). In Britain, urban policy was about planning the growth and then restructuring of the major industrial conurbations and was understood in terms of land and planning regulations, including the construction of new towns. France in the 1960s had at least three, often contradictory, urban policies: the building of utilities, transport networks and housing; the development of regional capitals supported by state investment (research centers, hospitals, cultural centers); and the organization of the Paris region – hence the creation of new towns, motorways, rail networks and *La Défense* business center (5934, 1951, 1919, 1922, 5956).

Urban policies came back on the agenda, labeled as such, in the 1970s. After President Nixon declared that the war against poverty in US cities was over (!), the hopes of poverty erosion, of welfare and economic growth vanished with the economic crisis, long-term unemployment, new forms of poverty and social exclusion, the strengthening of anti-immigrant ideas and groups, and the revival of a political form of mobilization that many thought had disappeared: riots (3139, 2916). The social question was transformed and presented again as an urban question. In this sense, the rise of urban policies in the 1970s can be characterized as policies to deal with the social and economic crises of industrial cities, in particular in large housing estates, in the city center (inner city) or in the suburbs of ports and industrial cities – such as cities in the Ruhr, Antwerp, Liège, Lille, Le Havre, St. Etienne, Marseille, Birmingham, Sheffield, Liverpool, Manchester, the West Midlands, Glasgow, Rotterdam, Göteborg,

Turin, Genoa, Napoli, Porto, Bilbao – but also in parts of the largest metropolises, in London, Paris, or Berlin (5759, 3996, 1638, 6581).

New waves of immigration also made the urban crisis more visible within public debate (see Chapter 9). The post-war economic boom and imperial legacy attracted many new populations to Western Europe, especially in the North, and much later, particularly in the last decade, in the South. Business leaders encouraged immigration of cheap labor but that was often debated and contested in political circles, not least in France, Britain and Germany (Hansen and Weil 2001). From the late 1960s onwards, the issue of "immigration," or "race," has become an important political issue with a clear urban bias in most countries (Body-Gendrot and Martiniello 2000). The current debate in Italy and Spain echoes older debates in northern, more industrial cities. The urban became "colored" in many ways, not to the American extent, not for the time being at any rate, but in a very obvious way (5067, 4856, 3722). Immigrant communities, organized as such, became a component of urban life first in large industrial cities, capitals and ports such as Birmingham, Stockholm, Antwerp, Brussels or Marseille, then gradually in most European cities (3047, 4102). Policies to accommodate these new groups had a distinct urban element.

The social dimension of urban policy was therefore central in the new "urban policies" of the 1970s. Social redistribution in favor of the rising tide of poor populations within cities appeared central. However, rapidly the issue of urban regeneration and economic development was also brought forward, either because it was ideologically driven by the neoliberal Thatcherite revolution in the UK case, or because cities came to be seen as crucial engines of economic development in the new post-industrial economies. In the UK, the basic assumptions and urban policy instruments were radically modified; public investments and social services were not seen as the solution to the urban crisis but as causes of the problems. British urban policy aimed to promote market disciplines, competition, and private-sector investments in most cities at the expense of the professions, local authorities, planning rules, and social redistribution, sometimes mimicking US urban initiatives in terms of flagship projects, private developers' investments in quays and harbors, and business-led partnerships (2586, 2731, 5549, 6272).

Beyond the UK, most governments became concerned with the role of cities in economic development (2457, 2015, 0908). From the mid-1980s onwards, Western European cities enjoyed economic and demographic growth in particular capitals of small countries such as Helsinki, Copenhagen, Stockholm, Dublin, and Lisbon, but also the bulk of European cities, regional capitals of between 200,000 and 2 million inhabitants (within the urban area) (Le Galès 2002). Even former industrial cities in crisis and harbor cities (3003, 4963, 0292) turned around and have become more prosperous, for instance in Germany. Urban growth ran parallel with processes of suburbanization and metropolitanization, hence opening new conflicts for urban policies, including processes of centrifugal fragmentation (Dematteis 2000).

Urban Policies as Public Policies: Do Not Take the Label for Granted

This brief historic account reminds us of the wide range of policy programs that make sense as *urban policies*, but also of the limits of labels such as *urban policy*. Urban policies are part of the complex cross-boundaried, cross-sectored world of public policies and should be analyzed in those terms.

First, in Europe, every level of government is required to be able to demonstrate it has an urban policy. Once the questions of urban crisis, poverty, and social exclusion have entered the political field, which has been the case nearly everywhere now for the past two or three decades in Europe, they acquire dynamics of their own as issues that will be regularly activated through research reports, claims by organized interests, images, and policy discourses. Political elites, whatever the level, cannot be seen to be doing nothing. In his classic account of symbolic policies, Edelman (1985) chooses the example of the creation of a national urban agency in the 1950s in the USA to show that something was being done. The creation of task forces, committees, and agencies surrounded by publicity is a classic tool of government. In the case of urban policies, where the timescale of change is rather slow, several years or a decade, and where many actors and issues are mixed, it is particularly tempting for political elites to demonstrate ad hoc commitment to large programs, priorities, new agencies, emergency programs, and units. For instance, the photograph of Mrs Thatcher within the urban ruin of an industrial city, wearing a building worker's helmet, in the early 1980s, clearly signaled that the government was in charge and was dealing with the problem. Creating an urban program or initiative is a way of avoiding blame in case of problems, for instance urban riots.[2]

Most of the time, a "new policy" results from the reorganization of existing pieces of public policy which are reassembled, brought together and rebranded as "new urban policy". Reassembling and reframing elements of public policies is a major activity within ministries for two reasons:

1 Policies die hard.
2 There is constant pressure for ministers to be visible in the public debate, to start new initiatives, to launch new policies, to initiate innovative programs.

Even cases of innovation most of the time build upon existing marginal programs which are brought to the fore, as was the case, for instance, with the "new urban policy" in France, labeled *"politique de la ville"* before it acquired a dynamics of its own (Estèbe 2003).

Second, urban policies, like most public policies, are part of the world of overlapping powers within European governance in the making: municipalities, metropolitan authorities, regions, federal states, or auto-nomies, the nation-state, the EU, and sometimes the Organization for Economic Development and Cooperation (OECD) urban group, and the United Nations (UN) (Habitat Summit) international rules comprising environmental norms can have a role in urban policies. There are endless cases of urban policies where the norm is now for the overlapping funding and influence of different levels of government, for better – more targeted and coordinated effort – or worse – more piecemeal and fragmented actions. In most countries, the territorial organization of the nation-state has been facing serious reshaping, an ongoing process that leads to the pluralization of territorial interests within the state. Associations and vol-untary sector organizations – from neighborhood groups to giant utility firms – have a say and some power in urban policies. Urban policy there-fore covers a wide range of actors from different sectors of society, with different statuses, acting at different levels. Emerging problems raise ques-tions that cross horizontally over bureaucracies and sectors, and vertically over different levels of government.

Urban problems, programs and networks of actors are characterized by vast heterogeneity – hence the attraction of decentralization and experi-mentation. The development of new policy tools provides evidence of attempts to redefine public policy in a rather flexible way in order to face ill-defined problems and to cope with difficult heterogeneous goals. If "combating poverty" or "regenerating urban neighborhoods in crisis" is a set goal, the degree of generality provides considerable room for maneuver to define, design, *"bricoler"* (Lascoumes and Le Bourhis 1998) various types of representations, goals, and programs. In all countries, urban public policies are not given. Some constructionist approach is required to see how locally, or nationally, the problem is constructed by different actors, how adjustment processes are taking place to define a cognitive frame which is adopted by the actors, what the relations of power are. The dynamic of partnership offers some remarkable insights into these pro-cesses (Benington and Geddes 2001).

Urban public policies are a difficult business and one often tends to conclude that the less serious the problem is, the more likely the policy will appear to be a success. It follows that governments are ever more eager to promote their initiatives, their new programs. Analyses of urban policy over time (Le Galès 1995; Atkinson 1999a; Imrie and Thomas

1999; J. Andersen 2001) underline the wealth of procedures, new schemes, new combinations of policy instruments, a never-ending process of policy initiatives, auditing, creation of organizations, an immense field of experimentation undertaken by local actors . . . as if this movement could dissimulate the lack of capacity to act on some basic issues of labor market, education, or wealth redistribution. The power to design what is relevant and what should be excluded from the urban policy field as defined by the government is an important one. The rise of evaluation research, a good thing by other means, also leads to endless evaluation processes which do not question the boundaries and the categories of public policy as designed by the government, whatever the level or the power relationship between different groups. French urban policy ignored for years the ethnic minorities' questions (Morel 2002), while UK urban policy tended for a while to leave out the question of poverty (Atkinson 1999a). Public policies, whatever the label put upon them or the announced goals, are constantly shifting, redesigned as a result of conflicts between groups, organizations, business interests, political entrepreneurs who try to define a cognitive frame, or several, a legitimate view of problems which will lead to action in their interests.

This is the reason why the question of governance, coordination, and coherence has become so crucial, as is reflected in the language and the policy instruments, such as partnership, global approach, integration project, strategic program, coalitions, leadership, contracts, governance, and so on. Urban public policies, together with many public policies, have been characterized by various mixes of networks, uncertainty, serendipity, interferences between various policy domains, multiplication of actors and objectives, contradictory constraints.[3] Although urban policy was never as institutionalized a policy sector as, let us say, social services in Scandinavia, financial policy in the UK or agricultural policy in Germany and France, fragmentation has been emphasized. In this sense, the urban policy process is probably nowadays more like the American one.

Third, urban policies are increasingly brought together and implemented at the urban level. All the points made previously stress the role of urban elites in designing, implementing and coordinating policies. Urban policies are therefore also a result of urban governments or governance transformation (John 2001; Le Galès 2002).

In most Western European countries, more than half of all public investment is now made at the local or regional level (Table 11.1), in particular by urban governments – hence the flourishing of projects and initiatives. Altogether, urban policies are at least as important when initiated by urban elites as national programs.

In terms of revenue raising and sharing, the context in which the cooperation and/or competition between various levels of government

Table 11.1 Fiscal revenue of different public administrations (%)

	Federal state or central administration	State	Local authorities	Social security
Austria	52.7	9.3	10.2	27.8
Belgium	36.7	23.3	4.9	35.1
Finland	52.6		22.2	25.2
France	43.6		10.6	45.8
Germany	29.4	22.0	8.0	40.6
Greece	68.8		1.1	30.1
Ireland	86.8		2.0	11.2
Italy	58.8		11.7	29.5
Luxembourg	68.1		6.3	25.6
Netherlands	56.5		3.0	40.5
Portugal	67.0		6.1	26.9
Spain	48.0		17.0	35.0
Sweden	58.1		30.8	11.1
UK	63.0		13.3	23.7

Source: OECD Economic outlooks (2001).

takes place is making the choice more acute and politically contested. This takes two different forms which constitute different challenges, if not a serious threat to the nation-state. Significantly, associations of urban mayors have flourished and have been asking for more resources for cities: in Germany in the mid-1990s, in Britain with the Core Cities' groups, in Italy with the movement of the cities, in France, in Denmark, Spain, and now the six cities of Finland. These organizations express an interest different from the traditional redistribution within the welfare system, emphasizing the needs of cities' inhabitants and the crucial role of cities for the competitiveness of countries. The process of European integration also fuels that dynamics because of funding regulations.

Urban government has not disappeared from European cities. Organized within nation-states, urban governments still perform functions for the state, as well as having more responsibility because of the decentralization, restructuring and differentiation of the state and the fragmentation of public policies. As cities are increasingly becoming a site of aggregation and representation of different interests, then the job remains of bringing them together to organize a mode of city governance, to institutionalize collective action and to integrate them with a more or less shared cognitive framework, a set of priorities that may appear to be for the common good of a city. In cities, local governments have been profoundly restructured, becoming more political, strategic and organized for action in their implementation of policies (Klausen and Magnier 1998; John 2001). Urban governments retain a strong presence, and their political expertise and influence are also tending to increase. By comparison with US public–private partnerships, which frequently vest most of the power in the private sector, European public–private partnership experiments remain fairly limited (except in the UK), and urban governments still have strong capacities for initiative and control. Urban governments have developed their mode of action in three directions in particular: consideration of group, neighborhood and resident demands; diversification of public policies; and management of urban services, despite privatization (Lorrain and Stoker 1995). The processes of making collective choices, choosing, linking, aggregating, and representing interests within a territory, and taking and implementing decisions are inherently political. Therefore, within European cities, urban governments and elected politicians are under pressure to deal with a set of problems that used to be under state control (economic development, law and order, social exclusion, representation of the city in Europe). In terms of urban polices they are now required both to deliver and implement national and European urban programs and to implement their own urban policies. There are issues that cannot be addressed at that level, but most of the literature on urban policies or urban governance stresses the dynamism and the relevance of urban policies understood as policies implemented by urban elites (Le Galès 2002; Moulaert et al. 2003) within the constraints of the nation-state.

What Does the Label "Urban Policies" Cover?

Urban policies: an empirical list

The point has been made: urban policy is a rather elusive category (but are not they all?). In most countries, urban policy was organized, shaped, and determined by a set of actors, interests, institutions, representations, and ideas that were related to the particular situation of a nation-state. During what may be called a century cycle of the nation-state, national variables were central in determining what urban policy would be, or would be considered to be. This different national structuring of what urban policy meant, and its outcomes, has not disappeared overnight. Any attempt to provide some views on urban policies in Europe has to take into account this heritage, which has only recently been mixed with a different set of powers. New issues have arisen in close interaction with the dynamics of state restructuring. Because cities are back on the agenda, because more resources, social conflicts and wealth production are concentrated there, the notion of urban policy is now recovering an

Table 11.2 Urban policies

Land and planning regulation, from conservation to new towns
Strategic planning, urban collective projects
Housing, social housing (construction and destruction)
Construction and management of utilities, infrastructures
Transport: railways, buses, airports, metro, tramway, stations, dealing with NIMBYs
Area-based, transversal/global policies
Social services, targeting of categories: young children, old people
Training for the workforce, attracting specific professionals groups
Policies against social exclusion
Cultural policies: prestige projects, new museums, but also carnivals, festivals
Neighborhood initiatives, initiatives to deal with multiculturalism
Regeneration policies, renovation of old urban centers, quays, property developments,
  flagship projects
Economic development: training, attracting investment, image-making, support to firrns,
  enterprise zones, tax policies
Antiviolence, social control, policing, dealing with marginal groups, surveillance, safety
Integration of immigrants, control of immigrants
Quality of life, environment, antipollution, sustainable development
Patrimony, protection of the historic center
Urban tourism promotion, leisure and consumption spaces, public spaces, malls,
  entertainment
Policies to raise participation of the inhabitants, democratic procedures, consultations
Health policies to target groups at risk, to deal with epidemics (e.g., Aids)
Investments in science, universities, research centers, innovation districts
Positive discrimination in disadvantaged neighborhoods: education, heath, economic
  development, public services
International exchange, twinnings, international relations
Programs to coordinate fragmented policies: partnership, contracts

ever-increasing range of issues. Table 11.2 provides a list of items in a deliberate effort to avoid classification.

The list echoes classic Marxist work on the contradictions of the state, maintaining social order and incorporating different social groups for the long-term dynamics of capitalism. The list is indeed a purely descriptive device; it does not tell us about the dynamics, the budgets, the actors, the representations, the outcomes, or the institutions. It could have been written for the USA or Canada alike. At one level of analysis, many urban policy programs are very similar, thus suggesting important elements of policy transfers and/or similar types of pressures and constraints leading to similar responses. The following section makes a distinction between two domains of urban policies, identifying what is European about them and how to explain differentiation between states and between cities.

*Social urban policies: redistribution, local regeneration, and
the control of the poor*

Urban policies are in part related to state strategies and policies. Policies die hard and long-term welfare state commitments are not that easy to undermine on a short-term basis, not even during the era of Thatcherism in the UK. European states are characterized by a diversity of institutional arrangements and generalization is perilous. However, in most cases urban policies and antipoverty strategies alike are developed from a set of premises:

1 The state has legitimacy to develop policy; urban policy is a legitimate domain of state intervention.
2 There is a large body of state funding and public agencies that can be involved.

Beyond all the local initiatives and partnerships, there is a robust welfare state with powerful mechanisms of redistribution through pensions, social security expenditure, public investments in major facilities (schools, hospitals, railway stations, or universities). Most of these mechanisms are relatively long-term, discrete, and automatic. The relative stability of the importance of the welfare state, measured as a percentage of GDP (Table 11.3), with some exceptions such as Britain, suggests a relative macro stability of this powerful base that, even if it is not called urban policy, provides massive support to inhabitants within cities in terms of services, jobs and revenue. By contrast to the USA, European cities are far more dependent on and/or supported by the welfare state and the public sector. This has two consequences:

1 Urban elites are not so dependent upon business interests and the middle classes (hence a much smaller degree of urban boosterism and less pressure from economic competition).
2 Groups within cities and associations of cities are powerful interest groups for the defense of existing welfare patterns and opposition to radical cuts or reshaping. The stronger the welfare state, e.g., in Northern Europe, the stronger the welfare pillar of cities.

The long-term trend of increasing resources for subnational governments, and cities in particular, is not uniform and masks large variations among and within countries. It is not just a result of pressures from within the state, but also the result of the strategy of state elites. Pickvance and Préteceille (1991) have clearly shown that decentralizing the management of cuts and shortages was a popular move among nation-states' elites.

Table 11.3　Fiscal revenue of EU member states (% of GDP)

	1965	1975	1985	1995	1999
Austria	33.9	37.7	41.6	41.5	44.3
Belgium	31.3	41.6	46.3	44.8	45.4
Denmark	29.9	41.4	47.4	49.4	50.6
Finland	30.3	37.07	40.0	45.0	46.5
France	34.5	36.9	43.8	44.0	46.0
Germany	31.6	36.0	32.9	38.2	37.7
Greece	18.2	21.0	28.6	31.7	37.1
Ireland	24.9	30.2	35.1	33.1	31.9
Italy	25.5	26.2	34.4	41.2	43.0
Luxembourg	27.7	39.6	45.3	41.9	42.1
Netherlands	32.8	43.0	42.4	42.0	40.3
Portugal	15.8	21.3	27.1	32.7	34.5
Spain	14.7	19.5	27.6	32.8	35.1
Sweden	35.0	43.4	48.3	47.6	52.1
UK	30.4	35.4	37.7	35.2	36.6
EU average	29.1	33.4	36.8	39.4	40.7
Australia	22.4	26.6	29.1	29.4	29.9*
Japan	18.3	20.9	27.6	28.4	27.7
USA	24.7	26.9	26.1	27.6	28.9*

* Figures are for 1998.
Source: OECD Economic outlooks (2001).

However, by contrast to the USA, the support for urban policy has been relatively strong over time because:

1　Suburbanization has not taken place at the same scale – cities and the metropolitan area are growing.
2　Lower-middle classes from the public sector, often depending on public employment, still constitute the bulk of the cities' social structure in most countries, less so in the South.

Lower-middle classes from the public sector are organized within the social democratic parties, the Greens and sometimes the extreme Left (Sellers 2002). These groups have an active role within urban and national politics and are able to make demands at the national level to support the welfare state and cities. A good deal of the middle classes also live in the cities, hence an interest in good services, transport and schools, for instance. In the European urban systems there are therefore powerful forces at play, which, in contrast to many US cities, support public investment in cities, urban policies more than antipoverty policies as such.

Beyond this macro dimension, which is what urban policies are based on, what is labeled as *the urban crisis* questioned vertical policies and paved the way for all sorts of new, experimental, innovative urban policy programs that were aimed at tackling the crisis. There is no need in this chapter to return to the dimensions of this urban crisis: process of deindustrialization, marginalization of the working class, rising and renewed forms of poverty, immigration, the retreat from the state in social housing, increasing unemployment, flexibility of the labor market, forms of privatization of services and utilities. Waves of riots – mostly in France, Britain, and Germany, but also in Belgium, the Netherlands, and Denmark, less so in Southern Europe – epitomized and made visible forms of urban crisis that were associated in the media with large housing estates, youth unemployment, crime, and immigrants (1914, 3170). From the state point of view, urban policies are not central but state elites cannot accept too many problems in cities for revenue and social order reasons. From a purely functionalist perspective, some degree of urban policy is useful for state elites in order to avoid blame and maintain social order, but not crucial. This is the reason why most accounts of urban policies tend to emphasize the ad hoc nature of urban policies, the experiments, the incomplete institutionalization, the multiplication of initiatives and the contradictions.

Indeed, from the 1980s onwards, urban policies were labeled as such to design more micro programs to regenerate neighborhoods, including housing, social services, economic development, services, culture and health, a bit of everything targeted on the neighborhood (6557, 5939). Britain, the Netherlands, and France pioneered these approaches, which then spread to other countries but also vertically, either to the EU (the URBAN program) or downwards towards regions and cities themselves. Those area-based strategies for regeneration have spread in most places under different names with a view to giving coherence to a whole set of partners and policy initiatives, a transversal approach (H.T. Andersen 2001). The implementation process is much more difficult than the intellectual design and faces limitations, but the spread of these bottom-up political dynamics also reveals the mobilization of different sets of actors (Benington and Geddes 2001).

Unemployment and immigration have once again contributed to the dark image of the city, as a place of danger and crime. In most European countries, issues of safety and crime are gaining salience on the political agenda, associated with immigration and leading to the rise of extreme right and antiforeigner parties from Denmark to France, Italy, the Netherlands, Germany, or even Britain. Urban policies are therefore under pressure from those groups to deal or to be seen dealing with this issue. In most cities, urban policies have a more obvious dimension of safety and social control of the poor (Body-Gendrot 2000; Garland 2001; Eick 2002; Roché 2003). The multiplication of local, private or state agencies and the rising number of prisoners (which remain far behind the US figures, even in Britain) are two indicators of the salience of the issue. In welfare policies across the board, many community organizations and agencies depending upon public funds, now implementing elements of welfare policies (e.g., welfare to work; Mayer 2003), also play an ambiguous game in terms of managing the poor (Eick 2002).

Urban policies to foster economic development and competition

The restructuring of the state has weakened the protection from market forces which benefitted different groups within cities. The rise of unemployment in the 1970s symbolized the limits of state power to control the economy. Under increasing pressure from market forces, urban elites thus became more active in promoting urban policies that aimed at fostering economic development. Neoliberal state elites, often allied to ministries of finance, also contributed to greater market pressure to transform urban policies.

There is general agreement that competition between European cities is growing, but the concepts of interurban competition and urban success remain diffuse.[4] The metaphor of the "entrepreneurial city" (Jessop 1997) has three characteristic elements:

1 The discourse of competition and the market, including notions of image and identity.
2 The political priority given to the stakes of economic development and attracting favored investments, flows, and social groups.
3 Changes in local government towards organizational forms of a public–private partnership type, which give private-sector actors a major role in defining the common good of the city, its priorities and modes of management, as well as in designing and implementing projects.

Coalitions that govern cities have an interest in getting involved in these dynamics – that is, in improving their position on the scales of prestige, wealth, and political influence in international competition between cities to attract investments, well-off social groups, and visitors. Urban elites are trying to strengthen their cities' positions as consumption centers (with shopping centers and leisure complexes, entertainment, major urban projects and culture), and as command centers (as headquarters of big firms and public bodies) (6282, 1221, 2339). They are implementing urban policies to make themselves attractive to investors and people: urban planning, social policy, image, and culture can all be reviewed and measured against the demands of competition – and this is not a benign process, because it involves social transfers, police to control the poor and redistribution towards the favored groups. This logic can have the effect of legitimizing forms of pragmatic or so-called apolitical urban policies, thus privileging public–private partnerships and networks of economic and political elites, more flexible ad hoc urban policies.

So, how far have things gone in European cities? Most of the time, as far as cities are concerned, the reality of competition translates into public policies presented in the language of competition. Similar to their American counterparts at the urban level, urban elites have engaged in forms of urban policies following that path: creation of leisure and/or consumption complexes (fantasy cities; Hannigan 1998), private–public partnership to redevelop docks and quays all over the continent, flagship urban projects, museums and festivals, redesigning of public space, attraction of foreign direct investments (FDI), middle-class housing, and prestigious hotels (2746, 1255, 6303). The rise of urban strategies from Bilbao to Lyon or Cardiff, from the new urban region of Oresund (between Copenhagen and Malmö) to Turin or Lisbon, from Vienna or Dublin to Munich and Helsinki, this reveals the changing focus for urban policies towards issues of competition and economic development and the public investments that support these projects.

This type of urban policy has spread everywhere. Although there are differences between cities, the same dynamics and the same actors are at play. Such urban policies are weakly connected to social exclusion; by contrast, they tend to participate in those processes.

Conclusions: European Urban Policies?
Do They Make Any Sense?

At a superficial level, the contrast between the USA and Europe is quite sharp: American scholars write about the decline of national urban policy, local welfare to work, race, and attempts to revive metropolitan government, new urbanism, private developers, urban regime, and growth coalitions. European scholars in this book also emphasize urban social policies, public investments, growing cities, political legitimacy, and initiatives of urban elites, welfare, and antipoverty policy.

However, this chapter has tried to show the combination of both the European legacy, in particular the combination of economic and social policies supported by powerful groups and public funds, and the increasing pressures and fragmentation of the policy process that make the comparison with the US case much more pertinent. Issues of social and racial segregation, violence, or boosterism make the point.

A different kind of answer points to the making of a European "urban policy" along the lines of economic, social and environmental regeneration. A European-wide urban coalition has gradually formed, finding intermediaries among commissioners, member state representatives of the European Commission, and members of the European Parliament, promoting the URBAN Program for the renewal of urban neighborhoods. The Commission also produced a document entitled *Europe's Cities: Community Measures in Urban Areas* (1997), which has strengthened this dynamic. The URBAN program has as its objectives: promoting local employment; revitalizing depressed neighborhoods, both socially and economically; providing social and other services; improving living conditions and the urban environment and public spaces; and improving local strategies and decision-making processes so as to involve local communities. A second phase is now on the way (Aldskogius 2000). This URBAN program is therefore a classic case of hybridization between different urban policy traditions (Atkinson 1999b). The creation of the EU URBAN programs goes together with the making of a European network of cities benefitting from that program and its funding, the creation of professional networks and the dissemination of norms and rules, i.e. a classic case of horizontal European integration mechanisms. However, urban policies in Europe are also shaped by EU competition policy, immigration policy and environment policy.

Urban policies have come back on the political agenda because of their own dynamics but in relation to state restructuring and economic changes. Instead of analyzing urban policies as they are labeled by governmental agencies, the chapter has shown the diversity of programs under the "urban policy" label and their similarities with other public policies. Many trends, programs, and policy responses are comparable to that of the USA. However, the insertion of European cities within European states, and now within the EU, provide them with a different support in terms of resources, social groups, and political legitimacy, hence the dynamism of urban policies in Europe.

ACKNOWLEDGMENTS

At the time of writing, the author held a CAMPUS research fellowship with SURF/University of Salford. Thanks to Alan Harding and Yuri Kazepov for their comments on the chapter.

NOTES

1 The author apologizes for writing only about Western Europe; I do not know enough about the new member states.
2 The literature on blame avoidance gives convincing insights into the how and why of such a trend. It argues that blame avoidance, or minimizing blame, is a major concern for individual politicians who develop all sorts of strategies (Hood 2002) to justify themselves.
3 This is not so new. In their classic account of the implementation of the American urban program in the city of Oakland, Pressman and Wildavsky (1979) gave the evocative title: *How Great Expectations in Washington are Dashed in Oakland or Why it's Amazing that Federal Programs Work at all: This Being a Saga of The Economic Development Administration.*
4 "Interurban competition basically is rivalry between cities in the European urban system for the creation or attraction of economic activity which produces income. The capacity to generate income is in turn related to other aspects of urban economy and society such as levels of service, size of the tax base, infrastructure, quality of life, and educational and cultural facilities" (Jensen-Butler 1997: 3).

REFERENCES

Aldskogius, G. (2000) *Urban Policy in the Structural Policy of the EU.* CERUM, Umeå.

Andersen, J. (2001) *Urban Policy between Neoelitist Growth Policy and Community Empowerment: The Politics of Gambling and Ambivalence in Copenhagen.* Working Paper, Roskilde University.

Andersen, H.T. (2001) The new urban politics of Europe: the area based approach to regeneration. In: Andersen, H.T. and van Kempen, R. (eds.) *Governing European Cities: Social Fragmentation, Social Exclusion and Urban Governance.* Aldershot, Ashgate.

Atkinson, R. (1999a) Discourses of partnership and empowerment in contemporary British urban regeneration. *Urban Studies,* 36: 56–89.

Atkinson, R. (1999b) An urban policy for Europe. *North,* 4: 11–16.

Beauregard, R.A. and Body-Gendrot, S. (eds.) (1999) *The Urban Moment.* Sage, London.

Benington, J. and Geddes, M. (eds.) (2001) *Local Partnership and Social Exclusion in the European Union, New Forms of Local Social Governance.* Routledge, London.

Body-Gendrot, S. (2000) *The Social Control of Cities.* Blackwell, Oxford.

Body-Gendrot, S. and Martiniello, M. (eds.) (2000) *Immigrants in European Cities.* Macmillan, Basingtoke.

Dematteis, G. (2000) Spatial representations of European urbanism. In: Bagnasco, A. and Le Galès, P. (eds.) *Cities in Europe.* Cambridge University Press, Cambridge.

Edelman, M. (1985) *The Symbolic Use of Politics*. University of Illinois Press, Urbana.

Eick, V. (2002) New strategies of "policing the poor": Berlin's neo-liberal security system "Civil society style." Paper presented at the conference on Cities as Strategic Sites, Militarization, Anti-Globalization and Warfare, Manchester, SURF, November.

Estèbe, P. (2004) Les quartiers de la politique de la ville. In: Lascoumes, P. and Le Galès, P. (eds.) *L'action publique et ses instruments*. Presses de Sciences Po, Paris (forthcoming).

European Commission (1997) *Europe's Cities: Community Measures in Urban Areas*. EU, Brussels.

European Commission (1998) *Sustainable Urban Development in the EU: A Framework for Action*. EC Com/98/605 F, Brussels.

Garland, D. (2001) *The Culture of Control: Crime and Social Order in Contemporary Society*. Oxford University Press, Oxford.

Hannigan, J. (1998) *Fantasy City: Pleasure and Profit in the Postmodern Metropolis*. Routledge, London.

Hansen, R. and Weil, P. (eds.) (2001) *Towards a European Nationality: Citizenship, Immigration and Nationality Law in the EU*. Palgrave, Basingstoke.

Harloe, M. (1995) *The People's Home*. Blackwell, Oxford.

Harvey, D. (1985) *The Urbanisation of Capital*. Blackwell, Oxford.

Harvey, D. (1989) *The Condition of Postmodernity*. Blackwell, Oxford.

Healey, P., Cameron, S., Davoudi, S., Graham, S., and Madanipour, A. (eds.) (1995) *Managing Cities: The New Urban Context*. John Wiley, Chichester.

Healey, P., Khakee, A., Motte, A., and Needham, B. (eds.) (1997) *Making Strategic Spatial Plans: Innovations in Europe*. UCL Press, London.

Hood, C. (2002) Managing risk and managing blame: a political science approach. In: Weale, A. (ed.) *Risk, Democratic Citizenship and Public Policy Oxford*. OUP/British Academy, Oxford.

Imrie, R. and Thomas, H. (eds.) (1999) *British Urban Policy: An Evaluation of the UDC*. Sage, London.

Jensen-Butler, C. (1997) Competition between cities, urban performance and the role of urban policy: a theoretical framework. In: Jensen-Butler, C., Sachar, A., and van Weesep, J.B. (eds.) *European Cities in Competition*, Avebury, Aldershot.

Jessop, B. (1997) The entrepreneurial city: re-imagining localities, redesigning economic governance and restructuring capital? In: Jewson, N. and Macgregor, S. (eds.) *Realising Cities: New Spatial Divisions and Social Transformation*. Routledge, London.

Jessop, B. (2002) *The Future of the Capitalist State*. Polity Press, Cambridge.

John, P. (2001) *Local Governance in Europe*. Sage, London.

Klausen, K.K and Magnier, A. (eds.) (1998) *The Anonymous Leader: Appointed CEOs in Western Local Government*. Odense University Press, Odense.

Lascoumes, P. and Le Bourhis, P.P. (1998) Le bien commun comme construit territorial: identités d'action et procédures. *Politix*, 42: 37–66.

Le Galès, P. (1995) Politique de la ville en France et en Grande-Bretagne: volontarisme et ambiguïtés de l'Etat. *Sociologie du Travail*, 2: 249–276.

Le Galès, P. (2002) *European Cities, Social Conflicts and Governance*. Oxford University Press, Oxford.

Lorrain, D. and Stoker, G. (eds.) (1995) *La privatisation des services urbains*. La Découverte, Paris.

Marcuse, P. and van Kempen, R. (eds.) (2002) *Of States and Cities: The Partitioning of Urban Space*. Oxford University Press, Oxford.

Mayer, M. (2003) The onward sweep of social capital: causes and consequences for understanding cities, communities and urban movements. *International Journal of Urban and Regional Research*, 27 (1): 110–132.

Morel, S. (2002) *Ecole, territoires et identités: Les politiques publiques Françaises à l'epreuve de l'ethnicité*. L'Harmattan, Paris.

Moulaert, F. (2002) *Globalization and Integrated Area Development in European Cities*. Oxford University Press, Oxford.

Moulaert, F., Rodriguez, A., and Swyngedouw, E. (eds.) (2003) *The Globalized City: Economic Restructuring and Social Polarization in European Cities*. Oxford University Press, Oxford.

Organization for Economic Development and Cooperation (OECD) (2001) *Economic Outlooks*. OECD, Paris.

Pickvance, C. and Préteceille, E. (eds.) (1991) *State Restructuring and Local Power: A Comparative Perspective*. Pinter, London.

Pressman, S. and Wildavsky, A. (1979) *Implementation: How Great Expectations in Washington are Dashed in Oakland or Why it's Amazing that Federal Programs Work at all: This Being a Saga of The Economic Development Administration*. University of California Press, Berkeley.

Roché, S. (2003) *En quête de sécurité*. Colin, Paris.

Saraceno, C. (ed.) (2002) *Social Assistance Dynamics in Europe*. Policy Press, Bristol.

Saunier, P.Y. (2001) Sketches from the Urban Internationale, 1910–1950: voluntary sector associations, international institutions and US philanthropic foundations. *International Journal of Urban and Regional Research*, 25 (2): 403–424.

Sellers, J.M. (2002) *Governing from Below: Urban Politics and Post-Industrial Economy*. Cambridge University Press, Cambridge.

Topalov, C. (1990) From the "social question" to "urban problems": reformers and the working classes at the turn of the twentieth century. *International Social Science Journal*, 135: 319–336.

12

Changing Forms of Solidarity: Urban Development Programs in Europe

Jan Vranken

Introduction

Recent European history is rich in urban development programs (UDPs).[1] They have been established in the wake of a growing political recognition that exclusion threatens social cohesion, economic performance, and the democratic legitimacy of many cities. The social unrest and occasional rioting that many cities have experienced[2] are just the tip of the iceberg of social and spatial disparities within the city.[3] Visibility of these developments has been very much enhanced by the specific approach of "urban development programs."

These UDPs have developed in style and orientation throughout the 1980s and 1990s, from interventions focusing on combating social exclusion and poverty in specific neighborhoods to a more "positive" approach, that of promoting social cohesion, cultural creativity and economic dynamism at the city level. The solution of the "urban crisis" then, would simply be to restore solidarity and cohesion.

The problem, however, is that this new focus has never been sufficiently conceptualized. Simplification dominates the public and political discourse. Social inclusion, social cohesion, and solidarity have been used as interchangeable terms, thus greatly complicating analysis and policy-making. However, social reality is more complex than the public and political discourse would like it to be, and the specificity of an urban society certainly adds to this complexity. From its very beginnings, the city has been characterized as the context where difference (see Chapter 5), inequality and social exclusion in their many forms – spatial, social, cultural, and political – are concentrated. It would be wise, therefore, to lift the veil of simplicity from both solidarity and cohesion.

This contribution tries to do so. We approach the problem from a very specific angle: how UDPs have recognized and eventually handled problems of cohesion and solidarity. We begin with an overview of the context in which UDPs have started and then proceed with a brief discussion of the relation between solidarity and cohesion and their specificity. Although not all of these rather conceptual remarks are used in the more empirical part, we think they substantially contribute to a better understanding of our approach. The latter part of this chapter then, is a first analysis of some of the ways in which matters of cohesion and solidarity have been handled. This will be illustrated by initial research results collected about UDPs in the UGIS (Urban Development Programs, Urban Governance, Social Inclusion and Sustainability) project.[4]

Urban Development Programs in Their Context

In the 1980s and especially the 1990s, the perception of urban problems changed in almost all European countries. Instead of being defined simply as physical decay, the multidimensionality of urban problems became obvious. Poverty and other forms of social exclusion (homelessness, beggars) (4743, 0635, 2925), an increasing concentration of marginalized groups and ensuing spatial segregation constituted the most visible facets of a larger set of problems which also included growing unemployment, increasing criminality (5023, 6141), deteriorating private dwellings and public space (6141, 6559, 2641), dwindling social cohesion, and a declining quality of life in some neighborhoods (1883, 3135).

Whereas at the level of a society, old and new forms of inequality, exclusion, and fragmentation sometimes exist in a diffuse manner, at the city level they are often present in such a concentrated way that they capture the imagination (Bourdieu 1993). Across a range of European cities, concentrations of excluded people in particular neighborhoods have appeared (Madanipour et al. 1998). Spatial fragmentation has been fostered by the facilitation of access to the city for private transport, creating vacant spaces (motorways, parking lots) that are difficult to reintegrate in the city (2881, 6555, 0741). The same goes for monofunctional areas; recent ones, such as shopping areas, join older ones, such as social housing areas (5289, 4087, 5442, 1652, 2281). Social fragmentation appears in many forms of individualization of urban life, such as when "consumers" of goods (shopping malls) and services (cultural events) take precedence over "citizens" as the main users of the city.

The degree of segregation and exclusion differs among cities. This is related to their income level and income distribution, the type of welfare state, and housing and spatial policies (Breebaart et al. 1996; van Kempen and Özüekren 1997; Vandermotten et al. 1999). Nevertheless, there is an inherent and re-emerging spatial dimension in many forms of social exclusion (see, among others, Madanipour et al. 1998; Andersen and van Kempen 2001).

This concentration of deprived and excluded groups has self-perpetuating effects. As a result, they are unable to profit from the traditional mechanisms of socio-spatial mobility that formerly characterized cities. Not only are their personal or group characteristics responsible for their immobility; structural circumstances and the attitude of the population, the media and urban policies also play a part. Their neighborhoods no longer fulfill the "integrative" function, but became dead-end areas.[5]

These different forms of fragmentation threaten solidarity and social cohesion. This is reflected in the collapse or withering away of many features of traditional (urban) society, from rather cultural ones (common value patterns, traditional socializing institutions and mechanisms of social control) to more structural ones (neighborhoods, traditional social classes).

These developments do not point in the same direction – they also provide opportunities for more cohesive cities at the same time as they threaten solidarity and cohesion. Neighborhoods, for example, have always been seen as important "integrators" and their supposed disappearance would thus constitute an important threat to urban cohesion. However, it is not that simple. Indeed, the accepted thesis from reference group theory (Merton and Kitt 1950) is that identification with smaller units stands in the way of identification with a "higher level" (cities instead of neighborhoods, society instead of social classes). This is only part of what is happening. People do not only integrate into society as individuals but also through the smaller collectives they participate in. The question then, is whether developments such as increasing fragmentation are obstacles to cohesion and solidarity or rather take away obstacles that formerly prevented identification with more "modern" levels of social life (the city, the nation state).[6]

Solidarity and Cohesion are Different but Related

Komter et al. (2000) identify four different aspects of the question of "social order," all of which are applicable to the constituent dimensions of solidarity and cohesion. First, different societal levels are at stake, such as cities and neighborhoods, and it is relevant to analyze their external relations. Second, mutual understanding is needed to establish communication and trust. The increasing diversity of lifestyles and ethnic cultures (1903, 2827, 2994) within the city could form an obstacle to this because then a common cultural context is missing. Third, "shared utility" – self-preservation and sound self-interest – also contributes to solidarity, resembling a variation on the theme of "private vices, public virtues." Last, solidarity always coexists with (individual and group) conflict and deviance, with rapid and therefore destabilizing social change and cultural innovation.

In spite of this common context, we should not forget our initial point, which is that cohesion and solidarity are not to be used as synonyms, although both concepts imply reciprocal dependency between individuals, groups, and institutions. Where then, do they differ? Some authors see cohesion as an empirical descriptive concept and solidarity as a normative one (see Schuyt 1997: 1). Others insist that both can be used in a descriptive and normative sense (Komter et al. 2000: 10–11). We would rather focus on the fact that cohesion refers to the static dimension (as in chemistry) and solidarity to a process. There is some indication in Durkheim that he viewed it this way: "Cohesion, which results from this solidarity" (Durkheim 1893: 131). Solidarity, then, is a set of processes through which the (urban) social system is integrated and social cohesion is the *result* of different forms of solidarity. A cohesive social unit would be an organization, group or city in which a variety of forces are active that are strong and lasting enough to hold that unit together. It renders that social unit into something "sustainable" (for a more detailed discussion see Vranken et al. 2003: 43–51).

Solidarity

Recently, classifications of solidarity in terms of formal and informal solidarity, horizontal and vertical solidarity, "spontaneous" and "imposed" solidarity, "bottom-up" and "top-down" solidarity have been presented. They are relevant distinctions but do not have the analytical power of Durkheim's classic pairing of "mechanical" and "organic" solidarity.

At first sight, organic solidarity is the dominant form in modern cities, because labor division has been on the increase since Durkheim's time. On the other hand, it is clear that the "natural" and rather hidden solidarity mechanisms resulting from far-reaching differentiation in the labor process did not suffice to hold society together. They have been supplemented by "top-down" and explicit initiatives, such as complex systems of social security and a myriad of initiatives that in one way or another are intended to redistribute increased welfare or to guarantee minimal levels of living conditions. It has even taken the form of a specific type of society, the welfare state, which in this sense is the most striking sign of the insufficient workings of "organic solidarity." In recent years, there has even been a growing call for more state intervention in non-material matters such as public safety or the safeguarding of central values.

In other words, new forms of "mechanic" solidarity seem to be needed to complement the "organic" solidarity that is rooted in a functional division of labor. We could put it otherwise: because the "structural bonds" that sufficed for many decades are no longer strong enough, there is increasing call for an explicit organization of "cultural bonds." Still another way of looking at it is that the "bottom-up" solidarity present in social networks, informal exchange or mutual trust is losing ground and has to be complemented by new forms of solidarity that are imposed from above through all kinds of social control (by the state or by the mass media); new forms of "top-down" solidarity.

The crisis of bottom-up forms of solidarity continues to be widely discussed in modern literature in terms of dwindling social capital, but some organized top-down forms of solidarity are neglected. These now cover an even wider array of initiatives than before, from "repressive" to "protective" ones (social protection, social services). We will not discuss the protective forms, for obvious reasons – the topics are well known, and the literature is too extensive to be synthesized in a few paragraphs.

The "repressive" ones are most visible through the initiatives to "police the private and public sphere," the many social and physical control systems that are being introduced in urban environments in order to promote safety (2959, 0709). Best documented are the increase in CCTV-controlled areas, private security services, and the call for "more police/blue on the street." Less easily identifiable, they are found in the success of monocultural discourses and the increase of legal and other mechanisms to prevent or to combat forms of "deviant behavior" (including specific cultural behavior) (2069, 1939, 3032). The integration debate has shifted from "reciprocal adaptation" of dominant and minority cultures to the slogan "integrate or leave," and integration is reduced to "adaptation." The treatment of beggars and other types of "street people" has become less lenient than it used to be (6009, 5369). For young offenders who are considered to be "incorrigible" special prisons are built, and their prime function is no longer to re-educate the inmates but to protect society from them. Even the necessity to organize links between people, such as through the financing of "spontaneous" neighborhood festivities such as barbecues, fits into this picture (6557, 3437).

We should be aware that these different forms of solidarity are not only complementary, they are often conflicting and in some cases even mutually exclusive. The discussions about promoting participation or about neighborhood-centered interventions later in this chapter provide good illustrations. In both cases, the general and the particular interest do not always coincide. Awareness of the different forms of solidarity, however, are of utmost importance when setting goals and assessing the results of urban initiatives, such as at what level cohesion should be preserved (and social mix be promoted) or whether the replacing of previous forms of solidarity should be left to "market forces" or be organized from above (and whether both approaches are not mutually exclusive). This awareness is distinctly absent from urban policy-making.

Social cohesion

Social cohesion is needed to ensure the reproduction ("sustainability") of a neighborhood, a city or any other urban system. Whereas solidarity is perhaps the single most important and certainly the most discussed force leading to social cohesion, it is not the only factor at stake. In order to make solidarity produce cohesion, we need resources. The action of cementing does not suffice; we need building blocks and cement. We would like to subsume these resources under two headings: a relational dimension (social networks and "social capital," which is largely dependent upon the existence of social networks) and a cultural dimension (common value pattern, group identification).[7]

The relational dimension of social cohesion consists of a structured multiplicity of social links between individuals or their positions. Through these links, people occupy a position in society. This in turn requires that many different foci exist (Feld 1981), where people of different social groups (or subcultures) meet. Cohesion is then measured by the extent to which "social circles" (Simmel 1908: 312–13) are cross-cutting. In modern social network terms, this would mean a certain degree of heterogeneity of relations within one's network, a mix of strong and weak ties. Weaker ties perhaps are limited in the claims that can be made for them, but they also tend to provide better access to a greater diversity of resources than do strong and socially more homogeneous ties. Weak ties therefore are particularly important for people living in society's margins, because these weak ties – which for them are rather indirect (that is, of the "via-via" type) – provide access to important "social goods" (labor, income, education), whereas strong ties do not because they are rather with "the same kind of people" (originally Granovetter 1973).[8] For them the only way to connect to a city's resources – and so to improve their individual or collective position – is through the development of their weak ties. However, as Burns and Taylor (1998) point out, socially excluded groups and persons do not have the dense and overlapping networks of a possible mythical past, nor the sparse overlapping networks required in the present world. Moreover, their situation is being complicated by recent developments within neighborhoods (the increasing in- and out-flow, leading to more anonymous relations) and by changes in the structure and functions of the family (leading to less stable networks).

Regarding the cultural dimension of cohesion, a Parsonian view would focus on the presence of a set of shared values and norms. This would enable the members "to identify and support common aims and objectives, and share a common set of moral principles and codes of behavior through which to conduct their relations with one another" (Kearns and Forrest 2000: 997). It should be clear that this "value dimension" of social cohesion cannot be reduced to a "mutually respected moral code" or to a common political culture (read voting behavior), both of which have been at the center of politicians' concerns. Elements such as the recognition of one's societal responsibility, democratic conflict-resolving, and tolerant behavior are equally important. The sociologic problem also lies in the hypothesized collapse of routines that used to function as mediators between the general value patterns and everyday life and, moreover, fulfilled an important function of social control. It is the weakening or even disappearance of these "spontaneous" routines and reciprocities that invite "top-down" initiatives to strengthen or to complement them.

This brings us to another facet of social cohesion: a feeling of belonging to or identification with a group. In fact, this feature could also be regarded as integrating the relational and cultural dimensions just discussed. Indeed, cohesion implies the merging of a cultural pattern and a social network into a specific "social form." The forces leading to this formation are internal and external. Internal forces are the networks facilitating interaction and communication, and common cultural frameworks providing shared values and facilitating common meanings, interpretations, and common norms. They result in a feeling of being part of a common enterprise and readiness to cooperate with one another to reach common goals. That urban residents identify themselves with others of "their" city or, put differently, the city viewed as my "home" (*Heimat*) provides a good illustration.

The external force promoting identification with the in-group is the perception of an out-group as a "threat," an important result of which is the generation of stereotypes and stigmatization (see Chapter 10). This could even mean that forms of social exclusion[9] are necessary, as is most visible in ethnically or religiously homogeneous groups or societies. In order to have cohesion at the group level, two conditions must be fulfilled: a negative and a positive one. Hence, exclusion and cohesion are not opposite but complementary realities (see also Healey 1998). Exclusion implies the active existence of cohesion. This suggests that we need to understand both social exclusion and cohesion as group-building and mobilizing processes that generate boundaries and create labels of "we," "you," and "they."

Some cohesion may be constraining and limiting, unable to respond to new conditions. While a strong, neighborhood-related cohesion might exclude inhabitants from opportunities outside the neighborhood, they may also exclude others from opportunities to which they are entitled. This suggests that research and policy attention need to be directed at discriminating between forms of cohesion and exclusion that are supportive and which give strength and identity to people in vulnerable situations, and those that actively seek to prevent others participating in their opportunities and social worlds.

Does the Area-based Approach of Urban Development Programs Provide an Answer to Problems of Cohesion and Solidarity?

Over the last decade, area-based approaches have gained prominence, largely because they are supposed to provide a relevant framework for concerted action to counteract the multiple problems that cities in general and deprived neighborhoods in particular are confronted with. UDPs are the most prominent expression of this approach. They are closely related to a geographically defined area of the city that is characterized by an accumulation of physical, economic, and social problems, and very often also ethnic problems. This kind of area, moreover, is hypothesized as being devoid of solidarity and cohesion.

Area-based approaches can produce considerable synergy, as they imply direct involvement of and cooperation with the local community, as well as with various public authorities, businesses and other organizations (see also Andersen 2001; Andersen and van Kempen 2001). Moreover, the spatial approach has been popular among politicians because it has often allowed them to produce visible results within a relatively short time.

Despite these advantages, the area-based approach has been strongly debated among urban researchers. H.T. Andersen (2001) argues that deprived neighborhoods constitute a very important element of the interaction between social, economic, and physical changes in the cities that cause urban decay. In other words, these areas are not simply a result of social inequality and segregation; they are also by themselves creating new segregation and inequality. In these neighborhoods, strong self-perpetuating processes occur that, through complicated mechanisms, pull them into a downward spiral from which they seldom escape by themselves.

On the other hand, van Kempen and Priemus (1999) conclude – from studies of Dutch cities – that the battle against segregation and concentration is fought on the basis of ideas that are questionable in the Dutch situation and probably in other European countries as well. According to them, it is premature to establish a direct link between concentration and segregation of specific population categories (such as ethnic minorities) and social problems and limited life chances. Parkinson (1998) formulates the same conclusion even more strongly.

We are not choosing sides in this debate in the context of this contribution. At present our rather pragmatic opinion, based on visits and talks during the UGIS cross-evaluation, is that the context – once more – determines whether the deprived neighborhood is totally dependent upon what happens in its surroundings, has some kind of (active) interaction with the rest of the city or is the rotten apple that spoils the whole barrel. As a working hypothesis, the second option looks the more realistic.

We have selected three problems that seem to be essential regarding the possible impact of area-based urban policies on solidarity and social cohesion. First, do area-based projects have an impact on the life chances of the inhabitants? This would give us some insight into the "economic, social and cultural capital" that people have at their disposal in order to create solidarity between the residents and cohesion within the neighborhood. Second, do area-based policies just displace problems between different neighborhoods? This is about solidarity and cohesion at a higher level, between neighborhoods or between a neighborhood and the city. Third, does the integrated approach that is typical for UDPs – which implies partnership and collaboration between different actors, domains and levels – therefore foster solidarity and cohesion?

Do area-based projects have an impact on solidarity and cohesion within a neighborhood?

Distressed areas are targeted in most UDPs, which seems logical because they are confronted with higher unemployment rates, more criminality, more single parents, often more ethnic conflicts, low political participation and more run-down buildings and public spaces. All indicate a threat to solidarity and cohesion. However, one important question remains. Is the higher occurrence of these problems related to characteristics of the area or are these areas disadvantaged because of the characteristics of their residents? Do people become unemployed because they live in that area or did they migrate to that area because they are unemployed? Do people enter relations of solidarity because of their deprived surroundings or do they move to these neighborhoods because there they do not have to conform to rules of public behavior and to participate in networks?

We cannot ignore that a long-standing tradition of ecologic research has documented the negative impact of concentrated urban poverty and related disadvantages such as segregation on children. These multiple forms of concentrated disadvantage include infant mortality, low birth weight, teenage childbearing, dropping out of school, child maltreatment, and adolescent delinquency (Brooks-Gunn et al. 1997). Much less understood, however, are the reasons for these correlations, leaving the concentration effect thesis, as introduced by authors such as Wilson (1987), unanswered (see also Friedrichs 1997; Musterd et al. 2001). The relation with a more "abstract" analytical level, because of relational variables such as solidarity or cohesion, is even less known.

There is a clear link between low or missing participation and lack of solidarity, and thus of cohesion. It is less clear whether this link is a direct or an indirect one, via variables such as income level, education or family structure. In our research, people seemed to feel more involved when it comes to policies targeted on their specific area than is the case with distant and general policies. Therefore, local participation might not only be easier to organize in an area-based policy context, but would also have more effects. Local participation thus could be a means to promote social inclusion and social cohesion.

In general, it looks like the inclusion of people in the form of participation in the urban programs has indeed been successful. In nearly all UDPs that were included in the UGIS project, groups of inhabitants participated in the planning process and quite often also in their implementation (all quotations are from the UGIS cross-evaluation):

> In some countries, such as the Netherlands and Denmark, participation is considered a "normal practice" when it comes to urban planning and urban renewal. In places like Naples, participation of the residents was limited. However, it was considered very important that there was some participation, as the inhabitants would normally not trust programs coming from public authorities. Within the local culture of clientelism, participation was seen as a means to shift people's allegiance from the local '*Camorra*' to public authorities.

However, problems do remain. Who is involved? Who is excluded? Whose interests do participants want to promote: their own, their group's, the neighborhood's? Which intended and unintended effects exist with respect to the processes of inclusion and cohesion? At least for the Netherlands and Flanders, it is well known that specific minority ethnic groups are very hard to reach when it comes to local participation. Another difficult group are the young people who recently migrated to the neighborhood; they are often not interested at all in what happens there.

Generally, the older Dutch inhabitants who have been living in the area for decades do participate in neighborhood activities. We may hardly call them a representative group and certainly not in areas where 80 percent of the population belongs to ethnic minorities, like the Schilderswijk in The Hague. This implies that they are also setting the standards for other, very different, groups of residents – which might lead to the creation or aggravation of problems.

Apparently, strong group cohesion and a slow rate of acculturation do not necessarily stand in the way of political participation. Fennema and Tillie (1999), following Putnam's hypothesis on the relation between social trust and (political) participation, find that political distrust is lowest among Turks in Amsterdam and they show a higher turnout rate at municipal elections, participate more in other forms of politics and are more interested in local politics. In this respect, the relatively high level of political incorporation of Turks is exactly the opposite from what one would expect starting from an individual resource model.

A more indirect way of improving the life chances of the residents is to improve the physical environment. Improving the housing situation may be seen as a first step to a better life. However, unequivocal successes are very hard to find. In the Netherlands, urban restructuring in some neighborhoods means that part of the rented stock has been demolished and more expensive alternatives have been built. Opinion about the quality of life among the sitting inhabitants, however, has not changed. In other words, changing the housing stock does not automatically mean that people are more satisfied (Bolt and van Kempen 2002).

However, the research also reveals that investing in bricks and mortar is not always evident. If a neighborhood was badly conceived from the beginning – like many high-rise estates – it is not only very difficult to change its negative image, it is also very expensive to change its physical structure and the structure of the (local) housing market. In other cases, it was a deliberate choice not to invest in the quality of the housing or in changing the structure of the housing market.

In Antwerp and in Ghent, the aldermen stated that the amount of money needed to provide good and affordable housing is so huge that they choose not to invest in it, since it is like 'bringing coal to Newcastle'. At the same time, they stressed that housing is the major problem of their cities. In both cities, the money went to the amelioration of the social infrastructure (e.g., neighborhood centers) or of the public domain (e.g., the refurbishment of streets and squares).

Most UDPs of the 1990s are more comprehensive than the urban renewal programs of the 1970s. Physical renewal of the housing stock is only one aspect of these programs – often not the most important one. When the housing stock is not an important target, it might be expected that displacement effects occur less often.

> In the Netherlands, the "Dutch Restructuring Policy" specifically aims at the restructuring of the housing stock: low-rent areas should become more mixed, cheap dwellings should be demolished, more dwellings that are expensive should be built, all with the aim to create mixed neighborhoods. In this case, displacement is almost an intended result of urban policy.

This brings us to another important assumption of area-based policies; that of the effects (if not the desirability) of social and/or ethnic mix. Social mix is indeed expected to enhance social cohesion, to reduce delinquency, and to improve social integration. A strong argument in favor of a social mix and the creation of balanced communities is that a concentration of deprivation is not desirable (van Engelsdorp-Gastelaars 1996; Forrest 2000). Both the combating of deprivation and better integration would lessen, if not prevent, the self-perpetuating process and neighborhood effects discussed earlier.

Yet, if we consider the historical development of cities, the feasibility of social mix becomes problematic. Affluent social groups have nearly always left distressed areas, moving to the more prosperous urban periphery. Nevertheless, if a greater variety of different dwellings are being offered in a wide range of locations, this may enhance the freedom of choice and thus at least provide the context for enhancing social mix. Strongly simplified, the current structure of the housing market forces the poor to live in deprived neighborhoods with poor housing conditions, while affluent households can choose where to live and even may gentrify distressed areas. At least social mix can offer successful local households the opportunity to stay in their neighborhood. The Dutch restructuring policy is built on this assumption (1218, 3625). Demolishing cheap dwellings in the inner city and replacing them by more comfortable (and more expensive) dwellings would support successful local households in sharing the neighborhood with the poorer households. However, differentiated housing definitely does not mean that people interact and communicate, share experiences and strive for the same goals (for a specific discussion on this topic see Chapter 8).

Do area-based policies displace problems between different neighborhoods?

The problem of solidarity and cohesion is not restricted to the neighborhood itself. Indeed, selecting areas for inclusion in a UDP means leaving out other areas that sometimes are only slightly better off. At the city level this may have important consequences for solidarity and cohesion.

One consequence is that area-based approaches may simply displace problems between different neighborhoods and not add to the overall economic and social wellbeing of the city as a whole. For Parkinson (1998), it is like rearranging the deck chairs of the Titanic. He concludes that trying to solve the problems of social exclusion within particular areas of cities is bound to fail, because the causes of the problems and the potential solutions – whether they are economic or social changes or institutional resources and programs – lie outside excluded areas.

More specifically, Andersen and van Kempen (2001; see also De Decker et al. 2001) have identified a number of possible pitfalls with respect to area-based policies that refer to problems of solidarity between neighborhoods and the city's cohesion. First, problems do not occur exclusively in the targeted areas. Selecting only areas with the biggest problems might mean that areas with a score that is slightly better on variables such as unemployment, crime and quality of life do not get any attention. Second, it is not illogical to assume that area-based policies would only move problems from areas that are subject to the policy into areas that are not. Moreover, not all excluded individuals live in excluded areas (De Decker et al. 2001) and area-based approaches do not address their needs. In other words, general poverty policies remain necessary and can only be complemented, not replaced, by area-based policies. Substitution would imply an important breach of basic principles of solidarity. Third, by focusing all resources on a selection of neighborhoods, the potential of other parts of the city might not be optimized. This is particularly important for labor market and housing market initiatives. Finally, the electoral requirement that successes must be quick and visible can become a problem as it often turns projects into promotional means for the careers of politicians and other policy-makers. The increasing number of programs offers decision-makers the possibility of obtaining a higher profile in the media. In other cases, the areas themselves may be used to enhance prestige. Cities might deliberately target all policies to particular areas, to be able to show off their success story. Of course, it may very well turn out to be one, but the rest of the city might suffer from a lack of attention and money.

Indeed, urban renewal often interacts with general trends in the urban setting. Sometimes long-term and mostly unplanned gentrification processes occur where a deprived area becomes highly attractive, specifically in areas dominated by owner-occupied dwellings or private rented dwellings (2936, 6271, 1861).

> An extreme example of conflict and imbalance between districts and city can be found in Budapest, Hungary. Because of the political constellation,

districts possess a huge degree of autonomy and function more or less as cities within a city. This leads to the anomaly that the central district of Pest, on the right bank of the Danube, is so rich that rents of relatively high quality housing are lower than in adjacent districts where large parts of the housing stock are in decay. In the Ferencvaros district gentrification is even seen as a token of a successful policy.

Other forms of displacement also occur. When criminality is seen as a major problem in a given area, and when measures are taken to combat it, this may very well result in a decline in its crime figures. However, criminal activities may increase in adjacent areas, because criminals move their field of activity. Dwellings that house prostitutes or where drugs are sold may be closed and demolished (2177, 3314), but pimps and dealers will move to other areas. Forms of this displacement of activities have been detected in Rotterdam, the Netherlands (Botman and van Kempen 2001).

The conclusion is that signs of displacement indeed exist as a consequence of area-based policies. Harder data are needed, however, to provide stronger evidence for this process. Nevertheless, it is hardly inevitable that if only a few areas are targeted, other areas will suffer from some displacement effects.

Does an integrated approach foster solidarity and cohesion?

The case for an urban development approach is not usually only made from a geographic perspective (the area-based focus that we discussed before), but also in terms of an integrated approach. The argument is that urban problems are very complex, that the constituent elements are intrinsically connected and that it is impossible to untie them, as is the case in traditional "departmentalized" policies. Urban areas such as a neighborhood are an integrated whole of persons, groups, social networks, buildings and public spaces. At the same time, people's living conditions – particularly those of people living on the margin – are considerably interwoven. Any policy thus has to tackle different fields simultaneously and in an integrated way.

If we translate this argument into the language of solidarity and cohesion, then we could say that urban policies should strive towards an approach that brings together different aspects of urban structure and living conditions of the urban villager that have been fragmented (or differentiated) because of the developments described throughout this book.

Geographic integration is dominant in the urban renewal of neighborhoods and districts. However, what should be done on the district level can conflict with what should be done on a city or regional level. Indeed, a district or neighborhood is part of a larger urban fabric and has a certain function in that fabric. An approach that is very much restricted to one neighborhood may be counterproductive in terms of the development of the city or the metropolitan region. In many cases, the more integrated the approach is at the level of the (distressed) neighborhood, the more one loses sight of the broader geographic context.

> In a specific neighborhood of Rotterdam, part of a "three star district" from the "Integrated Area Approach," it was suggested to establish a super-market. It could help to redevelop the public space in the neighborhood, it would increase the neighborhood's diversity, people would be able to shop in their own neighborhood, and it would create a few jobs. At the neighborhood level, everybody, social workers included, agreed. It was pre-sented to city hall, which decided against the supermarket. Indeed, in the adjacent district, initiatives had already been taken to strengthen the shop-ping infrastructure. A new supermarket would either not be viable, because of the competition with the adjacent neighborhood, or it would damage the initiatives taken elsewhere. So, a perfectly logical idea at the neighborhood level was not considered a good one at the city level.

One of the flaws of an integrated neighborhood approach is that it tends to isolate neighborhoods and districts from their wider urban con-text. It tends to treat districts as cities on their own, complete in terms of public and private facilities and which should keep all the present inhabitants aboard. A high mobility rate is often seen as an indicator of malfunctioning and even officially used as such. When new dwellings are constructed, the tendency is towards replicating the composition of the local population. However, different districts can and do possess dif-ferent and specific functions in a wider urban context, and wiping out those differences can have serious consequences at a higher level. If, for instance, all marginal housing and facilities are cleared in all districts, homelessness may increase. It may then become increasingly difficult for certain newcomers to find a place to live in the city, because there is no longer a "transition zone" (1683, 2544). Moreover, "margins" – also in the spatial sense – often function as breeding places for innovation and entrepreneurship. Without these margins, cities might lose some of their creative capacity. Last, but not least, where are social outcasts, such as drug addicts and asylum seekers, going to live? They are always and everywhere the victims of the NIMBY syndrome (2178), which cannot be solved at the level of the backyard itself – be it as large as a neighborhood.

Different domains, actors and levels should cooperate because of the multidimensionality of the problems that are being focused by UDPs. An integrated approach can vary from just adding up the efforts made in different domains all the way to the development of a program in which every issue has an explicit relationship with all others. An integrated UDP connects different projects in such a way that the successes and failures of each project are at least partly dependent upon the successes and failures of the others. Implementing such a strategy constitutes a great challenge. The major difficulty in organizing "transversal" or "horizontal" cooperation between administrations and departments is the juxtaposition of different fields of interest, which creates tensions and confrontations between various approaches, methods, procedures, professional cultures, and organizations. This would be another dimension of solidarity at the city level.

There are some positive attempts to set an integrated program in motion, defying traditional departmental egotism. The French and German cases can be seen as examples of a strong bureaucratic tradition, where interdepartmental cooperation occurs at administrative levels.

> In France, the so-called "*politique de la ville*" covers all the fields of urban reality. "Thematic covenants" are worked out within the framework of "*contrats de ville*." These conventions may address different themes, such as housing, environment, transport, education, sport, culture, and leisure. These conventions may also privilege an approach that takes into account a specific category (for example children or the elderly) and then recombines sectoral policies (for example, health or safety).
>
> The Social City program (*Soziale Stadt*) in Germany can be considered as a first step to integrate the potential of various departments and administrative levels in order to tackle the complex issues of UDPs, aiming at physical and social "rehabilitation" at the same time. Launched in March 2000, the program foresees collaboration on the national level among the Ministry of Transport, Construction and Housing; the Ministry of Economy; and the Ministry of Social Affairs. It requires close cooperation between the departments at the "*Land*" level – again of housing, economy, and social affairs – and the (federal) Ministry of Housing responsible for the program. City and "*Land*" departments in turn cooperate.

Partnerships between departments may not only be the result of top-down incentives, but can also be the consequence of bottom-up activism. In that case, it could lead to the much-desired integrated approach, but may also be successful in terms of solidarity and cohesion. That is because such a bottom-up approach implies at least the existence of networks and a sort of identification with common goals at the neighborhood level.

> In Spain, in 1996, a group of social actors led by the neighborhood association of Trinitat Nova (Barcelona) decided to promote development in their neighborhood. They elaborated a community development plan covering a wide range of goals and including all sorts of social and political actors. The aim of this bottom-up initiative was to launch a renewal plan for the area through an integrated approach. This grassroots initiative has been

successful in making public administrations work in a coordinated manner, integrating the interventions of different bodies and departments. Some departments (Housing and Urban Development) have been most committed to the Plan and more open to coordinating their efforts with other departments, whereas others have been more reluctant to participate in an integral and integrated Urban Development Program. This shows that an external initiative to foster the coordination of different public administrations and departments may produce positive changes.

Conclusions

In most UDPs, a strong (declared) concern exists for local problems related to exclusion, solidarity, and cohesion. The number of projects regarding education, vocational training, job creation, and the many different committees, associations, and other groups involving the citizens in the planning and implementation of local improvement projects is quite impressive.

More important, however, is the fact that urban policies are only one factor influencing processes of solidarity and cohesion. Many other factors play a major part and they are beyond the reach of these UDPs and even of city government. The answer to the problem that we focused upon in this chapter very much depends on the explanatory model of exclusion and of solidarity and cohesion that is used. If the causes of their presence or absence are seen as inevitably linked with the present type of (capitalistic) Western societies, area-based UDPs do not stand a chance of combating exclusion and promoting solidarity and cohesion. If, however, these causes are at least partly considered to be a combination of societal, spatial, and group characteristics, we may expect an area-based program to have some effects. Urban policies in general and area-based policies in particular do have a role, but not necessarily the most important one.

In this concluding section, however, we are expected to bring together some of the more conceptual and theoretical reflections from the first part and some more empirical statements from the second. We would like to briefly look at the existence of UDPs and then turn to their (un)intended effects, both from the perspective of solidarity and cohesion and in that order.

The mere existence of UDPs – supposing that they answer a need – could be seen as an indication that "structural" forms of *solidarity* (that is, of organic solidarity) are not effective enough to guarantee the "sustainability" of cities. One of their main characteristics is that they organize solidarity at different levels and from different perspectives. First, they are intended to integrate or to reintegrate excluded people and groups into urban society, to re-establish links between deprived neighborhoods and the rest of the city. Second, they are themselves very much characterized by stimulating forms of collaboration between different levels, domains, and partners – which before had been working independently. This does not look like "solidarity" at first sight, but it is. The remarkable thing about UDPs is that they have often put together pieces of a puzzle that could be expected to find their way by themselves: different departments with complementary assignments, actors from the public and private and from the for-profit and not-for-profit spheres – all working within the same city and to a certain degree pursuing the same goals.

From both the UDPs' and the city's perspective, the city's *cohesion* has been enhanced. At the policy-making level, UDPs certainly have contributed to new forms of collaboration, stretching from temporary coalitions over multi-actor networks to more or less enduring regimes. At the level of the city itself, they have contributed to both the relational and the cultural dimension of cohesion.

First, the relational dimension of cohesion is about the development of networks and the fostering of economic, social and cultural capital in the neighborhood and the city. The network dimension has been most prominent in our discussion of social mix and of the close links between neighborhoods and between a neighborhood and the city overall. Cohesion implies differentiation, which is what social mix is all about, and the same goes for the neighborhoods, which have to be fitted into a common frame with their specific structure, functions, and location.

Second, it is about the cultural dimension of cohesion. The introduction of UDPs has often revived feelings of identity in the targeted neighborhood, has brought people together around a common objective (if not a set of goals), has reactivated the remnants of the old civil society and given birth to new forms of participation.

However, this brings us back to the starting point of our discussion. In order to have policies that promote solidarity and cohesion, we need a much better knowledge of the complex interaction between both solidarity and cohesion, and of the context in which they are being produced or destroyed. We have provided some clues for a solution – in suggesting that a unique combination of mechanic and organic solidarity, and "top-down" and "bottom-up" solidarity characterizes the modern city and that therefore innovative and appropriate policies must be developed. Urban governance was expected to be an appropriate approach to the many diverse and complex problems with which the modern city is confronted. The more complex forms of self-organizing and interorganizational networks of different political, social, cultural, and economic agents from different political levels are seen as a guarantee of more effective urban policies. These would not only promote economic growth and ecological sustainability but also social inclusion, solidarity, and cohesion.

NOTES

1 We use this term for a number of programs that mostly originated in the 1990s and which originally aimed at combating social problems in deprived neighborhoods. They constitute a set of interrelated projects on a local level to be implemented within a certain period of time within a certain area. The projects may focus on physical measures, such as demolishing and rebuilding parts of the housing stock (6501, 0901, 2469), or on social and economic targets, such as decreasing unemployment (2731, 0908, 1489). They may also be a combination of physical, social, economic, and cultural initiatives, and they usually are (0908, 3439). This is what we call an "integrated approach." By "local level," we mean cities or urban municipalities and by "area," urban districts or neighborhoods. The temporal dimension of a UDP refers to the fact that it has a clearly defined beginning and end. The dimensions of space and time are highly variable when we look at practices in different European countries and cities, but, in spite of that, by their very nature, they raise the same kind of questions and call for the same kind of decisions. Some examples are: the Dutch *Big Cities Policy* (1993); the French *Politique de la Ville* (1993), *Politique de la Ville et Contrat de Ville* and *Politique Territorialisée de Développement Solidaire et de Renouvellement Urbain* (1998); the German NRW program *Benachteiligte Stadtgebiete* (1993); the Danish *Urban Committee Initiative* (1994) and the *Urban Area Improvement Programme* (1996); in Belgium, the Flemish *Vlaams Fonds voor de Integratie van Kansarmen* (VFIK) (1992) and *Sociaal Impulsfonds* (SIF) (1996), and the *Projet de Quartiers* in the Brussels Metropolitan Region; and at the European Union level, the URBAN Community Initiative Program that started in 1994.
2 For an overview see, for example, Campbell (1993), Power (1997), Body-Gendrot et al. (1998) and Jelen (1999).
3 See, among others, Sassen (1991), Castells and Mollenkopf (1992), Mingione (1996), Lee and Murie (1997), Musterd and Ostendorf (1998), and Marcuse and van Kempen (2000).
4 This discussion is necessarily preliminary, because it is based on an as yet incomplete analysis of the evidence from the cross-evaluation carried out in the nine countries involved in the UGIS (Urban Development Programs, Urban Governance, Social Inclusion and Sustainability) project (2000–2003), which was funded by the Fifth Framework Program. The project followed three objectives. The first was to analyze the impact of UDPs on promoting social inclusion and urban sustainability. A second question concerned emerging forms of governance and whether these have shaped the characteristics of UDPs, their definition, their implementation and their successes and failures. A feedback loop referred to possible effects of UDPs on forms of urban governance. The UGIS research proceeded through different phases, each resulting in at least one publication. The central concepts of "urban governance," "social exclusion," "social cohesion," "social inclusion" and "sustainability" were discussed at an early stage (Vranken et al. 2003). During a second phase, national reports were written. These reports convey information on the economic and social situation of the selected cities and neighborhoods and on the

relevant urban policies in the areas. During the same period a book was published, *On The Origins of Urban Development Programmes in Nine European Countries* (De Decker et al. 2003). In a third research phase, so-called key-witnesses – people who were involved in the planning and the implementation of UDPs – were interviewed. We used their observations and opinions on UDPs in the following phase to question and cross-examine high-level policy-makers such as politicians and high-ranking civil servants. The end products of this international "cross-evaluation" are, first, a "handbook for policy-makers" and, second, an academic publication on the functioning and effectiveness of UDPs across Europe.

5   Of course, urban poverty is not always concentrated in these crisis-ridden districts and, at the same time, their populations are not that homogeneous. The so-called ethnic and social mix is still present, at whatever level: a building, a neighborhood or a larger district. What links them is the fact that they are living in an area that is excluded in several ways: economically through the lack of local economy and/or employment; socially through the weakness of its networks and its civil society; politically through the powerlessness of its population (often expressed in the lack of voting rights or even in the illegality that many families are living in); and culturally through its stigmatization by outsiders.

6   With some historical irony, we could see this as an urban "dis-enclosure movement." That it is the opposite of the "enclosure of common fields" that was so important for modernization in rural areas could be attributed to the specific urban context.

7   Kearns and Forrest (2000) discuss five dimensions of social cohesion: a common value pattern, structured solidarity, social networks, group identification, and social capital.

8   This connection between strong ties and emotional support, and between weak ties and important "social goods," evidently is not to be generalized to all social groups and regional contexts; people from well-to-do milieus clearly will find both functions in weak ties alone, and in Southern European countries strong ties seem to facilitate entry to the labor market for all population groups.

9   Whereas social exclusion refers to a vertical relationship, social cohesion is about a horizontal one. Social exclusion focuses on the participation and integration of elements in a larger whole, such as people in groups, and groups or individuals in societies. Social cohesion focuses on relations between the elements of a group (be it a primary group, a collective or class, or a society) that are at a relatively comparable level.

REFERENCES

Andersen, H.T. (2001) The new urban politics of Europe: the area-based approach to regeneration policy. In: Andersen, H.T. and van Kempen, R. (eds.) *Governing European Cities: Social Fragmentation, Social Exclusion and Urban Governance*. Aldershot, Ashgate.

Andersen, H.T. and van Kempen, R. (2001) Social fragmentation, social exclusion, and urban governance: an introduction. In: Andersen, H.T. and van Kempen, R. (eds.) *Governing European Cities: Social Fragmentation, Social Exclusion and Urban Governance*. Aldershot, Ashgate.

Body-Gendrot, S., Le Guennec, N., and Herrou, M. (1998) *Mission sur les Violences Urbaines*. La Documentation Française, Paris.

Bolt, G. and van Kempen, R. (2002) Moving up or moving down? Housing careers of Turks and Moroccans in Utrecht, the Netherlands. *Housing Studies*, 17 (3): 401–422.

Botman, S. and van Kempen, R. (2001) *The Spatial Dimensions of Urban Social Exclusion and Integration: The Case of Rotterdam, the Netherlands*. Amsterdam Study Centre for the Metropolitan Environment, Amsterdam.

Bourdieu, P. (ed.) (1993) *La misère du monde*. Le Seuil, Paris.

Breebaart, M., Musterd, S., and Ostendorf, W. (1996) *Etnische segregatie en beleid: Een internationale vergelijking*. AME, Amsterdam.

Brooks-Gunn, J., Duncan, G.J., Lebenthal, T., and Aber, L.J. (eds.) (1997) *Neighbor hood Poverty: Policy Implication in Studying Neighborhoods*. Russell Sage, New York.

Burns, D. and Taylor, M. (1998) *Mutual Aid and Self-Help: Coping Strategies for Excluded Communities*. Policy Press, Bristol.

Campbell, B. (1993) *Goliath: Britain's Dangerous Places*. Methuen, London.

Castells, M. and Mollenkopf, J. (1991) *Dual City: Restructuring New York*. Russell Sage, New York.

De Decker, P., Meert, H., and Peleman, K. (2001) Combating urban poverty: the power and specificity of territorial policies. Paper presented at the Conference on "Social Inequality, Redistributive Justice and the City," International Sociological Association, Research Committee on Urban and Regional Development, Amsterdam, 15–17 June.

De Decker, P., Vranken, J., Beaumont, J., and Van Nieuwenhuyze, I. (eds.) (2003) *On the Origins of Urban Development Programmes in Nine European Countries*. UGIS Collection 2, Garant, Apeldoorn, Antwerpen.

Durkheim, E. (1893) *De la division du travail social: Étude sur l'organisation des sociétés supérieures*. F. Arcan, Paris.

Feld, S.L. (1981) The focused organization of social ties. *American Journal of Sociology*, 86: 1015–1035.

Fennema, M. and Tillie, J. (1999) Political participation and political trust in Amsterdam: civic communities and ethnic networks. *Journal of Ethnic and Migration Studies*, 25 (4): 703–726.

Forrest, R. (2000) What constitutes a "balanced" community? In: Anderson, I. and Sim, D. (eds.) *Social Exclusion and Housing: Context and Challenges*. Chartered Institute of Housing, Coventry.

Friedrichs, J. (1997) Context effects of poverty neighbourhoods on residents. In: Vestergaard, H. (ed.) *Housing in Europe*. Danish Building Research Institute, Horsholm, 141–160.

Granovetter, M. (1973) The strength of weak ties. *American Journal of Sociology*, 78 (6): 1360–1380.

Healey, P. (1998) Institutionalist theory, social exclusion and governance. In: Madanipour, A., Cars, G., and Allen, J. (eds.) *Social Exclusion in European Cities: Processes, Experiences and Responses*. Jessica Kingsley, London.

Jelen, C. (1999) *La guerre des rues: La violence et "les jeunes"*. Plon, Paris.

Kearns, A. and Forrest, R. (2000) Social cohesion and multilevel urban governance. *Urban Studies*, 37 (5–6): 995–1017.

Komter, A., Burgers, J., and Engbersen, G. (2000) *Het cement van de samenleving. Een verkennende studie over solidariteit en cohesie*. Amsterdam University Press, Amsterdam.

Lee, P. and Murie, A. (1997) *Poverty, Housing Tenure and Social Exclusion*. Policy Press, Bristol.

Madanipour, A., Cars, G., and Allen, J. (eds.) (1998) *Social Exclusion in European Cities: Processes, Experiences and Responses*. Jessica Kingsley, London.

Marcuse, P. and van Kempen, R. (2000) *Globalizing Cities: A New Spatial Order?* Blackwell, Oxford.

Merton, R.K. and Kitt, A.S. (1950), Contributions to the theory of reference group behavior. In: Merton, R.K. and Lazarsfeld, P.F. (eds.) *Continuities in Social Research*. Free Press, Glencoe, IL.

Mingione, E. (ed.) (1996) *Urban Poverty and the Underclass: A Reader*. Blackwell, Oxford.

Musterd, S. and Ostendorf, W. (eds.) (1998) *Urban Segregation and the Welfare State: Inequality and Exclusion in Western Cities*. Routledge, London.

Musterd, S., Ostendorf, W., and de Vos, S. (2001) *Armoedeconcentraties en sociale effecten in dynamisch perspectief*. AME, Amsterdam.

Parkinson, M. (1998) *Combating Social Exclusion: Lessons from Area-Based Programmes in Europe*. Policy Press, Bristol.

Power, A. (1997) *Estates on the Edge: The Social Consequences of Mass Housing in Northern Europe*. Macmillan, London.

Sassen, S. (1991) *The Global City: New York, London, Tokyo*. Princeton University Press, Princeton, NJ.

Schuyt, K. (ed.) (1997) *Het sociaal tekort, veertien sociale problemen in Nederland*. Uitgeverij de Balie, Amsterdam.

Simmel, G. (1908) *Die Kreuzung Sozialer Kreise. Soziologie: Untersuchungen über die Formen der Vergesellschaftung*. Duncker and Humblot, Berlin.

van Engelsdorp-Gastelaars, R.R. (1996) Steden in ontwikkeling. *Stedebouw en Ruimtelijke Ordening*, 77 (5): 19–23.

van Kempen, R. and Özüekren, A.S. (1997) *Turks in European Cities: Housing and Urban Segregation*. ECOMER, Rotterdam.

van Kempen, R. and Priemus, H. (1999) Undivided cities in the Netherlands: present situation, and policy rhetoric. *Housing Studies*, 14 (5): 641–657.

Vandermotten, C., Vermoesen, F., De Lannoy, W., and De Corte, S. (1999) Europese steden: vergelijkende cartografie. *Het Tijdschrift van het Gemeentekrediet, Gemeentekrediet*, 53: 207–208.

Vranken, J., De Decker, P., and van Nieuwenhuyze, I. (2003) *Social Inclusion, Urban Governance and Sustainability*. UGIS Collection 1, Apeldoorn, Antwerpen.

Wilson, W.J. (1987) *The Truly Disadvantaged: The Inner City, the Underclass and Public Policy*. University of Chicago Press, Chicago.

13

Challenging the Family: The New Urban Poverty in Southern Europe

Enrica Morlicchio

Introduction

Within the current spread of adverse socio-economic conditions, cities in Southern European countries are characterized by distinctive patterns of poverty and social exclusion involving high levels of unemployment and income poverty, lack of universal minimum income schemes,[1] traditional family models, a low proportion of working women, and an absence of "ghettoized poor" (defined as vulnerable groups living in neighborhoods where almost one in two residents is poor; see Wilson 1987, 1996). In this chapter, I focus in particular on the phenomenon of the "familization" of poverty (Mingione et al. 2002), according to which the whole family is made vulnerable through the need to support a long-term unemployed young adult in urban contexts characterized by a scarcity of social services, income support, and employment opportunities.

Literature on urban poverty in Southern European countries is rather limited. This is understandable for a number of reasons, one being that in all of these countries until just a few decades ago poverty equated mainly to rural misery. This is because at that time the majority of the population was still a rural population and the main sector of activity was agriculture. The late shift to an industrial economy entailed an intense process of deruralization, urbanization, and modernization, which caused an extreme decline in rural employment while at the same time producing urban unemployment and giving rise to urban occupational sectors characterized by low salaries and high insecurity. These trends have also marginalized women in the role of housewives, because the need to provide childcare and other family support is crucial in the absence of social services and traditional forms of family solidarity (like the peasant extended family networks) and community networks.[2] Moreover, as Pugliese argued for the Italian case, "While the rural class of self-employed workers and their dependants might have benefitted in the last decade from a flow of social security income that kept them substantially sheltered from poverty and misery . . . we cannot say the same for the urban population. It is here that we record the main conditions of distress that are not compensated, if not exceptionally acute, by welfare provisions" (Pugliese 2002: 144–5).

This implies that generalizations about the characteristics of urban poverty in Southern European countries inferred from other social contexts could be misleading. Indeed, within these countries, urban poverty is quite different, both in its causes and in its consequences. Problems of development and economic growth continue to play a crucial and more fundamental part. In Southern European countries, the actual "victims of the labor market" (Offe 1985) are not so much the vulnerable sectors comprised of the "Fordist working class" – the "losers" that Kern and Schumann (1984) contrast with the "winners" – but, above all, workers in the building trade, casual laborers, and the long-term unemployed (mainly young and female) in low-income households. This is particularly evident with regard to the low proportion of workers in big industry relative to the employed and the model of industrial relations, which provides strong protection of the insiders, usually adult males.

Obviously, the differences between Northern and Southern European countries with respect to the characteristics of the new urban poor are not only related to the structure of the labor market; access to social services and the level of protection provided by the welfare system must also be considered.[3] This chapter begins with an in-depth analysis of the disadvantages, connected mainly with the current conditions of the labor market, which overburden household strategies, leading to a very high risk of downgrading and of generating forms of irreversible and intergenerational poverty. We then go on to discuss briefly two typologic cases of family trajectories with a high probability of being or falling into poverty in Naples. These cases do not constitute a privileged area of research and, naturally, they do not exhaust the typologies of new urban poverty in Southern European countries. They have been selected because they are sufficiently characteristic to formulate a research hypothesis from my personal experience in studying poverty and unemployment. Furthermore, these two typologies clearly show how, at the very most, poor households manage to survive without meeting serious local integration difficulties or being defeated by life adversities. I define this situation as a condition of "integration into precariousness."

The Poverty of "Ordinary" People in Southern Europe

Who is more affected by poverty in Europe and what opportunities do people have to escape this condition? Statistical data help to provide a first response to this question.[4]

Table 13.1 shows that the highest poverty rates are observed mainly in the Southern European countries, particularly considering the 40 percent of median income threshold which identifies the pure subsistence level. Conversely, Scandinavian countries show the lowest poverty rates (e.g., Finland has less than 1 percent falling below the poverty line).

Analysis of the non-monetary aspects of poverty shows that Southern European families are more likely to suffer from bad housing conditions (e.g., overcrowding, presence of damp) (2654, 4572, 5021) and low quality consumption (e.g., second-hand as opposed to new clothing, lack of durable goods such as a telephone or color television, no holiday away from home in the last 12 months). Statistics also show that the greatest difficulties in paying rent and utility bills are found among the poorer residents of Greece and Ireland (44 percent), while these rates are particularly low in Portugal, presumably because of the extremely precarious housing conditions and the high incidence of informal self-constructed housing, which does not entail paying rent and bills. More complex is the issue of social isolation indicators (e.g., meeting friends and relatives), for which Greece and Spain register very low rates, and those of job dissatisfaction, which identify Italy as the most dissatisfied, directly followed by Greece and Spain (for a more thorough account of these figures, see Eurostat 2000a).

Data on persistent income poverty in the European Union (EU) are also available. Rates range from approximately 3 percent in Denmark and the Netherlands to 10 percent in Greece and 12 percent in Portugal. Spain and Italy are both slightly above the European average (Eurostat 2000b).[5] Also noticeable is the disproportionately high incidence of large families (couples with three or more dependent children) among the long-term poor in all Southern European countries, especially if the household has no working members or some unemployed members.

From the data presented so far we can observe that in Southern Europe the phenomenon of poverty is much more widespread than in other European countries and it affects mainly large nuclear families: "ordinary people" – people who live in persistent income poverty but do not present

Table 13.1 Social indicators using the 1998 EUROMOD baseline[a]

	1 Households with disposable income <60% of median (%)	2a As 1 but for 40% of median	2b As 1 but for 50% of median	2c As 1 but for 70% of median	3 As 1 but for 60% of the (baseline) median[b]	4 Median poverty gap using 60% median[c]	5 Mean poverty gap using 60% median[3]	6 Quintile share ratio	7 Gini coefficient
Austria	11.28	1.28	3.60	19.29	11.28	845	1433	3.640	0.250
Belgium	15.53	2.76	6.69	23.11	15.53	3759	5333	3.133	0.247
Denmark	11.18	2.19	4.30	19.80	11.18	712	1272	2.394	0.237
Finland	7.85	0.58	2.52	15.84	7.85	435	563	2.206	0.222
France	11.78	1.38	4.89	21.54	11.78	616	773	4.206	0.276
Germany	10.02	2.42	5.16	18.45	10.02	237	287	3.454	0.252
Greece	20.31	11.00	15.11	26.96	20.31	40,662	45,974	5.868	0.333
Ireland	18.06	1.10	9.44	29.97	18.06	65.22	6569	4.765	0.333
Italy	19.96	7.46	12.97	28.09	19.96	248	309	5.991	0.341
Luxembourg	11.70	1.35	4.06	21.22	11.70	4949	6768	4.188	0.256
The Netherlands	9.86	1.90	3.83	20.53	9.86	162	333	3.447	0.249
Spain	17.95	7.17	11.21	25.80	17.95	14,587	18,692	5.843	0.325
United Kingdom	20.02	1.93	9.84	29.41	20.02	74.30	84.20	4.970	0.313

Source: EUROMOD.

Notes:

[a] All indicators are based on household disposable income, equivalized using the modified OECD equivalence scale.

[b] In the baseline, this is the same as indicator 1.

[c] In 1998 national currency per month.

demographic or personal characteristics that predispose them to become socially isolated (such as one-parent families or the homeless). The risk of abandonment and social isolation seems to be much higher in Northern European countries (this is also partly true of the North of Italy and certain regions of Spain) where, in a much more favorable economic context and in particular a more favorable labor market, subjective and individual variables have a much larger importance in explaining the incidence of poverty. Obviously this does not imply that forms of poverty centered on processes of individualized downdrift or discrimination and racism do not exist in Southern Europe. Indeed, in some areas poverty among immigrants is an increasing problem. Immigrants certainly present income conditions and models of consumption that indicate severe deprivation (5021, 5890, 4743). However, the lack of income and benefits does not necessarily imply an equal level of social exclusion. Many of these economically poor subjects, irrespective of individual and group differences, display the material, psychological, and cultural resources (working traditions, capacity for adjustment, interethnic forms of solidarity) necessary to confront the initial discomfort of their conditions and to safeguard them from the risk of being socially excluded. As has been observed, "Immigrants and minorities do not constitute a significant problem in Spanish and Portuguese cities. Vulnerability due to unemployment affects mainly the local population" (Mingione et al. 2002: 55). A further factor complicating the issue is that the specific condition of immigrants results from the interaction of many and complex variables, including the characteristics and the efficiency of social policies, and is not an indicator of common characteristics (obviously the main factors that allow immigrants to avoid social exclusion are a steady formal job and the possession of a stay permit).

Another social group that has been the object of attention are the homeless, although this group does not preclude members of immigrant groups (4743, 2423). The problem of homelessness is a combination of material and social exclusion. These conditions of severe material poverty and social isolation are often exacerbated by other kinds of problematic factors, but the number of homeless, in absolute terms, is far lower than that of poor families. Research by Laparra and Aguilar (1997), for example, suggests that in Madrid the number of people living on the streets or in shelters is approximately 2000–2500, a number very much lower than in cities such as Paris or London. In general, these extreme forms of poverty and social isolation have a limited incidence even in the other large Southern European cities. According to a recent estimate (Saraceno 2002a), in Italy the number of homeless people amounts to approximately 17,000 (contrasted with over a million poor children living with both parents). A slightly higher estimate had been made by Antonio Tosi (1996).

In most Southern European cities, therefore, poverty less frequently involves groups that are clearly identifiable on the basis of personal characteristics or a specific context, such as marginalized immigrants, discriminated-against minorities, socially isolated single parents, and single-person households segregated in deprived and stigmatized areas, or people whose personal history and lifestyle puts them outside the acknowledged norm, such as drug addicts, mentally ill people, or former offenders. Poverty affects to a large extent married "able-bodied" parents and their children, who, as we will see shortly, have faced serious problems of integration and sometimes discrimination in ill-equipped and underfunded schools.

The School as a Central Factor in the Process of Exclusion

The social and material difficulties of poor people are different in each country, depending on the nature and evolution of the labor market, and on the system of social protection that exists in relation to that market. However, there are also key differences in relation to other aspects of the social structure that have an impact on poor people, such as the practice of social reproduction, its prevailing gender relations, the role of the family and, perhaps most importantly, the educational system.

In Southern European countries there are two main limitations to schools and the education process. The first concerns the problem of planning and the built environment, including insufficient buildings (which implies rotating shifts) or the use of inappropriate buildings, vandalism and, at the heart of the problem, late intervention to solve these problems. The second and perhaps more important problem that can be identified concerns the relationship between the educational system and the family. Negative attitudes towards the education system by both students and parents, because of peer pressure among young school dropouts and a lack of high-school culture and professional experience, is reinforced by demotivated teachers and by the scarcity of additional resources and services (such as full-time schools or personal tutors) able to compensate for the initial social disadvantage and to stimulate social integration. The children are more likely to fail and abandon school, and to gain an occupational qualification. In this way, the countries of Southern Europe present a particularly high level of young dropouts, most of whom leave school several years before reaching the legal minimum age (5016). As Klasen (2001) documents, more than 10 percent of the Southern European population (11 percent in Greece and Portugal and 17 percent in Spain) are in this situation as opposed to just 3 percent in Sweden. Moreover, the proportion of the population not in school at the age of 17 is 44 percent in

Greece, 27 percent in Portugal, and 25 percent in Spain. Klasen comments that: "Educational systems that fail a proportion of their students not only lead to social exclusion through denying them this basic right of citizenship in sufficient quality, but also through fostering social exclusion as adults" (2001: 435).

This generation of undereducated young people, socialized in the same context of cultural and consumption expectations as the generation born in other industrialized countries with a higher level of education, end up entering the labor market with modest personal resources, i.e. with a lack of professional experience and limited social capital (Amaturo and Gambardella 2001; Spanò 2001). "Of course this phenomenon is quite comparable to the qualification and employment problems experienced by migrant youngsters in Northern European metropolises. Still, the phenomenon is typically Southern in that it affects large layers of the labor class population, irrespective of race" (Moulaert and Cavola 2002: 7).

In some cases and contexts these young dropouts become involved in illegal activity, such as drug dealing and theft (5018, 5023). In Naples, according to the Ministry of Justice, two-thirds of young people condemned by the juvenile magistrates are of Italian nationality and come from families in which one or more family members (generally the father or the brother) already have a criminal record. Of these young offenders, 58 percent have not completed their compulsory education qualifications and 51 percent come from families with five or more members, which in Southern Italy present the highest risk of poverty (one in three large families is poor; Ministero della Giustizia 2001).

The negative consequences of a low level of schooling increases among Southern women. Despite improved integration in the labor markets, there is evidence of a much greater polarization in women's employment rates between those with high levels of education and those with low levels. This gap is above 30 percent in Italy and in Spain, while in the Northern European countries work is much more evenly distributed. The gap becomes much more pronounced (equal to 48 percent in Italy and 39 percent in Spain) if, in addition to the level of education, the presence of non-school-age children is considered (see Cantillon et al. 2001).

Another comparative study shows that in all European countries, education encourages labor market participation, controlling for motherhood and age. However, in Italy and Greece the impact is significantly higher (Bettio and Villa 1999: 161–2). It must also be noted, among other things, that the lower levels of activity rate for poorly educated women is not attributable, in this case, to the operation of the so-called "poverty trap."[6] Following Esping-Andersen (1990) we can argue that the tax system of Southern European countries does not penalize wives' employment. In these countries, given the limited rights to and low replacement rates of child benefits or unemployment subsidies, the loss of income if the spouse works is quite insignificant (while it is very high, for example, in the UK, Finland and Belgium). The low level of labor force participation is instead related more to the burden of childcare and caring for elderly relatives that in Southern Europe continues to be allocated mainly to women (5017), as well as the scarcity of occupational opportunities in economies with structurally high levels of unemployment, which deprive such families of much needed extra income.

The Overburdened Family

Another characteristic that has attracted the interest of many scholars is that in Southern European countries young adults live at home with their parents for a much longer period of time than in other industrialized countries.[7] This loads the family with an enormous responsibility, particularly if they have to deal with unemployment for long periods. As Gallie (1999) has shown, in 1996, while more than half of the unemployed in Denmark and the Netherlands and approximately one-third of the unemployed in Western Germany, Finland, Sweden, and Belgium were living alone, in Spain, Greece, Portugal, and Italy the figure is less than 10 percent. Denmark and Italy represent the two ends of the spectrum in this respect. In Denmark, 52 percent of the unemployed live independently and only 2 percent live at home, while in Italy it is the exact opposite with 2 percent living alone and 56 percent in the family home (40 percent of the Danish unemployed live with a partner and 6 percent with other adults, while in Italy these percentages are 28 and 14 percent). However, living with one's parents does not necessarily imply receiving much support from them. A study by Bison and Esping-Andersen (2000) shows that in the Southern European countries, families with young long-term unemployed adult members manage to compensate for the "welfare gap," coping with the overload of domestic work and the scarcity of welfare services, but are not able to compensate for the "income gap." In other words, families are not in a position to provide effective support in terms of income because of the scarcity of component wages and the often precarious occupational situation of the head of the family.

The protective function that the family demonstrates has nothing to do with the family ethos – the so-called "familism" – that refers to the incapacity of the family to go beyond its own immediate interests for the benefit of the development of the local community, which according to Banfield (1958) is attributable only to the more backward areas. It is also very different from the productive role that the family has in the so-called "Third Italy" (the central zone of North-East Italy where a consistent development is based on micro businesses; see, for example, Bagnasco 1977), which is the result of particular historic, political, and territorial dynamics that cannot be traced elsewhere, even in other regions of Italy (see Hadjimichalis and Papamichos 1991). Other factors, such as the importance of the agricultural sector, are more helpful in explaining the persistent central role of the family in society and in the economy. In a country such as Italy, which even in the 1950s still had a much larger agricultural than industrial workforce (nine million in agriculture compared with three million in industry), it would not be surprising to find a persistent central role for the family – a factor that applies even more to other Mediterranean countries. This persistence is also connected to the general underdevelopment and limitations of the Mediterranean model of social provision (e.g., low quality of in-kind services, high fragmentation, strong presence of Catholic and conservative traditions), which places the main responsibility for the care of dependent members on the family (and in particular women) rather than the welfare state. In Southern European countries, it is the family overburdened with responsibility rather than the instability of family life that produces the greatest risk of poverty. This overburdening of the family does not create processes of expulsion or social isolation, but has given rise to what has been called the "familization of poverty" (Mingione et al. 2002: 52; see also Pugliese 2002).

The Spatial Clustering of Poor People

In most poor neighborhoods of Southern European cities, the exclusion of young people from the labor market, beginning with difficulties in education, a disadvantaged family and initial experiences of failure, could have very similar consequences to those experienced in other European cities. The literature on the topic, though, does not focus on South European countries. Generally speaking, we can say that rather than any striking phenomenon of neighborhood concentration of low-income families or other vulnerable groups, there is instead a general distribution of scattered areas in which trouble spots and risks of "ghettoization" may be found. These deprived areas are situated almost at random, both in the center and in the suburbs in social housing estates (6042, 2645, 4987, 5442) lacking facilities and bearing a social stigma, but also within historic neighborhoods (5893, 5021, 0909) where the social composition is still heterogeneous, as well as in quite prestigious and functionally complex areas.

Also, the processes of urban segregation on the basis of ethnic characteristics that operate in cities such as Brussels or Amsterdam (see Kesteloot et al. 1997; Musterd et al. 1998) are not so strongly felt in Madrid,

Barcelona, Naples or Palermo. The low incidence of immigration relative to the resident population (approximately 5 percent in the large cities as opposed to much higher percentages in other European cities) and the recent and fragmented nature of immigration (involving a wide range of nationalities) do not give rise to highly segregated areas, even if forms of racism, housing problems, and discrimination in access to welfare services frequently occurs (2069, 3725).

Another important difference is to be found in the high incidence of owner-occupation in Southern European poor areas (85 percent in Spain and 70 percent in Italy according to the last population census), often based on self-built constructions, which makes low-income families less willing to abandon the area of residence and more interested in maintaining a positive image of their neighborhood to impede depreciation of house values.

In Southern European cities, then, the concentration of low-income families in the neglected areas of the city center or in suburban areas lacking public facilities has not resulted in the creation of "ghetto-like" neighborhoods in which socially excluded and poor people concentrate, or with which they become identified. From this point of view, the comparison that we might reasonably draw with forms of urban poverty in US inner cities is with the Hispanic population, where one can find a similar role of the family and a high diffusion of odd jobs among the adult members who are then not totally excluded from the labor market (Moore and Pinderhughes 1993).

Rather than perceiving the situation in terms of such "concentration effects" (Wilson 1987),[8] the situation of most Southern European poor neighborhoods could be better described in terms of "integration into precariousness." Indeed, these poor areas are not fully characterized either by a high concentration of individuals or families totally outside the labor market (at least the formal labor market) or by the collapse of the personal social networks that makes unemployed people unable to seize any occupational opportunities. In a situation of "integration into precariousness" the family members are able to solve their daily problems through a combination of kinship and family support and odd jobs, but in such a way that it does not really result in an escape from them. They just try to maintain a more or less precarious equilibrium.

In Figure 13.1, I have attempted to illustrate this area of "integration into precariousness" by using Castel's "four areas" model (1995, 2000) based on the two dimensions of integration/non-integration in the formal labor market and social and kinship support/absence of support. In Southern European poor neighborhoods, the existence of this zone of integration, although limited and characterized by high precariousness, prevents poor neighborhoods being classified as highly distressed, notwithstanding

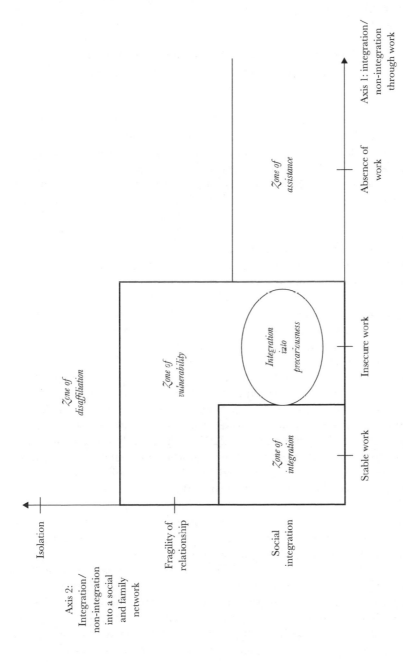

Figure 13.1 Castel's four areas of social integration

the high concentration of low-income families, unemployed people, or casual workers.

Intergenerational Transmission of Poverty: Two Low-Income Families in Naples

Within the contextual conditions described above, what are the effects of poverty for low-income Southern Italian families? We attempt to answer this question by looking at two specific cases of low-income family social trajectories (Bertaux 1995; Bertaux and Bertaux-Wiame 1997). We try to examine the household economy through the history of the family and to explore the extent to which poverty and the breadwinner's occupational uncertainty are fixed characteristics for different generations. The two trajectories exemplify some of the factors identified in the statistical analysis, which we can integrate in our hypothesis of the distinctiveness of the Southern European social context.

The two low-income families living in the Southern Italian city of Naples that I choose as an example do not exhaust the typology of new urban poverty in Southern Europe and, clearly, they must be put into the general framework already described. The central issue running throughout the two cases is the question of how the families are able to survive without falling apart, but without being able to avoid the vicious circle of the intergenerational transfer of poverty. I am especially interested in showing how a process such as poverty can be "absorbed" and "metabolized" by different families living in different neighborhoods.

The first family I discuss lives in Scampia (6038) on the North-Eastern fringe of the city of Naples, while the second lives in Mercato Pendino in the historic city center (3717, 2422, 0867). Both are characterized as poor areas, but the former is a neighborhood originating in the post-World War II period characterized by high-rise public housing and a severe lack of public services, while the latter is a pre-World War II area with a relatively large amount of private rented housing.

Case A, that of the Esposito family living in Mercato Pendino, is a household formed by a young couple with three small children. Case B, that of the Buono family living in Scampia, is a household made up of a middle-aged couple with two adult children (one of whom is married). In both families, the male head of the family is registered as unemployed, although in each case he works outside the formal labor market, while the female head does not participate in the labor market. In the Esposito family, the father has never had a regular job. In the Buono family, the male breadwinner held a regular job that had guaranteed a degree of security in the past, but this was many years ago.

The Esposito family

The Esposito family is currently going through the most economically problematic phase of the domestic cycle: the expansion phase. At present the family is composed of five people: the mother, the father, and three children aged 10 and 5 years, and the youngest aged 12 months. The male head, Ciro, took his secondary school certificate at the age of 26 by means of an adult education course, while his wife, Maria, has only obtained her primary school certificate.

Ciro is a 30-year-old long-term unemployed male working as an unauthorized car park attendant, while Maria stays at home looking after the young children. Maria used to live in the same neighborhood as Ciro and they saw each other frequently. They finally got married in 1990 when they were both 20 years old. Ciro considers the premature marriage a mistake because it has made the possibility of migrating in search of work much more difficult.

> She was pregnant. I felt an obligation, a moral obligation . . . If I had not married at the age of 20 I would have moved in search of work. Now, with the experience I have, I wouldn't have got married so young . . . These years of marriage have been a constant battle to try to have a decent life (Mr Esposito).

For Ciro, as for many long-term unemployed people, the economic basis of marriage has been undermined. Ciro Esposito's family is a family of irregular workers: people in low-skilled, precarious jobs with low earnings, outside the framework of public regulation. Figure 13.2 (included in the CD-Rom) shows the genealogy of his family: Ciro's father, Vincenzo, at 52 years of age, has always worked as a street vendor (5894), selling socks or T-shirts. His mother is a housewife. Ciro has a sister (Luisa) and a brother (Giovanni). Luisa is a housewife and is married to an unauthorized night parking attendant. Giovanni is unemployed but three times per week transports mattresses for a small firm. None of Ciro's cousins have a formal job, with the exception of Gennaro and Maria who moved to Ravenna, in the North of Italy, where they work in metallurgic and textile factories, respectively. Ciro's other cousins have failed to move out of the secondary labor market, although their experiences in the labor market have been varied. Similarly, Ciro has never had a formal job. As a boy he worked as a bricklayer and street vendor. At 17 he started to work as an unauthorized parking attendant (2421), a job he is still doing. Ciro works every day for 4 h and earns 150–170 Euros per week.

In the family of Ciro's wife, Maria, the main occupation is wholesale or street vending of table and bed linen or cleaning products (5895). Maria's father died at the age of 38 in a car accident. Uncles and aunts who are also trades people have helped Maria but she herself has never worked at this activity. Although there is enough evidence to suggest that in her family the men's economic contribution is not enough to cover the needs of every member of the household, she is not looking for work, given the poor prospects of the local labor market. She defines herself as a housewife:

> I'm a housewife. With three children and no qualifications I've got no chance of getting a job! (Mrs Esposito).

A description of Maria's typical day is a valid indication of her considerable family duties and also of the absence of any form of social isolation.

> I get up quite early, because I have to get the children ready and then take them to school. Fortunately the school is quite near, so it's not an effort to take them. Then I go and do some shopping and drop in to see my mother, who still lives in the neighborhood. Around lunchtime, I go and pick up the children. In the afternoon I do the housework and sometimes I go and visit friends who live in the same neighborhood (Mrs Esposito).

Ciro and Maria have lived in the neighborhood since birth, remaining there after their marriage. The apartment, of approximately 45 m^2, is the property of a housing company and has been sublet by the leaseholder, an elderly lady, to the Esposito family for a rent of 50 euros per month.

> This situation is pretty common in the neighborhood. When it gets around that someone has gone away, abandoning their home, contact is made with that person and their place is taken by someone local so they don't have to move away from the neighborhood where their family lives. It doesn't cost a lot of money (Mr Esposito).

The relatives of both Ciro and his wife live in the same neighborhood. The whole family prove to be strongly attached to their neighborhood even though they are aware of the neglect and lack of public services which characterize it.

> Given my work, I'm always in the street . . . I feel like a part of the neighborhood and I've got friends that I've known since I was a kid . . . We meet every day, have coffee at the bar and talk about this and that . . . the neighborhood is ruined, everything is missing . . . Also, in the last ten years in this neighborhood, criminal activity has got worse in the sense that there's more violent crime than there used to be. There's more shootings. At first there was only illegal cigarettes sellers, but now there's a lot of drug pushers (Mr Esposito).

Maria has indeed little hope of obtaining better housing conditions.

> If I could, I'd change the neighborhood to improve the quality of life for my family, especially for my children . . . It's something that for the moment isn't realistic and since we can't do it, it's better not to even think about it (Mrs Esposito).

The Esposito family is in daily or at least regular and frequent contact with relatives, from parents, brothers, and sisters to uncles, aunts, and cousins, all of whom live in the same neighborhood. Nevertheless, any help furnished by this close relationship with the family is limited, as the people who make up the network of family and friends also find themselves in difficult economic circumstances. Relatives provide children with food, shoes, and money, but only in cases of emergency.

The possibilities of access to public services and to social benefits are limited, given the characteristics of the Italian welfare system, which provides only limited support for families with young children. Although the Esposito family get free medical services and some medicines through the National Health Service, they sometimes have additional costs in this area. The family also receives vouchers for school books awarded on a means-tested basis by the municipality.

The only form of income support that the Esposito family have received was a *Reddito Minimo d'Inserimento* – a basic income-like subsidy – granted from July 1999 to December 2000 and corresponding to 500 Euros per month. At the time of the interview (February 2001), the payment of this grant had been suspended by the local administration, causing the family to fall again into a state of uncertainty.

> When we had the grant we felt at ease, without needing to count every single lira like we had to before. The first time I received the grant it was summer and I did a lot of shopping, for food and cleaning, and I took the children to the seaside. At that time I was behind with the rent so I took care of it. I then bought shoes for the children; the washing machine broke down . . . all these things are necessary in a house. Then another main thing is food. When I got home I had to think about shopping. Also, for my son for example, I needed to buy one or two books that the school didn't provide. I bought them for him because you are given a certain amount in vouchers for buying school books, but the rest you have to buy yourself – schoolbag, exercise books, all those things. I was able to do all the things that I couldn't do before (Mrs Esposito).
>
> We hope that we'll continue to receive it, we know this is an experiment they're doing but in the rest of Europe they already give unemployment benefit so why not in Italy? (Mr Esposito).

The possibility of receiving the monetary grant has not in any way affected Ciro's commitment to looking for a job. He perceives work as a central issue, as a key element for enhancing his life prospects.

> Together with other people from the neighborhood who get the monetary grant, we are trying to organize ourselves to see if instead of giving us the grant they would give us a job, so as in a way we can feel more comfortable about our future. We keep in contact with each other in the neighborhood; we even visit other neighborhoods and talk to other long-term unemployed people. We've even taken unauthorized strike action (Mr Esposito).

As a result of the low-income of the main breadwinner, the Esposito family has a level of consumption below the poverty threshold. This is illustrated by the following two examples.

> When the children are small they don't have many problems, you can put them in the jumpers that other people give you. But when they grow up and begin to understand that the jumper that people give you is second hand, they don't want it any more. [Interviewer: Your situation has always been like this?] More or less like this. We have always managed somehow (Mrs Esposito).
>   When we don't have enough money to buy meat or fish, my wife prepares "gnocchi" [fresh pasta made of flour, potato and water] or at other times a pizza so my children aren't naughty and we can save money (Mr Esposito).

Though there is much hardship, neither parent seems to be demoralized and they are able to cope with their situation in one way or another.

The Buono family

The Buono family comprises Domenico, aged 60, his wife Maria, aged 53, and their son Salvatore, 27. They also have a daughter, Tina, aged 30, who is married and lives separately with her husband. Neither Domenico nor Maria have a school diploma. The family lives on the very meagre income of Domenico, who has a permanent job (though it is "off the books") and on the occasional earnings of Salvatore.

Domenico started his laboring life at the age of 22.

> I found the job easily enough; at that time there weren't so many complications in finding work like who you know, recommendations, money, that type of thing. I remember that together with a group of friends I went to the glassworks factory to ask for a job and they gave everybody one, and – up to the crisis in this sector – I never had any problem (Mr Buono).

The sector crisis, which Mr Buono alludes to, dates back to 1974 when the local glass factory laid off its employees. In 1975 the factory closed down entirely. In 1978, at the age of 38, Mr Buono found work as a storeman in a goods haulage company but was not hired legally, that is to say, he has no pension contributions paid, no holiday pay and no sickness benefit. Mr Buono has lived, then, through what Pugliese (1993) describes as a "skidding" process, passing from a regular occupation to an irregular one, the low level of income reflecting the low level of skills and qualifications. The skidding process has implicated a net worsening of family life conditions.

> Today many people live on around 800,000 to 1,000,000 lire [approximately 400–500 euros] a month. They are making us return to 50 years ago, when I was a boy . . . but what kind of life are we living? (Mr Buono).

The family is in one way or another able to make ends meet, but the level of consumption is very low. Shopping is done in the local shops where prices are lowest and is almost exclusively limited to food. The choice of food itself is conditioned by the available weekly budget, as Mrs Buono cautions: "You have to be aware of your low income when you're doing your grocery shopping." Almost no money is spent on culture, leisure or social activities. The home itself is poorly equipped with electrical domestic appliances and electronic equipment, apart from color television, radio, fridge and washing machine. There appear to be no traces of luxury consumer goods, although these are to be found amongst the marginal sectors of the Neapolitan population where they are largely obtained by illicit purchases or by hire purchase.

The passage of Mr Buono from the formal to the informal labor market has therefore brought a net reduction in the family's consumption and major uncertainty with respect to the future. This worsening situation is also tied to the absence of "component wages" of the other members of the family capable of compensating for the reduction in the income of the only breadwinner (see Figure 13.3 on the CD-Rom for a genealogy of the Buono family). Indeed, Maria, the wife of Mr Buono, is a housewife. She comes from a family of precarious workers. Her paternal grandfather unloaded crates at the fruit and vegetable market, leaving this occupation as an inheritance following his death at the age of 48, to his son, the father of Mrs Buono. One of Mrs Buono's brothers also works at the fruit and vegetable market as an unloader. One of her father's sisters migrated to England with her husband while another brother collected scrap metal from the streets. Both have since died. Mrs Buono's maternal grandfather works as a street fishmonger. Mrs Buono's sister is disabled in one arm due to polio; nevertheless she works as a domestic twice a week. Her husband assists patients at night at the Camaldoli Hospital, receiving payment from the patients' families.

The Buonos' son started work at the age of 12 as a helper in a mechanic workshop, then at 14 he took up work laying floorboards. At 19 he was called-up for military service and was sent to Somalia, where he suffered a knee injury that impeded him from working well at his job when he returned. His employer was no longer willing to employ him so he had to look for another job. At present he works occasionally as a painter. He has since made a request for compensation from the Italian navy.

The daughter of Mr and Mrs Buono is married and has three children, aged 5 and 3 years and 12 months. Her husband used to work as an electrician earning 500 Euros per month, but now works occasionally as a porter instead.

The Buono family has changed neighborhood many times. When Domenico and Maria got married they went to stay in Domenico's parents' house in the Fuorigrotta neighborhood. Domenico's parents did not charge any rent, which was a very convenient arrangement for the new couple. Then they went to live with Maria's mother in another of Naples' neighborhoods and she did not charge the couple any rent either. Domenico's occupation remained the same but it had started to become less secure. In 1974, after 5 years of marriage, they went to live on their own for the first time. They moved to Miano (in the Neapolitan hinterland). That year they already had two children and Domenico was experiencing problems in his work. After the earthquake of 1980 they moved to the Scampia district of the city, where they occupied a flat illegally.[9] From the way they relate the events in the interviews, it is clear that Maria was very active in all the stages of the occupations and then in the struggle through which the inhabitants of Scampia obtained the introduction of public services and other urban infrastructure. In 1985, they were formally allocated the occupied flat. At first they paid 34 euros in rent, while at present they pay 50 euros.

Other members of the family have a similarly precarious housing situation. One of Mrs Buono's sisters lives in an illegally occupied house inside the area of the Frullone Psychiatric Hospital. The occupied house was transferred to her from her mother 7 years ago, after she had obtained public housing in Melito.

The Buono family maintains good relations with their neighbors.

> Living opposite there's a very nice young lady who lets me put out my washing from her balcony in the morning when the sun shines, also with the neighbors on the other stairway we have a good relationship and with the other people living in the building as well (Mrs Buono).

However, these neighborhood relationships are not able to help Domenico get a better job and are limited to giving moral support and mutual assistance.

Conclusions

From the above discussion it can be seen that in Naples, which we assume to be similar to other Southern European cities, poverty tends to be concentrated in nuclear families where the adult male breadwinner is a low-income worker, often precariously employed, the adult female is a full-time housewife and young adult offspring are long-term unemployed, living in neighborhoods where kinship networks do not exist or have little to offer and public services are insufficient and of poor quality. The risk of being poor for this kind of family increases when there are three or more minors, or one or more members suffer from physical or psychological problems (e.g., drug addiction, chronic sickness, Down's syndrome). These poor families are mainly concentrated in run-down neighborhoods in the big cities and remind us, in certain respects, of the situation of the ghetto poor in the USA. However, the low incidence of disadvantaged minorities and the absence of institutional discrimination warn against pushing the analogy too far. In addition, by being dispersed over a wide area in the cities, both in the center and at the fringe, the aggravating effect of territorial concentration is avoided.

My purpose in this chapter has been, through examining the material we have obtained in the interviews from two Southern Italian families and setting it within a comparative framework, to emphasize the particular characteristics of the Mediterranean model of poverty which I describe in terms of "integration into precariousness": faced with heavy responsibilities, families manage to cope with the lack of income without breaking up and to resist the compulsion to engage in illegal activities, but they do not have the resources they need to break the vicious circle in which they find themselves trapped, for which social and occupational policies are required.

As we have seen, both the Southern Italian families have frequent contact with friends, neighbors, and relatives, although the Esposito family appears to be less isolated from their kinship networks than the family living in Scampia, which has undergone a process of geographic mobility. The social trajectories of the Esposito and Buono families appear, on the other hand, to prove that kinship and friendship networks, or "strong ties" (Granovetter 1974), are a necessary alternative to the inadequacy both of the income support and social services (like education, occupational training, and health services) and to the poor prospects of the local labor market. Even in the case of Naples, however, the strength of informal personal networks is decreasing.[10] These ties generally have little to offer in terms of useful contacts, information regarding job vacancies or the exchange of material resources. This is because the subjects who are part of these networks are in the same circumstances of chronic occupational precariousness and lack of income. They aim merely to maintain a level of daily subsistence, such as childcare, the performance of domestic tasks, and exchange of food or children's clothes. In this context, work is without doubt a crucial resource. The precarious occupational situation of the main breadwinner is a basic feature of the two families and other members of the household have little hope of obtaining regular employment either. The main problem of the two families is therefore that of meeting living expenses on incomes that are both insufficient and uncertain.

Finally, it must be stressed that the lack of social services and the inadequacy and uncertainty of the family income affects the time women have to spend on running the family, making domestic work time-consuming and making it impossible for them to resort to domestic aids, such as outside laundering services or pre-cooked food. This makes the work harder than is necessary and is a burden that women tend to shoulder alone. The weight of domestic work seems to have had a strong effect on their participation in the labor market.

Both the cases analyzed help us to understand why in Southern Europe poverty affects mainly those that we have called "ordinary" families: it is the poverty of precarious and underpaid workers with little or no protection by any system of welfare, this new urban poverty, that has replaced the rural poverty. The difference between Southern European countries and the more economically successful countries in Northern and Central Europe is not so much due – as in the recent past – to the rural or urban character of the phenomenon, but more to the different degree of social isolation and the degree of stigma attached to being poor.

We conclude by observing that those groups which have up to now been privileged by the Italian welfare system – such as the "core" industrial working class – are now also gradually losing ground. Their losses seem not to be offset by other forms of opportunity, especially in the labor market. At the same time, welfare provision for newly targeted groups appears to be unreliable and inconsistent. The generally poor conditions of those who have been disadvantaged in the labor market but relatively advantaged in the welfare system are likely to worsen in the near future.

NOTES

1   Within the EU at present, only Italy and Greece do not have such a scheme as part of institutionally acknowledged social rights. In Spain the system is still regulated at the regional level and in Portugal it is a very recent addition to the system of social protection (see Saraceno 2002b).

2   The history of the relationship between Southern European women and the labor market in the last 50 years is exemplified by a typical sequence in which the grandmother was a peasant worker, the mother is an urban housewife, and the daughter is a long-term first job seeker (see Siebert 1991).

3   The literature has made frequent reference to a "Latin rim" (Leibfried 1993) or to a "rudimentary assistance regime" (Gough et al. 1997). More recent studies criticize the view that the welfare state in Southern Europe has been rudimentary or underdeveloped and instead argue for the existence of a specifically Mediterranean model of social protection, with a particular mix of strong family support, weak public policies, and market dependency, which worked fairly well in the post-war period at guaranteeing social cohesion (Mingione 2001; Kazepov 2002; Morlicchio et al. 2002).

4   For the difficulties involved in comparing different measures of poverty, see Gordon (2002).

5   The low-income threshold is set at 60 percent of median income.

6   A question that cannot be addressed here is whether in the Southern European countries a proportion of the poorly educated women are employed in the informal economy.

7   The distinctive characteristics of the Southern European family have been examined by an extensive literature (see Mingione 1991; Jurado Guerrero and Naldini 1997; Saraceno 1998; Naldini 2002). Factors specifically bearing on the poverty of such families include the network of relationships, the strength of solidarity among the members of the networks and between generations, and the higher institutionalization of lifestyles as illustrated by low divorce rates, low levels of cohabitation, and the low number of children born outside marriage.

8   In most Southern countries, the relative absence of forms of spatial concentration of poverty at the city level does not imply the absence of forms of spatial concentration at a broader level. To cite the example of Italy, one-third of Italian families live in the Southern Italian regions but there is a concentration of well over half (63 percent) of Italy's poor families in these regions, constituting a structural polarization of the country. In Southern Italy the incidence of poverty is equal to 25.5 percent, contrasted with much lower rates registered in the Northern regions (5.9 percent) (Saraceno 2002a). Not so marked, but just as significant, such differences exist between the regions of Spain: the incidence of poverty is equal to 14 percent in the regions of the North, but increases to 27 percent in the area of Levante (of which Valencia and Murcia are poorer), and 35 percent in the South (Consejo Economico y Social 2001: 13). In any case, according to Jargowsky (1996) and Wilson's (1987) broader definitions, I have used "ghettoization" and "effects of concentrations" as shorthand collective terms for explaining the causal mechanisms that underlie the existence of areas of intense and widespread poverty. This use of the concept of ghetto has been criticized, among others, by Wacquant who refers to it as "An example of this common elision of the racial and institutional dimension of the notion of ghetto" (1997: 342).

9   At the beginning of the 1980s in Scampia there was a wave of occupations of houses not yet completed by the local authorities.

10   It is also important to remember that not only do networks of solidarity develop among and within poor families, but also competitive and even constrictive networks can develop. The problem lies in identifying and verifying which conditions favour the development of one type or the other.

REFERENCES

Amaturo, E. and Gambardella, D. (2001) Poveri e disuguali. In: Bianco, M.L. (ed.) *L'Italia delle Disuguaglianze*. Carocci, Roma.

Bagnasco, A. (1977) *Le tre Italie: La problematica territoriale dello sviluppo italiano*. Il Mulino, Bologna.

Banfield, E.C. (1958) *The Moral Basis of a Backward Society*. The Free Press, Glencoe.

Bertaux, D. (1995) Social genealogies commented and compared: an instrument for studying social mobility processes in the "long durée." In: Diani, M. (ed.) The Biographical Method. *Current Sociology* (special issue), 43: 70–88.

Bertaux, D. and Bertaux-Wiame, I. (1997) Social mobility over five generations. In: Bertaux, D. and Thompson, P. (eds.) *Pathways to Social Class: A Qualitative Approach to Social Mobility*. Clarendon Press, Oxford.

Bettio, F. and Villa, P. (1999) To what extent does it pay to be better educated? Education and the work market for women in Italy. In: Gonzalez, M.J., Jurado Guerrero, T., and Naldini, M. (eds.) *Gender Inequalities in Southern Europe: Women, Work and Welfare in the 1990s*. Frank Cass, Essex.

Bison, I. and Esping-Andersen, G. (2000) Unemployment, welfare regime and income packaging. In: Gallie, D. and Paugam, S. (eds.) *Welfare Regimes and the Experience of Unemployment in Europe*. Oxford University Press, Oxford.

Cantillon, B., Ghysels, J., Mussche, N., and van Dam, R. (2001) Female employment differences, poverty and care provisions. *European Societies*, 3 (4): 447–469.

Castel, R. (1995) *Les Métamorphoses de la Question Sociale: Une Chronique du Salariat*. Fayard, Paris.

Castel, R. (2000) The roads to disaffiliation: insecure work and vulnerable relationships. *International Journal of Urban and Regional Research*, 3 (24): 520–535.

Consejo Economico y Social (CES) (2001) *La pobreza y la exclusion social en Espana: Propuestas de actuacion en el marco del plan national para la inclusion social*. CES, Madrid.

Esping-Andersen, G. (1990) *Three Worlds of Welfare Capitalism*. Polity Press, Cambridge.

Eurostat (2000a) *Income, Poverty and Social Exclusion in Member States of the European Union*. Office for Official Publications of the European Communities, Luxembourg.

Eurostat (2000b) *Statistics in Focus: Population and Social Conditions*. Office for Official Publications of the European Communities, Luxembourg.

Gallie, D. (1999) Unemployment and social exclusion in the European Union. *European Societies*, 2: 139–167.

Gordon, D. (2002) The international measurement of poverty and anti-poverty policies. In: Townsend, P. and Gordon, D. (eds.) *World Poverty: New Policies to Defeat an Old Enemy*. Policy Press, Bristol.

Gough, I., Bradshaw, J, Ditch, J., Eardòey, T., and Whiteford, P. (1997) Social assistance in OECD countries. *Journal of European Social Policy*, 7 (1): 91–108.

Granovetter, M. (1974) *Getting a Job: A Study of Contacts and Careers*. Harvard University Press, Cambridge.

Hadjimichalis, C. and Papamichos, N. (1991) Il mito dello sviluppo locale dell'Europa meridionale. *Inchiesta*, 93 (September): 51–56.

Jargowsky, P.A. (1996) *Poverty and Place: Ghettos, Barrios, and the American City*. Russell Sage Foundation, New York.

Jurado Guerrero, T. and Naldini, M. (1997) Is the South so different? Italian and Spanish families in comparative perspective. In: Rhodes, M. (ed.) *Southern European Welfare States Between Crisis and Reform*. Frank Cass, London.

Kazepov, Y. (ed.) (2002) *Le Politiche di Attivazione in Europa: Frammentazione e Coordinamento*. Roma, Ediesse.

Kern, H. and Schumann, M. (1984) *Das Ende der Arbeitteilung*. O. Beck, Munchen.

Kesteloot, C., De Decker, P., and Manço, A. (1997) Turks and housing in Belgium, with special reference to Brussels, Ghent and Visé. In: Özüekren, A.S. and van Kempen, R. (eds.) *Turks in European Cities: Housing and Urban Segregation*. European Research Center on Migration and Ethnic Relations, Utrecht University, Utrecht.

Klasen, S. (2001) Social exclusion, children and education: implications of a rights-based approach. *European Societies*, 3 (4): 413–445.

Laparra, M. and Aguilar, M. (1977) Social exclusion and minimum income programmes in Spain. In: Rhodes, M. (ed.) *Southern European Welfare States between Crisis and Reform*. Frank Cass, London.

Leibfried, S. (1993) Towards a European welfare state? In: Jones C. (ed.) *New Perspectives on the Welfare State in Europe*. Routledge, London.

Mingione, E. (1991) *Fragmented Societies: A Sociology of Economic Life Beyond the Market Paradigm*. Blackwell, Oxford.

Mingione, E. (2001) The Southern European welfare model and the fight against poverty and social exclusion. In: *Encyclopedia of Life Support Systems*, Vol. 14. UNESCO, Paris.

Mingione, E., Oberti, M., and Pereirinha, J. (2002) Cities as local systems. In: Saraceno, C. (ed.) *Social Assistance Dynamics in Europe: National and Local Poverty Regimes*. Policy Press, Bristol.

Ministero della Giustizia (2001) *Flussi di utenza dei servizi della Giustizia Minorile*. Dipartimento di Giustizia Minorile, Roma.

Moore, J. and Pinderhughes, R. (1993) *In the Barrios: Latinos and the Underclass Debate*. Russell Sage Foundation, New York.

Morlicchio, E., Pugliese, E., and Spinelli, E. (2002) Diminishing welfare: the Italian case. In: Schaffner Goldberg, G., and Rosenthal, M.G. (eds.) *Diminishing Welfare: A Cross National Study of Social Provision*. Auburn House, London.

Moulaert, F. and Cavola, L. (2002) Combining general and specific perspectives: the Neapolitan experience. Unpublished paper, Newcastle upon Tyne.

Musterd, S., Ostendorf, W., and Breebaert, M. (1998) *Multi-Ethnic Metropolis: Patterns and Policies.* Kluwer, Dordrecht.

Naldini, M. (2002) Le politiche sociali e la famiglia nei paesi mediterranei. *Stato e Mercato*, 64: 73–99.

Offe, C. (1985) *Disorganized Capitalism: Contemporary Transformation of Work and Politics.* Polity Press, Cambridge.

Pugliese, E. (1993), *Sociologia della disoccupazione.* Il Mulino, Bologna.

Pugliese, E. (2002) La povertà nel Mezzogiorno: dalla miseria contadina all'esclusione urbana. *La Questione Agraria*, 2: 129–152.

Saraceno, C. (1998) *Mutamenti della famiglia e politiche sociali.* Il Mulino, Bologna.

Saraceno, C. (ed.) (2002a) *Rapporto sulle politiche di lotta contro la povertà e l'esclusione sociale.* Carocci, Roma.

Saraceno, C. (ed.) (2002b) *Social Assistance Dynamics in Europe: National and Local Poverty Regimes.* Policy Press, Bristol.

Spanò, A. (ed.) (2001) *Tra esclusione ed inserimento: Giovani inoccupati a bassa scolarità e politiche del lavoro a Napoli.* F. Angeli, Milano.

Siebert, R. (1991) *È femmina Però è Bella.* Rosenberg e Sellier, Torino.

Tosi, A. (1996) Senza dimora: le forme dell'esclusione abitativa. *L'Assistenza Sociale*, 2 (aprile–giugno): 155–170.

Wacquant L. (1997) Three pernicious premises in the study of the American ghetto. *International Journal of Urban and Regional Research*, 20: 341–353.

Wilson, W.J. (1987) *The Truly Disadvantaged: The Inner City, the Underclass and Public Policy.* University of Chicago Press, Chicago.

Wilson W.J. (1996) *When Work Disappears: The New World of the Urban Poor.* A. Knopf, New York.

Figure 13.2 Esposito genealogy
Figure 13.3 Buono genealogy

14

Minimum Income Policies to Combat Poverty: Local Practices and Social Justice in the "European Social Model"

Marisol García

Introduction

This chapter addresses the challenge, created by the persistence of poverty, to social citizenship in the societies belonging to the European Union. The many debates among academics and the policy community and the prominence of the concept of "social inclusion" indicates a generalized perception of increasing inequality between those who are included in the economic, social and political spheres and those who are excluded from one or more of these spheres. Thus, policies to combat poverty have been formulated as social inclusion policies. The perception of social inequality involves a notion of social justice; however, sociologists have seldom discussed conceptions of social justice (Therborn 2002). This chapter aims to make more explicit the implicit notions of social justice that are emerging in the context of the policy discussions and the design and implementation of policy to address poverty within the European Union context. As policies directed towards the poor have been redefined with an increasing focus on the multidimensional causes of poverty beyond insufficiency of resources, highlighting participation in society, the local level has become the obvious context for the implementation as well as the design of such policies. This framework generally neglects the importance of social citizenship as a principle and as a set of practices integrated in the lives of the citizens of Europe. In this formulation there is an assumption that social citizenship has been realized in the recent past in all Member States, albeit to different degrees, from the social democratic welfare regime representing what has become an ideal type of social citizenship with comprehensive universal welfare programs, to the other extreme of the Southern familistic welfare regime with more fragmented and particularistic programs (see Chapter 3). This chapter focuses on the current implicit definitions of social justice – old and new – by looking at the European and local levels as the arenas where the innovative thinking and action are taking place.

One important factor in understanding social policy in Europe is the move towards multilevel governance (Leibfried and Pierson 1995). Most responsibility for the provision of social policy falls to the national governments, but there is an important tendency towards design and mutual vigilance between Member States, the main actors in the vigilant role being the European Commission and the European Court of Justice. Multilevel governance also means that regions and cities are gaining more responsibility for the administration of social policy resources as well as for the management of services. This context allows cities to undertake initiatives in areas such as unemployment and social exclusion, as well as in the areas of housing and urban services. These increasing responsibilities for social policy concern spur institutional transformation through which more heterogeneous actors are entering into the overall picture. The new forms of governance underlying social policies, such as the incorporation of civil society in policy implementation, however, differ according to cultural traditions (see Chapter 11). The argument stressed in the following pages is that these actors are contributing to the emerging definitions of social justice.

The chapter first focuses on some of the ways in which social citizenship has been openly challenged by neoliberal thinking, inviting the reader to reflect on the extent to which this thinking is gaining support in intellectual and policy-making discourses. It then discusses the increasing relevance of the European and local levels in the formulation, design, and implementation of programs. Finally, it shows some of the complexities of European Union attempts to evaluate policy, given the heterogeneity of both the contexts in which poverty needs to be addressed and the existing institutional frames.

Social Citizenship and the Question of Social Justice

The challenge to social citizenship, as it was formulated by T.H. Marshall, has become explicit under contemporary social and economic conditions. The welfare state that put into effect the entitlements associated with social rights has been challenged from provision-side arguments, especially in the UK. In the world of Marshall, still the same world of Beveridge,[1] citizenship in its social dimension located the individual above the "dignity minimum," that is, a minimum of life conditions in which an individual could preserve his or her human dignity (Marshall 1950). This was accomplished not only through income opportunities, but also through education, healthcare, and social services, and above all full employment. That world no longer exists since the early 1980s and, as a consequence, social conditions in the spheres of work, family, and community as well as in the public sphere within cities offer a different picture (Bulmer and Rees 1996). To mention just one facet, less productive workers, who were previously protected by trade unions in secure employment, have been retired or placed on unemployment benefits at public expense (6028, 6029, 3179). Moreover, rationalization of public administrations and privatization of national infrastructures are decreasing the employment opportunities that existed in past decades. Both trends occur in the context of a diminished effective capacity for redistributive politics.

In his book, *Spheres of Justice*, the North American scholar Walzer states: "Distributive justice in the sphere of welfare and security has a twofold meaning: it refers, first, to the recognition of need and, second, to the recognition of membership" (1983: 78). In order to achieve a common understanding on the levels and quality of welfare provision, citizens must argue about the extent of mutual provision. Discussions about conceptions of need, dignity and the desired collective good are hardly universal and therefore need to be socially grounded and related to the context of reference. In fact, this is what the social contracts of the post-war period involved. In many European countries, social contracts constituted "an agreement to distribute the resources of the members in accordance with some shared understanding of their needs" (Walzer 1983: 82). The question of how much welfare is distributed and of what kinds and how it is paid for are empirical questions. The outcomes, however, do not only depend on collective values and conceptions of needs. Because the culture of protection is not given, there will be competing conceptions and, at the end of the day, political choices will have to be made.

In the Western world, generalization of welfare rights happened in different forms and to different extents according to the outcomes of political discussions and the balance of social forces. In well-established democracies, collective decisions were taken to determine the level of state responsibility in relation to the family and the market (Esping-Andersen 1990, 1999). In societies with dictatorial regimes, the road to achieving universal welfare rights was long and arduous and when democracy was re-established the outcome in some areas was incomplete (García and Karakatzanis 2004). However, in democratic societies, national solidarity contracts were established on the basis of collective understandings of social justice. The question of democratic participation in the construction and restructuring of welfare, however, is far from obvious (Crouch 1995: 63–81).

Some provisions seem generally more defendable than others, thus collective health provision, social security, and old age pensions get more support from the majority of citizens than provisions for the unemployed or the poor. This is because the problems of poverty and unemployment can be isolated and even blamed on their bearers, and therefore they are not seen as so intimately related to the political community (Walzer 1983: 80–81). Despite the high priority given to unemployment during the last two decades in Europe, it is revealing that whereas almost half of European Union welfare expenditure is directed towards old age and survivors (46.4 percent), the average expenditure on unemployment is no more than 6.3 percent of this amount (Eurostat 2000). Moreover, public expenditure for the protection of the unemployed varies considerably, again according to specific national values on the one hand, and to who the unemployed are on the other (Gallie and Paugam 2000). Thus, the cultural values that favor a male breadwinner model of income opportunities – as is the case in Southern European countries – need to be correlated with the relatively small collective provisions for unemployment support when the majority of those outside the labor market are young people and women.

The problem of poverty is avoided even more in mainstream political discussions, not necessarily because the numbers are less significant, but because the condition of need of the poor is so marginalized that it can be easily stigmatized (2448, 5896, 5023, 2643, 1613, 5723, 2925, 6009). The isolation of the poor in North American cities (1608, 1624, 1618) has been widely discussed (Fainstein 1996; Wacquant 1996). In Europe, where the national and local policies of social cohesion are becoming more extensive, poverty is nevertheless seen as a different category of need. For example, the impact that the National Action Plans for Employment has had in recent years is far greater than that of the National Action Plans for Social Inclusion, which have been virtually ignored in the press. In terms of public expenditure, the proportion of GDP assigned to housing and social exclusion is as little as 3.7 percent (Eurostat 2000).

There are, of course, exogenous factors to the policy choices taken by each political community. The result, however, seems to be that previous national solidarity contracts are being eroded, increasing the gap between a core sector of "insiders" – well-protected and well-paid workers – and "outsiders" – with jobs in the secondary labor market or in the informal economy (5895, 2852, 3996, 4002, 5398) or simply unemployed. As a result, social and economic citizenship has been put under considerable pressure. In the demise of national solidarity contracts there is an implicit redefinition of social justice in which collective social solidarity (exercised partly through fiscal policies) is no longer as obvious as before. Public policy has been forced to search for a new balance between protection and risk, and social solidarity is being increasingly replaced by individual responsibility (Streeck 2000). The shift from welfare to workfare in unemployment policies is just one example. There are variations too. In continental Europe, where the Social Democratic and Corporatist models prevail, social forces have proved resilient to drastic changes (6372, 6371, 6029, 6028), and welfare state restructuring – with the exception of Britain – has been less dramatic than predicted. Nonetheless, elected politicians have been administering cuts in social entitlements and consequently "welfare states are producing less welfare" while there has been a general tendency towards more relative poverty (Therborn 1997). The following paragraphs describe the tension between the defenders of neoliberal thinking and the supporters of what has been called the "European Social Model."

Following Marshall, social citizenship as a set of social and economic rights involves an economic and social status outside the market. Although social rights did not imply reducing differences in terms of economic inequality, they did reduce differences in terms of status, the more important aspect being that citizenship enhances "a growing interest in equality as a principle of social justice" (Marshall 1950: 40). The significant element is that the interests in equality are translated into welfare rights, transforming citizens' life chances. This was done by introducing measures "to empower all citizens to participate in the economic, social and political process" (Dahrendorf 1988: 14). Or, in today's terminology, it created a method of social inclusion – for example, by providing comprehensive education that could prepare citizens for participation in the work sphere. One crucial criticism from the neoliberal perspective on the implementation of social rights is that these rights intrinsically involve commitments of scarce resources and that there cannot be a right to scarce resources. This view distinguishes social from civic and political rights. The latter rights are considered legitimate by neoliberal supporters because they defend the freedom of the individual, but social rights interfere with the freedom of the taxpayer. Against this argument Plant has stressed that in today's world enforcing civic and political rights involves costs and therefore political negotiations. Moreover, the political question will be about the fair redistribution of resources between different types of rights (Plant 1992: 15–29). Should resources go to welfare services or to societies' security against crime? In what balance? Once it is understood that all types of rights involve costs, political choices have to be made in the face of economic scarcity.

The other basic argument is that without enforceable rights the distribution of services is left to discretion. Institutions and personnel will be freer to choose their targets, given the limited resources available for social services. Thus, whereas the existence of social rights entitles the citizen to the service and therefore empowers him or her accordingly, the absence of such a right leaves one at the whim of social services institutions. The right to a substantial child benefit can be reassuring to mothers, especially if they receive it directly as opposed to having it granted on a discretionary basis according to existing resources, as is the case in most Southern European cities. In this instance, the situation of the citizen depends on the values that inform policies, and who is deemed deserving or non-deserving. In this case, the citizen loses some autonomy and is very much at the mercy of the ethical code and value system of others. Moreover, the accountability of those who make discretionary decisions is more opaque in the absence of clear regulation. This is a very important question for several reasons. As we shall see, it implies a free rein for institutional choices in relation to who should be assisted, for how long and what the assistance should involve. It also places the discussion of choices exclusively in the economic sphere rather than in the political sphere. As Therborn (1997) has pointed out, the disaggregation of popular coalitions in the 1960s and 1970s, combined with a general weakening of workers' unions, has resulted in the expansion of "protest crowds" with weaker although not totally ineffective social pressure to maintain social entitlements in Europe (6372, 6371).

Finally, the political agenda that was presented in the work of Marshall held that social rights required a general provision of public service. However, as we saw, the world of Marshall is no longer with us and in today's world the assumption is that along with public organizations, other actors and institutions – not only public, but also private – will be involved in the provision of those services. Thus, a transition has come about from a context in which social rights were legitimated and enforced through public allocation to one in which public allocation can be redefined by stealth in some areas of social welfare without public questioning of the legitimacy of such redefinitions.[2] Thus, the European Council of Economic and Financial Ministers' (ECOFIN) calls for budgetary constraints affect redistributive justice but run parallel to the promotion of the European Social Model. However, as Habermas has pointed out, Europeans have a "comparatively low threshold of tolerance towards social exclusion" at home (Habermas 2001: 21). This fact can constitute an incentive to work on normative goals, such as generating solidarity and a common agreement on distributive justice. Thus, as this chapter shows, there are European policies underway in this direction.

The other level of analysis at which definitions and practices of social justice can be observed is the local level. "Every account of redistributive justice is a local account," argues Walzer (1983: 314). David Harvey has provided the most comprehensive urban analysis of the constraints to achieving redistributive justice, arguing that no society can do without a workable conception of justice and that "the way these concepts get constituted through social practices has to be the primary focus of our attention" (1973: 333). I use this focus later on when examining the way in which the institutionalization of minimum income policies in different cities are constituting social practices through which social justice definitions are implicitly emerging.

Before entering into discussion of the European and local level as contexts where policies to combat poverty are generating new shared meanings and definitions of social justice, it is important to point out the following. The national contracts concluded by the social partners and governments that I have referred to were shaped not only in a historical period of economic growth and full (or almost full) employment (even if based on the breadwinner model); these contracts were also constructed by societies that were highly homogeneous on the whole in terms of ethnic origin, "habits of the heart," and religion. Thus, European societies have created a social equality culture closely related to their national identities and based on intergenerational solidarity mediated by the state that favors "insiders" and sees "outsiders" as a threat to maintaining community identity as well as welfare rights (1885, 5417, 1218, 4985, 0657). This pattern is stronger in some Nordic countries that have built a tradition of very generous welfare programs. Citizens in some of these countries have started to vote for radical right-wing parties in response to what they see as threat to their shared way of life; for example, Austria, Denmark and France.

The European Dimension

The Barcelona European Council in 2002 concluded that the European Social Model is based on good economic performance, competitiveness, a high level of social protection, and social dialogue. It also stated that this model allows for a diversity of approaches to achieve shared European values. Promotion of employment, improved living conditions, proper social protection, and combating social exclusion are among the objectives included in the European Union Treaty.[3]

The European Union plays a significant part in the development of policies to combat poverty. The 1990s took a considerable step towards this goal. The European Commission launched a series of programs such as the Observatory on National Policies to Combat Social Exclusion (1990– 94) and the Third Poverty Program (1989–94), later linked to the two Council Recommendations[4] on common criteria for sufficient resources and social assistance in social protection systems, and on convergence on social assistance policies (Ferrera et al. 2002). In 1995, the Policy Framework for the eradication of poverty was adopted at the Social Summit in Copenhagen.

With the Lisbon agenda (2000), the European Union Member States acknowledged the impact of unemployment on the expansion of poverty in European societies and recognized the importance of promoting social inclusion. The Lisbon Council concluded that: "Steps must be taken to make a decisive impact on the eradication of poverty by setting adequate targets to be agreed by the Council by the end of the year 2000." This was to be achieved through an "Open Method of Coordination,"[5] as the methodological paradigm for European Social Policy (Szyszcak 2001). A fully decentralized approach will be applied in line with the principle of subsidiarity in which the European Union, the Member States, the regional and local levels, as well as the social partners and civil society, will be actively involved, using variable forms of partnership. A method of benchmarking best practices on managing change will be devised by the European Commission networking with different providers and users: the social partners, companies, and non-governmental organizations (NGOs) (Ferrera et al. 2002).

Thus, the Open Method of Coordination is designed to help Member States develop their own policies, reflecting their individual national situations, and at the same time be aware of their specific outcomes and those of the other Member States. From an optimistic perspective, this method should help to define in a more precise way the substance of the European Social Model. However, the Open Method of Coordination is becoming a "process of multilateral surveillance" (Biagi 2000: 156).

At the Nice Summit in December 2000, a European Social Agenda was agreed that called on Member States to implement by June 2001 a national 2-year action plan for combating poverty and social exclusion. The Social Agenda for the 2000–05 period[6] was adopted as well, while the open method of coordination was extended to the field of *social inclusion* and the Social Protection Committee foreseen in the Nice Treaty is being fast-tracked into operation. Finally, in the Spring European Council Meeting of 2001, held in Stockholm, mid-term objectives for the Lisbon Strategy were set up, including the explicitly stated aim of combating poverty and social exclusion.

The National Action Plans for social inclusion represent an important step forward in the approximation of policies. After 2 years, the Commission has elaborated a Joint Report on social inclusion which recognizes the absence of evaluation of the implementation policies by national reports. In fact, national governments have had considerable difficulty in gathering information on the mobilization of resources at the regional and local level. This has been the case especially in Southern Europe, due to the decentralization of most welfare policies and particularly of social assistance.

Thus, evaluation of social assistance has become part of the strategy of social Europe, which favors approximation among standards of protection in Member States, and also seeks to raise awareness about what is being done and what could be done to combat poverty. However, the diversity of contexts and policies remains an important concern. In the report on Indicators for Social Inclusion in the European Union, Atkinson et al. (2001: 42) draw attention to the inadvisability of calculating a poverty line for the European Union as a whole, which would result in utterly unrealistic targets for some countries. It would seem better to work on the basis of national or even regional and local variations in order to ascertain:

1 How antipoverty policies operate and the value system of their institutional frame.
2 What poverty and social assistance mean for those who experience it.

This approach acknowledges the importance not only of the local level to ascertain poverty diagnosis but also of the design and implementation of policies to combat poverty. I develop these crucial questions in the following section.

Despite European Commission involvement in the evaluation of antipoverty programs, it is important to keep in mind that there are competing views among Member States and European Union political actors concerning the extent to which the European Union should be involved in social policy. Thus, in current debates in the Convention, several models of European integration have been put forward which give greater or lesser priority to social issues. As we have made the link between collective involvement in social justice and shared values, it is important to remember what the existing Treaties say about shared values.

Their preambles include the principles of liberty, democracy, and respect for human rights and fundamental freedoms of the rule of law. They also mention commitment to fundamental social rights and the desire to strengthen solidarity with high levels of employment and social protection. In the 2003 European Convention, the preliminary report of the Working Group on "Social Europe" recommends that social justice and solidarity be included along with human dignity among the values of the Union in the future Constitutional Treaty.[7] Whether or not this materializes, these values are considered crucial and are being debated today at the European level. What is more significant is that the European context is somehow safeguarding the relationship between values, shared meanings, and policy instruments to combat poverty within the (even if often vague) European Social Model.

A more radical assessment points to the highly rhetorical character of the European Union approach to social policy in general and social assistance to the poor in particular. This area of social policy continues to be seen as *soft policy* and has been criticized repeatedly for being slow, timid, and inefficient. Indeed, the history of redistributive struggles has been characterized by the popular demand for "performance" rather than for "deliverance" (Walzer 1983: 74). So far, substantive financial support has not been allocated at the European level to combat poverty.[8] Also, the impulse to institutionalize a social agenda within the Union aiming at the improvement of social conditions of the most vulnerable sectors of society in European Member States[9] is highly dependent on the political will of national governments to gather bottom-up information and identify good practices.

Spheres of Justice at the Local Level

As pointed out earlier, the pursuit of social consensus ("social contracts" agreement) on the redistribution of resources resulted in some shared understanding of human needs. There is an agreed compromise in Europe to implement policies to support the poor as their life chances have been severely curtailed. The concept of need, explains Gough (2000), is useful as the real issue is that certain needs must be satisfied because being deprived of them threatens the basic wellbeing of the poor. The success of the different social assistance programs directed to the poor can be measured using criteria such as enhancement of human capacities and promotion of participation in the economic, social, cultural, and political spheres. Each political community, however, has developed its own shared understanding of how to meet these needs, that is, where the responsibility falls. This involves:

1 How much a society is willing to pay.
2 Who the main actors will be in the practices involved in making the programs work.

The local level constitutes a rich constellation of economic conditions, social actors and processes as well as particular patterns of family, community, and civil society organization. The local level can be an arena for conflict over redistributive issues. Against this, the local level allows identification of particular welfare mixes in which the combination of state, market, and civil society, as well as family and community, generate a particular system of local welfare. By establishing and elaborating a particular welfare culture, each locality is explicitly or implicitly stating what the predominant values of the local society are with regard to social redistribution and therefore social justice. This is not entirely straightforward, as many of the resources to be allocated to social welfare locally may come from the national or regional government's fiscal resources. In this sense, each case needs to be tested empirically in order to explain the ways national and local systems influence each other on matters of policy and principles.

When referring to the local, we often envisage cities. Cities are distinct and diverse social formations, in terms of both spatial and social contexts, with specific economic and cultural histories and frameworks, which give rise not only to partially different forms of vulnerability and poverty, but also to different ways of perceiving and addressing them. Employment prospects, in addition to the social insertion agencies operating in the city, are key factors to achieve the objective of social integration. In the 1990s, the elaboration of strategies for social integration has become more complex as the characteristics of the claimants of social assistance diversify. The labor market context and the restructuring of unemployment benefits referred to at the beginning of this chapter pushed new types of potential beneficiaries to claim for minimum income programs. As a result, the social integration of a larger and more diverse poor population has become more challenging. This challenge "is forcing local actors to engage in comprehensive public interventions as well as to establish new relationships between the institutionalized, bureaucratic forms of public action and the more flexible, informal networks of associations working for the poor" (Mingione et al. 2002: 73).

Three questions need to be addressed here. First, cities are the locus where many different programs have been elaborated in the pursuit of social inclusion from different social policy perspectives – neighborhood integral regeneration programs (0898, 2687, 1983, 3437, 3438, 4338), collective service implementation, subsidized housing rehabilitation projects (2564, 2559, 2544, 2636, 1216), work activation and training programs, community care for the elderly, to name but a few. Although the city councils are often the institutional coordinators of many of these programs, the increasing role of civil society and the continuity of more traditional community work – often with the involvement of churches – are contributing considerably to their implementation (6011, 4609, 2494, 5166, 2374, 6139, 5226). Only in some instances, however, are there explicit formulations concerning the promotion of social justice, such as the Local Government Association in the UK. Often the actors proclaiming social justice as a target are working in units within city councils[10] or in civic, community, or religious groups.[11] In all cases, there is considerable fragmentation of actors and programs requiring ever more coordination and giving a new role to city councils.

Second, the real problem is to achieve a consensus on social values as well as agreement on a desired level of social justice. As Fainstein has pointed out, "the concept of the just city embodies a revived recognition of the need to formulate social values explicitly" (2001: 885). In the current terminology within the EU this translates to reaching agreement on the definition of inclusion: who must be included, at what level, and in what relationship to the majority of city residents. In the European context, the increasing emphasis is on the relation between successful economic competition among cities and social cohesion in cities. Along with competition, decentralized governance and partnerships between the public and private sectors have emerged. In contrast with the USA, there is no evidence that growth coalitions are predominant forces in European urban governance (Salet et al. 2003). In some European cities there is more stress on recreation of local identities and on the development of local strategies for social cohesion than on economic growth (6557, 1891, 4980, 2746, 2930, 2934). Good examples are Scandinavian cities, but also Amsterdam, Berlin, or Rennes, to mention just a few.[12] Increasingly, much weight is given to the value of civil society and community as key actors in bringing back the socially excluded into social inclusion, which means innovative experimentation in the local context. Social inclusion implies a more structured and clear definition of social justice in which the recipients of social assistance can see themselves as recognized members of their societies. However, the problem is that emphasis solely on social cohesion often obscures the realities of social conflict and unequal power structures within cities (2942, 2919, 4906, 2020), and also legitimizes the entrepreneurial state (3178, 0898, 2070) to the detriment of the enabling state (Fainstein 2001).

Third, there is a marked emphasis on the value of social capital. Family, neighbors, and friends – although providing important support – are not always effective in restoring to autonomy those in need, as we see in the short biographies that follow, especially so when the community itself is short of economic and cultural capital. In the best case, people have retained their social bonds but these often do not constitute social capital in the way Bourdieu defines it as: "the aggregate of actual or potential resources that are linked to the possession of a durable network of more or less institutionalized relationships of mutual acquaintance and recognition ... which provides each of its members with the backing of the collectively owned capital, a 'credential' which entitles them to credit, in the various senses of the word" (1985: 248, quoted in Harloe 2001: 893–894).

Moreover, recently, social capital has been more often associated with social practices directed towards social integration. There is also another relevant way to interpret social capital, namely as a source of mobilization admitting the existence of conflicting views in the city in relation to living standards as well as the welfare of people (Mayer 2003).

The Case of Minimum Income Policies

Social assistance has no fixed universal meaning. Generally, it is understood as the use of means testing to target benefits and services at the poor and deprived groups in society. In the European Union it translates to the provision of a national "safety net." However, variations remain as to the different approaches, allocated resources and territorial levels at which social assistance is organized within European societies. Gough (2000: 50–51) identified five social assistance clusters based on extent (how many people are covered), program structure and generosity:

1 Extensive, inclusive, above-average benefits (UK, Ireland).
2 Below-average extent, average inclusion/exclusion, average benefits (Belgium, France, Germany, Italy, Luxemburg, and Spain).
3 Average extent, average inclusion/exclusion, generous benefits (Denmark, Finland, Netherlands, and Sweden).
4 Low extent, exclusive, above-average benefits (Austria, Norway, Switzerland).
5 Minimal extent, exclusive, very low benefits (Greece and Portugal).

Gough's clusters show the complexity of elements involved in the effectiveness of social assistance policies and tell us that:

1 There is a high fragmentation of programs and this presents a real challenge to the coordination of policies at the European level.
2 This diversity involves different approaches to poverty with explicit definitions of who are the "deserving" poor, and therefore with values that imply definitions of social justice.

However, the approach might be misleading: it does not provide enough information on the relationship with other social policies and on intra-country differentiation. Recent research has shown that the extent and quality of this fragmentation becomes more informative and explanatory by looking at the local level where social assistance to combat poverty is implemented but also often designed (Saraceno 2002). Local level analysis also offers more insight into the important differences between countries classified in the same cluster. This will be shown below in the analysis of particular cases.

In fact, a person's inclusion in or exclusion from the minimum income programs is highly informed by the shared meaning that shapes the notion of poverty in each national/local context. "This will depend [not only] on prevailing economic conditions, but also on political structures and dominant cultural and ideological representations . . . One cannot study poverty and resulting measures independently of the social universe that names it and gives it meaning" (Bonny and Bosco 2002: 82).

Thus, both the socio-economic characteristics of each city and the institutional framework mediated by local cultures will provide a variety of resources, opportunities and constraints to enhance the life chances of the beneficiaries of minimum income policies. Minimum income policies are closely linked to other systems of social protection, such as level and duration of unemployment benefit and family benefits. What the following illustrative cases show is that definitions of social justice are emerging from that link, in particular from the social assistance programs' definitions of who are the deserving and the undeserving poor. Also, the existence of variation in thresholds according to localities indicates the extent to which collective economic redistribution is placed in the area of social assistance. The fact that some cities provide less financial resources does not necessarily mean that they have a lower rank in social justice, but there is a diverse understanding of who is responsible for administering it. The result of the different allocation of responsibilities and the sharing of these responsibilities by different actors highlights the role of redistributive agencies and the consequent effects. For example, by putting considerable responsibility on families as redistributive agents less equity is guaranteed. As Laparra and Aguilar (1996: 91) maintain: "there is no way of granting a right to family solidarity."

I have chosen to illustrate the argument with four cases of lone mothers in different urban contexts. Of all groups, lone mothers are a category that appears over-represented among beneficiaries of minimum income policies in almost all cities studied by the ESOPO project (Saraceno 2002). The comparison of these personal trajectories in each different city shows what it means for the beneficiary to be embedded in a particular urban milieu, where there are specific institutional arrangements in terms of design and implementation of the program as well as in terms of the actors involved, with their own set of values. The fact that these trajectories include the paths into the social assistance programs shows the interaction between the life chances offered by the city as well as the institutional filters and the personal capacities of the person (García and Kazepov 2002). Of all the aspects of the complex organization of the programs, most relevant are the extent (universal/categorical, duration, and activation measures), structure (selectivity, bureaucratic regulation, obligations), and generosity (income and provisions), as well as their ability to help the beneficiary to become autonomous. The inclusion of organizational aspects and practices here constitutes a step beyond the more limited dimensions of the classification established by Gough.

Helsingborg, Sweden

Ms A lives in Helsingborg and was 25 years old at the time of the interview. She became pregnant at the age of 17 while she was living with her partner. When the baby was approximately 12 months old Ms A separated from her partner and moved into a flat. She has a secondary school certificate, but her work experience in the service sector as a cleaner and as a shop assistant gave her no particular qualifications. She entered the minimum income scheme partly as a result of the child's birth, in order to have time both to care for her child and to look around for convenient job opportunities. Previously she had benefitted from other welfare schemes such as unemployment and educational benefits. This woman has a strong support network, which helped her considerably when she became a lone mother. At the time of the interview she was no longer claiming the benefit, and was living with a new boyfriend and working in a part-time job as a cleaner. After separation she actively reorganized her life, succeeding in finding help in circumstances of need.

Living in Helsingborg gives Ms A income opportunities because the economy of the city, which combines the industrial sector with traditional commercial and service activities, translates to a dynamic labor market. The city's coastal location facing Denmark favors this dynamism. Enhanced life chances for women through being active workers in a labor market are here combined with the fact that in Helsingborg, as in other Swedish cities, women do not suffer the negative economic consequences of marriage breakdown, given the generous and comprehensive welfare programs. The benefit constitutes a universal right. Moreover, the generosity of the program is coherent with the value system that underlies it and which operates on the principle of providing "a reasonable standard of living." This means that beneficiaries like Ms A can stay in the program as long as she needs help. However, Ms A, like other beneficiaries in Swedish cities, remained only a short time on minimum income benefit because of the existence of a wide range of training and job insertion programs, together with unemployment benefits. This factor and the relatively high threshold of resources results in a high heterogeneity of claimants (many of them refugees). Here we have an example of a strong collective solidarity model based on *thick* social citizenship. As for the structure of the program, it is highly bureaucratic with a hegemonic role of the public social services and a weak role of civil society. The system places low demand on family obligations, which does not prevent Ms A from finding social support from her networks of family and friends in her condition of young mother. This model provides answers to individual needs, showing a robust practice of redistributive justice concerning minimum income policies.

Halle, Germany

Ms B is aged 55 and mother of five children, living in Halle. She entered the minimum income scheme as a result of an accumulation of crisis events, including separation from her second partner and forced exit from work. She had left school at the age of 14, and after a short and unfinished apprenticeship in industry, started to work as a typist. She worked for 18 years in an industrial plant and after that for 11 years in a welfare organization. With the reorganization of the welfare system following reunification in 1991, she was made redundant. Unemployment and separation occurred within a short period of time. She has been on income support for 5 years, and claims that social assistance support has made a clear improvement in her life conditions. She is strongly involved in family and neighborhood networks and enjoys being with two of her children, aged 14 and 16. She manages her life from day to day with little hope of getting off social assistance given her age and qualifications, but without feeling either isolated or stigmatized because of this.

In contrast with the previous case, Ms B is suffering the consequences of economic and political restructuring of Halle. This city, located in an Eastern *Länder* of Germany, was an important industrial center in Eastern Europe but has faced a serious economic crisis after reunification. Deindustrialization (0169, 0262, 0270) has brought about a severe crisis in the labor market, affecting women in particular. As a result, Ms B has to adapt to a new situation, having been socialized in the mentality of being a worker rather than a citizen, and also to having to deal with an unfamiliar welfare system. Her life chances, like those of many other women, have been seriously curtailed as a worker and yet the German welfare system, after assuming responsibility over the Eastern *Länder*, provides generous work insertion programs as well as income support. For this reason, Ms B did not experience drastic changes in her quality of life. Although her active social life in trade union associations is over, she continues to rely on networks of family and friends for emotional support and maintains a decent social life.

In contrast with the Swedish system, the German system operates on the principle of subsidiarity, placing considerable responsibility on families for the welfare of their members. In terms of redistributive justice, Halle is a city in transition from an environment of relatively low but generalized living standards to one in which social inequalities and social segregation are on the increase – a city that demands new skills and in which some members run ahead and others like Ms B are left behind. She was offered a 1-year contract to work in an office of the unemployment service and then went back into the program. An emerging civil society allowing for active participation in a network of associations that provide information and emergency services complements the picture.

Barcelona, Spain

Ms C is 38 and lives with her daughter aged 5 years in a traditional neighborhood of Barcelona. She entered the minimum income program after her marriage breakdown following a household situation that caused her considerable instability. Having left her long-term employment as a shopkeeper following the wishes of her second husband, who mistreated her, she ended up in an association for the protection of women suffering domestic violence. She gained the courage to denounce her husband with the support of her mother and sister. It was the women's association that directed her towards the social assistance office. Within the program she has gained self-esteem and the courage to look for new employment. She has been in the program for 5 years, attending training courses. She considers the courses to be of limited value to prepare beneficiaries for entering the labor market, but she praises the moral support she receives. She combines looking after her daughter with job searching, administering her life with the support of her family.

The case of Ms C illustrates several characteristics of women inside the minimum income program. While the city combines a traditional industrial sector with an expansive service economy (0519, 0912, 0908, 4981, 2480, 0902), income opportunities in the formal labor market are relatively limited for lone mothers. Part-time jobs are not widespread and low-qualified women often end up having to work in the informal economy. Moreover, Ms C, like other women, lacks an extensive social provision of childcare, which means that she needs to dedicate more hours to the care of her daughter and relies on the help of other female relatives. She is very grateful for the support of the program; despite the insufficient economic support it has helped her to gain self-confidence. Like other beneficiaries, she has to find complementary financial support either within the family or in the informal economy, which is widespread in the city (2476). Ms C's case is also illustrative in the sense that she came to the program thanks to a voluntary association. This is not an isolated case, because the Barcelona context has been developing a collective sense of solidarity to activate resources, such as neighborhood, formal, and informal community associations (2477, 5226, 0897). Even if Ms C has a formal right to a minimum income, she cannot survive on this income because it is not particularly generous. However, social workers generally have an understanding approach towards such situations and in order to help women like Ms C to make ends meet will turn a blind eye to other sources of income complementary to the benefit, even if this is not sanctioned by law. In some cases, social workers provide "advice" on job openings both in the formal and in the informal economy. They are not strict about the something-in-return obligation, or about declaring income sources from which the recipient is known to benefit, as long as they do not exceed a certain amount. Such treatment expresses the social workers' intention to practice a kind of local justice in the face of a measure they judge insufficient (Bonny and Bosco 2002).

Therefore, what it is emerging in this city is a new definition of social justice in which efforts are combined from multiple resources to make the person feel socially integrated and to help him or her gain autonomy. Two problems emerge from this model: the first is discretion in institutional decision-making, which favors divisions between "deserving" and "non-deserving" (in this case young people, who are not eligible for minimum income); the second is the prolonged time beneficiaries stay in the program as the limited income and limited efficiency of the training courses do not favor personal autonomy. However, given the small amount of income support it is not possible to refer here to welfare dependence.

Milan, Italy

Ms D is aged 35, living in Milan with her three sons aged 11, 13 and 14. Originally from Southern Italy, she migrated to Milan when she was 17 years old, following other members of the family, without any formal education qualifications. She married at the age of 19 to a man who was a factory worker and became a widow 9 years later. Although entitled to her husband's pension she needs complementary support, which she receives from the community church and from her parents. This support being insufficient to cover her needs and those of her children, she contacted social services in 1991. She has been receiving a *minimum vitale* from social services for 6 months each year, also earning income from off-the-books cleaning jobs. However, her health problems do not always allow her to work. She feels unable to enter the formal labor market and needs the financial and psychological support of social services. She is trapped in poverty without being able to depend fully on social assistance. Instead, she pulls together resources from different community and public resources.

The experience of Ms D is illustrative of a woman who organized her family life according to the breadwinner model. In a city with a very dynamic labor market, she became dependent on her husband's wage and found it difficult to restructure her life around job opportunities given her lack of qualifications and her maternal role. Milan's social service sector offers only scarce resources to beneficiaries and no openings to job activation. In fact, the municipality takes a residual role in social services, leaving considerable room for action to the Catholic Church organizations and the innovative approaches of the third sector. In relation to this sector, the municipality acts as a financing agent (Mingione et al. 2002). For a person in need like Ms D, the combination of income resources from family members and the informal sector, as well as from the Church and social assistance, is vital. Minimum income support is not a social right in Milan and its provision depends on the city's budget allocation, which makes it precarious. Moreover, the amount received by a beneficiary is low and it changes according to the category of the claimant. As in other cities, lone mothers are considered a deserving category. All this and the fact that social assistance is often understood as a temporary patch, the need for which can be surmounted by charity and support from the third sector, means that the municipality does not lead in affirming a more comprehensive definition of social justice in the city in relation to the poor.

Conclusions

This chapter has revised some of the current challenges for policy-makers and active citizens who are involved in the task of combating poverty in Europe. With more members joining the European Union, the picture is going to widen and deepen in complexity. The argument in the previous pages is that there is strong need for collective debates in which definitions of social justice can emerge. The territorial level at which these debates should be taking place seems to point towards localities, with the support of the European Commission, which is taking a proactive role in this area. Cities are becoming the locus of dynamic local welfare systems where innovative social processes are developing. However, the constitution of social justice appears to be more robust when both national and local institutions are involved in assuming responsibility for redistributive policies, as the Swedish and (to a lesser extent) the German cases have shown. Where decentralization means relegation of responsibilities to the local or regional levels of government, there is more space for discretion within the institutions administering the services (e.g., in Spain and Italy). It also favors increasing social inequalities within national societies. Therefore, decentralization as such not only does *not* foster social justice, but can have the opposite effect. In order to strengthen social justice there is need for substantive debate and policy formation that goes beyond the formal arrangements of decentralization and subsidiarity.

The previous pages only offer a hint of the wide and heterogeneous map of local programs in Europe. The reader who wants to have a comprehensive understanding of these programs should consult Saraceno (2002) and Kazepov and Sabatinelli (2001). There is an emerging literature that captures a variety of examples that show the importance of elaborating integrative plans at the local level (Madanipour et al. 1998). However, the general picture is one of fragmentation of actors, associations, and programs. The conclusion from a policy-making point of view is that it will be desirable to see more leadership from municipalities as coordinators of innovative measures at the local level, and more evaluation from national and European institutions. Moreover, leadership needs to be supported with more generous fiscal allocation to the problems of social integration caused by poverty.

Academically, we need systematic research on these questions. We have to look carefully again at the overwhelming production of research on social integration to see what active citizenship is producing in terms of urban conflict. In the past we find a world in which collective action for the improvement of living conditions (1687, 1192, 6334) was a key factor (Dahrendorf 1988; Esping-Anderson 1990). Social processes involving collective action are taking place, even if scattered and with relatively little visibility in public opinion, as the literature on social movements shows (*International Journal of Urban and Regional Research* 2003).

The four cases used illustrate different urban contexts in which different social assistance programs provide comparative conceptions and practices of social justice with regard to antipoverty measures. Helsingborg represents a local welfare mix based on social citizenship. The benefit is a universal right, is generous and the program offers work activation schemes and social integration. Halle represents a local welfare mix in transition – perhaps an interesting example for many cities in Central and Eastern Europe. As a result of the economic and political transition, life chances have been reduced in various spheres, but beneficiaries of minimum income policies can have access to a variety of programs that will help them to feel socially integrated, if not autonomous. As in Helsingborg, the principle behind the program is that the beneficiary can lead a dignified life. Barcelona and Milan present contrasting examples. Both cities have comparable features in their welfare mix in so far as the minimum income programs do not provide beneficiaries with sufficient resources for a dignified autonomous existence. In both cities there is an implicit understanding that the family is the main agency for redistribution of resources, which leaves some people very vulnerable and can bring considerable inequality. They are different in that in Barcelona the minimum income is a right and the beneficiary can stay in the program as long as the condition of need persists; in Milan this is not the case. Moreover, in Barcelona the local and regional administrations are active in creating a network of existing associations in order to generate a more efficient provision. Out of the combined work of public and non-profit organizations, emerging definitions of social justice can be expected to develop.

These examples show some of the different models currently applied in Europe. They illustrate that despite common understanding at the European level, there is diversity in the understanding of social justice and in how this is organized locally. This means that evaluating diversity by European institutions continues to present a big challenge. However, the concern about improving the effectiveness of the programs at the European level, and the dissemination of this concern to localities, is promising. As has been pointed out: "It is perfectly rational for European cities to try to avoid an American scenario and the creation, within the next 10 or 20 years, of types of ghettos" (Le Galès 1998: 498).

NOTES

1   Beveridge wrote his *Full Employment in a Free Society* in 1944.
2   This discussion is highly informed by social and political transformations that have taken place in the British context and does not include recent approaches to the diversity of welfare regimes which have been discussed elsewhere (Esping-Andersen 1996, 1999).
3   See articles 136 and 137 of the Nice Treaty.
4   These were: "Council Recommendation of 24 June 1992 on common criteria concerning sufficient resources and social assistance in social protection systems" (92/441/EEC) and "Council Recommendation of 27 July 1992 on the convergence of social protection objectives and policies" (92/442/EEC).
5   The open method of coordination involves fixing guidelines for the European Union, establishing quantitative and qualitative indicators to be applied in each Member State, and periodic monitoring.
6   In the 2000–05 Social Agenda, six strategies, covering the whole social policy sphere, are formulated; here only the headings are highlighted:

(a)   More and better jobs.
(b)   Anticipating and capitalizing on change in the working environment, creating a new balance between flexibility and security.

(c) Fighting against poverty and all forms of exclusion and discrimination in order to promote social integration.
(d) Modernizing social protection.
(e) Promoting gender equality.
(f) Strengthening the social policy aspects of enlargement and the European Union's external relations.

7   They also include equal treatment, in particular equality between men and women, and equal opportunities (European Convention 2003).
8   A proposal to introduce financial support for a unified program to combat poverty has been spelled out by Schmitter and Bauer (2002: 3–17).
9   In the field of social inclusion, an important role has been given to the Social Protection Committee (formed by senior representatives of Member States to prepare the business for the Council of Ministers of Social Affairs), which has established a Sub-Group on Social Indicators which started meeting in February 2001.
10 This is, for example, the case in some London boroughs.
11 This appears to happen more in the Anglo-Saxon world than in continental Europe, where the tradition developed from the French Revolution onwards has developed a stronger affinity with the concepts of equity or solidarity than with social justice.
12 The reader will find other, more elaborated examples in this volume.

REFERENCES

Atkinson, A., Cantillon, B., Marlier, E., and Nolan, B. (2001) Indicators for social inclusion in the European Union. Report presented at the Conference on Indicators for Social Inclusion: Making Common EU Objectives Work, Antwerp, 14–15 September.
Biagi, M. (2000) The impact of European employment strategy on the role of labour law and industrial relations. *International Journal of Comparative Labour Law and Industrial Relations*, 16 (2): 155–173.
Bonny, Y. and Bosco, N. (2002) Income support measures for the poor in European cities. In: Saraceno, C. (ed.) *Social Assistance Dynamics in Europe*. Policy Press, Bristol.
Bourdieu, P. (1985) The forms of capital. In: Richardson, J.G. (ed.) *Handbook of Theory and Research for the Sociology of Education*. Greenwood, New York.
Bulmer, M. and Rees, A.M. (eds.) (1996) *Citizenship Today: The Contemporary Relevance of T.H. Marshall*. UCL Press, London.
Crouch, C. (1995) Exit or voice: two paradigms for European industrial relations after the Keynesian welfare state. *European Journal of Industrial Relations*, 1 (1): 63–81.
Dahrendorf, R. (1988) *The Modern Social Conflict*. Weidenfeld and Nicolson, London.

Esping-Andersen, G. (1990) *The Three Worlds of Welfare Capitalism.* Princeton University Press, Princeton, NJ.

Esping-Andersen, G. (ed.) (1996) *Welfare States in Transition.* Sage, London.

Esping-Andersen, G. (1999) *Social Foundations of Postindustrial Economies.* Oxford University Press, New York.

European Convention (2003) Working Document 38 REV. 1, Brussels.

Eurostat (2000) *Social Protection in Europe 2000.* Eurostat, Luxemburg.

Fainstein, N. (1996) A note on interpreting American poverty. In: Mingione, E. (ed.) *Urban Poverty and the Underclass: A Reader.* Blackwell, Oxford.

Fainstein, S. (2001) Competitiveness, cohesion and governance: their implications for social justice. *International Journal of Urban and Regional Research,* 25 (4): 884–888.

Ferrera, M., Matsaganis, M., and Sacchi, S. (2002) Open coordination against poverty: the new EU "Social inclusion process." *Journal of European Social Policy,* 12 (3): 227 240.

Gallie, D. and Paugam, S. (2000) *Welfare Regimes and the Experience of Unemployment in Europe.* Oxford University Press, Oxford.

García, M. and Karakatzanis, N. (2004) Social policy, democracy and citizenship in Southern Europe. In: Gunther R., Diamandouros, N., and Puhle, H.J. (eds.) *The Changing Functions of the State in the New Southern Europe.* Johns Hopkins University Press, Baltimore.

García, M. and Kazepov, Y. (2002) Why some people are more likely to be on social assistance than others. In: Saraceno C. (ed.) *Social Assistance Dynamics in Europe.* Policy Press, Bristol.

Gough, I. (2000) From welfare to workfare: social integration or forced labour? In: European Seminar: Policies and instruments to fight poverty in the European Union. Report of Conference. Almancil, Portugal, 1–2 February 2000. Ministry of Labour and Solidarity, Lisbon.

Habermas, J. (2001) Why Europe needs a constitution. *New Left Review,* 11 (September–October): 5–26.

Harloe, M. (2001) Social justice and the city: the new "liberal formulation". *International Journal of Urban and Regional Research,* 25 (4): 889–897.

Harvey, D. (1973) *Social Justice and the City.* Edward Arnold, London.

International Journal of Urban and Regional Research (2003) Symposium on Urban Movements, 27 (1).

Kazepov, Y. and Sabatinelli, S. (2001) How generous are social assistance schemes? In: Heikkilä, M. and Keskitalo, E. (eds.) *Social Assistance in Europe: A Comparative Study on Minimum Income in Seven European Countries.* Stakes, Helsinki.

Laparra, M. and Aguilar, M. (1996) Social exclusion and minimum income programmes in Spain. *South European Society and Politics,* 1 (3): 87–114.

Le Galès, P. (1998) Regulation and governance in European cities. *International Journal of Urban and Regional Research,* 22 (3): 482–506.

Leibfried, S. and Pierson, P. (eds.) (1995) *European Social Policy: Between Fragmentation and Integration.* Brookings Institution, Washington.

Madanipour, A., Cars, G., and Allen, J. (eds.) (1998) *Social Exclusion in European Cities: Processes, Experiences and Responses.* Jessica Kingsley, London.

Marshall, T.H. (1950) *Citizenship and Social Class and Other Essays.* Cambridge University Press, Cambridge.

Mayer, M. (2003) The onward sweep of social capital: causes and consequences for understanding cities, communities and urban movements. *International Journal of Urban and Regional Research*, 27 (1): 110–132.

Mingione, E., Oberti, M., and Pereirinha, J. (2002) Cities as local systems In: Saraceno, C. (ed.) *Social Assistance Dynamics in Europe*. Policy Press, Bristol.

Plant, R. (1992) Citizenship, rights and welfare. In: Coote A. (ed.) *The Welfare of Citizens: Developing New Social Rights*. River Oram Press, London.

Salet, W., Thorney A., and Kreukels A. (eds.) (2003) *Metropolitan Governance and Spatial Planning*. Spon Press, London.

Saraceno, C. (ed.) (2002) *Social Assistance Dynamics in Europe*. Policy Press, Bristol.

Schmitter, P. and Bauer M. (2002) Una propuesta para expandir la ciudadanía social en la UE y al mismo tiempo ampliarla hacia el Este. *Sistema*, 167 (March): 3–17.

Streeck W. (2000) Opening speech of the 2000 SASE conference. LSE, London.

Szyszcak E. (2001) The new paradigm for social policy: a virtuous cycle? *Common Market Law Review*, 38: 1125–1170.

Therborn, G. (1997) *The Western European Welfare State and its Hostile World*. Working Paper no.109, Centro de Estudios Avanzados en Ciencias Sociales–Instituto Juan March, Madrid.

Therborn, G. (2002) Dimensions and processes of global inequalities. Paper presented at the XV World Congress of Sociology. Brisbane, July 8–13.

Wacquant, L. (1996) Red belt, black belt: racial division, class inequality and the state in the French urban periphery and the American ghetto. In: Mingione, E. (ed.) *Urban Poverty and the Underclass: A Reader*. Blackwell, Oxford.

Walzer, M. (1983) *Spheres of Justice: A Defence of Pluralism and Equality*. Martin Robertson, Oxford.

Visual Paths Through Urban Europe

This book comes along with a CD-Rom on *Visual Paths Through Urban Europe*. The CD is the result of a highly innovative project, which aimed at using images to complement the theoretical and empirical documents provided in the single chapters. Referencing to the pictures occurs through the picture's number. This number is searchable through a search engine in the CD, which you can find on the bottom-right of your screen.

The adoption of visual methods in social sciences is gaining more and more relevance in urban studies and contemporary social research. Images are mainly used as illustrative means but they are, in fact, sometimes also able to show aspects of social life that words alone cannot necessarily convey. From this point of view, a crucial element to be taken care of in putting the two perspectives together is the way in which social categories become embodied in images. Becker encourages social scientists and photographers to reflect on the importance of the "starting point" in the process of making a link between social sciences and visual arts. "Sociologists tend to deal in large, abstract ideas and move from them to specific observable phenomena that can be seen as embodiments, indicators, or indices of those ideas. Photographers, conversely, work with specific images and move from them to somewhat larger ideas. Both movements involve the same operation of connecting an idea with something observable, but where you start makes a difference." (Becker 1974: 20).

The CD, involving more than 80 people with different scientific backgrounds from 11 countries, aims at providing readers and scholars with images on some – more or less contested – concepts and taken from quite diversified "starting points." You will find the three sections into which the book is divided visualized through different key topics. The first section on the *Changing Context of European Cities* is visualized through pictures on non-places, local identity and deindustrialization. The second section on *The Spatial Impact of Ongoing Transformation Processes* is visualized through pictures on gentrification, social housing and suburbanization. The third section on *Social Exclusion, Governance and Social Cohesion in European Cities* is visualized through pictures on local communities, ethnic villages and poverty.

The pictures of the three sections show the diversified impact of changes which is addressed in the different chapters of the book. In order to frame this variation and to relate the photographs in the CD to the specific topics they refer to, you will find also a series of theoretical and analytical tools written by young PhD students, which are also included in the CD.

All the people whose photographs are included in the CD participated in EUREX, an innovative online seminar on processes of social transformation and social exclusion impacting on cities and metropolitan areas in Europe (http://www.shakti.uniurb.it/eurex). Many of the chapters of this book have been discussed online with PhD students from all over the world and the authors benefitted from the interdisciplinary debate and interaction.

In the CD, besides the photographs you will find data, maps, literature reviews, interviews, which are also complementary to the chapters of the book. By providing this data we do not have the ambition to give the complete picture, but to show the fruitfulness of looking at the same issues and processes of change from different perspectives. Maps are not produced with sophisticated GIS systems and are not comparable across cities. They are based on the best knowledge of informed scholars (see credits section of the CD), who also have used statistics to provide them, when available. Maps, however are not constructed using the same scales, so they can be considered only as illustrative and not statistically representative.

The CD cities included pictures of 16 major European cities which are: Amsterdam (NL), Antwerp (B), Barcelona (ES), Berlin (D), Birmingham (UK), Brussels (B), Bucharest (RO), Helsinki (SF), London (UK), Milan (I), Naples (I), Paris (F), Rotterdam (NL), Tirana (AL), Turin (I), and Utrecht (NL). The CD includes also pictures on New York – as the only non-European city – because it provides an ideal-typical reference to globalization and to the changing scenario. Many chapters refer to the United States as a contrasting counterpart to highlight the European specificities. Even though New York is not a typical north American city, its inclusion helps in visualizing these differences. A contribution by Robin Harper highlights also how the perception of space changed in New York City after September 11, in particular in relation to public and private space. As Harper put it, however, "the desire to "return to normal" overrode the desire to create public expression and permit the bending of space and transformation of the lines between public and private, personal and political. This might still be the big difference between European and North-American cities.

Technicalities

To launch the application contained in the CD-Rom:

1)   *Windows users*: insert the CD and wait for the automatic start. In case Autoplay is not enabled, open the CD main directory and double-click on file "VisualPaths.exe".
2)   *Mac users*: Double-click on file "VisualPaths" in the CD folder.

System requirements

The application requires a 800 × 600 resolution screen and speakers.

It has been successfully tested on PC with Pentium 2 and a 500 Mhz processor, 128 Mbyte Ram and Windows 98, with a 24x CD-Rom drive; and on Power Mac G3-300 Mhz, 576 Mbyte Ram, Mac OS X, with a 24x CD-Rom drive.

Better performances have been obtained with more powerful machines. Notice that, due to the large amount of data, the loading after the Introduction requires a little wait.

If you want to use the content of the CD for teaching, copy the content of the CD on your hard disk and launch the application from there, it improves the performance substantially. When the entire content of the CD has been copied on hard disk, the CD itself is not needed for the application to run correctly.

For Mac users: the application does not run on systems older than Mac OS X.

Help

Notice that when the mouse is over buttons or active areas, a brief explanation appears in the status bar (near the low-left corner of the screen).

To skip the Intro simply press any button.

REFERENCE

Becker, H.S. (1974) Photography and sociology. *Studies in the Anthropology of Visual Communication*, 1: 3–26.

Index